Northwest Wine

Winegrowing Alchemy
Along the Pacific Ring of Fire

Ted Jordan Meredith

Fourth Edition

Nexus
Press

Library of Congress Catalog Card Number: 90-91641
ISBN 0-936666-05-6

All maps and illustrations by the author.

All photos by author except
page 14, bottom photo by Austin Post, U.S. Geological Survey;
page 14, top photo, and photo on page 23 by U.S. Geological Survey.

First Edition, 1980
Second Edition, 1983
Third Edition, titled The Wines and Wineries of America's Northwest, 1986

Additional copies of this book may be obtained by sending
$14.95 plus $1.25 for shipping to:

Nexus Press
P.O. Box 911
Kirkland, WA 98083
(Washington residents please add $1.21 sales tax)

Bookseller rates available on request.

Printed in the United States of America

Dedicated to—

*The tectonic plates,
the growth of the vines,
and other rhythms of the earth*

In this book

Northwest Wine

Oregon

47 Oregon's Wine Industry
Informed idealists in pursuit of a vision

51 Oregon Winegrowing Regions
Elegant wines from a land of rich pastoral beauty

67 Oregon Wineries
Individual pride and small family owned wineries predominate

Washington

123 Washington's Wine Industry

Visionaries & agriculturists join forces in one of America's most dynamic wine industries

129 Washington Winegrowing Regions

Intense & refined wines from a dramatic primordial terrain

149 Washington Wineries

Diversity is the rule, sized from tiny to tremendous

Idaho

America's Northwest

Diversity & distinction in America's upper left corner

AMERICA'S NORTHWEST

The Northwest's bold and dramatic geology and geography are striking to the eye. Their effects on the Northwest's winegrowing climates are no less bold and striking.

Clustered together in America's Northwest, it is easy to think that the wines of the Northwest states, Oregon, Washington, and Idaho, would be similar. There are similarities, but also very great differences. The Northwest's bold and dramatic geology and geography are striking to the eye. Their effects on the Northwest's winegrowing climates are no less bold and striking. The

---

America's Northwest

Wine Grape Acreage
17,000 acres

Winegrowing States
Washington, Oregon, Idaho

BATF Viticultural Areas
Columbia Valley, Yakima Valley, Walla Walla Valley,
Willamette Valley, Umpqua Valley

Predominant Grape Varieties
Riesling, Chardonnay, Pinot Noir, Chenin Blanc,
Cabernet Sauvignon, Sauvignon Blanc,
Merlot, Semillon, Gewurztraminer

Northwest winegrowing region is not characterized by a uniform sameness, but by great diversity in land and climate.

Measured in terms of the U. C. Davis climate classification system, Washington state by itself embraces the full climatic range from Region I on the scale through Region V, a range that includes the world's coolest winegrowing climates, typified by Germany's Moselle and France's Champagne district, through the world's warmest, typified by the winegrowing climates of Morocco, Algeria, and the San Joaquin Valley of California.

Distances to U.S. Cities

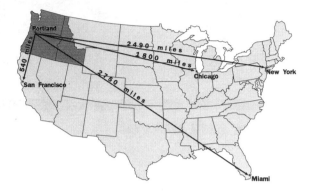

Northwest Dimensions

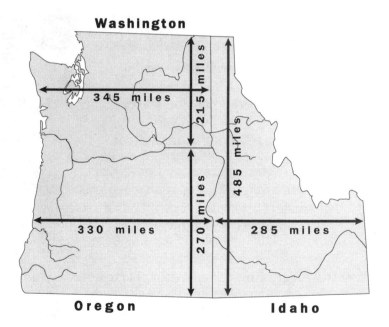

In the Northwest, nearly all vineyards are on winegrowing sites classified as Region I or II, as are most of the world's premium winegrowing areas. The U. C. Davis system, however, only begins to capture the critical characteristics of premium winegrowing climates. This is no more evident than in the Northwest, where profoundly different winegrowing climates fall into the same climatic Region on the U. C. Davis system.

Parts of the Willamette Valley in Oregon and the Columbia Valley in Washington, for example, are classified as Region I, but the climate and wines from the Willamette Valley, a temperate winegrowing region under the moderating influence of Pacific marine air, are very different from the climate and wines of the near desert Columbia Valley environment.

The Northwest region is divided into two major, and radically different, climates. The towering Cascade Mountain Range, running north to south through Washington and Oregon, divides and defines the two major climates. West of the Cascades, the climate is moderated by marine air from the Pacific Ocean. To the east, the Cascades block the flow of marine air, creating a rain shadow that extends for hundreds of miles. West of the Cascades, the land is lushly vegetated. East of the Cascades, the land is a near desert.

Nearly all of Washington's grapes are grown east of the Cascade Mountain Range. Except for a few growing sites, most of western Washington is too cool and cloudy for wine grapes. In Oregon, a low lying range of coastal mountains partially interrupts the flow of marine air, and most of Oregon's grapes are grown west of the Cascade Mountain Range, in the temperate valleys bordered by the Cascade Mountain Range to the east and the Coast Range to the west.

America's Northwest is an exceptional wine producing region in many ways. The Northwest's grape wine industry is based virtually entirely on the *Vitis*

Northwest Appellations
BATF Approved Viticultural Areas

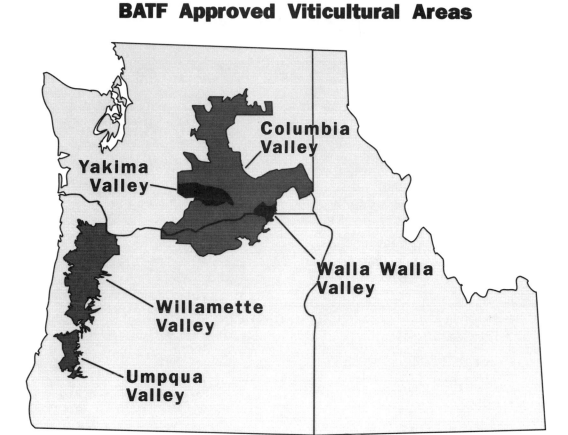

vinifera grape species, the species responsible for all the world's greatest wines. The famous French Bordeaux and Burgundy wines are made from vinifera grapes. Cabernet Sauvignon, Chardonnay, Pinot Noir, and Riesling are examples of vinifera varieties. Except for California, the Northwest produces more premium vinifera grape wines than any other winegrowing region in America. Most other regions rely heavily on native grape species or hybrids, but premium vinifera grape wines are the glory of the Northwest region.

The Northwest winegrowing regions have similarities, but it is important to remember that the differences are many and quite dramatic. The chapters for each state outline the differences in detail, but it is well to keep in mind that reference to the Northwest winegrowing region in no way implies a single growing climate or a single style of wine. The differences are great, and so are the opportunities for the wine aficionado.

Geology of the Vine

Winegrowing Alchemy along the Pacific Ring of Fire

**The eruption
of Mount St. Helens
was awesome, yet it was a
relatively small event,
the metaphorical tip
of a geologic iceberg
that speaks of the
much more powerful forces
that created it,
that created and shaped
the Northwest's landscape,
its climates—and thus, too,
created and shaped
the Northwest's wines.**

America's Northwest is one of the most geologically active regions in the world. The massive explosion of Mount St. Helens on May 18, 1980 symbolizes the powerful dynamics of the region. Equivalent to the force of a 10 megaton hydrogen bomb, the explosion was heard as far as Montana, two states away. The blast propelled powdered rock twelve miles high. For hundreds of miles to the east, the sky darkened, and ash fell like a heavy snow.

Before the eruption blew the mountain apart, Mount St. Helens rose 9,677 feet above sea level, one of several volcanic peaks along the Cascade Mountain Range. Barely touched by erosion, its nearly perfect symmetry prior to the eruption attests to its youthful existence. By far the youngest mountain in America, much of Mount St. Helens is less than 2,000 years old.

Mount St. Helens is one of many active, dormant, or extinct volcanoes embracing the Pacific Ocean along what is known as the Pacific Ring of Fire. The eruption of Mount St. Helens was awesome, yet it was a relatively small event, the metaphorical tip of a geologic iceberg. The eruption of Mount St. Helens speaks of the much more powerful forces and events that created it, and indeed, created and shaped the Northwest's landscape, the Northwest's climates—and thus, too, the Northwest's wines.

The earth's crust is composed of about a dozen plates, moving at different rates in different directions. Plates slipping past each other tear away portions of themselves at their perimeters. California's famed San Andreas Fault is an example of this type of interaction.

In the Pacific Ocean Basin, the oceanic plates are pulling away from each other at the crests of ridges along the ocean floor. As the plates separate, molten basalt wells up to fill the rift, expanding the oceanic plate and pushing it outward.

In the Northwest, the spreading oceanic plate is forced into a collision with the North American Continent. In the contiguous 48

■ The May 18, 1980
eruption of
Mount St. Helens.
The explosion was
heard in Montana,
two states away.
For hundreds of miles
to the east,
the sky darkened,
and ash fell
like a heavy snow.

■ The eruption took away
the top quarter mile
of the mountain, but
most of the eruptive blast
was directed sideways,
taking out the side of the
mountain and devastating
more than
200 square miles of
surrounding landscape.

The Earth's Tectonic Plates

A world floating on itself

The earth's surface (lithosphere) is composed of about a dozen slabs called tectonic plates. We tend to think of the earth as a solid constant. As temporal beasts with a very limited lifespan, there is little to dissuade us from this notion. But, terra firma is really not so firm.

Geologic time is far more vast than human time, and in this context, the tectonic plates are in constant motion, moving

Subduction causes volcanic activity that builds mountain ranges, and radically transforms landscape and climate. In the contiguous 48 states, except for the northernmost corner of California, this interaction is unique to the Northwest.

apart, slipping past each other, and crashing together. The tectonic plates ride on a plastic layer of the earth known as the asthenosphere. Heat rising from the earth's core and lower mantle create convection currents in the asthenosphere causing the plates to move.

The most dramatically active area of plate movement is known as the Pacific Ring of Fire, a ring of volcanic activity that encircles the Pacific Ocean. Approximately three-quarters of the world's active volcanoes are part of the Pacific Ring of Fire.

The most extraordinary type of plate movement occurs when the plates collide and one slips under the other, a process known as subduction. This process causes volcanic activity that builds mountain ranges, and radically transforms the landscape and climate. In the contiguous 48 states, except for the northernmost corner of California, this interaction is unique to the Northwest. Here, the heavier Pacific Plate slips beneath the North American Plate, sinking, only to rise again as a chain of high mountains and volcanoes paralleling the coast.

At a rate of an inch or two a year, the pace of subduction seems insignificant, but in geologic time, the pace is rapid and the effect far from trivial. Every few million years, a hundred miles worth of the seafloor sinks beneath the North Ameri-

Every few million years, a hundred miles of seafloor sinks beneath the North American Continent—and rises again as magma to form volcanoes and mountain ranges. The eruption of Mount St. Helens in 1980 was a product of this effect, as is most of the Cascade Mountain Range.

can Continent—and rises again as magma to form volcanoes and mountain ranges. The eruption of Mount St. Helens in 1980 was a product of this effect, as is most of the Cascade Mountain Range. Because we see few such events in our individual lifetimes, we tend to think of the Northwest's volcanoes as dormant, but they are highly active—and anything but dormant.

Subduction
The building of mountains and climates

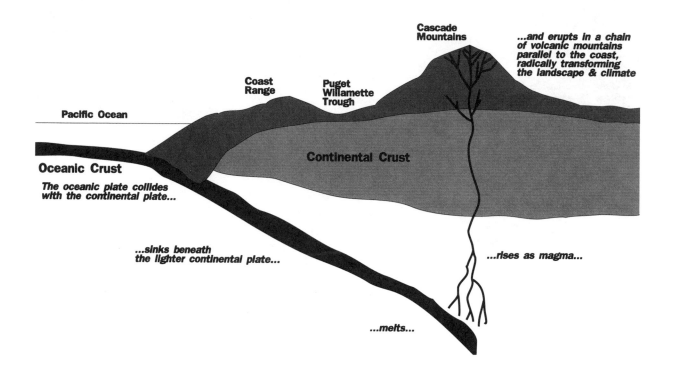

Cascade Mountains

...and erupts in a chain of volcanic mountains parallel to the coast, radically transforming the landscape & climate

Coast Range

Puget Willamette Trough

Pacific Ocean

Continental Crust

Oceanic Crust

The oceanic plate collides with the continental plate...

...sinks beneath the lighter continental plate...

...rises as magma...

...melts...

Without the Coast Range Mountains, western Oregon's climate would be too cool and moist to grow fine wine grapes. We owe our glass of Oregon Pinot Noir to the collision of the ocean floor with the North American Continent.

states, except for the very northernmost corner of California, this collision of plates is unique to the Northwest, and a determinant factor that shapes the land, the climate, and the wines.

As the ocean floor and the continent collide, the heavier oceanic plate sinks beneath the lighter continental plate, scraping away its topmost sedimentary layers against continent, uplifting the continental perimeter and widening and raising it with the materials from the ocean's crust. The Coast Range Mountains of Oregon were created by this phenomenon, as was the Willamette Valley itself, uplifted out of the sea.

In the context of wine, the Coast Range shelters Oregon's Willamette Valley from the cloudy, cool, wet, marine air, creating an ideal climate for winegrowing. Without the Coast Range Mountains, western Oregon's climate would be too cool and moist to grow fine wine grapes. Were it not for this geologic phenomenon that created the Coast Range, Pinot Noir would not have found such a fine home outside its native Burgundy. We owe our glass of Oregon Pinot Noir to the collision of the ocean floor with the North American Continent.

As the oceanic crust sinks beneath the continent, it moves deeper and further inland, partially melting as it descends. Approximately

Influence of
Pacific Marine Air
on Oregon
Winegrowing Climates

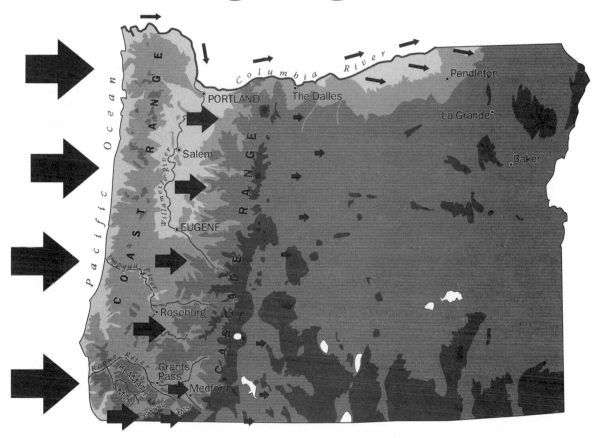

P a c i f i c   M a r i n e   A i r

Relative Influence

Pathways Through River Valleys →

The origins of Washington Cabernet Sauvignon are rooted in the tumultuous volcanic thrustings of the Cascade Mountains.

100 miles inland, part of the molten basalt of the ocean floor returns to the surface as a chain of volcanoes paralleling the coastline. The towering Cascade Mountain Range, running north and south through Washington and Oregon, was formed by this fiery phenomenon. In recorded history, all the volcanic eruptions in the contiguous 48 states have occurred in the Cascade Range.

Many of the world's great mountain ranges reach their high elevations from already high beginning points of the surrounding landscape, but the Cascades rise from the coastal lowland, sometimes thrusting more than 10,000 feet into the Northwest sky. The highest volcanic peak, Mount Rainier, rises 14,410 feet above sea level. Even at a great distance, the mountain dominates the skyline. Its active glaciers cover 35 square miles.

The Cascade Mountains shape the Northwest climate. The wall of mountains blocks the flow of marine air, causing heavy precipitation on the western side of the mountains, and a near desert on the eastern side. The vast Columbia Valley, east of the Cascades, is the largest and most productive winegrowing region in the Northwest. The Columbia Valley's winegrowing climate is unique and complex. A discussion of its climate in the Washington section of this book details the climate's characteristics and its effects on the grapes and the wines. For now it is sufficient to say that we owe our glass of Washington Cabernet Sauvignon to the tumultuous volcanic thrustings of the Cascade Mountains, the Northwest's most prominent geologic feature.

■ The Columbia River, east of the Cascade Mountains— from the Washington side, looking across into Oregon

Influence of Pacific Marine Air on Washington Winegrowing Climates

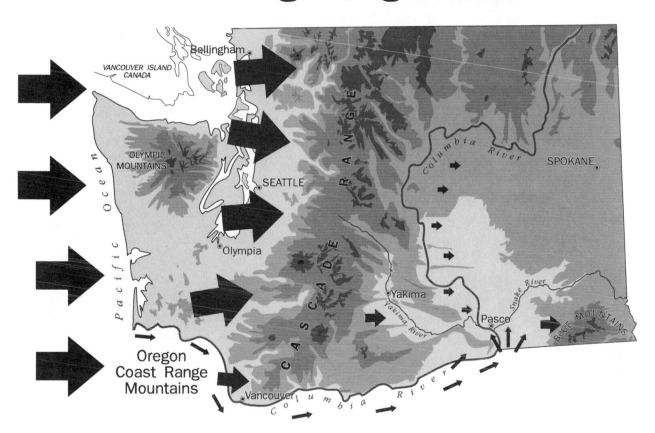

Pacific Marine Air

Relative Influence

Pathways Through River Valleys →

We also owe a measure of thanks to the Columbia River. The 500 mile wall of mountains that divides the Northwest's two major climates is breached only at one point, where the powerful Columbia River cuts through the Cascades on its way to the Pacific Ocean. Just enough marine air flows through this breach to lengthen the growing season east of the Cascade Mountains and moderate the cold, wintertime, inland climate.

The Columbia provides drainage for three-quarters of the Northwest region. One of its major tributaries, the Snake River, cuts a path into Idaho. Even at this far distance, more than 300 miles inland, the Pacific marine influence makes winegrowing in Idaho's western valleys possible.

The Cascade Mountains were formed in several geologic episodes. About 25 million years ago, the old Cascade volcanoes stopped erupting. Around 15 million years ago, volcanic activity resumed, but further inland. The newer volcanoes were of a different kind. Fissures miles long released floods of basalt lava. The massive quantities of highly fluid lava may have moved as fast as 30 miles an hour across the Northwest landscape. One of the larger flows covered an area of more than 20,000 square miles within a matter of hours. Some flows were more than 200 feet thick.

Concentrated in central and eastern Washington and Oregon, the Columbia Plateau lava floods covered nearly 250,000 square miles, reaching into Idaho and northern California, burying the existing landscape of hills and valleys with basalt. In recorded history, there is nothing even remotely comparable.

The Columbia Valley, the Northwest's largest winegrowing region, covering nearly a third the state of Washington, encompasses the northernmost part of the vast Columbia Plateau. Arching across eastern and central Washington, the path of the Columbia River itself was shaped by the floods of basalt lava. The largest volcano in the Columbia Plateau, sometimes called the Grande Ronde Volcano by geologists, was centered in southeastern Washington and northeastern Oregon.

Lava from the Grande Ronde volcano flowed over and created what is now the Columbia Valley, pushing the Columbia River's antecedent drainages northward and westward, forcing it to follow the lowest path where the farthest reaches of the gently sloping Grande Ronde Volcano met the Okanogan Highlands to the north and the Cascade Mountains on the west. Washington's prime winegrowing region, the nearly flat 23,000 square mile Columbia Valley, is actually the gently sloping side of a vast ancient volcano.

Although the eastern part of the Columbia Valley is almost flat, the western part, where most of the valley's vineyards are located, is contoured with high ridges. Within the last 10 million years, the northward movement of the west coast has caused the basalt lava flows to buckle and form large steep folds. This folding process created and shaped the Yakima Valley, one of Washington's most

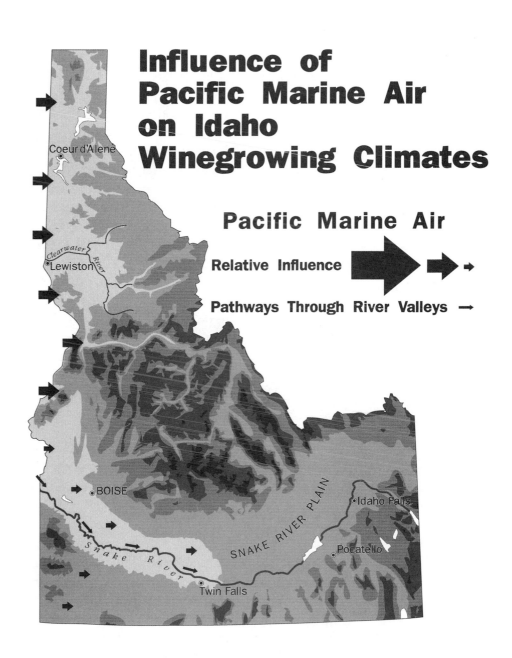

Influence of Pacific Marine Air on Idaho Winegrowing Climates

Pacific Marine Air

Relative Influence

Pathways Through River Valleys →

Many small volcanic hills dot the western Oregon landscape, providing slopes for modern day vineyards. In the northern Willamette Valley, Oregon's largest city, Portland, is flanked by clusters of volcanic hills built on the older basalt from the Columbia Plateau lava floods.

important winegrowing regions. The Ahtanum Ridge, Rattlesnake Hills, and Horse Heaven Hills, all basalt folds, define the shape of the valley and separate it from the rest of the Columbia Valley from which it was created.

Running in a generally east to west direction, the folded basalt ridges offer shelter from the cold of the north and provide sunny southern slopes for winegrowing. In other parts of the western Columbia Valley, the Wahluke and Royal Slope, the lower reaches of the Saddle Mountains and Frenchman Hills, are winegrowing sites created by the buckling and arching of old basalt lava flows.

The rivers were not halted by the buckling of the lava plain. As fast as the basalt ridges rose, the rivers cut through them. Nowhere is this more dramatic than along parts of the Columbia River, where towering basalt cliffs plummet vertically to the river below, exposing the angular basalt columns formed by the great lava floods. Along the Idaho and Oregon border, another kind of uplift of the Blue Mountains forced the Snake River to carve a corridor through hard, dense, greenstone rock, creating the aptly named Hell's Canyon, the deepest canyon in North America. Further up river, in Idaho's winegrowing country, the Snake River Lava Plain dips across southern Idaho in a broad crescent.

About 12 million years ago, the great basalt floods subsided, and the volcanic activity along the Cascade Mountains resumed before again slipping into quiescence, marking the last eruptive period for what are now known as the western Cascades. Covered by a succession of lava flows and eroded over many millions of years, the western Cascades consist of a broad chain of high ridges and ravines. Their appearance does not suggest their volcanic origins.

Within the last several million years, however, yet another eruptive period began building a different type of volcano along the Cascade Range. Built on the base of the old western Cascades, the modern high Cascades form a towering chain of volcanic cones. Before destructive eruptions and glacial erosion took their toll, some of the volcanic peaks thrust more than three miles into the Northwest sky.

The current peaks, still very young mountains, are only slightly less spectacular. Their height blocks the Pacific marine air and transforms the Columbia Valley climate more dramatically than the lower, older western Cascades ever could. The modern Cascade Mountain Range, more than any other single geologic feature, determines and defines the Northwest winegrowing climate. Even in western Oregon, where their climatic effect is less obvious, the Cascades shelter the winegrowing environment from inland temperature extremes, lengthening the growing season, and maintaining a temperate climate.

The volcanic past leaves its traces—and foundations, throughout the Northwest wine country. The lava floods from the Grande Ronde volcano made their way to the Pacific Ocean, covering parts of

Oregon's northern Coast Range and the northern Willamette Valley. Many small volcanic hills dot the western Oregon landscape, providing slopes for modern day vineyards. In the northern Willamette Valley, Oregon's largest city, Portland, is flanked by clusters of volcanic hills built on the older basalt from the Columbia Plateau lava floods.

Not only lava flooded the Northwest. During the last ice age, some 16,000 years ago, a massive glacier pushed southward from Canada into Idaho, damming the Clark Fork River. The waters of the Clark Fork backed up into the high mountain valleys of western Montana, forming Glacial Lake Missoula. Two thousand feet deep, the lake contained some 500 cubic miles of water. Inevitably, the rising water floated and broke its glacial dam, instantly releasing a wall of water, and creating one of the world's greatest floods.

The floodwaters raced across the Columbia Valley, scouring away the soil and exposing the hard basalt from the ancient lava floods. All the "normal" flood effects were magnified exponentially. The

An aerial view of the Ahtanum Ridge. The city of Yakima is above the ridge. The Yakima River and highway funnel through the narrow gap, known as Union Gap. The terminus of the Rattlesnake Hills forms the other side of the gap. A mosaic of farmland surrounds the ridge's spine. These folded basalt ridges shape much of the Columbia Valley's terrain, providing shelter from northern inland air, and southerly slopes for vineyards.

flood of Glacial Lake Missoula scattered boulders weighing many tons across the Columbia Valley. Ripple marks, like those seen in the sand at the bottom of a stream, still remain today, but these are as much as 30 feet high and hundreds of feet from crest to crest.

After racing across the Columbia Valley, the floodwaters dammed up behind the narrow Wallula Gap near what is today the Tri-Cities area of Pasco, Richland, and Kennewick, creating a temporary lake

**The wines of
America's Northwest
are the newly born product
of an ancient
and powerful alchemy,
the great workings
of earth, air, fire, and water,
antiquity's
four primordial elements,
distilled in the crucible
of America's Northwest.
These are the roots
of the Northwest vine.**

a thousand feet deep. The briefly stilled floodwaters released much of their sediment in the Pasco Basin, soils for the vines that would follow many millennia later.

The floodwaters then raced through the Columbia Gorge, the narrow breach in the Cascade Mountain Range, reaching a depth of nearly 1,000 feet, scouring away the soil from the underlying bedrock, and ripping away the lower portions of tributary streams, creating precipices and waterfalls. Where the Columbia takes a sharp northward bend before entering the Pacific Ocean, the floodwaters were dammed once again, flooding across Oregon's northern Willamette Valley to a depth of 400 feet. The floodwaters receded, leaving soils and boulders traceable to the mountains of Montana.

This spectacular flood happened not only once, but as many as 40 times, as the massive moving glacier again and again dammed the waters of the Clark Fork River in Montana only to release them in a series of violent torrents. The layers of sediment in some of the Northwest winegrowing valleys correspond to the shoreline markings in the mountains of Montana, modern day traces representing each filling and emptying of the great glacial lake.

Roughly comparable to the latitudes of France's Burgundy and Bordeaux regions, the northerly latitude of America's Northwest winegrowing region is an important factor in the quality of the region's wines—yet the northerly latitude is far from the whole story. Mooselake, Minnesota, Roundup, Montana, and parts of Mongolia are also at a similar latitude, but little can be said for them as premium winegrowing regions. Clearly, other factors are at work in the winegrowing regions of America's Northwest.

Pacific Ocean marine air, the Coast and Cascade Mountain Ranges, the Columbia River, the great floods of water and molten earth, these elements, and many more, shape the Northwest landscape, shape the Northwest climate, and shape the taste and style of Northwest wine.

The wines of America's Northwest are the newly born product of an ancient and powerful alchemy, the great workings of earth, air, fire, and water, antiquity's four primordial elements, distilled in the crucible of America's Northwest. These are the roots of the Northwest vine.

Northwest Wine Grapes

The grapes and wines of the Northwest vineyard

These are the principal Northwest wine grapes. Unless otherwise noted, references to Oregon, Washington, or Idaho pertain to the predominant grape growing areas of each state, i.e., Oregon's Willamette and Umpqua Valleys, Washington's Columbia and Yakima Valleys, and Idaho's Snake River Valley.

Aligote Grown in miniscule quantities in Washington, Aligote is a high yielding, lesser quality white grape of France's Burgundy region. It is generally similar to Chardonnay, though with a leaner profile and less finesse. Aligote can offer good wine at a moderate price.

Cabernet Franc One of the Bordeaux grape varieties grown in limited quantities in Washington and Oregon, Cabernet Franc produces a wine similar to Cabernet Sauvignon, though less intense, with typically lower acids and tannins. The grape is gaining interest, particularly in Washington.

Cabernet Franc can occasionally be overly vegetal. Though Washington red wines sometimes have a tendency toward this characteristic, Cabernet Franc has not been a particular problem when grown on suitable sites. It offers what are variously described as raspberry or lilac components. While good on its own, Cabernet Franc is excellent for adding complexity to blends with Merlot and Cabernet Sauvignon. It promises to play a small but worthy role on the Washington red wine scene.

Cabernet Sauvignon Arguably, Washington's finest wine grape. Washington Cabernets are typically deeply colored and flavored, full bodied, rough, and tannic when young, frequently needing several years of bottle age to begin showing their best. Recent refinements in winemaking methods have made more Washington Cabernets accessible earlier, without sacrificing character or aging potential.

Washington Cabernets have a structure and backbone similar to classically styled Bordeaux, but with a ripeness and body more reminiscent of a California Cabernet. Ultimately, they are Cabernet Sauvignon in their own style.

The better Washington Cabernets avoid burnt and overtly weedy flavors. Sometimes, Washington Cabernet Sauvignons have a berry-like character that is atypical of Bordeaux or California Cabernet. The finest combine rich fruit with spicy flavors and scents. Supple, yet possessing a sturdy acid backbone, they are long-lived wines that require bottle aging to fully develop their potential.

Growing site is critical for the finest Washington Cabernet Sauvignon. Warmer sloped sites are best. Sub-regions and vineyards produce Cabernet Sauvignon with distinctive characteristics. The cooler areas produce more of the berry-like or herbal flavors. Warmer areas are more textural and spicy.

With occasional exception, Oregon's Willamette Valley is too cool for the best Cabernet Sauvignon. Most Willamette Valley Cabernets are good, but rather unremarkable, with herbaceous tendencies. Warm years on warm growing sites are best. Further south, the Umpqua Valley, and, particularly, the Rogue, Applegate, and Bear Creek valleys of southwest Oregon, near the California border, are capable of producing fine Cabernet.

Idaho has severe winters and a relatively short growing season. Cabernet Sauvignon is fairly winter sensitive, and needs a moderately long growing season. The prospects for Idaho Cabernet Sauvignon have not looked good, but the grape has proven more cold hardy than expected, and Idaho's intense growing season compensates, somewhat, for its relative shortness. The potential for Idaho Cabernet Sauvignon remains largely untested, but quite encouraging.

Chardonnay

Oregon's premier white wine grape is also its most challenging. The predominant Chardonnay clone grown in the state was developed for warmer climates, but the Oregon winegrowers have effectively worked around its shortcomings. A flexible grape, Chardonnay is at home in all of Oregon's winegrowing areas, including the warmer Rogue River Valleys of southwest Oregon.

Chardonnay is a winemaker's grape. Much of the final character of the wine depends on the winemaker's hand. In Oregon, traditional Burgundian winemaking methods predominate—relatively warm fermentation temperatures, barrel fermentation, lees contact, and the like. The best are elegant and complex wines, often delicate, yet rich in flavor with a sturdy acid backbone. It is a challenging grape, and some winemakers achieve the ideal more routinely than others.

Other Chardonnay clones, particularly those from Dijon, are more closely matched to Oregon's winegrowing climate, and are just becoming available for commercial planting. The new clones offer the prospect of another qualitative step for Oregon Chardonnay.

Washington Chardonnays were routinely and reliably good,

One of the Northwest's great wine grapes— Washington Cabernets are long-lived wines that need time in the cellar to fully develop their potential.

though often a bit simple and coarse compared to the best attainable from the grape. The choice of winemaking style was the main culprit rather than any climatic constraint. Washington's predominant style treated the grape as if it were highly fruity and aromatic—which it is not. Cold fermentation temperatures, stainless steel tanks, avoidance of lees contact, and so on, are fine for Riesling, but not Chardonnay—at least not great Chardonnay.

Washington winemaking has matured significantly in the past few years, and now most Chardonnay winemakers incorporate more of the traditional Burgundian winemaking methods into their wines. Today's Washington Chardonnays are by far the best the state has offered, and the positive trend continues.

Idaho Chardonnays are generally similar to those of Washington. The Chardonnay grape adapts well to a wide range of climates from very cool to quite warm. It has adapted well to Idaho's intense but relatively short growing season.

Chenin Blanc

In America, specifically, California, Chenin Blanc is considered a lowly varietal with little character. Though not a great grape, it is regarded far more highly in Europe.

Washington Chenin Blanc is usually made in a tasty, fresh, fruity style with some residual sweetness. Chenin Blanc also lends itself to a drier, wood-aged style. A few Washington Chenin Blancs are made in this style with good success.

Washington Chenin Blancs have considerably more interest than the typical examples from California, but the variety inherently yields high quantities of grapes, and most Washington grape growers do not discourage this tendency. Many Washington Chenin Blancs lack the focus and intensity that smaller yields would bring. Washington is capable of producing even better Chenin Blanc, but for now, the grape is stuck in its role as a high yielding variety for moderately priced, off-dry, easy quaffing wines.

In Oregon and Southwest Washington, very little Chenin Blanc is produced, but some fine examples in a variety of styles add interest to the wine spectrum. Idaho also produces good Chenin Blanc, but the grape's lack of winter hardiness is even more of a problem than it is in Washington.

Early Muscat

A U.C. Davis cross, Early Muscat is grown in Oregon's Illinois Valley and in very limited quantities in the Willamette Valley. It produces good quantities of muscat flavored grapes in cool climate environments.

Ehrenfelser

A German cross of Riesling and Sylvaner, planted in miniscule quantities in Oregon. It has a Riesling-like character but ripens earlier with less acidity.

Flora

A U. C. Davis white wine cross grown in miniscule quantities in Oregon's Willamette Valley.

Gamay Beaujolais

Once thought to be the grape of France's Beaujolais district, the

Gamay Beaujolais grown in the Northwest and the rest of America is actually a clone of Pinot Noir and not a separate grape variety. This Gamay clone of Pinot Noir produces wines that are lighter in color and higher in acid. Though it is generally not highly regarded, some significant Oregon Pinot Noir producers purposely seek out moderately cropped vineyards of this clone. At its best in Oregon, the Gamay clone can contribute desirable structural components in a Pinot Noir blend. Though more delicate, the Gamay clone ages well and develops complexity in the cellar.

Gamay Noir

The true Gamay grape of France's Beaujolais region, and a different grape than the Gamay and Gamay Beaujolais grown in America. Showing excellent promise in Oregon, the grape is beginning to find its way out of the experimental stage, into commercial plantings.

Like French Beaujolais, it promises high yields of fine quality, fruity, flavorful, red wine. The classic grape of nouveau wines, the true Gamay is also capable of more substantive wines of distinction. Still untested on a large scale, Gamay Noir promises to be a worthy and major Oregon wine grape.

Gewurztraminer

A fickle grape that needs the right climate and growing site to develop its spicy flavor intensity without turning flat and dull. It was one of Washington's earliest successful vinifera grape varieties.

Both Washington and Oregon produce good Gewurztraminer in styles from bone dry, to slightly sweet, to very sweet botrytised versions. The few examples from Idaho have shown good balance and fine, spicy, Gewurztraminer character. Some of the best Gewurztraminer grapes in the Northwest are grown along the Columbia Gorge, on either side of the Oregon-Washington border, and in the Illinois Valley of southwest Oregon.

Unfortunately, Gewurztraminer is not the easiest grape to manage in the vineyard, and it is a tough sell in the marketplace. Gewurztraminer often shows its best in finely crafted dry versions, but most are made in a slightly sweet style for the widest consumer appeal.

Some of America's best Gewurztraminer is grown along the Columbia Gorge, and in the Illinois Valley of southwest Oregon.

Grenache

The grape requires a very warm growing climate and a long season. Both along the Columbia Gorge and in Washington's Columbia Valley, Grenache produces good, soft, red wines and flavorful roses with pleasant flavors of black pepper and spice. There is little acreage in Washington, and major expansion seems unlikely because of the grape's acute sensitivity to winter damage.

Island Belle

A local variant of the native American, non-vinifera, red grape, Campbell Early. Developed in the late 1800s by Adam Eckert, Island Belle enjoyed commercial success as a table, jelly, and wine grape. Grown in western Washington's Puget Sound area, Island Belle fell out of favor when Columbia Valley Concord began to dominate the grape market. Except for those who find favor with its distinctive non-vinifera character, it does not make a particularly good wine grape.

Lemberger   Also spelled Limberger, the variety is a little-known red wine grape grown in small quantities in several European countries. Lemberger has become a speciality grape of Washington. The wines are darkly colored, with flavors of berries and vanilla. The character is straightforward without the texture or complexity of the great wine grapes, but the wines are, nevertheless, fruity, well-balanced, and tasty.

The variety can be cropped higher than other red varieties while still retaining balance and character. Lemberger is at its best young. Aging brings out an unflattering metallic character and there are few bottle aged nuances to compensate. Lemberger is best appreciated for what it is, a good wine grape for moderately priced, early drinking red wines, and an enjoyable change of pace from Cabernet and Merlot. Acreage is gradually expanding.

Malbec   One of the lesser red Bordeaux varieties, Malbec yields wines with lower acidity and a less pronounced profile than Cabernet Sauvignon. It is grown only in very small quantities in Washington, where it occasionally finds its way into blends with Cabernet Sauvignon and Merlot.

Madeleine Angevine   Also spelled Madeline Angevine, this cool climate grape is grown in western Washington's Puget Sound region. It is a French, vinifera, white grape bred in the Loire Valley in the 1850s from two older vinifera varieties, Precoce de Malingre and Madeleine Royale.

The wines range in style from dry to slightly sweet. Occasionally, sweet botrytised versions are made. The wines have good fruit character. The flavors are vaguely reminiscent of Semillon, with an added spicy component. Some of the current examples suggest excellent promise for the grape in Washington's Puget Sound area. It is at its best when fermented completely dry, or in the occasional sweet botrytised versions.

Marechal Foch   A French-American hybrid once planted in Washington before premium vinifera grapes buried all interest in hybrid varieties. It is currently released commercially in Oregon in very small quantities, and yields a dark colored red wine with unexpectedly (given its hybrid origins) fine flavors.

The grape is widely planted in the eastern United States, where it has a less than stellar reputation. A key to its success in Oregon seems to be the higher level of ripeness it achieves. In the warmer Oregon vintages, it offers a very good wine with little or none of the hybrid taste.

Melon   Melon is the white wine grape of Muscadet in France's Loire Valley. Because of a mix-up in plant material identification, virtually all the vines, grapes, and wines in America called Pinot Blanc are actually Melon. Planted in Oregon in the early years of the wine industry as Pinot Blanc, Oregon winegrowers are beginning to work with the grape again, on a small scale—this time, as Melon.

Merlot   One of the Bordeaux grape varieties, Merlot marries well with Cabernet Sauvignon, contributing texture and suppleness. It is a highly regarded grape, but on its own, whether in Bordeaux, California, or the Northwest, it often comes across as if it were Cabernet Sauvignon lacking in varietal intensity.

Washington produces fine Merlot with good character and structure. Washington Cabernet Sauvignons from some growing sites can be very hard. Blending in Merlot gives them a more complete, less austere profile. Merlot ripens earlier than Cabernet Sauvignon, and can quickly become overripe if care is not taken at harvest time. The best Merlots often have a portion of Cabernet Sauvignon or, more recently, Cabernet Franc blended in for an additional flavor dimension. Merlot is one of Washington's best red wine grapes.

Very little Merlot is grown in Oregon. Unless the spring weather is just right, Merlot refuses to set berries. In Oregon, during berry set, conditions are seldom just right. The warmer Rogue River Valleys of southwest Oregon, near the California border, experiences these problems to a lesser degree. Idaho also holds some promise for the grape.

Morio Muskat   Also spelled Morio Muscat, the grape is grown in miniscule quantities in Washington. A cross between Sylvaner and Pinot Blanc, Morio Muskat ripens early and produces high yields. The appealing wines have an intense muscat flavor and aroma.

Muller-Thurgau   This century-old German crossing of Riesling and Sylvaner is, today, Germany's most widely planted grape. In Germany, Muller-Thurgau is typically cropped high and picked early to offer large quantities of inoffensive Liebfraumilch. Muller-Thurgau may not be the world's greatest white wine grape, but it is capable of better wines than the German norm.

If cropped conservatively and allowed to ripen in a very cool growing climate, Muller-Thurgau produces flavorful fruity wines with a pronounced floral-musky aroma. In most years, western Oregon is a bit too warm to bring out the best of the grape. Western Washington's Puget Sound area is a more ideal climate. The wines are best drunk young, while they are at their fruity and aromatic best.

Muscat Alexandria   One of the world's oldest grape varieties, Muscat Alexandria lacks refinement, even for a Muscat. The fruit lacks a clarion grapy voice, and the character is slightly earthy. Grown in Washington, the variety has been all but superseded by the superior Muscat Canelli.

Muscat Canelli   The principal Muscat grown in Washington. The grape has a variety of names, including Muscat Blanc and Muscat Frontignan. Its white wines have an intense aroma, and a luscious, fresh, fruity, muscat character. Washington's excellent Muscat Canellis are usually made in a sweet style. The vines are sensitive to cold damage, and are often one of the hardest hit varieties in a bad winter.

Muscat Ottonel

A white wine grape grown in tiny quantities in Oregon, Muscat Ottonel is of relatively recent origins. Bred in France's Loire region in the 1800s, Muscat Ottonel does well in cool climates, unlike most other Muscat varieties. It is now the predominant Muscat of France's Alsace region. Its wines are less intensely muscat than other Muscats, and thus, to some tastes, less overt and more refined. Oregon's only commercial release of the grape is finished in a dry style, and offers a welcome addition to the wine spectrum.

Nebbiolo

The great red wine grape of Italy's Piedmont region is barely out of the experimental stage in Washington. Like Pinot Noir, it is very fickle about growing conditions. And, like Pinot Noir, it is not uncommon to achieve perfect "numbers" for the grapes, but have indifferent wine. Its huge clusters require careful cropping management in the vineyard. Early results have been encouraging.

Okanogan Riesling

Also spelled Okanagan Riesling, this traditional Canadian white wine grape has made its way south to western Washington. Of uncertain origin, the grape is now generally believed to be an interspecific hybrid and not a true vinifera. Although Washington efforts have been successful in taming its sometimes coarse nature, the grape is not likely to play a major role in the future of the western Washington wine industry.

Petite Sirah

Once thought to be the noble Syrah grape of France's Rhone region, Petite Sirah is now know to be the considerably less noble Durif grape. Making its way north from California, there have been a few commercial releases of Washington Petite Sirah. Petite Sirah wines are darkly colored, big, tannic, and rather dull, lacking in fruit. They have fine structure, but offer no special flavor or character. There has been a recent small flurry of interest in Petite Sirah, but energies would be better rewarded if directed toward the true Syrah grape.

Pinot Blanc

Pioneer Oregon winegrowers planted Pinot Blanc, an early ripening variety, only to find that it did not behave as the textbooks said it should. The puzzle was resolved some years later when it was discovered that virtually all the Pinot Blanc in America was not really Pinot Blanc at all, but the grape Melon. True Pinot Blanc is a relative of Pinot Noir. Oregon is now beginning to work experimentally with true Pinot Blanc.

Pinot Gris

A genetic relative of Pinot Noir. Virtually non-existent in the rest of America, Pinot Gris has become one of Oregon's speciality grape varieties. The grape is grown in a wide range of European countries, but its best known wines are from France's Alsace region, where it is also known as Tokay d'Alsace.

At its worst, Pinot Gris offers a heavy, flat, dull white wine. At its best, Pinot Gris is a crisp, full-bodied, full-flavored wine of distinction. Oregon's best renditions of the grape are finished dry, and strike a balance between the extremes of crisp and simple, and heavy and flat. Early picking in warm vintages helps maintain the wine's balance. Unlike some white wines that seem hollow without oak, Pinot Gris is complete even when it has seen only stainless steel.

Pinot Meunier
Grown in small quantities in Oregon, the grape is a red relative of Pinot Noir. It plays a major role in French Champagne. In Oregon, Pinot Meunier finds its way into both sparkling wines and red still wines.

Pinot Noir
Oregon Pinot Noir is arguably the Northwest's finest wine grape. Unlike the Cabernet Sauvignon grape, which produces fine wines throughout the world, Pinot Noir, the great red grape of Burgundy, rarely produces wines of distinction outside its French homeland. Pinot Noir is by far the most sensitive of the great wine grapes. If growing conditions are not just right, Pinot Noir becomes nondescript, at best, or develops less desirable, and sometimes unpleasant, flavors and scents.

Oregon's Willamette Valley meets the grape's criteria with perfection. Although the cooler growing regions of California produce

Cellaring Oregon Pinot Noir

Do Oregon Pinot Noirs really age?

With cellaring, do Oregon Pinots develop the complex textural array of flavors and scents that we associate with fine aged Burgundy—or do they simply grow tired and fall apart? Ever since the first Oregon Pinot Noirs were released to consumers, this has been an ongoing topic of conversation and debate.

For understandable but unfortunate reasons, Oregon Pinots that do not age well are often the very ones put up for the test, and the inevitable conclusions are then extrapolated to Oregon Pinot Noir as a category.

Vineyard and winemaking practices have changed much over the years. In retrospect, early Oregon Pinot Noir was often grown and made into wine in ways that virtually guaranteed the wines would not age well. If you have heard the complaint that Oregon Pinots turn brown and don't age, this may have often been true historically—but, as a statement of current conditions, it is far from valid.

Most (but not all) early Oregon Pinot Noirs have not cellared well. The wines were made at a time when the psychology of the industry called for low acid wines made from the ripest possible grapes. Some of the specifics are detailed in a companion volume to this book, *Northwest Wine Companion*, but it suffices to say here that many of the early wines were overripe with grossly high pH (low acid). These wines really had no hope in the cellar.

Here I will grant that it is quite possible to have an affec-

good Pinot Noir, the wines rarely have the length, finesse, or complexity of Oregon's best. California's famed Carneros region is a cooler area of a very warm climate. Oregon more closely matches the Burgundian norm, growing Pinot Noir on the warmer sites of a cool growing region.

In California, Pinot Noir ripens in the heat of late summer. In Oregon, the grapes ripen in moderating fall temperatures. This extended period of ripening, under moderate conditions, develops and retains the complex flavors of great Pinot Noir.

In the earlier years of the Oregon wine industry, there were fears that the Willamette Valley was too cool for the best wine grapes. But, if anything, in some years the climate may be a bit too warm for Pinot Noir. High pH, low acid, overripe Pinot Noirs were a product of earlier Oregon winegrowing practices. Improved grape growing and winemaking methods have made these concerns less frequent, and warm vintages less troublesome.

Already, the finest Oregon Pinot Noirs are outstanding, but the best is still to come. Further advances in grape growing and winemaking practices are on the horizon.

Oregon's Umpqua and Illinois valleys also offer promise for the

---

tion for such wines. We tend to develop an appreciation for the tastes most familiar to us, and well-cellared older style Oregon Pinot Noir has its fans. I am not one. With age, the older style Pinot Noirs develop cola, tea, and caramel flavors, with a sweetlike character that marks them as high pH (low acid) wines.

Are all older Oregon Pinots like this? Out of wisdom as well as happy accident, not all the early Oregon Pinot Noirs were made in the prevalent style. Vineyard and winery practices have advanced considerably over the years, but a few of these early Pinots show clearly that Oregon Pinot Noir does cellar well indeed—and is at its best with cellar age, bringing out the wonderful array of flavors found only in aged Pinot Noir.

The 1983 Oregon Pinot Noir

vintage has become a double-edged sword. Highly acclaimed when first released, the wines garnered much attention for the industry in a well-publicized

---

For understandable but unfortunate reasons, Oregon Pinots that do not age well are often the very ones put up for the test.

New York tasting. To many tastes, my own included, the vintage is not aging well. This has led detractors to proclaim that Oregon Pinot Noir is far less than what was hoped. If the highly touted 1983 vintage is not aging well, it is said, then what chance do any Oregon Pinot Noirs have in the cellar?

The 1983 vintage was the best and last hurrah of the old

style Oregon Pinot Noir. The wines have good concentration, but they are generally overripe and too low in acid. The rich, soft, ripe characteristics that made them so appealing in youth return now to haunt them.

The 1985s are more like what the 1983s promised to be, richly concentrated wines of considerable merit. A few of the 1985s were overripe, but most were not, and the vintage had better natural acidity. The 1985s will age much better than the 1983s.

The 1986 Pinot Noirs are underrated. A period of rain during the harvest prompted some growers to pick at inopportune times. Coming after the highly publicized and richly ripe 1985 vintage, the 1986s seemed far less concentrated. Indifferent comments by some winegrowers following the vintage were negatively inter-

grape. Like California, Washington's Columbia Valley occasionally produces good Pinot Noir, but the area is really not well suited to the grape, though there are ongoing flurries of attention prompted by recent consumer interest in the grape. Idaho, too, looks only moderately hopeful, though too soon to rule out.

Southwest Washington, an extension of what is geologically known as the Willamette Trough, is effectively part of the Willamette Valley climate. This corner of Washington can authentically lay claim to quality Pinot Noir.

Riesling

Also known as White Riesling and Johannisberg Riesling, it is by far the most widely planted wine grape in the Northwest, finding a home in nearly every winegrowing region.

Riesling is a winegrower's dream. It is the most winter hardy of all the vinifera grape varieties, produces good yields, and grows successfully in a wide range of growing sites, from the coolest areas of Washington's Yakima and Oregon's Willamette Valleys, to Idaho's Snake River Valley, to the very warm Wahluke Slope in Washington's Columbia Valley. Riesling is a late season grape, but it develops varietal character early in the ripening cycle. Good Riesling can be

preted by the media, and the wines had little chance for fame.

There were certainly weak wines in 1986, but many of the 1986s are splendid. While they do not have the rich concentration of the 1985s, they possess the delicate fruit complexity that is the hallmark of good Pinot Noir. They have excellent acidity and structure for cellaring, and the best will develop the fine complex flavors unique to Pinot Noir.

Following the poor press for the 1986 vintage, the 1987s were heavily hyped. I think the vintage is remarkable, not because it is so superb, but because the wines are really quite good in a vintage that was simply too warm to bring out the best in the grape. The hottest year in the modern Oregon wine industry's history, the wines could have turned out like the 1978s—or worse.

If handled like the 1978 vintage, the 1987s would have been pruney and hopelessly

---

Do Oregon Pinot Noirs age well? I have voted with my cellar. It holds more Oregon Pinot Noir than any other Northwest wine.

---

overripe, turning brown in the bottle very quickly—but they were not handled like the 1978 vintage, and they are vastly better. Picking early and adding acid as necessary were keys to success.

A few of the 1987s have port-like flavors that creep through their augmented acidity, but not many. Of necessity, some grapes were picked before the berries had fully colored. Most 1987s lack the complex flavors of the cooler vintages. Augmented by the deft use of oak, however, they are tasty wines that remind me more of Carneros Pinots than Oregon Pinot Noir.

As I write this piece, the first of the 1988s show splendid concentration, firm structure, and many layers of fruit. They look very promising indeed.

The preceding comments on vintages are offered with the caveat—buy wines not vintages. The old adage holds very true. In every vintage, there are wines that differ from the norm.

Do Oregon Pinot Noirs age well? I have voted with my cellar. It holds more Oregon Pinot Noir than any other Northwest wine.

made in a wide range of climates.

Washington and Idaho Rieslings tend toward a riper, fuller-bodied style, with more honeyed, muscat-like tendencies. Oregon Rieslings tend more toward the delicate and floral end of the spectrum. These differences are only general tendencies. It is quite possible to find delicate, floral, Washington Rieslings as well as ripe, honeyed, Oregon Rieslings.

The typical and ubiquitous Northwest Riesling is made in a crisp fruity style, with some residual sweetness. Some of the most interesting Northwest Riesling are made in a wide range of less common styles—bone dry, intensely sweet and botrytised, ice wines, sparkling, and even barrel fermented and barrel aged on the lees.

> **Some of the most interesting Northwest Rieslings are those made in the less common styles.**

The finest Northwest Rieslings occasionally approximate the elusive balance of ripeness, refinement, crisp acidity, and complex flavors and scents that is the hallmark of the finer Rieslings from Germany or those from France's Alsace region. In America, except perhaps for the Rieslings of the Northeast, they have no equal. Most Northwest Rieslings, however, are simply good, if not particularly exciting wines. Today, particularly in Washington, Riesling is in oversupply relative to the other grape varieties.

Sauvignon Blanc

Also known as Fume Blanc, Sauvignon Blanc has evolved into a fashionable grape, both in America and in Europe. Grown throughout the Northwest, it is a major variety only in Washington. Sauvignon Blanc has an herbaceous, grassy, varietal character. It also has a character that British enophiles, affectionately and with a reasonable measure of accuracy, describe as cat's piss. It is a very good wine grape, yet its current fashion exceeds its quality.

Sauvignon Blanc plays a role in white Bordeaux, where it adds fragrance and freshness to Semillon, Bordeaux's true, great, white wine grape. Sauvignon Blanc has a direct, simple, rather coarse character. It rarely develops well with bottle aging, and is usually best when consumed young. Sauvignon Blanc stands up better to warm growing climates than the more subtle and complexly flavored Semillon. Partly because of this, it emerged in California, and thus, in America, as a supposedly superior grape to Semillon.

Current fashion, in the Northwest as well as California, calls for grape growing and winemaking methods that minimize its herbaceous characteristics. What are purportedly dry Sauvignon Blancs are often finished with slight residual sweetness for a rounder, less cutting profile. Such wines can become quite cloying during the course of a meal, as they warm and the sweetness becomes more apparent.

Sauvignon Blanc is at its best when blended with Semillon. Sauvignon Blanc is genuinely a very good wine grape—just not a great wine grape as current fashion seems to suggest.

Semillon

In America, and more specifically, in California, Semillon is viewed as a lesser, secondary grape of white Bordeaux—as a grape of modest distinction that is not in the same league as Sauvignon Blanc. Quite the opposite is the case. Semillon is the predominate grape in great white Bordeaux. Sauvignon Blanc plays only a secondary role, adding a fresh aromatic element, or, in larger proportions, for providing aggressive flavors for lesser wines meant for early consumption.

Semillon is a far more subtle grape that develops increasing complexity with age in the cellar, but it can be flat and dull if it is grown in a climate that is too warm. Because the warmer California growing climates burn away much of Semillon's character, the more aggressive flavors of Sauvignon Blanc have been a necessary substitute for the superior Semillon. In fairness, some California growing climates also do well with Semillon.

Washington, Idaho, and southwest Oregon produce excellent Semillon, but it is widely grown only in Washington. Washington Semillons are not shy in character. Some growing sites offer Semillon with a pronounced grassy character. The best Semillons offer the subtle complexity that is their hallmark in Bordeaux.

The potential of Washington Semillon is far from realized. One of the state's first commercial vinifera varieties, Semillon has only recently gained popularity. Washington Semillon is typically made in a fresh style with no wood aging. The best of these are fine wines, but they show only one of Semillon's many dimensions.

Semillon is benefited greatly by traditional winemaking methods, particularly, wood aging, slightly warmer fermentation temperatures, lees contact, and the like. Semillon is arguably Washington's finest white wine grape. Great Washington Semillon, however, awaits a change in winemaking practices.

> **Semillon is arguably Washington's finest white wine grape.**
> **Great Washington Semillon, however, awaits a change in winemaking practices.**

Siegerrebe

A German vinifera cross that makes very good white wine in western Washington's cool Puget Sound area. The grapes ripen with high sugars, low acids, and an intense spicy character. It is capable of producing very good, sweet botrytised wines.

Sylvaner

Grown only in very small quantities in Oregon, Sylvaner offers a slightly earthy, moderately flavored, Riesling-like wine.

Syrah

The great red grape of France's Rhone Valley is just getting out of the experimental stage in Washington. Early results have been very encouraging, and the grape is seemingly less prone to winter damage than was feared. It is too early to say, but Syrah could become one of Washington's important wine grapes.

Zinfandel

Although the basis for many jug wines and the ubiquitous White Zinfandel, it can also be an exceptionally fine wine grape, as many examples from California have shown. Unfortunately, Zinfandel requires a long, warm, growing season, and has been generally regarded as not well suited to Northwest climates.

In miniscule quantities, Zinfandel is grown in Washington's Columbia Valley, along the Columbia Gorge, and in southern

Oregon. Reports from Oregon's Umpqua Valley, of a very old clone of Zinfandel which ripens better and more uniformly, offer encouragement. Additionally, recent efforts on warmer Columbia Valley growing sites have produced excellent red wine. Zinfandel may yet play a larger role in the Northwest.

The Wine Cellar

Browsing through Columbia's library

How well do Washington wines age? Vineyard and winery practices have developed greatly since the inception of Washington's modern wine industry, but the early wines offer a glimpse at the region's potential. In 1988, I had the opportunity to taste a number of wines from Columbia's library, the winery known, in the early years, as Associated Vintners. Here are some highlights.

A 1970 Cabernet Sauvignon showed fine fruit and bottle aged complexity. A twenty-one year old 1967 Cabernet had the typical color of an older red wine, but showed wonderful depth of fruit. After two decades in the cellar, these were splendid wines. Given the advancements in the vineyards and in the winery in the intervening years, the best of the newer Cabernets should age even more impressively.

The success of the red wines might have been predicted, but the white wines were a remarkable surprise. All were made in a dry style.

A twenty-one year old 1968 Gewurztraminer, in spite of modest acid, remained very drinkable. An 11 year old 1977 Gewurztraminer with slightly better acid had aged superbly. A 1967 Riesling, bottle number 00001, tasted relatively young and would easily hold for longer aging. Perhaps most remarkable was a 1970 Chardonnay with a complex sealing wax character. The wine had

> The success of the red wines might have been predicted, but the white wines were a remarkable surprise.

developed wonderful flavors, not merely surviving, but benefiting greatly from its 18 years in the bottle.

Savage on Northwest Wine

An Interview with Mark Savage, Master of Wine

Meredith: What was the first American wine you tasted?

Savage: The first American wine I ever recall tasting was in 1969 when I was running the Oxford University Wine Circle as an undergraduate. We had a blind tasting of Australian, Californian and French wine.

Meredith: What was your impression of the wines?

Savage: One of the French wines, I think it was a Chateau d'Issan 1962, clearly came out as the best balanced, most complex, and most sophisticated wine, but the California wines were by no means disgraced. They were very interesting, and that immediately made them memorable to me, and I thought one day we'll want to look at that area in serious depth.

I spent the following several years gaining experience in the wine trade in England and France, before developing the idea of running a small company based on very purist ideals, selecting single estate wines from small producers that I knew I could trust, and taking a long-term view of building up a reputation based on the track record of buying from trustworthy producers.

Meredith: How did you come to American wines and Northwest wines?

Savage: The decision was made by me in 1979 during a period when French wines were beginning to go through the roof in price and American wines from California were becoming more accessible—there were certainly more of them. The quality was also improving dramatically, and because the dollar was becoming considerably weaker, they became commercially viable in England.

This was in the very early stages of my own company, and we had

Mark Savage

Master of Wine & noted wine authority

Born in Uganda, Mark Savage was educated at Ampleforth and Oxford, where he was president of the Oxford University Wine Circle. Savage began his career in the British wine trade in 1971. In 1975, he was awarded that year's Vintner's Scholarship, which allowed him to visit wine producers in France, Italy, and Germany. When the money from the scholarship ran out, Savage worked his way through France during the harvest season, including a stint working twelve-hour night shifts in the presshouse of an Alsatian producer. In 1980, Sav-

Founded in 1953, only some 140 candidates have earned the Master of Wine Diploma

age was awarded the distinguished Masters of Wine diploma.

The Institute of Masters of Wine was founded in 1953. The process for becoming a Master of Wine is extremely rigorous. In the more than 35 years of its existence, only some 140 candidates have earned the Master of Wine diploma. Preliminary

processes eliminate all but the top candidates, leaving approximately 50 candidates each year. Of those candidates, only approximately 10 percent are awarded the Masters of Wine diploma. In some years, no MWs are awarded. A Masters of Wine candidate must have comprehensive knowledge of the wines of the world as well as an experienced and well-trained palate.

Savage, through his wine import and marketing firms, Windrush Wines and Savage Selection, is widely regarded as England's premier importer of American wines, particularly the wines of the Northwest. He was the first European wine authority to study the Northwest in depth.

Savage travels extensively throughout Europe's major winegrowing regions to select wines. Northwest wines are a small, but rapidly growing portion of his import selections. Savage is author of *The Red Wines of Burgundy*, an up-to-date guide to the Burgundy region and its wines.

Though a resident of England, Savage has spent more time in Northwest wineries and vineyards than most regional

wine writers. I can personally testify to his palate, and his familiarity with the region and its wines. I once served him a wine blind. Through a series of logical progressions, Savage iden-

Though a resident of England, Savage has spent more time in Northwest wineries & vineyards than most regional wine writers

tified the grape, the state where the wine was made, and the winery that produced it.

Savage had not previously tasted that particular wine, but he was sufficiently familiar with the grape, the regional characteristics, and the style of the winery that a logical (and correct) conjecture was possible. Interestingly, Savage commented that a similar assessment of a California Chardonnay would have been much more difficult. In the Northwest, he said, the winegrowing climates tend to produce more distinctive signatures and complex character variations.

very little cash to play with, but I made use of the cheap flights of Freddy Laker from London to L.A. On my first trip, I spent three weeks giving myself a crash course in California wineries. When I returned, I was able to tell my colleagues that I tasted a huge number of wines up and down California and honestly could say that I hadn't tasted a single badly made or uninteresting wine. That's something you couldn't do in France over a three week period, at least certainly not at that time.

The trip made a major impression, and I was back again the following year, with a more commercial hat on to begin making a few purchases.

Meredith: How and why did you make your way to the Northwest?

Savage: The logical progression seemed to me to move to the north, away from the heat of California, if I was going to find wines with an emphasis on finesse and elegance rather than on mere power.

I'd been impressed by California wines, and still continue to be, but I saw that the problems faced by producers in the warm climate of California were the opposite faced by producers in the best part of France. That is to say, in the best parts of France there is usually an overabundance of acid and not enough sugar. The reverse is obviously true in a hot climate. If a correction has to be made to a wine in a warm region like California, it will be more a question of adding acid than adding sugar.

When I got up to see the cooler regions of the Northwest, in about 1980, I liked the prospects very much. It seemed to me that there was an area up there of enormous potential and versatility.

My first port of call when I went to Oregon was to see David Lett of The Eyrie Vineyards. He had just begun to put Oregon on the map by that stage.

I came back to the Northwest very soon, to Seattle, as a member of the judging panel for the Enological Society of the Pacific Northwest. Being on the panel gave me the opportunity to taste all the best wines of Oregon, Washington, and Idaho. In subsequent years, I participated in other judging panels, which allowed me to assess the progress of a broad range of wines over time.

Meredith: Given your international perspective, what are the Northwest's best varietals? Where does the main potential lie for the various growing regions?

Savage: Straight away, the Northwest seems to be more versatile than California. I think no one will doubt California's ability for making great Cabernet Sauvignon, Chardonnay, and Zinfandel, but I think in the Northwest we have Oregon quite clearly with a different growing climate as well as the Columbia Basin in eastern Washington and the Snake River Valley in Idaho.

We have seen a good number of Pinot Noir wines with genuine elegance and finesse emerging from Oregon. We have found Char-

■ **Mark Savage**

donnay a more difficult customer in that climate, perhaps because the main clone planted in Oregon to date is not actually a good ripening clone in that climate. It happens to be the clone that is most widespread in California, so maybe it's not reasonable to expect it to perform so readily in such a different climate.

It's nearly certain that the next stage for Oregon to develop greater complexity in its wines and real depth will be when it manages to get a wider variety of clones, both in Chardonnay and Pinot Noir. I suppose if we look at Oregon from a European perspective, we'll tend to think of it as the USA's answer to Burgundy and Alsace. I think there are many similarities with the latter, and this raises the possibility of interesting wines coming from Pinot Gris and Muscat, not forgetting Gewurztraminer and Riesling in the dry style.

Meredith: Which Muscats do you see for Oregon?

Savage: I have not seen many, but only last week I tasted a Muscat Ottonel from the Eyrie Vineyard which seemed to have the same kind of spiciness and style that I associate very firmly with Alsace.

Moving on from Oregon to the warmer ripening climates of eastern Washington, I see enormous possibility for Cabernet Sauvignon and Merlot and a totally different style of Chardonnay, closer in a sense to California, but with a different balance because of the higher natural acidity that the grape growers and wine makers have at their disposal.

Idaho has so far shown me real potential for interesting Chardonnay with flavors, delicacy, and elegance which I had not thought would have been forthcoming from the first examples I had tried some years ago. Whether Idaho can do anything with Pinot Noir is much more doubtful, but I certainly wouldn't dismiss the possibility. I've tasted two or three in cask which gave me real hope that wines of finesse with that nice Pinot Noir perfume could be produced.

Meredith: You've spoken of Oregon as being somewhat Burgundian in their most notable varietals, and regarding Washington you've mentioned the red Bordeaux varietals. What about the white Bordeaux varietals in Washington? How do you see those?

Savage: It's certainly another area which will contribute to that overall versatile picture. I've tasted some excellent Sauvignon Blanc, although the danger of a rather excessive vegetal, grassy flavor creeping in is evident. If that rather savage character from the Sauvignon grape can be tamed, then I think it's perfectly possible to produce wines that will be a match for the, shall I call it, Sancerre style of stainless, fruity flavored Sauvignons rather than the oaky Bordeaux manifestations of that grape.

As for Semillon, it's a variety that I've long felt to be underrated, whereas I've felt that Sauvignon Blanc has been too fashionable and overrated for a variety that tends to do very little with bottle age. Semillon, both by itself, and when blended judiciously with Sauvignon has a real future in Washington state, and that mix will lend

"The logical progression seemed to me to move to the north, away from the heat of California, if I was going to find wines with an emphasis on finesse and elegance rather than on mere power."

itself very nicely to barrel fermentation and prolonged aging both in cask and in bottle. With this type of wine, I think that Washington state can very likely rival the best from Bordeaux.

Meredith: In Europe, Semillon is regarded as much the superior grape relative to Sauvignon Blanc?

Savage: I think it's still relatively underrated in Europe as well. The country where it seems to have achieved its greatest success and reputation has been Australia, in the Hunter Valley. Anyone who's had a really old, mature Hunter Valley Semillon will know what I'm talking about.

I'd like to see more done with Semillon in Europe. Dry white Bordeaux has been in the doldrums for a long time. One of the reasons is maybe that not enough has been made of Semillon. Too much emphasis has been put on dull Sauvignon, which can be very flattering early, but when the wine has been in bottle for six months and has lost its precocious fruit, and with clumsy wine making and too much sulfur, those wines don't look too good when they're a year old. That smell of dirty dish cloths has been all too familiar to many of us who have been trying to buy good dry white Bordeaux.

Fortunately, there has been a resurgence of interest in Semillon in Bordeaux, and in vinification techniques involving barrel fermentation, skin contact, and new oak. Semillon adapts to new oak very nicely, but Sauvignon, I think, does not.

Meredith: We've been talking about the Washington grape varieties, what about Riesling, the state's most widely planted grape?

Savage: I don't know any other area in the world that can produce such competition for Germany in terms of the fine balance between sweetness and acidity as Washington state.

I've been tremendously impressed by the late harvest and botrytis affected Rieslings that I've tasted from a number of good producers. They seem to be able to produce them with less risk and more continuity from vintage to vintage than Germany, at a much lower price than Germany. I've tasted a number of flawless wines which make me sure that Riesling has a very valid home in the Northwest.

The late harvest wines have impressed me the most, but in the drier styles, Riesling is certainly useful. Whereas, the medium-dry/medium-sweet style is useful for the first-time wine drinker market, it tends to become less useful when the beginners have moved on to regular wine drinking and their palates naturally move towards a drier taste.

I don't, myself, find the type of Riesling that is neither dry nor sweet, i.e., somewhere in the middle, commercially very useful. Although the wines, as a group, are not unpleasant or faulty, they have very little flavor interest beyond that of sugar and water. They're not good with food. They're neither one thing nor the other.

Meredith: At this point, what wines in the Northwest, if any, can compete head to head with their European counterparts.

> **"Semillon is a variety that I've long felt to be underrated—it has a real future in Washington state."**

> **"Oregon hasn't got a great deal to fear...California has produced some very good Pinot Noir wines in recent years, though I still believe them to be the exception rather than the rule."**

Savage: I think if you were to line up a good late harvest Riesling against a German Beerenauslese, the Washington wine, far from being disgraced, would hold its head up very well. For the lighter styles of Riesling, I think Germany would probably win hands down for flavor complexity and interest.

In Pinot Noir, while I think that Burgundy clearly maintains an edge in complexity, which is not surprising when you consider how much experience there is there, coupled with the average age of the vineyards and the effects of those unique soils and the growing climate, the flavors that are coming out of Oregon Pinot Noirs are often every bit as fine as those coming out of Burgundy.

While it's not difficult to find some unexciting Oregon Pinot Noirs, it's also easy to find at least as many poor examples of Burgundy. Both red Burgundy and Oregon Pinot Noir tend to be relatively expensive. This is likely to remain the case because the yield of grapes is low and production costs of that type of wine are relatively high.

I think it's perfectly easy to put together a tasting of Pinot Noir based wines from all over the world in which Oregon will perform very credibly. I certainly think that outside France, Oregon hasn't got a great deal to fear from many other countries. California has produced some very good Pinot Noir wines in recent years, though I still believe them to be the exception rather than the rule for that state. New Zealand, in time, ought to prove itself capable of doing interesting things with Pinot Noir. Its track record to date with red wines is disappointing, but this will change.

With Chardonnay, I think we haven't seen any serious competition to great white Burgundy coming out of Oregon. We've certainly seen some very acceptable wines that would stand up to competition of lesser white Burgundies.

If one's looking to more weight of flavor in Chardonnay, then there have been some wines produced in Washington state that I believe will stand up to competition from some much more expensive Cote d'Or Burgundies. And recently, I recall that an Idaho Chardonnay placed third in a tasting of 87 highly respected Chardonnays from all over the world.

In terms of the Bordeaux grape varieties, there have been several Washington state Cabernet Sauvignon wines that would have no problem standing up to classed growth wines from the Medoc. Stylistically, it looks as if they have enough individuality to create a niche in style that falls somewhere between California and Bordeaux—maybe in the ratio of two-thirds Bordeaux, one- third California, rather than the other way around.

Meredith: Has Bordeaux itself changed in recent years?

Savage: I think you could say that Bordeaux has moved towards a style that is likely to be more precocious than in the past, with the commercial necessity of making wines drinkable sooner. And, there's no doubt that Bordeaux has paid attention to the success that

California has had with its Cabernets, and it's not been just a question of California trying to imitate Bordeaux, but maybe there's been an element of Bordeaux trying to imitate California. This sometimes leads one to the feeling that California wines are getting too austere and Bordeaux wines are getting too opulent. Maybe the right balance is somewhere in the middle.

There is a flavor characteristic in many Washington Cabernet Sauvignons that I don't find in Bordeaux, and don't generally want to find. This is sometimes disconcerting. The flavor in question is usually described as vegetal or herbaceous, and may be a result of vineyard practices and vineyard sites which may tend to accentuate that characteristic. I must say there have been many wines that I've tasted that have had unnecessarily high levels of tannin, and that the wines themselves have had enough structure provided by their acid backbone not to require so much tannin.

Meredith: Good acidity the key to their structure rather than the tannins.

Savage: I would think that I would prefer to see the acidity providing that structure because I feel that it contributes more to the aromas and flavors of the wines and to their longevity and the growth in complexity of those flavors, while much of the tannin is simply going to overpower and outlive the fruit.

Meredith: You mentioned the vegetative aspects of Washington Cabernet. Is that always found, or are there Cabernets that have not had that character?

Savage: I think it's a characteristic that one has grown accustomed to being on the look-out for almost automatically every time you taste a Washington Cabernet, and, more often than not, the flavor, if not strikingly evident, can be found lurking in the background if you really want to dig it out. But I certainly have tasted a number of Washington Cabernets, albeit a minority, that have not a trace of that characteristic, and have exhibited very interesting fruit flavors of their own, and real finesse.

Meredith: Has that been a trend in recent years?

Savage: I hope so. I think that I've noticed an increase in the number of wines, particularly from certain individual vineyard sites, where the fruit seems to be showing real class without any of the cruder flavors.

Meredith: For Oregon Pinot Noir, what directions should Oregon take, or to what areas should they devote attention in order to produce even better, more complex wines?

Savage: This takes us back to the pressing need for a wider variety of plant material in the vineyard. The two principal Oregon Pinot Noir clones that have been certified for use from virus free stocks are the Wadenswil clone and the Pommard clone. These individual

> "...there have been several Washington state Cabernet Sauvignon wines that would have no problem standing up to classed growth wines from the Medoc."

clones undoubtedly have different characteristics and a blend of the two, in itself, is a contributory factor to the ultimate complexity of the wines.

However, few of the wines are really showing as many layers of flavor as you expect from great Burgundy. And while this is largely due to the relatively young vines, it must be at least partly due to the lack of clonal variety. We are hoping that new plant material from Dijon will be forthcoming in the near future, and within ten years, I hope we can expect to see a much wider range of clones in the vineyard.

The other question will concern the development of ideal vineyard sites for Pinot Noir. Initially, the area with the most reclame has been that of the Dundee Hills, in Yamhill County. As a result, land prices are much higher there than other parts of the Willamette Valley.

But there is exciting potential in the Eola Hills near Salem, and in the hills to the south and west of Corvallis in the foothills of the Coast Range. There are also some good sites north of the Dundee Hills in Washington County, so it is quite likely that we will be able to find three or four areas in Oregon, at the very least, which prove themselves highly suitable for Pinot Noir.

Another key factor, I think, is that older, mature vines are particularly important for red wines, and especially for Pinot Noir. When Oregon's vineyards are properly mature, I think we will see if Oregon Pinot Noir will be the great success story that many of us hope.

Meredith: What about the La Center area of southwest Washington? What is your view of Pinot Noir there?

Savage: Clearly, the wines from that area, although from geopolitical terms have to be considered as Washington wines, in geophysical terms they are part of the Willamette climatic environment, and the wines are closely related to their Oregon counterparts. I like the style of wines from here very much.

Meredith: It's been some ten years since you first came to the Northwest. What are your impressions now?

Savage: My conclusion, after a decade of looking at Northwest wines, is that the early potential that I felt was there is rapidly being realized. We should see additional gains as people learn where to plant, what sites are best for which grapes, and as the vines themselves get older. If Northwest wines have done as well as they have in the last 10 years, the next 10 years should be at least as exciting and inspiring.

> **"...the early potential that I felt was there is rapidly being realized... if Northwest wines have done as well as they have in the last 10 years, the next 10 years should be at least as exciting and inspiring."**

Oregon's Wine Industry

Informed idealists in pursuit of a vision

Less than three decades ago, an Oregon State University publication advised that premium vinifera wine grape varieties were not well suited to Oregon climates. The publication recommended *Vitis labrusca* grapes instead. At about the same time, faculty at the University of California at Davis were warning starry-eyed students that the idea of winegrowing in Oregon was worse than foolish. The grapes as well as their high hopes, it was said, would be rotted by endless rains and killed by spring and fall frosts.

Three decades, several thousand acres of premium vinifera wine grapes, and numerous international accolades later, it is reasonably safe to say that the early advice may not have been the best. The starry-eyed students persevered. Oregon winegrowers have a well-earned reputation for being stubborn idealists—and we can be thankful. Were it not so, there would be no Oregon wine industry, and there would be no Oregon wine.

Winemaking and vinifera grape growing came to Oregon more than a century ago. In the 1850s early settlers brought cuttings to Oregon by way of the Oregon Trail, and from California, to southwest Oregon. By the 1880s, Oregon's fledgling wine industry was centered in Jackson County, near the California border, in the far southwestern part of the state. By that time, winegrowing was active in the Willamette Valley as well.

Some of the early varieties were not the best for wine, and Prohibition struck before the wine industry was well developed. At Repeal, a farm winery law encouraged a flurry of small scale

Oregon
Wine Grape Acreage 5,250 acres
Winegrowing Regions Willamette Valley, Umpqua Valley, Illinois Valley, Applegate Valley, Rogue River Valley, Columbia Gorge, Walla Walla Valley, Columbia Valley
Predominant Grape Varieties Pinot Noir, Riesling, Chardonnay

47

wineries. There were 28 such wineries by 1937, most making wines in a sweet style, often from fruits and berries. Demand for this type of wine decreased over time, and by 1960, only four wineries remained. One year later, the Oregon wine industry was reborn.

In 1961, Richard Sommer bought land in the Umpqua Valley, near the town of Roseburg, and planted cuttings from premium vinifera wine grapes he brought from California. Two years later, Sommer bonded his winery, Hillcrest Vineyard. The Oregon wine renaissance had begun. Sommer focused his efforts on Riesling, a grape that still today remains a mainstay of the Oregon wine industry.

In 1965, two years after Hillcrest was bonded, David Lett came to Oregon with the singular intent of finding a climate suitable for the Burgundian grape varieties, and most particularly, a climate for Pinot Noir. Passing by the warmer Roseburg area in southern Oregon, Lett settled in the Willamette Valley, in the Dundee Hills, southwest of Portland, and founded The Eyrie Vineyards. Lett's choice of Pinot Noir proved farsighted. Today the grape is the glory of Oregon's wine industry.

Dick Erath, of the Knudsen Erath Winery, and a few others followed shortly thereafter in the 1960s. By the end of the 1970s, Oregon's wine industry was growing at a rapid pace, most of the newcomers gravitating to the northern Willamette Valley. A century ago, the wine industry was centered in the southernmost part of western Oregon near the California border. With the wine renaissance, emphasis shifted northward, first to the Umpqua Valley near Roseburg, then to the northern Willamette Valley, still the center of Oregon's wine industry. Now, every winegrowing region in the state is experiencing expansion, including Oregon's sliver of the Columbia Valley, east of the Cascade Mountains.

Most Oregon winegrowers are white collar professionals who have turned to winegrowing out of an interest in fine wines and a rural lifestyle. Few had connections with agriculture prior to winegrowing. Most Oregon wineries are winery estates. The winery and winegrower's residence are adjacent to the vineyards, and the winegrower literally lives with his vines and wines. An urban winery is rare, and even in those rare cases, urban wineries are usually associated with their own vineyards.

On average, Oregon's wineries and vineyards are much smaller than those of either Washington or Idaho. Roughly three-quarters of Oregon's vineyards are no larger than 20 acres. The existing agricultural environment is not one of expansive agribusiness, but of relatively small orchards and farms in a fairly populous, rural, agricultural community. Success is bringing change, however. Families still enter the wine business with a plot of land for their home, small estate vineyard, and winery, but corporations and outside investment are now part of the wine scene as well.

When the highly regarded Burgundian, Robert Drouhin, purchased prime Oregon vineyard land and started an Oregon winery,

When the highly regarded Burgundian, Robert Drouhin, purchased prime Oregon vineyard land and started an Oregon winery, the wine world received yet one more hint that Oregon might be something special.

the wine world received yet one more hint that Oregon might be something special. Oregon now has vineyards that exceed 400 acres. A French Champagne house has purchased Oregon vineyard land. An enterprise with an Australian connection is producing Oregon sparkling wine on a large scale.

California investors suffering sticker-shock from Napa Valley land prices see Oregon vineyard land as a bargain. One Willamette Valley land purchase encompassed nearly 2,000 contiguous acres. Oregon's expanding national and international reputation has added to growth pressures. Predictably, Oregon land prices are escalating.

In the early days of the Oregon wine industry, while the Oregon vineyards were maturing, many Oregon wineries supplemented their grape supplies by buying grapes from Washington, and, even, California. This led to a few guffaws from skeptics who saw the grape purchases as evidence that Oregon was unable to grow its own wine grapes in any meaningful sort of way. But times change. Oregon now sells grapes to Washington and several other states. California is one of Oregon's major out-of-state markets.

Oregon's wine labeling regulations are the strictest in the nation. If a grape variety is used in the name of a wine, the wine must be no less than 90 percent of that variety, except Cabernet Sauvignon, which may be blended with up to 25 percent of other Bordeaux grape varieties. Generic names, such as Chablis and Burgundy, are prohibited.

The economics of Oregon winegrowing are hard. Most western Oregon vines are cane pruned rather than cordon pruned, a method requiring greater skill, attention, and time. Crop yields are small. Some years are too cool. Rain during harvest is not uncommon, and each year's crop faces potential destruction by waves of migrating birds. For some winegrowing regions, freezes and frosts are additional threats to the vine.

In most instances, Oregon winegrowers chose the winegrowing enterprise not because it was the easiest way to make money (which in Oregon, it surely is not), but out of an abiding commitment to the enterprise itself, and the profound belief that Oregon is qualitatively the most important winegrowing region in America. For the production of fine wine, Oregon is not the easiest region in America, but it is easily one of the best.

Oregon Winegrowing Regions

Elegant wines from a land of rich pastoral beauty

ike Washington, Oregon is divided into two very different climates by the towering Cascade Mountain Range. The Cascades, running north and south through both states, create a barrier to Pacific marine air. On the eastern side of the Cascades, the climate is very warm and dry, and the land is a near desert. West of the Cascades, the climate is cooler, temperate, and more moist.

Unlike western Washington, western Oregon experiences less of the direct effect of the cool, moist, marine air. Western Oregon's Coast Range forms a continuous partial barrier to the onshore Pacific air flow. Running along the Oregon coast, from the state's northern border southward, the Coast Range partially blocks the marine air. Western Oregon's climate is consequently warmer, drier, and sunnier than western Washington's climate. Enough of the marine effect remains, however, so that western Oregon is ideally suited to well-known cool climate vinifera grape varieties such as Pinot Noir, Chardonnay, and Riesling. Unlike Washington, Oregon's main winegrowing regions are in the western part of the state.

Vineyards have been planted east of the Cascade Mountains on the previously undeveloped Oregon side of the Columbia River Valley. The openness and availability of land and the agribusiness economic environment suggest that a large portion of Oregon's wine production could one day come from grapes grown in the Columbia Valley, a climate greatly different from western Oregon's major winegrowing regions. As yet this has not happened, and

Oregon remains firmly identified with the wine grapes and wine styles of the western part of the state.

The Willamette Valley, Oregon's coolest winegrowing region, is the source for most of Oregon's wine grapes. Although the Willamette Valley does not totally dominate the state's wine industry to the same degree that the Columbia Valley dominates Washington winegrowing, the Willamette Valley is by far western Oregon's largest winegrowing region in size, vineyard acreage, and number of wineries.

Willamette Valley

Once a submerged inland bay, sediment and lava flows gradually raised its floor above sea level to create today's Willamette Valley. The valley filled first in the southern Willamette, the most inland part of the bay, working its way northward.

In January 1984, the Bureau of Alcohol Tobacco and Firearms (BATF) formally recognized the Willamette Valley as a designated viticultural area. Approximately 170 miles long and 60 miles wide at its greatest breadth, the Willamette Valley viticultural area covers 5,200 square miles. Forming an elongated "V" narrowing to the south, the Willamette Valley runs from Oregon's northern border on the Columbia River north of Portland to the Calapooya Mountains south of the city of Eugene, half way down the state.

Once a submerged inland bay, sediment and lava flows gradually filled the bay, slowly raising its floor above sea level to create today's Willamette Valley. The process began in the southern Willamette, the most inland part of the bay, and worked its way northward.

Bordered on the west by the Coast Range Mountains and on the east by the foothills of the Cascade Mountain Range, the Willamette Valley is a mosaic of prairie, open savanna with scattered oak trees, grasslands, and forest and woodlands of Oregon white oak and fir trees. Except for a slight extension into southwest Washington, the Willamette Valley vegetation pattern is unique in the Northwest.

Willamette Valley vineyards are located on wooded hillsides in the western part of the valley, along the foothills of the Coast Range; on the slopes of the valley's volcanic hills; or on the many hillsides that have been eroded into the basalt lava plain during the last 20 million years or so.

The Willamette Valley viticultural area generally extends no higher than 1000 feet into the foothills of the surrounding mountain ranges. Willamette Valley winegrowers have found that southerly hillside slopes between 300 feet and 1,000 feet elevation make the best growing sites.

Higher slopes are too cool and rainy. Lower slopes risk frost hazards. Nighttime cool air settles in lower elevations, and the vines do not warm as rapidly to the summer sun. Not only does cool air pool on the valley floor, but the heavier moist soils are slow to warm, and delay vine growth in spring. The heavier soils on the valley floor also produce more vegetative growth, delaying grape ripening. The relatively flat valley floor makes up much of the Willamette Valley, but the land is not well suited to grape growing.

In this northern marine climate, southerly hillside slopes capture the most energy from the sun. Parts of the Willamette Valley are subject to frequent, morning, low clouds, a reminder that the Pacific Ocean is not far away, and that the Coast Range Mountains only partially block the onshore flow of marine air.

Winter freezing is almost never a problem for the Willamette Valley's temperate climate. In February of 1989, however, the hardest winter freeze of this century caused major damage in some vineyards, and served as a reminder that Mother Nature occasionally takes broad, whimsical swings from the norm.

Willamette Valley
Northern Willamette

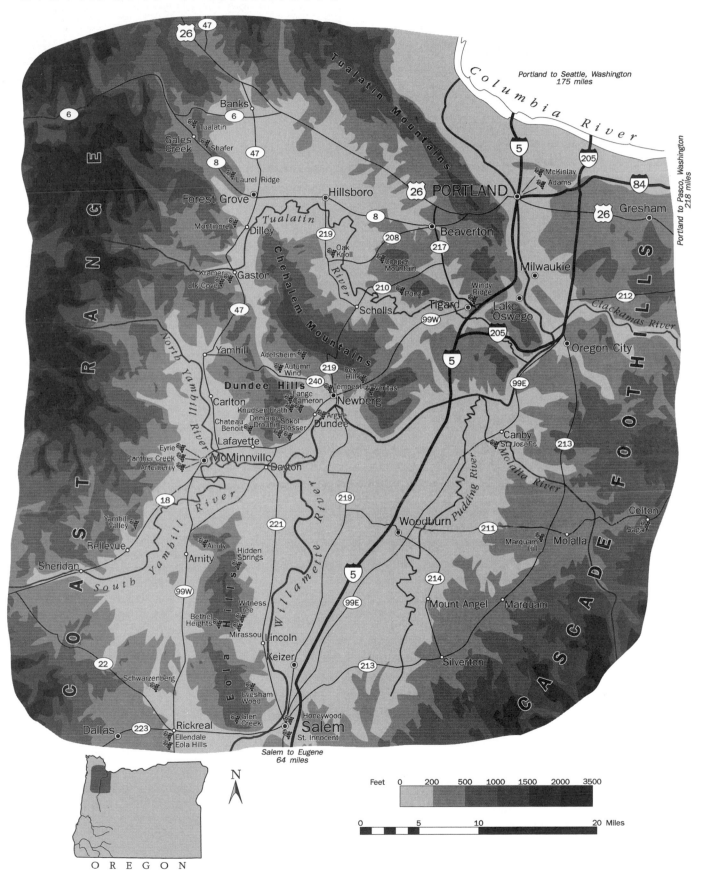

Columbia River

Portland to Seattle, Washington
175 miles

Portland to Pasco, Washington
218 miles

PORTLAND

Tualatin Mountains

Banks
Tualatin
Gales Creek
Shafer
Laurel Ridge
Forest Grove
Montinore
Dilley
Tualatin
Hillsboro
Beaverton
Gresham
Kramer
Elk Cove
Gaston
Oak Knoll
Cooper Mountain
Windy Ridge
Milwaukie
Chehalem Mountains
Ponzi
Scholls
Tigard
Lake Oswego
Oregon City
Clackamas River
Yamhill
Adelsheim
Autumn Wind
Rex Hill
Tempest
Veritas
Newberg
Dundee Hills
Lange
Cameron
Carlton
Knudsen Erath
Domaine Drouhin
Sokol Blosser
Argyle
Dundee
Chateau Benoit
Lafayette
Canby
St. Josef's
Molalla River
Pudding River
Eyrie
Panther Creek
Arterberry
McMinnville
Dayton
Colton
Saga
North Yambill River
Yamhill Valley
Woodburn
Marquam Hill
Molalla
Bellevue
Sheridan
Amity
Hidden Springs
Amity
Witness Tree
Bethel Heights
Mirassou
Lincoln
Mount Angel
Marquam
South Yambill River
Willamette River
Keizer
Silverton
Schwarzenberg
Eola Hills
Evesham Wood
Glen Creek
Honeywood
Salem
St. Innocent
Dallas
Rickreal
Ellendale
Eola Hills

Salem to Eugene
64 miles

COAST RANGE
CASCADE FOOTHILLS

N

OREGON

Feet 0 200 500 1000 1500 2000 3500

0   5   10   20 Miles

A winegrowing climate that ripens the grapes rapidly, early, and easily is also a climate that robs the grapes of their complex flavors and aromatics. In the Willamette Valley, grape ripening usually does not come with a rush, but gradually, as summer changes into fall.

For the better vineyard sites, frost is infrequently a problem, but on less than ideal growing sites, such as those at very high elevations or on the valley floor, spring frosts are a concern. Rain is moderate during the summer months, but increases in fall and winter, and often aggravates the grape harvest.

The Willamette Valley climate is classified as Region I, the coolest of five heat regions in the U. C. Davis classification system. A useful, but very rough guide, the Davis system lumps together a wide range of growing climates under the Region I moniker, and does not capture or address important distinctions that are key to the success of many of the worlds most important grape varieties and winegrowing regions.

In many respects, the Willamette Valley has more direct similarities with notable European winegrowing regions than do other American winegrowing areas. In itself, this does not necessarily mean that the Willamette Valley is inherently superior to other American winegrowing regions, but it begins to explain the interlinkage of the Willamette Valley winegrowing terrain and climate with its grape growing and winemaking practices, style of wine, and the philosophy and outlook of Willamette Valley winegrowers.

The Willamette Valley is a cool, marginal winegrowing climate. In California, as an example, cool climate grapes such as Pinot Noir are grown in the coolest growing sites (such as the Carneros area) of an otherwise very warm winegrowing region. In the Willamette Valley, as in the major European winegrowing regions, winegrowing sites are chosen in the opposite manner, and grapes are grown on the warmest sites of cool, marginal, winegrowing climates.

In Europe's premium winegrowing regions, grape varieties are not planted where they will ripen easily, but where they will ripen best. The grapes are planted where, in most years, they will just become ripe—but no more than just ripe. European winegrowers expect that in some years the grapes will not fully ripen, a necessary paying of dues for the excellence of other years.

Pinot Noir, for example, is not grown in Burgundy rather than Bordeaux simply out of tradition. In Bordeaux, a warmer climate than Burgundy, Pinot Noir would consistently produce "big" wines and ripen easily every year, but the quality would suffer. Pinot Noir ripens more quickly than the Bordeaux varieties, and requires the cooler climate of the Burgundy region. Similarly, the Bordeaux grape varieties (Cabernet Sauvignon, Merlot, etc.) are grown in the warmer Bordeaux region, but not in the even warmer Rhone Valley.

The best wine grapes and the best wines come from winegrowing regions where the grapes are carefully matched to the climate, the climate is marginal for the grape varieties, and the ripening of the grapes coincides with the end of the growing season. A winegrowing climate that ripens the grapes rapidly, early, and easily is also a climate that robs the grapes of their complex flavors, aromatics, and nuance.

Willamette Valley
Southern Willamette

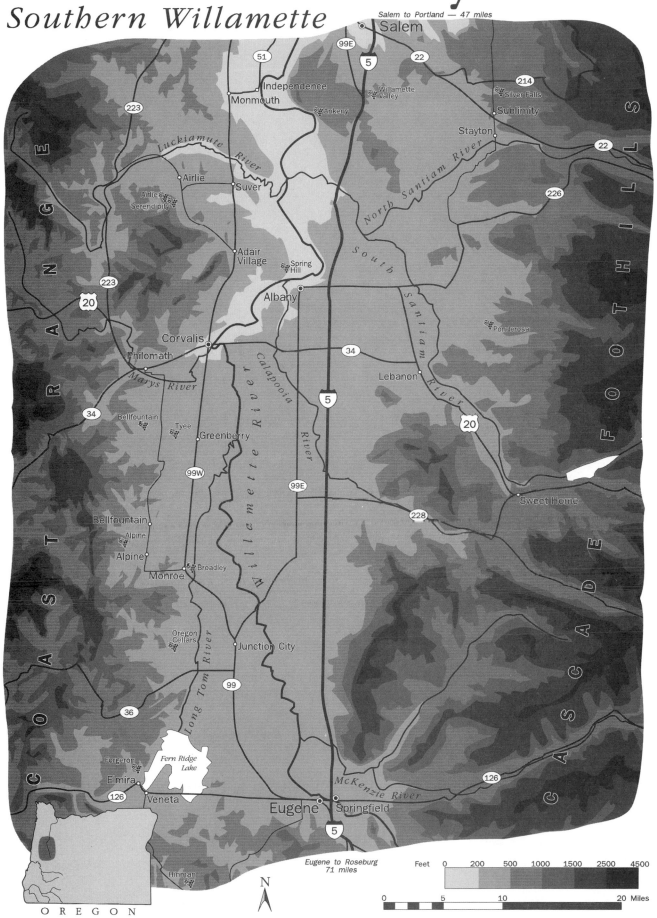

Salem to Portland — 47 miles

Salem

Eugene to Roseburg
71 miles

OREGON

In the Willamette Valley, grape ripening usually does not come with a rush, but gradually, as summer changes into fall. In spite of the relative coolness of the growing region, however, vintages are occasionally warmer than ideal, and the harvest must be hurried before the grapes become overripe. Arguably, too, a few grape growing sites are actually too warm for the best quality Pinot Noir, and better suited, for example, to Oregon's predominant Chardonnay clone which does best with more heat.

In the Willamette Valley, as in Europe's major winegrowing regions, vintages vary considerably from year to year, and in these cool marginal climates, the vintages that are less good are almost always so because the year was too cool, only occasionally because the year was too warm or the grapes overripened or ripened too soon.

The Willamette Valley is suited to a narrower range of grape varieties than many other American winegrowing regions, but the varieties that "fit" the Willamette Valley climate, such as the highly sensitive and fickle Pinot Noir grape, achieve an excellence of flavors and refinement rarely found elsewhere.

Umpqua Valley

The Umpqua Valley is not a simple, open basin, but an interconnected series of many small mountains, hillsides, and river drainages.

One of Oregon's oldest grape growing regions, dating back to the 1800s, the Umpqua Valley viticultural area was formally recognized by the BATF in April of 1984. Winegrowing in the Umpqua Valley remained largely dormant in the 1900s, until the early 1960s, when new and dedicated efforts hailed the rebirth of the Oregon wine industry and its modern day renaissance. Although most Oregon vineyard acreage is now located in the Willamette Valley to the north, the Umpqua Valley remains an important and interesting winegrowing region.

Located south of the Willamette Valley, and entirely within Douglas County in southwest Oregon, the Umpqua Valley covers approximately 1,200 square miles. Running north to south, the Umpqua Valley is approximately 70 miles long and 30 miles at its widest point. Bordered on the north and west by the Coast Range, on the south by the Klamath Mountains, and on the east by the foothills of the Cascade Mountains, the region is not a simple, open basin, but an interconnected series of many small mountains, hillsides, and river drainages. The more restrictive nature of the area lends itself to small or moderate size vineyards and wineries.

Like the Willamette Valley, the Umpqua Valley is classified as Region I on the U. C. Davis scale. The two climates are similar, but the Umpqua Valley is slightly drier and warmer, the growing season is slightly shorter, and summer and winter temperatures are slightly more extreme. None of the individual differences is major, but as a whole, they shape a different climate, particularly toward the southern end of the valley, where the higher mountains to the south and west block more of the Pacific marine air. Pine trees begin to replace

Umpqua Valley

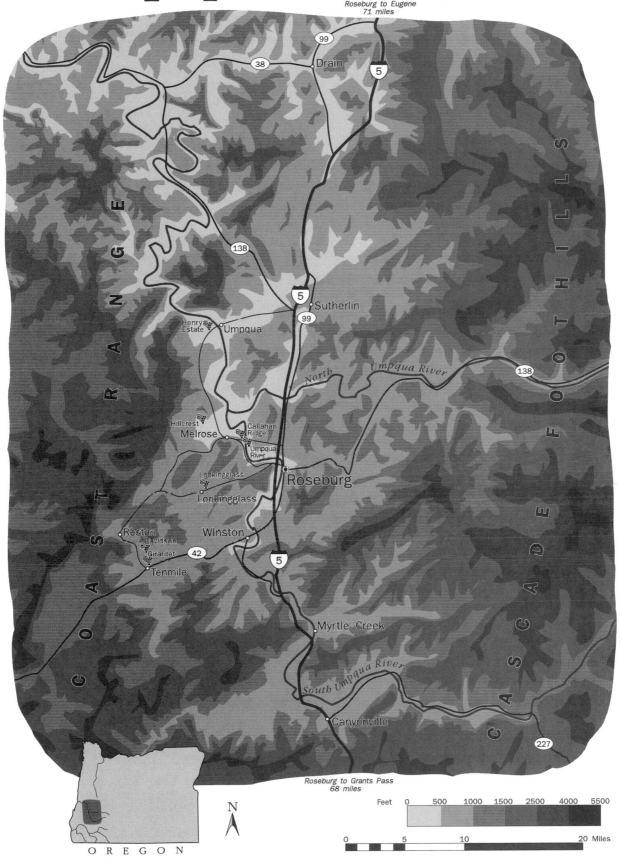

Roseburg to Eugene
71 miles

99

38 Drain

5

138

5 Sutherlin

99

Henry
Estate Umpqua

North   Umpqua River

138

Hillcrest Callahan
Melrose Ridge

Umpqua
River

Lookingglass

Roseburg

Lookingglass

Reston Winston
Davidson

Girardet 42

Tenmile

5

Myrtle Creek

South Umpqua River

Canyonville

227

Roseburg to Grants Pass
68 miles

C O A S T   R A N G E

C A S C A D E   F O O T H I L L S

O R E G O N

N

Feet 0 500 1000 1500 2500 4000 5500

0   5   10   20 Miles

the fir trees of the Willamette, and California oak (*Quercus kelloggii*) intermingles with Oregon oak (*Quercus garryana*).

The Umpqua Valley viticultural area extends no higher than an elevation of 1,000 feet. Above that elevation, the terrain rapidly becomes very steep and otherwise unsuitable for vineyards. Winter cold is seldom a problem, but frost, particularly in the spring, can be a threat. Vineyards are situated on the valley floor as well as hillside sites. The selection of grape varieties is quite varied, and is dependent as much on the individual growing site and preference of the winegrower as it is on any overall climatic imperative. Riesling, Chardonnay, and Pinot Noir predominate. Cabernet Sauvignon, among several other varieties, is grown on some sites, but it is not a major grape variety for the Umpqua Valley.

Illinois, Applegate, and Rogue River Valleys

The winegrowing climates of Southwest Oregon are as complex and varied as their geologic origins.

The winegrowing climates of Southwest Oregon are as complex and varied as their geologic origins. Here the coastal mountain range is not the same as the Coast Range to the north. The Klamath Mountains are much older. They were the southwest extremity of Oregon at a time when Oregon's land mass was far smaller, its boundary with the Pacific Ocean roughly cutting a diagonal across what is now Oregon. Looking at a modern map of the state, it is startling to think that much of what is now Oregon did not exist 200 million years ago, and that the Klamath, Wallowa, and Blue Mountains once formed Oregon's coastal mountain range.

The Klamath Mountains, and the Siskiyou Mountains within them, are a geologic jumble. They are by far the oldest mountains in western Oregon, formed initially from sedimentary rock folded and tumbled together by the collision of the seafloor with the continental shelf, collecting, along the way, scrambled bits of the ocean floor. The Klamaths later broke away from the continent to form an offshore island. Fossil seashells are abundant in parts of the Klamaths, a feature quite apparent in the rock border rimming the driveway of one southwest Oregon winery.

Oregon's famed Rogue River begins in the Cascade Mountains east of the southern end of the Umpqua Valley. From there, the Rogue courses south and west along a twisting path to the Pacific Ocean. Passing through the Siskiyou and Klamath Mountains not far from the California border, the Rogue and its tributaries flow through several small valleys. The surrounding mountains shelter the valleys in varying degrees from the cool, moist, Pacific marine air. The valleys nearest the ocean are the coolest and most moist, getting progressively warmer and drier toward the east.

It is tempting to refer to all these winegrowing regions by a single moniker, Rogue River Valley. All the area's winegrowing valleys are tributaries of the Rogue. Though varying somewhat in climate, the

Southwest Oregon

Illinois, Applegate, and Rogue River Valleys

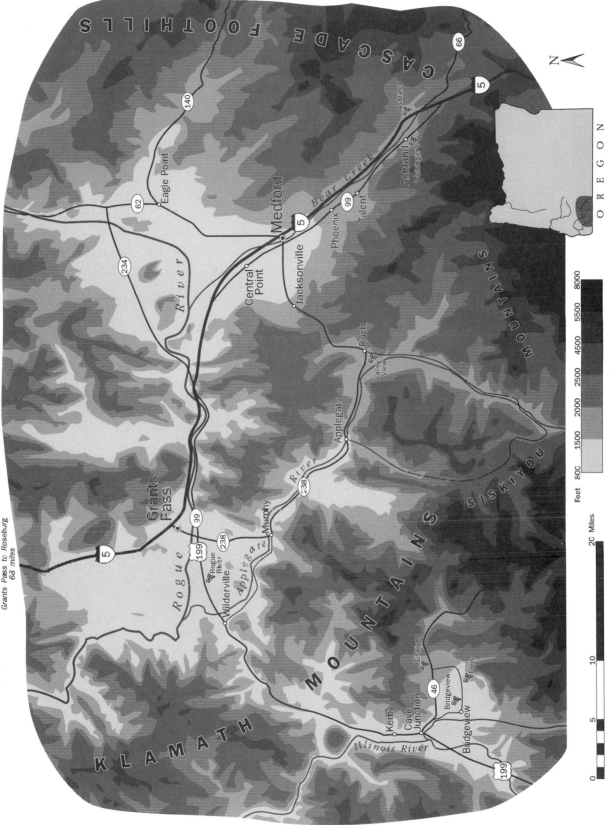

Grants Pass to Roseburg
68 miles

KLAMATH

MOUNTAINS

SISKIYOU

CASCADE FOOTHILLS

Eagle Point

Medford

Central
Point

Jacksonville

Phoenix

Talent

Ashland
Weisinger's

Grants
Pass

Rogue
River

Wilderville

Murphy

Applegate

River

Ruch

Valley
View

Applegate

Siskiyou

Cave
Junction

Kerby

Bridgeview

Foris

Bridgeview

Illinois River

Rogue

River

Bear Creek

OREGON

O R E G O N

N

Feet   800   1500   2000   2500   4500   5500   8000

20 Miles

0   5   10

5

140

62

234

99

5

66

199

238

99

238

238

46

199

Applegate, Bear Creek, and Rogue Valley systems could be conveniently grouped together.

The Illinois Valley, however, is a different beast. Though it is a tributary of the Rogue, the Illinois Valley winegrowing region is completely separated from the other valley systems by mountains and hills. The Illinois River does not connect with the Rogue River until it has itself wound its way through the Klamaths, meeting with the Rogue not far from the coast.

Although the distinction is not quite as radical, it would be a similar distortion to refer to the Illinois Valley as part of the Rogue Valley as it would be to refer to the Willamette Valley as part of the Columbia Valley, though the Illinois and Willamette are both tributary valleys of the larger drainage systems.

All Southwest Oregon winegrowing areas have a shorter growing season than the winegrowing regions to the north. The higher elevations and more mountainous terrain make seasonal temperature fluctuations more extreme, winter freezes a possibility, and spring and fall frosts an ongoing concern.

The Illinois Valley is the coolest of the major southwest Oregon winegrowing areas. Although it is near the California border, and less temperate than the Willamette Valley, the Illinois Valley is nevertheless significantly influenced and moderated by Pacific marine air. One Willamette Valley winery once contracted with an Illinois Valley winegrower for Pinot Noir grapes intended for an early release nouveau wine, only to find that in some years the Illinois Valley grapes actually ripen later than in the Willamette Valley. Chardonnay and Gewurztraminer from the Illinois Valley are particularly good, and the highly fickle Pinot Noir offers promise.

Moving inland, the climate grows successively warmer as additional ranges of mountains and hills block the flow of marine air. Both the Applegate Valley, nestled among the Siskiyou Mountains, and the Bear Creek Valley, emerging from the convergence of the Cascade Foothills and the Klamaths, offer good growing conditions for warmer climate grape varieties, including Cabernet Sauvignon and Merlot.

The surrounding mountains shelter the valleys in varying degrees from the cool, moist, Pacific marine air. The valleys nearest the ocean are the coolest and most moist, getting progressively warmer and drier toward the east.

Columbia Gorge, Columbia Valley, and Walla Walla Valley

The Columbia River forms most of Oregon's northern border with Washington. The river's passage through the Cascade Mountain Range carves an area known as the Columbia River Gorge. Further east, the vast Columbia Valley viticultural area, located primarily in Washington, dips across the Columbia River to the Oregon side of the border. The Walla Walla Valley, an easternmost part of the larger Columbia Valley, also extends into Oregon.

The slopes on the Oregon side of the valleys are more northerly facing, but otherwise the climate and terrain is very similar to the climate and terrain on the Washington side of the border. Unlike Washington, serious grape growing efforts on Oregon's part of the Columbia Valley are very recent. For more information on the Columbia Gorge, Columbia Valley, and Walla Walla Valley, refer to the entries in the Washington section of this book.

Columbia Gorge
Oregon

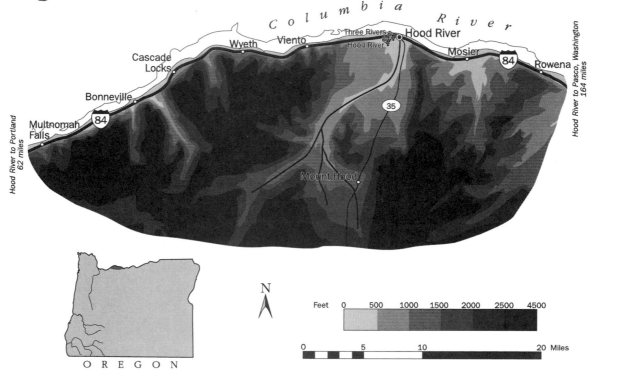

Columbia   *River*

Wyeth   Viento   Three Rivers   **Hood River**

Cascade Locks   Hood River   Mosier

Bonneville   84

Multnomah Falls

Hood River to Portland 62 miles

Hood River to Pasco, Washington 164 miles

35

Rowena

84

Mount Hood

OREGON

N

Feet   0   500   1000   1500   2000   2500   4500

0   5   10   20 Miles

Walla Walla Valley
Oregon

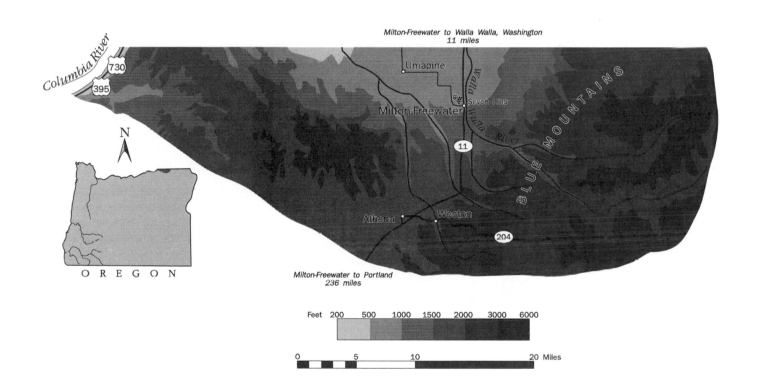

Milton-Freewater to Walla Walla, Washington
11 miles

Columbia River

730
395

Umapine

Seven Hills

Milton-Freewater

Walla Walla River

11

BLUE MOUNTAINS

N

Athena

Weston

204

OREGON

Milton-Freewater to Portland
236 miles

Feet 200 500 1000 1500 2000 3000 6000

0   5   10   20 Miles

OREGON
Other Oregon Wineries

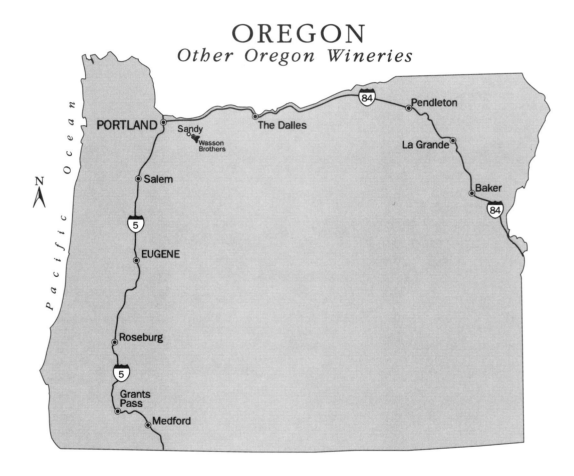

Oregon Wineries

Individual pride & small family owned wineries predominate

Adams Vineyard Winery

Washington has many urban wineries, some dating back to the beginning of state's wine renaissance, but Oregon's first urban winery, Adams Vineyard, did not begin operations until 1985. Unlike many urban Washington wineries, Adams is closely tied to its vineyards. Owned and operated by Carol and Peter Adams, the Adams' vineyard is located southwest of Portland, in the hills near the town of Newberg. Before opening their winery in Portland, the first vintages were custom crushed at the Adelsheim winery near the Adams vineyard.

Peter Adams is president of a construction materials firm. Carol Adams is an artist and wine and food writer. Her design graces their wine labels. The two owned a retail wine store in the early 1970s before deciding that a vineyard and winery was a more interesting venture.

By now, the phrase "food wine" is heavily overworked, stated glibly with equal fervor by the newly converted as well as those long dedicated to the cause, but the Adams practice this ethic in their selection of grape varieties as well as their wine style. Nearly every Oregon winery makes Chardonnay, Pinot Noir, and Riesling, Oregon's three major

> ### Adams Vineyard Winery
>
> 1922 N.W. Pettygrove Street
> Portland, Oregon 97209
> (503) 294-0606
>
> **Owners**
> Peter & Carol Adams
>
> **Winemaker**
> Carol Adams
>
> **Wine Production**
> 8,000 gallons
>
> **Vineyard Acreage**
> 13 acres
>
> **Year First Planted**
> 1976
>
> **First Vintage**
> 1981
>
> **Wines Produced**
> Pinot Noir, Chardonnay,
> Sauvignon Blanc

grape varieties. The Adams' vineyard is devoted to two varieties, Chardonnay and Pinot Noir. They do not grow, purchase, or make Riesling.

For their third variety, the Adams purchase Oregon Sauvignon Blanc grapes. Sauvignon Blanc requires a fairly warm climate. Because the variety has a difficult time in the Willamette Valley's cooler vintages, relatively few acres of the grape are planted in the valley. Carol Adams likes the inherently crisp nature of Oregon Sauvignon Blanc, a "third variety" that compliments food much better than Riesling.

Adelsheim Vineyard

David and Ginny Adelsheim are the owners and operators of one of Oregon's more innovative wineries. David Adelsheim prepared for the wine business by working with David Lett during one of Eyrie's crushes, by researching French and German viticulture and winemaking texts to gain a broader perspective than that offered by the teachings of the University of California at Davis, and by studying and working in France at the Lycee Viticole in Beaune.

An ardent and studied advocate of western Oregon's winegrowing climate, Adelsheim speaks not only of the future of his own winery, but of the future and destiny of the Oregon wine industry. On behalf of the Oregon Winegrowers Association,

---

Adelsheim Vineyard

22150 N.E. Quarter Mile Lane
Newberg, Oregon 97132
(503) 538-3652

Owners
David & Virginia Adelsheim

Winemakers
Don Kautzner & David Adelsheim

Wine Production
24,000 gallons

Vineyard Acreage
43 acres

Year First Planted
1972

First Vintage
1978

Wines Produced
Pinot Noir, Elizabeth's Reserve;
Pinot Noir, Eola Hills;
Pinot Noir, Oregon;
Chardonnay, Willamette Valley,
Chardonnay, Oregon; Pinot Gris;
Merlot, Layne Vineyard (Oregon);
Merlot (Washington/Oregon);
Dry Riesling; Gamay Noir;
Pinot Blanc

Adelsheim researched and successfully petitioned the Bureau of Alcohol Tobacco and Firearms (BATF) for "viticultural area" designations for Oregon's Umpqua and Willamette Valleys.

Adelsheim authored the strict Oregon wine labeling regulations, and is an advisor to Oregon State University on the importation of grape varieties and clones. His research writings include the publication of papers in the Proceedings of The International Symposium on Cool Climate Viticulture and Enology, and his com-

prehensive benchmark work on training and trellising methods for western Oregon vineyards published in the *Oregon Winegrape Growers Guide.*

Adelsheim was instrumental in arranging for the purchase of prime Willamette Valley vineyard property by the highly regarded Burgundian, Robert Drouhin. Drouhin's purchase of Oregon vineyard land and his opening of an Oregon winery brought immediate media attention, and yet more validation for the Oregon wine industry. Moreover, Drouhin and other Burgundians brought ideas and perspectives to the Oregonians that have improved the quality of Oregon wine and marked the maturation of the Oregon wine industry.

In many respects, Adelsheim epitomizes the spirit of Oregon winegrowers—not idle hobbyist, not agribusinessmen growing grapes because its the new cash crop, and not armchair investors who like the idea of owning a winery (if not the mental and physical effort), but deeply dedicated individuals committed to the belief that western Oregon is one of the world's finest winegrowing regions.

Oregon, Adelsheim believes, will increasingly become one of America's most important premium wine producing regions as consumers are better educated to the higher acidity and more delicate and complex flavors of European and Oregon wines. Pinot Noir, the star of Oregon's Willamette Valley, does not have a clear frame of reference for the average American palate. Adelsheim points out that Cabernet Sauvignon, the American standard of reference for red wines, is a much different kind of wine. Cabernet is strongly and

distinctively flavored, using high tannins as part of the balance of the wine, and striking the palate immediately with a highly defined taste.

Pinot Noir, on the other hand, does not have such a readily recognizable taste, but rather unfolds on the palate in manifold nuances. In Adelsheim's view, an important aspect of wine tasting often ignored by Americans is the feel of a wine in the mouth. Fine Pinot Noir, at least fine aged Pinot Noir, has a distinctive velvety feel—it is what Adelsheim calls a textural wine.

Adelsheim's Pinot Noirs are consistently among Oregon's best. They are softly textured wines, yet well structured with good acids and low pH. Tannins are minimized, and the layers of fruit show through.

Adelsheim makes several Pinot Noirs. The Oregon designation is a more moderately priced wine

---

Adelsheim does not inoculate with commercial yeast cultures, but instead ferments with wild yeasts.

---

for earlier consumption. The Polk County designation showcases fruit from the Eola Hills. The Elizabeth's Reserve is Yamhill County fruit, primarily from their estate vineyard in the Chehalem Mountains, but also including grapes from the Dundee Hills. Artist, Ginny Adelsheim, designs Adelsheim's distinctive wine labels for all the wines.

In 1984, Adelsheim upgraded his crusher-stemmer. This "better" equipment was, in fact, not better at all for his Pinot Noir. In 1986, Adelsheim returned to methods that would more gently crush the fruit rather than churning it to bits. Slightly more than half of the grapes for the 1986 Elizabeth's Reserve were not run through a

> **For all this vinous exploration, Adelsheim maintains a consistent stylistic theme—wines that are delicate, textural, and multi-dimensional.**

crusher-stemmer at all, but were simply put into the fermentation bins and walked on to crush the berries as gently as possible, leaving the them largely intact. The Burgundians, and now, more Oregon winemakers, are returning to various forms of ancient Burgundian winemaking practices, including using a portion of whole or lightly crushed berries.

Adelsheim does not inoculate his fermentations with commercial yeast cultures, but instead ferments only with wild yeasts. This practice can be risky in grape growing regions which do not have a long history of appropriate yeast cultures established in the vineyards, but the wild yeasts have worked well for Adelsheim.

For several years a broker for French oak barrels, Adelsheim experimented with the effects of six different French oaks on the flavors of Pinot Noir and Chardonnay. For Pinot Noir, Adelsheim uses a combination of three oaks, Allier for complexity and backbone, Troncais for spicy flavor and accents, and Bourgogne for butteriness.

For Chardonnay, Adelsheim prefers tight grained Limousin and Nevers. In his experience, Limousin accentuates the wine's acidity, offering pleasant, lemony qualities. Nevers, on the other hand, brings out the softer, rounder qualities of the wine, while playing down the acidity and any bitter tendencies. He specifies tight grained wood to prevent the extraction of too much woody flavor or excess bitterness.

In addition to the standard Oregon grape varieties, Pinot Noir, Chardonnay, and Riesling, Adelsheim is also working with Pinot Gris, Pinot Blanc, and, more recently, the true Gamay Noir grape of Beaujolais, a variety very different from the misnamed Gamay Beaujolais clone of Pinot Noir—and very different from California's Napa Gamay which is now believed to be the Rhone variety, Valdiguie. A counterpoint to his Chardonnay, Adelsheim's Pinot Gris is made in a crisp style, fermented in stainless steel, and released without any oak aging.

Adelsheim is an unrepentant experimenter and innovator, making wine in a seemingly endless number of small lots, each with one variation or another in method. One lot may receive "cold maceration" before fermentation begins. Another may have extended maceration on the pulp and skins after the wine has fermented dry. Another may receive the same treatment, but for a week longer, and so on. For all this vinous exploration, however, Adelsheim maintains a consistent and excellent stylistic theme— wines that are delicate, textural, and multi-dimensional.

Airlie Winery

Larry and Alice Preedy came to Oregon's Willamette Valley from Kansas where they ran a farming operation and a trucking business. They settled in hills of the northern Willamette Valley, bought land, and started growing Christmas trees. In 1983, the Preedys planted a few wine grapes and made homemade wine.

Each year they planted a few more wine grapes. As Larry

Airlie Winery

15305 Dunn Forest Road
Monmouth, Oregon 97361
(503) 838-6013

Owners
Larry & Alice Preedy

Winemaker
Larry Preedy

Wine Production
12,000 gallons

Vineyard Acreage
15 acres

Year First Planted
1983

First Vintage
1986

Wines Produced
Chardonnay, Gewurztraminer, Muller-Thurgau, Riesling, Pinot Noir, Marechal Foch, Crimson, Late Harvest Gewurztraminer

---

Preedy says, "Growing grapes is just like any other kind of farming. At some point you've got to decide either to get at it or quit—so we decided to get at it."

The Preedys are gradually planting more grapes and phasing out the Christmas trees. According to Preedy, in the spring, their growing site is about one to two weeks behind others in the nearby Eola Hills, but ripening occurs at about the same time in the fall.

The growing site was not originally selected for wine grapes, and frost can be a problem. Although frost danger is not typical in Willamette Valley vineyards, frost concerns are not uncommon in the world of grapegrowing. Like other frost prone growing sites, including many of California's premium winegrowing areas, Preedy will meet the problem, as needed, with wind machines, smudge pots, and other such devices.

A Pond near the winery offers a picnic area for the visitor, as well as a source of irrigation water for the vineyard below. Older vines do not need irrigating, but irrigation can help new vines get a quicker, sturdier start.

What is the style of Airlie wines? Says Preedy, "We're looking for people graduating up from jug wines to easy drinking, light sipping wines."

The unusual winery name comes from the nearby community of Airlie. Once the southern terminus of an old narrow gauge line of the Oregonian Railway Company, the rail station was named after the Scottish president of the company, the Earl of Airlie.

Alpine Vineyards

The nearby town of Alpine was named for its proximity to the top of one of the foothills of the Coast Range. Although the climate is far from Alpine, it differs significantly from the lower slopes nearer the valley floor.

On a sunny hillside three miles from the town of Alpine, the modern, "passive solar" home of Dan and Christine Jepsen overlooks their lush vineyards and the expansive valley below. The hillside site faces due south, above the cooling temperature inversions and fogs of the valley floor.

The grassy slopes and scattered oak trees confirm that this site is warmer, sunnier, and drier than the surrounding norm—sunny and warm enough for a solar home, and sunny and warm enough to grow Cabernet Sau-

---

Alpine Vineyards

25904 Green Peak Road
Monroe, Oregon 97456
(503) 424-5851

Tasting Room
Wood Gallery
818 S.W. Bay Blvd.
Newport, Oregon 97365

Owners
Dan & Christine Jepsen

Winemakers
Dan Jepsen;
Kerry Norton,
Assistant Winemaker

Wine Production
8,000 gallons

Vineyard Acreage
26 acres

Year First Planted
1976

First Vintage
1980

Wines Produced
Pinot Noir, Chardonnay,
Cabernet Sauvignon, Riesling,
Gewurztraminer

---

vignon as well as the more typical Willamette Valley varieties, Pinot Noir, Riesling, and Chardonnay.

Unlike most Oregon winemakers, Jepsen does not automatically put Chardonnay through malolactic fermentation. Alpine's Chardonnay is fermented in small stainless steel tanks at around 65 degrees, then aged in a combination of Allier and Never oak barrels. Usually, it is not put through a malolactic fermentation.

Alpine's grapes grow on their own rootstocks, but Jepsen has planted a patch of phylloxera re-

sistant, native American rootstocks for grafting, in case the dreaded root louse should ever invade Oregon. The vineyard soil is a Jory clay loam running fifty feet to rock, interrupted only by occasional stretches of shallow Bellpine.

All of Alpine's wine is made from the grapes of the adjacent estate vineyard. Jepsen believes that 80 percent of a wine's quality comes from the vineyard. Growing all his own grapes insures control over that 80 percent.

Amity Vineyards

Myron Redford, one of Oregon's leading Pinot Noir winemakers, did not set out to be an Oregon winegrower. First attracted to winemaking through part-time work at Washington's Associated Vintners winery, Redford planned to build a winery in western Washington near Port Townsend, and make wine from grapes grown in Washington's Columbia Valley.

While planning his winery, Redford learned of a vineyard for sale near Amity, Oregon, 45 miles southwest of Portland. In 1974, Redford abandoned his plans for the Washington winery, and formed a partnership to purchase the Oregon vineyard.

In the early years, Amity became best known for a carbonic maceration Pinot Noir Nouveau. Patterned after the French Beaujolais Nouveau, the wine is released in the fall, less than two months after the beginning of the vintage. It is a good quaffing wine when first released. Contrary to many nouveau style wines, Amity's Pinot Noir Nouveau improves in the bottle.

Dry Riesling and Gewurz-

■ **Myron Redford**

traminer are also Amity trademarks, but none of these wines reflect the driving interest of Amity's winemaker. From the beginning, Redford wanted Amity to be known for its Pinot Noir, not the "nouveau," but serious oak aged Pinot Noir. It was his interest in this wine that caused him to radically alter his plans and come to Oregon.

In 1977, Amity's second crush, and a poor Oregon vintage, Redford succeeded in making fine Pinot Noir from different clonal lots. The wines continue to age beautifully. If making good wine

---

> **"In 1978, we were getting over 24 Brix and cheering. Now, hardly anybody wants 24 Brix."**

---

in difficult years is the true test of a winemaker, then Redford has made his reputation. The 1978 vintage was as impossibly hot as the 1977 was impossibly cool. Redford's 1978 Winemaker's Reserve and estate bottlings were among the very few successful wines of the vintage. His 1982 Winemaker's Reserve was a fine wine from a mediocre vintage. Even in 1984, Oregon's coldest

and nastiest vintage, Redford was able to make a light but good Pinot Noir.

Redford buys grapes from many vineyards. Every clonal and vineyard lot is fermented and aged separately. He and his tasting panel then test various blending combinations. From each vintage, Redford releases up to three barrel aged Pinot Noirs, a moderately priced "Oregon" Pinot Noir intended for current consumption, an estate or Willamette Valley designation, and a Winemaker's Reserve.

Because he releases different styles of Pinot Noir, Amity's "house style" encompasses a wide range. Redford's preferences are best reflected in the wines intended for longer aging—fairly tannic, aromatic, full-bodied wines with a sturdy acid structure. Now, most Oregon winemakers are making wines with a good acid backbone, but in the earlier days, Redford was one of the few. This is one of the reasons Amity's early Pinot Noirs have aged well while others have not.

"We had a strong California influence that took us a while to shake off," says Redford. "In 1978, we were getting over 24 Brix and cheering. Now, hardly anybody wants 24 Brix. I pick by flavor and pH rather than sugar. I would rather pick at a lower pH and chaptalize than get those pruney flavors."

What flavors does Redford look for in Pinot Noir? "A little plummy is O.K., but when you get to pruney and raisiny, I don't like those flavors at all. Even plummy isn't my favorite character. I like black cherry, red cherry, black

pepper isn't bad, spicy. I don't like herbal too much. I really like the cherry flavor, not the soda-pop cherry flavor, but that black cherry flavor that's almost like currents. These are the flavors I look for in young Pinot Noir, the sort of flavors that will complex-up with age."

Most Oregon winemakers shun the Gamay clone of Pinot Noir. Redford does not. The Gamay is one of the higher producing "upright" clones that have a less than sterling reputation in both

---

Amity Vineyards

18150 Amity Vineyards Road S.E.
Amity, Oregon 97101-9603
(503) 835-2362

Tasting Room
Oregon Winetasting Room
at the Lawrence Gallery,
Bellevue, Oregon,
9 miles southwest of McMinnville
on Highway 18
(503) 843-3787

Owners
Myron Redford, President; Ione
Redford; Janis Checchia,
Secretary/Treasurer

Winemaker
Myron Redford

Wine Production
20,000 gallons

Vineyard Acreage
15 acres

Year First Planted
1970

First Vintage
1976

Wines Produced
Pinot Noir Oregon,
Pinot Noir Willamette Valley,
Pinot Noir Estate,
Pinot Noir Winemakers Reserve,
Pinot Noir Nouveau Style,
Gamay Noir, Cabernet Sauvignon,
Chardonnay, Gewurztraminer,
Riesling, Solistice Blanc

Burgundy and Oregon. Cropped moderately, and grown in the right sites, however, the Gamay clone can be an excellent structural component in Oregon Pinot Noir. Redford also likes the Mirassou clone, another upright clone he has planted in Amity's estate vineyard. Most of Amity's Pinot Noir comes from the Wadenswil clone, which Redford prefers over the predominant Oregon Pinot Noir clone, Pommard.

Clones, however, are only one element in quality Pinot Noir. What do you look for to make the best Pinot Noir? "You want old vines," says Redford, low crop levels, and by low I mean usually less than 2 1/2 tons an acre for great Pinot Noir, not just good Pinot Noir, and a variety of clones. You don't want too much new wood, but a variety of oaks and a variety of flavors."

Redford also prefers relatively cool growing sites. "There are

---

"There are some Willamette Valley sites that are too warm for Pinot Noir."

---

some Willamette Valley sites that are too warm for Pinot Noir," says Redford. "They should be planting Chardonnay, or maybe the Gamay clone of Pinot Noir with its higher acidity."

In recent years, many Oregon winemakers have begun fermenting Pinot Noir with a portion of whole clusters or lightly crushed grapes, a widespread technique in Burgundy. In Oregon, Redford was among the first to work with the technique, beginning in 1979, by blending in a portion of his carbonic maceration "Nouveau," and in subsequent years by employing the technique, from the start, with the Pinots intended for barrel aging.

Amity was the first Oregon winery to commercially release Gamay Noir. Not to be confused with the Gamay clone of Pinot Noir, Gamay Beaujolais, or with Napa Gamay, Gamay Noir is the true grape of France's Beaujolais region. Amity's first release from the 1988 vintage lived up to all possible expectations. It was a fruity, delicious, accessible wine. Like the more substantive Beaujolais crus, the wine is excellent young, but quite capable of aging in the bottle. Redford's efforts with Gamay Noir eloquently demonstrate its merits as an Oregon wine grape.

For the wine traveler unable to visit all the wineries, Amity operates the Oregon Wine Tasting Room at in the Lawrence Art Gallery in Bellevue, Oregon, nine miles south of McMinnville, on Highway 18, a major route to the Oregon coast. Staffed by Patric McElliott, the tasting room was the first of its kind in Oregon, featuring wines from wineries throughout the state for tasting and purchase, as well as knowledgeable discussions for the serious wine aficionado. The tasting room is open daily, from 11:30 AM to 5:30 PM.

Ankeny Vineyards

Named for the nearby 2,800 acre Ankeny National Wildlife Refuge, home for masses of wild geese and other waterfowl, Ankeny vineyards is situated in a relatively new grape growing area along the southernmost part of the Salem Hills. Ankeny Vineyards is a partnership of Joe Olexa and Bob Harris, a nearby grape grower.

The estate vineyard is situated on one of the Willamette Valley's

earliest homesteads, Federal Land Claim Number 38, dated 1846. Looking out across the broad

---

Ankeny Vineyards

2565 Riverside Road South
Salem, Oregon 97306
(503) 362-2508

Owners
Joe Olexa & Bob Harris

Winemaker
Joe Olexa

Wine Production
1,000 gallons

Vineyard Acreage
15 acres

Year First Planted
1982

First Vintage
1985

Wines Produced
Chardonnay, Pinot Gris, Riesling
Cabernet Sauvignon, Pinot Noir

---

sweep of the Willamette Valley toward Eugene, Ankeny's land has been in continuous cultivation since the original claim. The land has supported many crops since the settler's era, including walnuts, prunes, wheat, and now wine grapes. The setting invites a relaxed picnic on the "farmhouse" lawn, with a view of the valley, the vineyards, and a towering ancient oak.

Most Willamette Valley vineyards are planted on sloping hillsides along the western side of the valley. Ankeny is situated near the center of the valley, only 50 feet from the valley floor. The soil is a deep, heavy, clay loam, and vine growth is relatively vigorous.

Frost, often a problem for vineyards near the valley floor, has not troubled Ankeny. Olexa reports that not only is frost not a problem, but the site is in a particularly warm localized climate with early bud break in the spring and a longer fall season.

Instead of the Willamette Valley's usual cane pruning, the vines are trained in bilateral cordons. Cordon trained vines are easier

■ **Joe Olexa**

and less expensive to maintain, but the critical basal buds are not always reliably fruitful in the Oregon climate. Most of the vines are very young, but, so far, cordon pruning works well on Ankeny's growing sites.

Although produced only in small quantities, Cabernet Sauvignon is an Ankeny specialty. Chardonnay, Ankeny's main focus, is barrel fermented and left on the lees for several months. Olexa likes the effect of malolactic fermentation and oak aging in all his white wines, including Riesling. In the case of Riesling, the barrels are not new oak, so the oak character is not predominant, but the controlled oxygenating effect of barrel aging along with the malolactic fermentation give a softer, more textural effect to Riesling's typically hard-edged fruit.

Argyle

For more than a decade, since the first premium Oregon sparkling wine was released, there has been much interest and speculation about the potential for Oregon sparkling wine. Out of necessity, grapes for premium sparkling wines must be physiologically ripe at lower sugar levels than grapes intended for still wines. By this criterion, Oregon's Willamette Valley would be the best region on the west coast for premium sparkling wine.

Until recently, Oregon sparkling wine has been a small scale enterprise, an interesting adjunct to a winery's line of wines. With the arrival of Australia's Brian Croser and his Dundee Wine Company, all this has changed. The Dundee Wine Company, under the label Argyle, is producing premium sparkling wine on a

---

Argyle

P.O. Box 280
691 Highway 99 West
Dundee, Oregon 97115
(503) 538-8520

Owner
Brian Croser

Winemakers
Brian Croser & Rollin Soles

Wine Production
50,000 gallons

Vineyard Acreage
none

First Vintage
1987

Wines Produced
Argyle Brut, Chardonnay, Riesling

---

major scale. In this instance, it is the still wines that play a secondary role, not the sparkling wines.

An industrial complex in the small Willamette Valley community of Dundee houses winery operations. The Dundee Wine

Company leases and controls a 35 acre vineyard that was first planted in 1973. The operation also manages vineyards for some of the Willamette Valley's more noted winegrowers.

The Dundee Wine Company's Argyle Brut is a vintage dated cuvee of half Pinot Noir and half Chardonnay. Assisting Croser is on-site winemaker Rollin Soles, a U. C. Davis enology graduate who has previously made wine in Washington and Australia.

Arterberry Winery

McMinnville, a small college town in the heart of Oregon's northern Willamette Valley, is the home of two wineries with notable firsts. Located within a block of the renown Eyrie Vineyards winery, the first Oregon winery dedicated to Pinot Noir, Fred Arterberry's Arterberry Winery earns another first by producing the state's first sparkling wine from traditional Champagne grape varieties. The first cuvee, in 1979, was made entirely from Chardonnay. Subsequent cuvees featured Pinot Noir as well. Arterberry's expanded line of sparkling wines now also includes Riesling.

A low alcohol sparkling cider comprised most of Arterberry's production in the first years. The cider filled a gap while awaiting release of the bottle fermented sparkling wine. The first sparkling wine rested two years on the yeast.

An enology graduate of U. C. Davis, Arterberry believes that Oregon's Willamette Valley is ideal for sparkling wine. If grapes are too high in sugar, the base wine will be too high in alcohol, and the second fermentation can-

Arterberry Winery

905 E. 10th Street
P.O. Box 772
McMinnville, Oregon 97128
(503) 472-1587 or 244-0695

Owners
Arterberry Family

Winemaker
Fred Arterberry, Jr.

Wine Production
12,000 gallons

Vineyard Acreage
none

First Vintage
1979

Wines Produced
Pinot Noir, Chardonnay, Sauvignon Blanc, Riesling, Gewurztraminer, Sparkling

not take place. Grapes for sparkling wine must be picked at lower sugar levels, but in warmer climates, grapes don't become physiologically ripe at low sugar levels. In warmer climates, grapes can be picked early so that making sparkling wine is possible, but the underripe grapes do little for wine quality.

In Oregon's cooler climate, grapes fully ripen at lower sugars, an important criterion for premium sparkling wines. Arterberry prefers grapes at 19 degrees Brix, a sugar level that produces a base wine with an alcohol content of about 11 percent.

In 1982, to augment his sparkling wine production, Arterberry made his first still wines for release under the Arterberry label, Chardonnay, Pinot Noir, and Rose of Pinot Noir. Still wines now comprise most of Arterberry's production. In warmer vintages, those less than ideal for sparkling wine, Arterberry makes only still wine. Pinot Noir is now the predominant focus. Vintage permitting, Arterberry's Pinot is made in a rich, full-bodied style.

Ashland Vineyards

Bear Creek Valley, a tributary valley of the famed Rogue River, is one of the warmest grape growing areas in western Oregon. The valley is bordered by the foothills of the Cascade Mountains on the east, and the foothills of the Siskiyou Mountains on the west. Ashland Vineyards is located on the outskirts of the town of Ashland, renowned home of the Shakespearean theater.

Ashland Vineyards is situated adjacent to the town's airport, not

Ashland Vineyards

2775 East Main Street
Ashland, Oregon 97520
(503) 488-0088

Owners
Bill & Melba Knowles

Winemaker
Mark Knowles

Wine Production
9,000 gallons

Vineyard Acreage
12 acres

Year First Planted
1988

First Vintage
1988

Wines Produced
Merlot, Cabernet Sauvignon, Pinot Noir, Chardonnay, Pinot Noir Blanc, Muller-Thurgau, Sauvignon Blanc

entirely a coincidence, as owner Bill Knowles and his son were both commercial pilots. The pastoral grounds, complete with a pond and two white swans, contrast with the airport's nearby landing strip. Knowles' son, Mark, is the winemaker.

Although the Bear Creek Valley is one of western Oregon's warmest grape growing sites, Knowles' vineyard is planted largely to the cooler climate grape varieties

such as Muller-Thurgau, Pinot Noir, and Pinot Gris. Knowles has also planted Merlot, a variety that should do well in the Bear Creek Valley climate, setting fruit more reliably than in other parts of western Oregon. For a new, relatively small winery, the winemaking facilities are first class. The winery equipment, layout, and design convey a sense of professionalism and attention to detail.

Autumn Wind Vineyard

Tom & Wendy Kreutner came to Oregon in the late seventies to escape the urban milieu of Los Angeles. In 1980, the Kreutners began looking for vineyard land, a search that ended in June of 1983 with the purchase of a 52 acre site in the Chehalem mountains near Newberg.

The Kreutners planted their first vines in the Willakenzie and Panther soils of the lower portion of their acreage, adjacent to what is now the winery. The Kreutners' reserved their choicest vineyard sites for later planting on Wil-

Autumn Wind Vineyard

15225 North Valley Road
P.O. Box 666
Newberg, Oregon 97132
(503) 538-6931

Owners
Tom & Wendy Kreutner

Winemakers
Tom & Wendy Kreutner

Wine Production
3,000 gallons

Vineyard Acreage
10 acres

First Vintage
1987

Wines Produced
Pinot Noir, Chardonnay, Muller-Thurgau, Pinot Noir Blanc

lakenzie soils on the upper parts of their land.

Autumn Wind Vineyard is at an elevation of 250 to 450 feet, in the Chehalem Valley, a tiny river valley within the Willamette Valley. The Kreutners report that the hills forming the west side of the small valley create their own mini rain shadow effect, often diverting rain squalls to the north and south, away from the vineyard.

Visitors to Autumn Wind may note that the vines seem unusually tall. The Kreutners are training and trellising their vines to the Geneva Double Curtain system, a relatively new method for Oregon vineyards. As the new year's growth fills the vine, special catch wires bend the canes into a hanging position, more evenly exposing the leaves and grapes to light.

Bellfountain Cellars

After receiving masters degrees in chemistry and business, Robert Mommsen went to work for the mining industry.

Bellfountain Cellars

25041 Llewllyn Road
Corvallis, Oregon 97333
(503) 929-3162

Owners
Jeanne & Robert Mommsen

Winemaker
Robert Mommsen

Wine Production
2,500 gallons

Wines Produced
Pinot Noir, Chardonnay, Sauvignon Blanc, Riesling, Gewurztraminer

Mommsen was living in Ohio and running U.S. operations for a Canadian mining company when he had his fill of corporations. Changing their lifestyles, the Mommsens decided to start a vineyard and winery. They liked Oregon, and Oregon vineyard land held much more promise than Ohio's.

The Mommsens' winery, home, and land suitable for a 35 acre vineyard are situated in the Willamette Valley, south of Corvallis, on the lower reaches of the Coast Range Mountains. According to Mommsen, the bowl-shaped site is about 10 degrees warmer than surrounding areas. The soil is a cross between Bellpine and Jory—twelve feet deep, deeper than most Bellpine, but not as deep as Jory.

Part of the land was planted to Christmas trees, which are now being replaced by grapes. The vineyard will include the Gamay grape of Beaujolais, several of the new Oregon Pinot Noir clones that originated in Dijon, France, and a test planting of Cabernet Sauvignon for the warmest part of the vineyard.

All the wines, including Riesling and Gewurztraminer, are fermented completely dry. Mommsen does not care for malolactic fermentation or lees flavors in his white wines. The Chardonnay is barrel fermented, racked off the lees as soon as the wine settles, and kept from going through malolactic fermentation. "I like the fruit to come through, with crisp acid, no fat buttery character, and just a touch of oak—more of a Chablis-style."

Mommsen's Pinot Noir goes through malolactic fermentation, but he still prefers a good acid backbone for the wine. Of Oregon's current clones, Mommsen feels that Wadenswil offers better acidity and the best flavors. Sixty percent of the winery's production is red wine.

Bethel Heights Vineyard

Geologic remnants of a volcanic past are evident throughout the Northwest. The massive crater formed by the violent 1980 eruption of Mount St. Helens is the newest monument

Bethel Heights Vineyard

6060 Bethel Heights Road N. W.
Salem, Oregon 97304
(503) 581-2262

Owners
Ted Casteel & Pat Dudley,
Terry Casteel & Marilyn Webb

Winemaker
Terry Casteel

Wine Production
16,000 gallons

Vineyard Acreage
51 acres

Year First Planted
1977

First Vintage
1984

Wines Produced
Pinot Noir, Pinot Noir Reserve, Chardonnay, Riesling, Gewurztraminer, Chenin Blanc, Pinot Noir Blanc

to the Northwest's geologic history. In the Eola Hills of the Willamette Valley, Bethel Heights Vineyard has its roots in a far more ancient volcanic crater. At Bethel Heights, the vines are planted on a south facing slope along the crater's rim. With the passing of many millennia, the crater and the remnants of the volcano have merged into the landscape, but the distinctive bowl-shaped valley remains.

Befitting its volcanic origins, the vineyard's shallow soil is high in minerals, but is otherwise agriculturally poor—except for wine grapes, which seem to produce the best wines from the least rich soils. The soil is classified as

Nekia, a silty, clay, loam, overlying a bedrock of fractured basalt to an average depth of three feet. The land was once owned by Vic Winquist who had planned his own winery for the site. Winquist had recommended drip irrigation for the vineyard, and it remains one of the few irrigated vineyards in the Willamette Valley.

■ **Ted & Terry Casteel**

Although costly, the irrigation helped pay for itself by allowing vine cuttings to be planted directly in the vineyard and brought into production more rapidly. Now that the vines are mature, however, irrigation is no longer needed. The vines are left unirrigated to promote deep rooting.

Bethel Heights Vineyard is a family owned corporation operated by brothers, Ted and Terry Casteel, and their wives, Pat Dudley and Marilyn Webb. In the late 1970s, both families left their former occupations, purchased the vineyard, and moved to Oregon. Ted Casteel is the vineyard manager, Terry the winemaker.

Bethel Heights is one of the vineyards working with the Geneva Double Curtain system, a technique originally developed in New York for Concord grapes, but receiving attention in Europe and other winegrowing areas for vinifera grapes. With this system, the grapes and next year's buds are better exposed to the sun. In the sections of the vineyards that have been converted to the system, Ted Casteel reports increased and more reliable yields without a reduction in sugar levels, and good color in Pinot Noir.

Emerging as a distinctive growing area, the Eola Hills rise up from the Willamette River near Salem and run northward along the river for a brief distance. Bethel Heights is positioned in the path of coastal breezes that flow through a low lying gap in the Coast Range. The breezes flow through in late afternoon, tempering the climate, and cooling the evening temperatures. Cool nights help preserve the acids and fruit flavors. According to the Casteels, the vineyard is cooler than other vineyard sites in hot years, and warmer in cool years.

Although Chardonnays and excellently crafted Pinot Noirs are the major focus, Bethel Heights also produces limited quantities of Chenin Blanc, a grape seldom planted in Oregon. In California,

---

The vines are planted along the rim of an ancient volcano

Chenin Blanc is grown in warm growing areas and has a reputation for producing large quantities of indifferent wine. In Europe, however, Chenin Blanc is grown in cooler climates, and in the Loire, has a reputation that exceeds Sauvignon Blanc. Bethel Heights Chenin Blanc is made in a

crisp style with some residual sweetness.

Bethel Heights continues to sell a large portion of its grapes to other wineries, but Bethel Heights wines are 100 percent estate grown and bottled. "The vineyard is especially important to us," says Terry Casteel, "We really want our wines to be an expression of this particular piece of land. We came out of our former lives to this piece of earth, and this is where we have our roots."

Bridgeview Vineyards

The Illinois Valley is Oregon's southwesternmost winegrowing region. Located not far from the California border, it would be reasonable to assume that the Illinois Valley is a very warm growing climate—but this is not the case. The valley is not far

---

Bridgeview Vineyards

4210 Holland Loop Road
Cave Junction, Oregon 97523
(503) 592-4688 or 592-4698

Winery Tasting Room
Highway 199
Kerby, Oregon

Owners
Robert Kerivan, Lelo Kerivan,
Ernie Brodie

Winemaker
Laurent Mountalieu

Wine Production
50,000 gallons

Vineyard Acreage
74 acres

Year First Planted
1980

First Vintage
1986

Wines Produced
Pinot Noir, Pinot Noir Winemaker
Reserve, Chardonnay, Chardonnay
Barrel Select, Gewurztraminer,
Pinot Gris, Riesling,
Muller- Thurgau, Pinot Noir Blanc

---

from the Pacific Ocean, and the intervening Klamath Mountains only partially block the coastal marine air.

The Illinois Valley had long been a vacation destination for California residents Robert and Lelo Kerivan. In conjunction with long-time friend, architect Ernie Brodie, the three formed a partnership, planted a vineyard, and built a winery.

The vineyard is notable. Skillfully maintained, and relatively large by Oregon standards, the vines are planted to a tight spacing of six feet between each row, and four feet between each vine, for a total of 1,800 vines per acre. Rigorous cultural practices bring new vines rapidly into production, while vegetative growth is minimized for grape producing vines.

■ **Part of the Bridgeview crew— On the right is winemaker Laurent Mountalieu.**

A deer fence surrounds the property to protect the vines. The vineyard is comprised of six different soil types, ranging from a relatively rich loam, to a riverbed soil so rocky that it is classified as a commercial rock crushing source.

The grape varieties are the same as those grown in the Willamette Valley, though the climate differs. In the Illinois Valley, the growing season is shorter, the days are warmer and sunnier, and nights are cooler. At 1,400 feet, spring and fall frosts are a threat, so the vineyard is equipped with an overhead sprinkler system for frost protection.

Riesling and Muller-Thurgau comprise nearly half the vineyard production, but some of the vines are being budded over to Chardonnay and Pinot Noir, Bridgeview's leading wines. The Gewurztraminer, however, is not to be ignored. Nearly dry, intense, and concentrated, Bridgeview has produced some of the finest Gewurztraminer to come out of the Northwest—may Bridgeview's success with the grape continue, and the market respond in kind.

The arrival, in 1988, of French trained winemaker Laurent Mountalieu further solidifies the winery's direction. The Chardonnays are already particularly successful, showing good fruit, elegance, and structure. Bridgeview has two Chardonnay offerings. The moderately priced Chardonnay is fermented in stainless steel tanks, aged briefly in French oak, then released rapidly to the market without a malolactic fermentation. The Barrel Select Chardonnay is fermented in French oak barrels, put through a malolactic fermentation, and aged on the lees.

In the modern era, the Illinois Valley is a relatively new and untested winegrowing region. Often, in such regions, one finds marginal efforts, and it is not always easy to distinguish between the shortcomings of the region and the shortcomings of the effort. Bridgeview is an impressive effort. The winery, vineyard, and personnel convey the sense that the potential of the region will be thoroughly tested and explored. The first efforts are already more than promising.

Broadley Vineyards

Who would have predicted at the time, that a red brick building, built in the 1930s to house a car dealership in the small community of Monroe, would later be the home of a winery specializing in Pinot Noir and Chardonnay. The refurbished building is on Highway 99W, the main route through town. The back of the building overlooks the Long Tom River.

Craig and Claudia Broadly came to the southern Willamette Valley from the San Francisco area

---

Broadley Vineyards

265 S, 5th (Hwy 99W)
Monroe, Oregon 97456
(503) 847-5934

Owners
Craig & Claudia Broadley

Winemaker
Craig Broadley

Wine Production
5,000 gallons

Vineyard Acreage
15 acres

Year First Planted
1982

First Vintage
1986

Wines Produced
Pinot Noir, Chardonnay

---

to follow their dream of a small Oregon winery. Both had worked in the City Lights bookstore in the 1960s. The Broadleys own and operate a speciality book distributorship as well as their winery.

The Broadley vineyard is on a northeast to east facing slope. According to Broadley, the vineyard develops quickly in the early part of the growing season, but cools off more rapidly in the fall. The vines, says Broadley, are sheltered by trees that hold in the heat. The lay of the land protects them from fall storms that roll in from the southwest.

Although Chardonnay comprises a third of the vineyard, Pinot Noir is clearly the winery's focus. The Pinots are far from a fruity, nouveau style of wine. Says Broadley, "I'm looking for a big, rustic style of Pinot Noir." Sometimes "big" is a code word for overripe and jammy, but not at Broadley. As feasible, the grapes are picked at moderate sugars. The rustic bigness comes from the winemaking approach.

The grapes are fermented in 1000 and 500 gallon redwood tanks. Because of the winery's limited facilities, picking begins early, and the batches of grapes are run through the tanks and into French oak barrels. As soon as one batch has finished fermentation, another is started.

Grape clusters are put in the fermenter without destemming. Some batches are packed tightly, others loosely. Differing grape sugar levels and vatting time are additional variables. The batches vary considerably in character, and each is kept separate for later blending. The Pinot is neither fined nor filtered, and is not racked until bottling.

Broadley's Pinots are true to their intent. When young, they are rather rough, dark, and tannic— not too different in style from an older, "rustic" rendition of Burgundy. Broadley continues to re-

fine his winemaking approach while maintaining the stylistic theme. The more recent vintages combine more of the fruity quality of the grape with the underlying "rustic" character.

Callahan Ridge Winery

After dissolution of the partnership that constituted the Garden Valley winery, one of the partners, and Richard Mansfield,

---

Callahan Ridge Winery

340 Busenbark Lane
Roseburg, Oregon 97470
(503) 673-7901

Owners
Mary Sykes-Guido,
Richard Mansfield

Winemaker
Richard Mansfield

Wine Production
20,000 gallons

Vineyard Acreage
4 1/2 acres

Year First Planted
1985

First Vintage
1987

Wines Produced
Riesling, Dry Riesling, Select
Harvest Riesling, Vinum Aureolum
(individual berry select Riesling),
Sauvignon Blanc,
Dry Gewurztraminer,
Select Harvest Gewurztraminer,
Chardonnay, Chardonnay Reserve,
White Zinfandel, White Cabernet,
Cabernet Sauvignon, Pinot Noir

---

former Garden Valley winemaker, continued the venture under the Callahan Ridge name. The Callahan Ridge winery is housed in a rebuilt, attractively rustic, century-old barn.

A native of Newport, Oregon, Mansfield decided to become a winemaker at the age of 14, on a serendipitous visit to a California winery. Mansfield subsequently

succeeded in getting into an exchange program at what he thought was a German school of winemaking, only to discover on arrival that it was a viticultural school.

Mansfield applied his viticultural training in German vineyards, and was later able to shift his studies to the school of enology in Geisenheim, where he received a degree in enology. During his time in Germany, Mansfield made wine for several wineries. A venturesome soul, Mansfield reports living on three-day-old bread and 25 cent a pound cheese-ends for a year.

Mansfield's Oregon wines reflect his German training and perspectives. Riesling is Callahan Ridge's flagship wine. The Chardonnay and red wines go through a malolactic fermentation, but Mansfield generally prefers to control the process. In his view, malolactic fermentation diminishes fruity characteristics and may remove too much acid. Depending on the wine, Mansfield may halt malolactic fermentation prior to completion.

■ **Richard Mansfield**

Nearly all of Callahan Ridge's grapes come from the Umpqua Valley. One notable source of grapes is Doerner Ranch. Now owned and operated by Doug Doerner, Doerner Ranch traces its beginnings to the 1880s, when Doug's great-grandfather, Adam Doerner, emigrated from the Rheinpfalz area of Germany. Adam worked for a year at the Beringer winery in California before coming to Oregon's Umpqua Valley.

Grapes have been grown on the Doerner property since approximately 1888. One of the varieties still remaining from the original century-old plantings is a clone of Zinfandel. On his property, Doerner has both a more modern U.C. Davis clone, as well as the old clone Zinfandel. According to Doerner and Mansfield, the old clone ripens two weeks earlier and produces lighter crops with smaller and more regularly sized berries.

At present, Callahan Ridge is producing only a white Zinfandel with the grapes, but a red Zinfandel will be made in the future. Reliably ripening, good, red Zinfandel from the Northwest may yet be possible.

Cameron Winery

John Paul, winemaker and leading force behind Cameron Winery, is a PhD marine biochemist. Paul still does consulting work for a San Francisco firm, exploring antibiotic compounds extracted from seaweeds. Before coming to Oregon, he was assistant winemaker for California's Konocti and Carneros Creek wineries. But of all the wines he drank, Paul most loved those from Burgundy. In pursuit of his interest, Paul

■ **John Paul**

traveled to France to learn more about Burgundian wines and winegrowing.

After his trip to Burgundy, Paul made an exploratory trip to New Zealand, a cool climate winegrowing area, and one of the few in the world capable of producing fine Pinot Noir. Paul found that New Zealand had great potential, but lacked a discerning consumer market for fine wines. Without such a market, the quality of the

Cameron Winery

8200 Worden Hill Road
P. O. Box 27
Dundee, Oregon 97115
(503) 538-0336

Owners
Partnership

Winemaker
John Paul

Wine Production
8,000 gallons

Vineyard Acreage
4 acre test plot

Year First Planted
1985

First Vintage
1984

Wines Produced
Chardonnay, Chardonnay Reserve, Pinot Noir, Pinot Noir Reserve, Pinot Blanc

wines was much less than it could have been. Instead of New Zealand, Paul opted for one of the few other locations outside of Burgundy capable of producing fine Pinot Noir—Oregon's Willamette Valley.

But why come to Oregon at all? Paul already had vineyard and winemaking experience in Cal-

> **"They say a winemaker has maybe 30 vintages, 30 chances in a lifetime to make great wine. It's startling to think of it that way—I don't want to waste any chances."**

ifornia's Carneros region, a region touted as having a cool climate particularly suited to the Burgundian grape varieties, Chardonnay, and, especially, Pinot Noir.

"Carneros does produce good Pinot Noir," says Paul, "but I really love the wines of Burgundy, and neither the Carneros climate nor its wines have much in common with Burgundy. It is a misconception that Carneros is cool. It is cool only relative to other California growing climates, but it is still a warm climate. I don't mean to say that Oregon's Willamette Valley is exactly like Burgundy, but the climate and wines are very similar. Even the vegetation, which is a good indicator of climate, is very reminiscent of Burgundy."

Unique in Oregon, Paul built 1000 gallon stainless steel fermenters for his Pinot Noir. Similar in size to the fermenters he saw in Burgundy, the ratio of volume to surface area allows the wine to reach a high 95 degree peak fermentation temperature for good color and fruit extraction.

In Paul's view, Oregon Pinot Noirs, especially in the past, have been released with too little acidity. Paul favors the higher acid levels of Burgundies. "Acidity is important for a wine's longevity," says Paul. "If a wine tastes about right when it goes into the bottle, it will probably taste too flat after it has some bottle age. With a little higher acidity, wines taste better with food, and they are better able to develop in the bottle." Tartaric acid is the usual acid of choice when acid adjustments are called for, but Paul also uses citric and other acids for the differing flavor components they offer.

And about Chardonnays, "California Chardonnays are great as aperitifs, good to drink on their own, but with food, I much prefer the acid balance and delicate fruit of Oregon Chardonnays," says Paul. "I also enjoy them more as a winemaker. In California, Chardonnays pretty much make themselves but Pinot Noir is a big challenge. In Oregon, it is the opposite. Chardonnays are very responsive to slight changes in winemaking technique. They are winemakers' wines." Paul works with several yeast strains for complexity. An uncommon Australian yeast plays a key role in his Chardonnay's character.

Most wineries produce a line of several wines, including at least one cash flow wine, such as Riesling, that can be released soon after the vintage. But Paul came to Oregon with the sole purpose of making Pinot Noir and Chardonnay in the Burgundian tradition. With the exception of tiny experimental batches of wine and recent work with Pinot Blanc, the Cameron winery produces Pinot Noir and Chardonnay exclusively.

As we were tasting our way through many barrels, each with some variable different from the previous, Paul comments, "They say a winemaker has maybe 30 vintages, 30 chances in a lifetime to make great wine. It's startling to think of it that way. I don't want to waste any chances."

Chateau Benoit Winery

In 1972, Fred and Mary Benoit planted 10 acres of grapes near Veneta, a small community just west of the city of Eugene, in the southern Willamette Valley. What began as an investment and

---

Chateau Benoit Winery

6580 N.E. Mineral Springs Road
Carlton, Oregon 97111
(503) 864-2991 or 864-3666

Owners
Fred & Mary Benoit

Wine Production
50,000 gallons

Vineyard Acreage
22 acres

Year First Planted
1972

First Vintage
1979

Wines Produced
Sauvignon Blanc, Chardonnay,
Pinot Noir, Merlot, Riesling,
Late Harvest Gewurztraminer,
Sparkling Wines, Rainbow Run
Gold, Rainbow Run Red

---

hobby, a diversion from Fred Benoit's medical practice, evolved into a major enterprise.

The northern Willamette Valley is the center of Oregon's winegrowing industry. When the time came for expansion, the Benoits found the land, and the community of winegrowers and winegrowing traditions they were seeking, near McMinnville in the northern Willamette. The Benoits established a winery and new vineyard near McMinnville, eventually selling their original southern Willamette vineyard.

The Benoit's son, Mark, graduated from Fresno State in viticulture, and now runs a vineyard management consulting service in the Willamette Valley, managing, among his accounts, Chateau Benoit's vineyards. Oregon grape growers are working with many new vine training ideas and methods. For the Benoit vineyards, Mark Benoit is pruning the vines to four canes per vine instead of the more conventional two. With this method, Benoit is hoping to gain some of the cropping and ripening advantages of a denser vine planting without the expense of planting and maintaining additional vines.

The winery's northern Willamette vineyard is one of the warmest and sunniest in the area, receiving 2,500 to 2,700 heat units in warmer years, according to Benoit. The soil is Willakenzie.

Chateau Benoit's trademark wines have differed from the Willamette Valley norm. The Benoits grow twelve acres of Muller-Thurgau, Oregon's largest single planting of this variety. Muller-Thurgau produces a soft, Riesling-like wine much in the style of Liebfraumilch from Germany. Sauvignon Blanc is another winery speciality, showing the aggressive, zesty herbaceousness of the variety.

Chateau Benoit's best known wine came about by the good fortune of a misfortune. In 1981, a cool and rainy year, Benoit's Chardonnay did not ripen well enough to make a quality table wine, so Benoit decided to try a sparkling wine from the grapes. The Blanc de Blanc sparkling wine succeeded, and led Benoit to refine the cuvee in subsequent vintages. The Brut cuvee is predominantly Pinot Noir with lesser portions of Chardonnay and Pinot Blanc. The wine rests on the yeast for a year prior to disgorging. Less yeasty, but similar in structure to a racy French Champagne, the Chateau Benoit Brut helped demonstrate the potential of Oregon sparkling wine.

Cooper Mountain Vineyards

Visitors to Cooper Mountain Vineyards may first be greeted by the winery's resident Newfoundland dog named Burgundy. Seemingly larger than your average bear, it was still in its puppy stage on my first encounter. Extraordinarily friendly, my only concern was being inadvertently eliminated from the face of the earth by a friendly lick.

Cooper Mountain, the winery's namesake, is the remnant of an ancient volcano, now a prominent hill not far from Beaverton and the Portland suburbs. The hill is named after Perry Cooper, an Oregon pioneer who settled on Cooper Mountain in the spring of

> **Cooper Mountain is the remnant of an ancient volcano, now a prominent hill not far from Beaverton and the Portland suburbs.**

1853. The original Cooper farmhouse and homestead still stand on the lower slopes of the vineyard property now owned by the new custodians of the land, Bob and Corrine Gross.

A peach orchard in the 1940s, the land has been under cultivation of one kind or another for more than a century. Wines grapes are the newest offering of the land. Though only 72 acres, the vineyard is relatively large by Oregon standards.

After many years of selling grapes to others, the Gross's started their own small winery, featuring wines made solely from Cooper Mountain Vineyard grapes. Most of the crop is still sold to other wineries, but the Gross's are now able to showcase the product of their vineyard, instead of having it disappear anonymously into a blend.

Regrettably, Cooper Mountain's proximity to the Portland suburbs is a threat to the vineyard and winery. Although somewhat protected by farmland zoning, a development of 37 one-acre housing tracts has cut its way into the slopes adjacent to the vineyard. At $50,000 an acre, their vineyard land is clearly at a premium.

"I guess we're in the wrong business," says Bob Gross with a wistful sense of irony. Multiplying their vineyard acreage by the price of the adjacent housing lots is a textbook case of the dissonant values that come with the ineluctable onslaught of civilization, and the questions of what, indeed, is civil and civilizing.

Cooper Mountain's vineyard soils are of several types, Cascade, Laurelwood, and Saum. Located in the north central part of the Willamette Valley, east of the Chehalem Mountains, the vineyards are slightly cooler than the first Willamette Valley vineyard sites in the Dundee Hills, a potential benefit in the warmer vintages.

One of Cooper Mountain's grape purchasers is the new, major, Oregon sparkling wine producer principaled by Australia's Brian Croser. At the suggestion of Croser, the Gross's are working with a relatively new Oregon vineyard practice.

To eliminate any vegetative character in the grapes, the Gross's are stressing the vine by overloading it with grape clusters, causing the vine to act as if it was going to produce a huge grape crop. Then, later in the year, the grape clusters are radically thinned to a normal crop level.

Cooper Mountain Vineyards

Route 3, Box 1036
Beaverton, Oregon 97007
(503) 649-0027

Owners
Robert & Corrine Gross

Winemaker
Robert Gross,
Rich Cushman, consultant

Wine Production
4,000 gallons

Vineyard Acreage
72 acres

Year First Planted
1978

First Vintage
1987

Wines Produced
Pinot Noir, Chardonnay, Pinot Gris

How much to initially overcrop and when to thin the clusters are major variables to consider. A variant of this method has been employed in other parts of the world, and the Gross's view it as a promising approach for Oregon.

Cooper Mountain's Chardonnay is made in a rather austere, French Chablis-like style. The Gross's are in accord with the new direction of Oregon Pinot Noir winemaking, less thoroughly crushing the grapes and including whole clusters in the fermentation tank for a prolonged fermentation and fruitier character. Suppliers of Pinot Gris to Elk Cove and Ponzi, Cooper Mountain also makes a fine barrel-aged example of their own.

Davidson Winery

Residents of the San Francisco area for eight years, Guy and Sandra Davidson saved their money and prepared for the day when they would have a winery and vineyard of their own. Davidson worked at California wineries and took short courses at U.C. Davis to ready himself for the venture.

The Davidsons were looking for land in Sonoma when they

Davidson Winery

2637 Reston Road
Roseburg, Oregon 97470
(503) 679-6950

Owners
Guy & Sandra Davidson

Winemaker
Guy Davidson

Wine Production
7,000 gallons

Vineyard Acreage
10 acres

Year First Planted
1967

First Vintage
1989

Wines Produced
Pinot Noir, Chardonnay,
Sauvignon Blanc, Pinot Noir Blanc

heard that a winery and vineyard in Oregon had come onto the market. "It was a whirlwind trip," says Davidson. "We came to Oregon, looked at the property, and bought it the next day."

The winery, known for two decades as Bjelland Vineyards, was founded by Paul Bjelland, one of the new era pioneers who came to Oregon's Umpqua Valley from Los Angeles. Bjelland made fruit and berry wines, as well as grape wines, and sold most of the modest production directly from the winery.

The Davidsons arrival brought a much needed revitalization. In the first year of operation, the Davidson's bought new tanks, equipment, and barrels, tripled production, and began to put the winery and vineyard onto a sound commercial and operational footing. The existing wines were sold in bulk. Only the wines made by Davidson will see the Davidson label.

The white wines are barrel fermented. Except for a couple of experimental American oak barrels, all the cooperage is French oak. Pinot Noir and Chardonnay are Davidson's flagship wines.

Located not far from Wildlife Safari, a popular tourist attraction, Davidson Winery is just off Highway 42, one of the main routes from Interstate 5 to the Oregon coast.

Domaine Drouhin Oregon

Robert Drouhin's purchase of Oregon vineyard land caused no small sensation. The French have invested in wineries in California and elsewhere, but always for sparkling wine or some other wine, never before for Pinot Noir.

Oregon's Willamette Valley winegrowers have long contended that their region was one of the very few outside of France's Burgundy district capable of producing fine Pinot Noir. Robert Drouhin's major commitment to a

Domaine Drouhin Oregon

P.O. Box 700
Dundee, Oregon 97115
(503) 864-2700

Owner
Robert Drouhin

Winemaker
Veronique Drouhin

Wine Production
8,000 gallons

Vineyard Acreage
28 acres

Year First Planted
1988

First Vintage
1988

Wines Produced
Pinot Noir

Willamette Valley winery and vineyard land is a clarion endorsement of Oregon Pinot Noir. This endorsement is all the more important because Robert Drouhin is one of Burgundy's most highly regarded producers and shippers.

Drouhin bought 98.5 acres in the summer of 1987. In 1988 and 1989, Drouhin purchased an additional 80 adjacent acres. Eyrie's David Lett, the winegrower who started the Oregon Pinot Noir revolution, and David Adelsheim, another highly regarded Willamette Valley winegrower, were instrumental in arranging Drouhin's purchase of the Dundee Hills vineyard property.

Lett and his family were visiting Drouhin in France when the property became available. Lett's vineyard manager saw that the land had been listed for sale and called Lett. A prime piece of property, Drouhin moved quickly to buy the land. Back in Oregon, Adelsheim acted on Drouhin's behalf to secure the sales arrangement.

About 130 acres of the property are suitable for vineyards, but Drouhin plans to develop the land

Robert Drouhin's major commitment to a Willamette Valley winery, and vineyard land, is a clarion endorsement of Oregon Pinot Noir by one of Burgundy's most highly regarded producers and shippers.

slowly. Unlike the "quick-buck bottom line" and absence of long-range planning that is so much a part of American business culture, Drouhin's long-range view encompasses future generations.

Prior to his purchase of the land, daughter Veronique, a French trained enologist, spent several months visiting and working at Oregon wineries. Now winemaker for Domaine Drouhin Oregon, Veronique lives in the Willamette Valley during the fall harvest and crush. William Hatcher, is general manager. The first wines were made by Veronique and maintained by Hatcher at the Veritas winery in Newberg.

Domaine Drouhin Oregon's newly constructed estate winery is nothing less than superb. Drouhin's financial resources ensure that only the best is sufficient. Domaine Drouhin Oregon is certain to bring an infusion of ideas that will benefit not only Domaine Drouhin Oregon wines, but the Oregon wine industry as a whole.

Elk Cove Vineyards

At the outskirts of the small town of Gaston, a paved road winds its way up the hillside.

A turn-off just beyond its crest is the entryway to Elk Cove, a vineyard and winery named for the Roosevelt Elk that migrate through the area in the spring.

Solely owned and operated by the Campbell family, Pat and Joe Campbell, wife and husband, share winemaking and vineyard management duties. On the crest of a hill on the 136 acre estate, the winery and tasting room offer a sweeping view of the vineyard. Elk Cove has grown considerably since its early years, but still retains a personal and personable flavor that makes it a pleasure to visit.

Many premium American wineries are, to a degree, moving away from strict adherence to the methodologies and mind set of the University of California at Davis, and looking again toward traditional European winegrowing practices. In Oregon, Elk Cove was one of the early wineries to look to European methods, particularly those of Burgundy.

In Europe, vines are often planted much more densely than is common in California. Many believe that increasing the number of vines per acre insures more consistent yields at favorable sugar and acid levels. Elk Cove's vines are planted six feet apart, in rows seven feet apart, a density of 1,054 vines per acre. Some newer Oregon vineyards are planted even more densely, but Elk Cove was among those setting the trend.

Domestic farm machinery cannot cope with these narrow rows, and the Campbells are forced to put up with the scarcity of parts and repair service for their 48 inch wide Italian tractor. Because each vine must be pruned, trained, and cared for, the expense of this higher density planting is considerably greater.

It is commonly believed that increasing the vine's foliage increases its capacity to produce and ripen grapes, but as European studies show, this is only partially true. After approximately the fourteenth leaf on the main shoots

Elk Cove Vineyards

27751 N.W. Olson Road
Gaston, Oregon 97119
(503) 985-7760

Tasting Rooms
Dundee Wine Cellar & Deli
575 S.W. Hwy 99
Dundee, Oregon 97115
(503) 538-0911

Hood River Wine Tasting Room
1108 East Marina Way
Hood River, Oregon 97031
(503) 386-3355

Owners
Pat & Joe Campbell

Winemakers
Pat & Joe Campbell

Wine Production
30,000 gallons

Vineyard Acreage
45 acres

Year First Planted
1974

First Vintage
1977

Wines Produced
Chardonnay Estate,
Chardonnay Oregon,
Gewurztraminer, Pinot Gris,
Riesling Estate,
Riesling Late Harvest,
Ambrosia (Riesling Ice Wine),
Pinot Noir Estate Reserve,
Pinot Noir Wind Hill,
Pinot Noir Dundee Hills,
Pinot Noir Willamette,
Cabernet Sauvignon

and the fourth leaf on the lateral shoots, nutrient production merely supports foliage and no longer benefits the grapes. Elk Cove and other Oregon growers have taken to a practice called hedging, trimming vine shoots to benefit grape production, flavor characteristics, and ripening, a time consuming procedure, and an added expense.

The Chardonnay is fermented in French oak barrels and kept on

---

The Campbells were among the first Willamette Valley winegrowers to actively work with botrytised Riesling.

---

the lees (yeast cells and other sediment) without racking for four to seven months. During this time period, the lees are stirred. These practices contribute to the wine's flavor complexity.

During one of their first vintages, many years ago, the Campbells did not have enough cooperage to ferment all their Chardonnay in oak, so some of the wine was fermented in stainless steel barrels. After two weeks, when fermentation was completed, both the oak fermented and stainless steel fermented wines were put into oak barrels for aging. The wines were distinctly different. Although the oak fermented wine did not have a stronger oak flavor, it was fuller and more complex. This firsthand comparative experience made the Campbells strong advocates of oak barrel fermentation.

The Campbells ferment their Chardonnay with the Montrachet strain of yeast, a strain that has a reputation for producing fuller, richer wines, but at increased risk of the undesirable byproduct, hydrogen sulfide. To avoid the problem of hydrogen sulfide, the Campbells treat their grapes with little or no sulfur, and their Chardonnay benefits from the Montra-

chet yeast without suffering its undesirable byproduct.

Pinot Noir is Elk Cove's premier wine. Beginning with the 1985 vintage, the Campbells changed their method of harvesting and crushing the grapes. As a result, herbaceous flavors are greatly reduced, and the more delicately crushed grapes contribute truer fruit flavors to the wine. The wine is fermented in 200 gallon bins, and the cap of pulp and skins is punched down three to four times a day. After fermentation is completed, the pulp and skins are left to macerate in the must for approximately five days, a prac-

■ **Pat Campbell**

tice once uncommon, but now more widespread in Oregon winemaking. The wine is then pressed, and racked into Allier and Nevers oak barrels.

Grapes are highly sensitive to small changes in growing environment. The grapes Elk Cove purchases from other growers in the northern Willamette Valley are fermented and bottled separately. Differences in soil, climate, and growing methods are brought more clearly into focus when these different grapes are made into wine by the same winemaker.

Comparison of Elk Cove Pinot Noirs from their own estate, and from the Wind Hill Vineyard in the Forest Grove area west of Portland is a case in point. Both vineyards were planted the same year, to the same clone of Pinot Noir, obtained from the same source. The Wind Hill Vineyard is planted in a clay shot soil, the Elk Cove Vineyard in a sandier soil called Willakenzie Silty Loam. The Wind Hill Vineyard has had lighter yields. The site is warmer, and ripens a week ahead of Elk Cove's vineyard. The Wind Hill Pinot Noirs tend to be more tannic and display a more forward fruit intensity. The estate grown Pinot Noirs tend to be more restrained and earthier. Both are very good—and very different.

The Campbells were among the first Willamette Valley winegrowers to actively work with botrytised Riesling. In the often rainy harvest period, botrytis is more often a threat to the grapes than a benefit. The Campbells learned how and when to risk botrytis in Riesling to make sweet, late harvest wines. Although Willamette Valley botrytised Rieslings are now more common, they remain an Elk Cove speciality.

Ellendale Vineyards

While waiting for their own vineyards to mature, Robert and Ella Mae Hudson took advantage of an abundance of Oregon fruits, berries, and honey to satisfy local consumer demand for wines made from those products. By the mid 1980s, local consumer interest was shifting toward grape wines, a transition that coincided with the maturation of Ellendale's estate vineyard. Now, more than three-fourths of

Ellendale Vineyards

300 Reuben Boise Road
Dallas, Oregon 97338
(503) 623-5617

Tasting Room
99W & Rickreall Road
Rickreall, Oregon 97371
(503) 623-6835

Owners
Robert & Ella Mae Hudson

Winemaker
Robert Hudson

Wine Production
8,000 gallons

Vineyard Acreage
15 acres

Year First Planted
1979

First Vintage
1982

Wines Produced
Sparkling: Crystal Mist,
Crystal Mist Blanc de Blanc,
Crystal Mist Blanc de Noir;
Still Wines: Pinot Noir,
Chardonnay,
Barrel Aged Chardonnay,
Riesling, Cabernet Franc,
Cabernet Franc Rose,
Niagara (Beaver Gold),
Gewurztraminer, Mead,
Woolly Booger

Ellendale's wines are made from grapes.

Mead, made in different degrees of sweetness, is still an Ellendale specialty. No sugar is added to any of Ellendale's mead, only honey at bottling for the meads with residual sweetness. Aged in oak, the Hudsons make their mead in a relatively drier style than most, emphasizing the flavors of the honey.

From the beginning, the Hudsons planned to have a small winery focusing on sparkling wines. After many interim steps, Methode Champenoise sparkling wines now comprise 40% of the grape wine production, averaging about 2,000 gallons a year. Further increases are planned. Ellendale's sparkling wines spend from 18 months to more than two years on the yeast. Only Chardonnay and Pinot Noir are used for the sparkling wines.

The Hudsons still make a speciality wine called Woolly Booger, a blend of Loganberry, Blackberry, and Cherry, finished at about four percent residual sugar. The Hudson's have a certain attachment to Woolly Booger. Says Hudson, "Wooly Booger bought our Champagne equipment, and as long as the public wants it, I will make it."

Eola Hills Wine Cellars

The northern Willamette Valley's Dundee Hills put Oregon firmly on the wine map. Although the Dundee Hills remains the most well known winegrowing area in Oregon, new areas are emerging. The Eola Hills is one of the most prominent of the "new" areas. The Eola Hills, running north and south in the middle of the northern Willamette Valley, are generally warmer than the Dundees.

Oak Grove Vineyards, west of Salem, is situated on one of the Eola's warmer sites. When the small corporation of seventeen shareholders that owns Oak Grove Vineyards decided to become a winery, they took the name Eola Hills Wine Cellars. Most of the grapes from the relatively large (by Oregon standards) vineyard are sold to other wineries, but Eola Hills Wine Cellars continues to expand wine production.

An insurance agent, Tom Huggins, the corporation's general manager, became interested in grape growing and winemaking while writing insurance policies for other Oregon winegrowers. The enterprise started modestly, but rapidly grew into a small corporation of family and friends. Ken Wright, winemaker and owner of Panther Creek Cellars, was Eola Hill's first winemaker. Replacing Wright is Joe Dobbs, Jr. Dobbs spent a year in Burgundy before returning to Oregon and assuming Eola Hill's winemaking duties.

Because of the warmer growing site, Huggins planted Cabernet Sauvignon, Chenin Blanc, and Sauvignon Blanc, all warmer climate varieties, in addition to the more conventional Willamette Valley varieties such as Pinot Noir and Chardonnay.

Prior to crushing and fermentation, the grapes are hand sorted to remove damaged fruit, leaves, and other miscellaneous materials that can find their way into the picking bins. The Chardonnay is barrel fermented. The red wines are given extended maceration—after fermentation is complete,

Eola Hills Wine Cellars

501 South Pacific Highway West
Rickreal, Oregon 97371
(503) 623-2405

Owners
Corporation:
Tom Huggins, General Manager

Winemaker
Joe Dobbs, Jr.

Wine Production
20,000 gallons

Vineyard Acreage
67 acres

Year First Planted
1982

First Vintage
1986

Wines Produced
Pinot Noir, Chardonnay,
Sauvignon Blanc,
Cabernet Sauvignon,
Chenin Blanc, Pinot Noir Blanc,
Late Harvest Sauvignon Blanc

the wine is left in contact with the skins and pulp. Except for Pinot Noir Blanc, all the wines are aged in French oak. Many of the barrels are Vosges oak, a particularly tight grained oak that does not inundate the wine with strong oak flavors.

Evesham Wood Vineyard

The Eola Hills in the northern Willamette Valley have become one of Oregon's major new vineyard areas. For their vineyard and new winery, Russ and Mary

---

Evesham Wood Vineyard

2995 Michigan City Avenue
West Salem, Oregon 97304
(503) 371-8478

Owners
Russ & Mary Raney

Winemaker
Russ Raney

Wine Production
4,000 gallons

Vineyard Acreage
8 acres

Wines Produced
Chardonnay, Pinot Noir, Pinot Gris

Raney chose a site at the southeastern end of the Eolas, not far from West Salem. The winery and vineyard overlook a classic Willamette Valley scenic of the Willamette River, the valley's broad expanse, and the foothills of the Cascade Mountain Range.

After graduating from college, Russ Raney went to Germany to study, graduating from the State Technical School for Enology and Viticulture in Bad Kreuznach. Mary Raney studied horticulture at Southern Illinois University, and brings her training to their grape growing efforts.

Russ Raney also lived for a time

in France. Unlike some other German trained Northwest winemakers whose winemaking styles with Chardonnay and Pinot Noir are influenced by the Germanic methods traditionally applied to Riesling and Riesling-like wines, Raney translates his German technical training into Burgundian methods when working with the classic French Burgundian grapes, Pinot Noir and Chardonnay.

Evesham Wood is focusing on wines produced from grapes grown in the southeastern Eola Hills. In addition to the Evesham Wood label, the winery will also release wines made from a neighboring vineyard under the Redhawk Vineyard designation.

The Eyrie Vineyards

David Lett is one of the true pioneers of Oregon's wine industry. Although he came to Oregon in 1965, four years after Hillcrest's Richard Sommer had settled in the Roseburg area, Lett was the first winemaker in recent times to grow vinifera grapes in the Willamette Valley, and moreover, the first Oregon winemaker choosing to focus his efforts on a red wine—Pinot Noir.

With a degree in viticulture from the University of California at Davis, and some practical California winemaking experience, Lett began looking for an area to grow the northern European grape varieties, Pinot Noir and Chardonnay. Lett passed by Oregon's Umpqua Valley, believing it too warm for Pinot Noir, and chose the Willamette Valley's Dundee Hills as the site for his vineyards.

In selecting the site, Lett was not only singular in his convic-

tion, but virtually solitary. Oregon State University was then recommending *Vitis labrusca* as the only commercially viable grape species. Everyone from Lett's U. C. Davis professors to local farmers advised against his enterprise. Said one of his professors, "You'll be frosted out in the spring and fall, rained on all summer, and you'll get athlete's foot up to your knees." Lett ignored the advice.

The early years were not easy. For a time, David and Diana Lett and their two babies lived in a tent in their vineyard. Years would pass before Lett's beliefs about Oregon Pinot Noir could be validated.

Pinot Noir, a grape that rarely does well outside of Burgundy, is Oregon's stellar wine grape, a fact confirmed by the now famous tastings published in the French food and wine magazine, *Gault/Millau, Le Nouveau Guide.* In 1979, the magazine sponsored an "Olympics of the Wines of the World," pitting the 330 best of 586 original entries from 33 of the world's wine producing regions.

To the disappointment of many, including Robert Drouhin of the highly regarded Bur-

---

"You'll be frosted out in the spring and fall, rained on all summer, and you'll get athlete's foot up to your knees."

---

gundian wine firm, Joseph Drouhin, the French wines did not do as well as had been expected. Drouhin contended that the tasting had been unbalanced, and that less than the best Burgundies had been chosen to compete against the very best "foreign" wines. Drouhin proposed a rematch, pitting the top- scoring foreign Pinot Noirs against Burgundies selected from the Drouhin cellars.

On January 8, 1980, under the supervision of M. Jacques Puisais, President of the International Union of Enologists, twenty French, English, and American wine judges of considerable re-

---

The Eyrie Vineyards

P.O. Box 697
Dundee, Oregon 97115

935 East 10th Street
McMinnville, Oregon 97128
(503) 472-6315 or 864-2410

Owners
David and Diana Lett

Winemaker
David Lett

Wine Production
12,000 gallons

Vineyard Acreage
46 acres

Year First Planted
1966

First Vintage
1970

Wines Produced
Pinot Noir, Pinot Noir Reserve
Pinot Gris, Pinot Meunier,
Chardonnay, Muscat Ottonel

---

pute conducted a formal tasting of the wines. Drouhin's 1959 Chambolle-Musigny was the first place wine. In third place was a 1961 Chambertin Clos-de-Beze. The second place wine, two tenths of a point out of first, was an Oregon wine, the 1975 Eyrie Vineyards South Block Reserve.

After fifteen years of pioneer adversity, the results of the *Gault/Millau* tasting were sweet indeed. The landmark tasting brought Eyrie instant recognition, and helped bring well-deserved

and long overdue attention to the Oregon wine industry.

The *Gault/Millau* chapter was a beginning as much as it was a conclusion. In 1987, Lett and his family were visiting the Drouhins in Burgundy when Lett's vineyard manager phoned the news that a prime piece of vineyard land was for sale. Drouhin bought the land and subsequently built an Oregon winery. Daughter Veronique is the winemaker.

An international Pinot Noir celebration is held yearly in McMinnville. Burgundian and Oregon winemakers routinely visit each other, and California wineries are buying Oregon grapes and Oregon vineyard land. Now, when the early naysayers to Lett's Oregon Pinot Noir venture are mentioned, Lett's wry smile is irrepressible.

Lett believes that more than any other variety, Pinot Noir is a winegrower's grape. Cabernet Sauvignon has a strong and immediate varietal profile, but Pinot Noir is delicate, elusive, and subtle. Grown in less than ideal conditions, the varietal character disappears completely, yet this subtle quality makes the grape highly responsive to slight changes in growing conditions and winemaking methods. More than any other variety, Pinot Noir reflects the winemaker's style, the winemaker's art. And, more than any other variety, Pinot Noir is made in the vineyard.

Eyrie Pinot Noirs are reflective of Lett's preferences and predilections. Of Burgundies Lett prefers those with perfumed finesse rather than the bigger, and, to his taste, sometimes clumsy wines of the northernmost Cote de Nuits.

Eyrie's Pinot Noir is fermented without the stems in small, four-foot-square bins. Temperatures

reach the high 80s. At the height of fermentation, Lett sleeps in the winery, and punches down the fermenting cap of skins and pulp every two hours around the clock. Lett believes that frequent and vigorous punching- down extracts the most and best flavors from the grape. Eyrie's regular bottling of Pinot Noir is made from grapes purchased from other growers. The reserve Pinot Noir consists entirely of grapes from the original estate vineyard.

Most of Eyrie's estate Pinot Noir is the Wadenswil clone. Lett concedes that clonal differences

■ **David Lett**

exist, but emphasizes that other factors are more significant. Eyrie Pinot Noirs are not darkly colored wines. Lett decries the American, and particularly the West Coast, prejudice that high tannin, high alcohol, and inky color somehow equate with quality or aging potential. Lett believes that good acidity and concentrated varietal fruit are the keys to longevity and fine Pinot Noir.

Lett's wines give credence to his views. Often seemingly light and delicate when first released, Lett's Pinot Noirs have earned a justifiable reputation for developing fine, complex flavors—and continuing to age in the bottle long after the inky, high tannin, high alcohol, low acid Pinot Noirs have faded.

Lett produces Chardonnay, another Burgundian grape variety, and a mainstay of the

---

At a time when marketing expediencies and the quest to appeal to the lowest common denominator are rampant cultural diseases, it is heartening to find someone so steadfastly committed to substance, and courageous enough to follow an independent path.

Oregon wine industry. Lett's Chardonnay comes from his "Draper selection" rather than the more prolific and more common 108 clone. Eyrie's Chardonnays, too, have garnered a fine reputation.

Lett eschews Oregon's traditional third major variety, Riesling. Many feel that Riesling does not make a very good dry wine, but is at its best with residual sugar. Lett prefers dry wines to go with food, and has budded over his Riesling vines to another grape variety, Pinot Gris, a little-known white wine grape that is rapidly gaining attention.

For years, enamored with the grape variety and its wines, Lett produced miniscule quantities of Pinot Gris from a few experimental vines. A direct relative of Pinot

Noir, Pinot Gris is a viable alternative to Riesling. Riesling is popular with winegrowers because it produces palatable wines even in poor years, requires no oak and no aging, and can be released soon after the vintage, providing much needed cash flow for the winegrower. Pinot Gris has some of these same attributes, but it is an excellent food wine as well.

A color mutation of Pinot Noir, Pinot Gris is similar to its red cousin in that it does not have a high varietal profile as does, for example, Cabernet Sauvignon or Sauvignon Blanc, but instead communicates its merit through a subtle interplay of flavors.

Lett does not intend Pinot Gris as a replacement for Chardonnay. In his rendition, Pinot Gris is fermented in stainless steel, put through a malolactic fermentation, bottled without oak aging, and released soon after the vintage. Without oak aging, Chardonnay usually seems incomplete, but Pinot Gris makes a complete wine without oak. The texture and fullness of Pinot Gris often conveys the sensation that the wine has been in oak, even when it has not.

In very small quantities, Lett makes a dry Muscat Ottonel, a refined and uncommon member of the Muscat family. To avoid confusion among buyers expecting a sweet wine in the manner of most Muscats, Lett bottles his Muscat Ottonel in a Chardonnay-style bottle, a shape more readily associated with dry wines. Eyrie's Muscat Ottonel is an unusual and excellent wine.

Pinot Meunier is another speciality wine. Only about 175 cases are made each year. A red relative of Pinot Noir, the grape plays a significant role in French Champagne. Lett's Pinot Meunier

red wine, however, is probably the world's only commercial release of a Pinot Meunier still wine.

A quarter century ago, Lett assumed considerable risk, and pioneered Pinot Noir in Oregon's Willamette Valley. Two decades later, Lett again subscribed to risk and committed half his yearly wine production to an unknown and unrecognized grape. A marketing consultant would find Lett's major commitment to Pinot Gris unwise at best, but 25 years ago, his commitment to Oregon Pinot Noir was similarly foolish. Pinot Gris is already rapidly on its way to becoming one of Oregon's major grape varieties.

At a time when marketing expediencies and the quest to appeal to the lowest common denominator are rampant cultural diseases, it is heartening to find someone so steadfastly committed to substance, and courageous enough to follow an independent path. In Lett's case, it is more heartening still, when such a path has been so sublimely and emphatically validated.

Forgeron Vineyard

Climate measurements at the city of Eugene suggest that this southern portion of the Willamette Valley is nearly identical to the northern Willamette near Portland. Such is not the case. The climates surrounding Eugene vary considerably, and some are warmer and otherwise differ significantly in character from the growing areas of the northern Willamette. Forgeron vineyard is one such climate.

The choice of Forgeron's vineyard location was no accident. In the late 1960's, the Federal Government conducted an environmental impact study to evaluate the feasibility of a nuclear power plant near Eugene. The power plant was never built, but its latent legacy was a highly comprehensive source of climatological information. Taking advantage of this data, Lee and Linda Smith selected their vineyard site, and in 1972, planted their first grapes.

According to Smith, Forgeron has 55 more days of sunshine than Eugene, and seven to ten inches less rainfall. Although the days are

---

Forgeron Vineyard

89697 Sheffler Road
Elmira, Oregon 97437
(503) 935-1117

Owners
Lee & Linda Smith

Winemaker
Lee Smith

Wine Production
18,000 gallons

Vineyard Acreage
20 acres

Year First Planted
1972

First Vintage
1978

Wines Produced
Cabernet Sauvignon, Pinot Noir, Chardonnay, Riesling, Pinot Gris, Muller-Thurgau, Summer Blush

---

warm, the nights are quite cool, a condition Smith feels is a key factor in the quality of his Pinot Noir and Cabernet Sauvignon, and also an important element in encouraging the growth of *Botrytis cinerea*, a mold that, under the right conditions, is responsible for special, sweet, white wines of exceptional quality. Oregon vintages, like vintages of European winegrowing climates, vary much more than those of California. Smith reports that heat summation measurements in his vineyard

have ranged from 2,000 to over 3,000, though "typical" years average 2,400 to 2,500.

In part because of his vineyard's relatively warm climate, Forgeron is one of the few Willamette Valley wineries pursuing Cabernet Sauvignon. Forgeron produces much more Pinot Noir than Cabernet Sauvignon, but the Cabernet is Smith's personal favorite.

Forgeron's Pinot Noir is planted half to the Wadenswil clone and half to the Pommard. Smith, preferring a blend of the two clones, believes that Pommard has a more typically Burgundian character, but that Wadenswil contributes more aromatics. According to Smith, the topsoil of his vineyard is Bellpine, but at 18 inches is a layer with bits of a sandstone-limestone mix. At 30 inches, the soil changes to a permeable sandstone-limestone layer. Smith sees a correlation with the limestone soils of Burgundy, and attributes the character of his Pinot Noirs, at least, in part, to his vineyard soils.

Riesling is Forgeron's major grape variety. Smith ferments the Riesling at very low temperatures, about 40 to 45 degrees, to preserve the delicate fruit esters of the grape. He has found that the standard strains of dried yeast do not work well at these temperatures, and now imports live yeast cultures from France to do the job.

Smith believes that most Chardonnay planted in Oregon is a high acid clone poorly suited to the Oregon climate. Forgeron is focusing efforts on less widely planted Chardonnay clones, such as the Draper clone. Other white varieties include Chenin Blanc and Pinot Gris.

Foris Vineyards

Ted and Merideth Gerber own and operate Oregon's southernmost winery. Although their land is less than seven miles from the California border, the wine-

■ **Ted Gerber**

growing climate is far from Oregon's warmest. Nestled on the lower, west facing slopes of the Siskiyou Mountains, the vineyards are 40 miles from the Pacific Ocean. The intervening Klamath Mountains only partially shelter the vineyards from the cooling marine air.

This is not a growing climate for

Though less than seven miles from the California border, the winegrowing climate is far from Oregon's warmest.

Cabernet Sauvignon, but for the cooler climate varieties typical of those planted in the Willamette Valley to the north. At one time, a Willamette Valley winery, interested in earlier ripening Pinot

Noir for its "nouveau" wine, contracted for the Gerbers' grapes. The idea was a good one in theory, but not in practice. Ironically, in some vintages, Gerbers' Illinois Valley grapes ripen up to

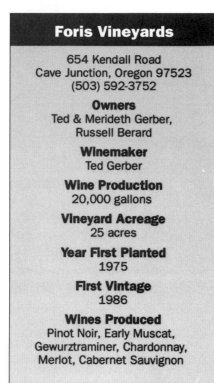

Foris Vineyards

654 Kendall Road
Cave Junction, Oregon 97523
(503) 592-3752

Owners
Ted & Merideth Gerber,
Russell Berard

Winemaker
Ted Gerber

Wine Production
20,000 gallons

Vineyard Acreage
25 acres

Year First Planted
1975

First Vintage
1986

Wines Produced
Pinot Noir, Early Muscat,
Gewurztraminer, Chardonnay,
Merlot, Cabernet Sauvignon

two weeks later than those in the more northerly Willamette Valley. Foris's Cabernet Sauvignon and Merlot wines are produced from grapes grown in southern Oregon's warmer areas further inland.

The Gerbers own 200 acres of land on two "ranches." Hay, seed crops, and cattle are part of their diverse agrarian interests. The soil in the Gerbers' main vineyard is unusual, no doubt one of the few in the world planted on mine tailings. In an earlier era, southwest Oregon was a hotbed of mining activity. The slurry of dirt and rock from a nearby mine was diverted into a sloping valley that is now the Gerbers' vineyard.

Early Muscat is one of Gerber's speciality wines, but Pinot Noir is his premier wine. Until 1988, the

Gerbers grapes were either sold to other wineries, or turned into wine elsewhere for release under the Foris label or the label of other wineries. Now, with a well-established vineyard, and control over the wine from vine to bottle, Gerber can more clearly explore and define what this intriguing wine-growing region has to offer.

Girardet Wine Cellars

While working as a design engineer for the chemistry and astrophysics departments at the California Institute of Tech-

■ **The Girardet family**

nology, Swiss born Philippe Girardet met his wife Bonnie, a teacher and graduate of the University of California at Berkeley. Within a year, the two opted for changes in career and lifestyle and moved to Oregon's Umpqua Valley near Roseburg. Girardet's Swiss background led him to a belief in good quality, moderately priced wines to serve with food.

Chardonnay is Girardet's leading wine. Girardet makes and prices his Chardonnay to be a reasonably affordable, "everyday" wine. Girardet is highly successful in hitting the mark with the wine, but it often exceeds the quality and character of its intended

niche, frequently beating out higher priced aspirants to Chardonnay excellence.

Girardet is a strong believer in oak aging for his wines, but not strong oaky flavors. He likes the softening and complexing effect of barrel aging. Girardet ages his Chardonnay and other wines predominantly in older, more neutral oak barrels. The Chardonnay receives extended lees contact in the barrel aging process.

The emphasis on "everyday," readily drinkable wines, as well as the nature of their vineyard site, prompted the Girardets to explore French-American hybrids, as well as the Oregon's customary vinifera varieties such as Chardonnay and Pinot Noir.

Parts of the Girardet vineyard are prone to frosts, and the soils are very shallow, with underlying

Girardet Wine Cellars

895 Reston Road
Roseburg, OR 97470
(503) 679-7252

Owners
Philippe & Bonnie Girardet

Winemaker
Philippe Girardet

Wine Production
18,000 gallons

Vineyard Acreage
18 acres

Year First Planted
1972

First Vintage
1983

Wines Produced
Chardonnay, Pinot Noir,
Cabernet Sauvignon, Riesling,
Gewurztraminer, Sauvignon Blanc,
Vin Blanc, Vin Rouge

shale. The hybrid varieties are much more suitable to these difficult conditions than the more sensitive vinifera varieties. Additionally, hybrids suffer less from mildew than vinifera vines, and the hybrids readily recover from spring frost damage. Girardet's vinifera vines produce about two tons an acre. The hybrids produce four to five tons an acre, ripening early at good sugar levels.

Although one might wince at the thought of French-American hybrids in Oregon, the wines have worked well for Girardet. None of the two dozen hybrids in the vineyard is released as a single bottling. All are blended into Girardet's Vin Blanc and Vin Rouge. The Vin Blanc is comprised of varying amounts of Chardonnay and, usually, five hybrid varieties, mainly Verdelet and Aurora. The Vin Rouge is usually about 50 percent Pinot Noir, blended with small amounts of other vinifera varieties, including Zinfandel and Merlot, as well as hybrid varieties, Baco Noir, De-Chaunac, Chancellor, and others. Although the composition varies from vintage to vintage, the Vin Blanc and Vin Rouge are usually fine, everyday, dry, table wines at a good price.

Glen Creek Winery

Founder of a leading southern California wine shop, Thomas Dumm was among the first wineshop owners in California to stock Northwest wines. In 1976, Dumm and his family left California for a better lifestyle in Oregon. Settling in a rural area in the Eola Hills near Salem, Dumm planted a few grape vines and continued with his interest in home winemaking, a hobby that would soon to grow into a commercial enterprise.

Dumm prepared for winemaking on a commercial scale by attending a series of courses at the University of California at Davis. In 1982, Glen Creek had its first crush, 6,000 gallons of wine from Washington grapes. Glen Creek now produces all its wines from Oregon grapes. Most of Glen Creek's grapes are grown in the Eola Hills where the winery is located.

An emerging winegrowing subregion of the Willamette Valley, the Eola Hills rise up from the Willamette River near Salem, and run northward along the river for a short distance. Situated in the middle of the wide Willamette Valley, the Eola Hills offer a slightly different winegrowing climate from the first Willamette Val-

---

Glen Creek Winery

6057 Orchard Heights Road N.W.
Salem, Oregon 97304
(503) 371-WINE

Owners
Thomas & Sylvia Dumm

Winemaker
Thomas Dumm

Wine Production
12,000 gallons

Vineyard Acreage
10 acres

Year First Planted
1983

First Vintage
1982

Wines Produced
Chardonnay, Pinot Noir,
Gewurztraminer, Riesling,
Muller-Thurgau, Pinot Noir Nouveau

---

ley vineyards which were situated along the western edge of the valley.

Dumm built Glen Creek's tasting room in the aging cellar so that visitors would not be isolated from the sights and smells of the winery. Just outside, tall, temperature controlled tanks glisten in the sun, and an arbor covered picnic area offers a tranquil setting for visitors. During the grape crush, a raised viewing deck affords a good view of winery operations.

Henry Estate Winery

The Henry Winery is a paradox, a winery firmly rooted in Oregon's rural, pioneering, winegrowing traditions, yet contrasting with, and contradicting, many of those same traditions. Scott Henry, the winery's founder, became interested in wine from his association with his close friend and colleague, the late Gino Zepponi. Both worked for the same California engineering firm. Zepponi became the "Z" in California's ZD winery, and later vice president of the large California sparkling wine producer, Domaine Chandon.

In 1971, Henry and Zepponi came to Oregon to look at the prospects for winegrowing. In 1972, Henry left California and the engineering firm, moved to Oregon, and planted 12 acres of wine grapes in Oregon's Umpqua Valley.

Many of Oregon's winegrowers have come to the state from California, but Henry is not a newcomer. The Henry family has lived and ranched in the Umpqua Valley for over a hundred years. The family ranch and orchards are on bottomland near the Umpqua River, and it is there that Henry planted his grapes, thus immediately violating Oregon winegrowing traditions, and the fundamental tenet that Oregon vineyards should be planted on southerly slopes above the valley floor.

The soil is a Roseburg Sandy Loam, running fifteen feet to gravel. Skeptics believed that the flatland vineyards would not have enough air movement to dispel destructive spring frosts, would not be sunny or warm enough to ripen the grapes, and would pro-

---

Henry Estate Winery

687 Hubbard Creek Road, HWY 9
P.O. Box 26
Umpqua, Oregon 97486
(503) 459-5120 or 459-3614

Owners
Scott & Sylvia Henry

Winemaker
Scott Henry

Wine Production
30,000 gallons

Vineyard Acreage
31 acres

Year First Planted
1972

First Vintage
1978

Wines Produced
Pinot Noir, Chardonnay,
Gewurztraminer, Red Table Wine,
Late Harvest Riesling, Sparkling

---

duce mostly vegetation instead of grapes. All these predictions proved wrong.

The nearby Umpqua River protects the vines from frost. As the temperature approaches freezing, the moist, river air fogs up, protecting the vines from frost much in the same way that overhead sprinkler systems are used to create a moist heating- freezing shield around the vines. The vineyard site has had an average of 2,200 heat units a year. During the growing season, a cut in the Coast Range Mountains corresponds with the position of the setting sun, thus increasing the effective day length. Adequate grape sugars have not been a problem.

The Henrys' decorative grape arbor consistently produced grapes every year, and Henry had little doubt that his vineyard would have a commercially viable

grape yield. This proved more than true. In Oregon, three tons an acre is considered a good average yield for most grape varieties. Scott Henry's vineyards yield six to eight tons of Chardonnay and Pinot Noir per acre.

Most feel that higher yields tend to dilute a wine's quality, particularly with respect to Pinot Noir, but Henry maintains that after experimenting with a wide range of yields, six to eight tons is best for his growing site. Because Henry's vineyards produce more than twice as much wine per acre as most Oregon vineyards, the sometimes hard financial realities of Oregon winegrowing do not impact Henry so severely.

Although Henry has expanded his range of wines, by far the greatest portion of the winery's production is Pinot Noir and Chardonnay. With rare exception, Oregon wineries use only French oaks for aging these varieties. At more than several times the price of American oak, French oak barrels seemed prohibitively expensive to Henry. His friend and consultant, Zepponi, urged Henry to use American oak cooperage, a widespread practice in California. Zepponi suggested that consumer acceptance and awards in wine judgings would be no different than if French oak were used.

Henry liked the flavors of American oak as well as the price and accepted Zepponi's advice. The wines, predictably, have proven both successful and controversial. The pronounced American oak character quickly polarizes wine tasters. Henry prefers a riper, fuller style of wine, a style that best suits the American oak, and is achieved most fully in Oregon's warmer vintages. Because of these stylistic predilections, some critics have suggested

Henry's wines more closely resemble the wines of California than the wines of Oregon. Others praise them highly, especially the fuller bodied wines from the warmest vintages.

Hidden Springs Winery

The Hidden Springs estate vineyard was among the first planted in the Eola Hills, a highly regarded winegrowing area in Oregon's northern Willamette Valley. Once the site of a cherry and prune orchard, the partners converted the adjacent prune drying building to their winery facility.

Most of Oregon's climatological information comes from data gathered at airport weather stations, but since airports are usually in valleys, and vineyards are usually at higher elevations, on hillsides with southerly exposures, winegrowers have not had the benefit of reliable basic information, much less information on important subtleties, comparing, for example, the implications of a southwesterly exposure versus a southeasterly exposure, the effects of cloud cover at different times during the growing season, and so on. Byard is participating in an experimental program with Oregon State University to gather more accurate and useful data. Thermographs have been placed at several vineyard locations in the Willamette Valley, including Byard's. Thermographs measure, automatically and continuously, temperature, humidity, and the intensity of the sunlight.

When conversation turns to clonal selection, Pinot Noir is the grape that comes first to mind, but other varieties have clonal variants as well, though not to the

Hidden Springs Winery

9360 S.E. Eola Hills Road
Amity, Oregon 97101
(503) 835-2782

Owners
Don & Carolyn Byard, Al & Jo Alexanderson

Winemakers
Don Byard & Al Alexanderson

Wine Production
9,000 gallons

Vineyard Acreage
20 acres

Year First Planted
1973

First Vintage
1980

Wines Produced
Pinot Noir, Chardonnay,
Dry Riesling, Riesling Reserve,
Riesling Dessert Style,
Pacific Sunset, Pinot Noir Blanc,
Cabernet Sauvignon

same degree as Pinot Noir. As part of another experimental program, three different clones of Riesling are planted at the Eola site.

Oregon's principal grape varieties, Pinot Noir, Riesling, and Chardonnay, comprise most of Hidden Spring's production, but other less usual varieties are produced as well. The Sauvignon Blanc is included in Pacific Sunset, a proprietary blush blend with Pinot Noir and Riesling. In warmer years, Cabernet Sauvignon is made. Muller-Thurgau, a Riesling-like variety that does well on cooler sites, has been planted on the less sunny area near the winery building.

A small winery, visitors can walk through the operations area and often see a phase of the winemaking process in progress.

Hillcrest Vineyard

In 1961, Richard Sommer bought acreage and planted wine grapes in Oregon's Umpqua Valley near Roseburg, and with that, became the proverbial father and founder of Oregon's wine industry.

Sommer studied agronomy and viticulture at the University of California at Davis, and after an intervening period, came to Oregon in search of a cooler winegrowing climate. Sampling some of the few vinifera grapes that were then growing in Oregon, Sommer was satisfied he had found the proper climate. Although remnants of earlier winegrowing efforts remained, when Sommer came to

---

In 1961, Richard Sommer planted wine grapes in Oregon's Umpqua Valley, becoming the proverbial father and founder of Oregon's modern wine industry.

Oregon, no prior precedent gave adequate assurance of success.

For the winegrowers that followed, Sommer not only provided direct assistance, but perhaps even more importantly, served as an example that commercial, premium, vinifera winegrowing in Oregon was not only possible, but viable. Some three decades have passed since Sommer came to Oregon. Although the state's wine industry has grown tremendously, and many wineries are vying for attention and recognition, for many years, Sommer's Hillcrest Vineyard and premium Oregon wine were virtually synonymous.

The trip from the town of Roseburg to the Hillcrest winery is a convoluted journey, well marked, but entailing many turns and side roads. At 850 feet above sea level, the Hillcrest vineyard is higher and slightly cooler than other estate vineyards in the Roseburg area, but well suited to Riesling. Fully two thirds of Hillcrest's 35 acre vineyard are planted to the grape, and Hillcrest's reputation is based on Riesling wines. Oregon is now known for several grape varieties, but when Sommer pioneered this cooler grape growing region, Riesling, a well known, premium, cool climate grape, was the most logical choice, and today, Riesling is still one of the mainstays of the Oregon wine industry.

Nearly every Oregon winery releases Riesling soon after the vintage as a cash flow wine to keep the bankers away from the door. Most Oregon Riesling is purchased and consumed within a year of the vintage. Although a tasty wine when young, Riesling is a better wine with some bottle

Hillcrest Vineyard

240 Vineyard Lane
Roseburg, Oregon 97470
(503) 673-3709

Owner
Richard Sommer

Wine Production
25,000 gallons

Vineyard Acreage
35 acres

Year First Planted
1961

First Vintage
1963

Wines Produced
Riesling, Select Harvest Riesling,
Chardonnay, Gewurztraminer,
Semillon, Sauvignon Blanc,
Umpqua Blanc, White Cabernet,
Mellow Red, Pinot Noir,
Cabernet Sauvignon, Cabernet
Sauvignon Early Release,
Zinfandel

age, though few Rieslings are stored long enough to show their best. Hillcrest Rieslings are given a better chance. Sommer does not release them until about two years after the vintage, fully ready to drink, though still receptive to longer aging.

Hillcrest's Rieslings are fermented at a temperature of 50 degrees in stainless steel tanks. The fermentation is stopped when the desired level of sweet-

---

A man of the seasons and the soil, after some three decades, Sommer's life is deeply rooted in his Hillcrest vineyard—so, too, the Oregon wine industry.

---

ness remains. In recent years, the Riesling has been selectively harvested. Pickers make several passes through the vineyard at different times, harvesting only the ripest grapes. Sommer has also made Riesling ice wine. The grapes are picked frozen on the vine and quickly pressed before they thaw. The sweetest berries freeze the least, and in the first pressing, only the juice from the ripest berries is released. True ice wines are much more concentrated than their regularly picked brethren.

Best known for his Rieslings, Sommer has also made a mark with his red wines, produced in small quantities. All the red wines are aged in a combination of French and American oak. Pinot Noir has been successful, and, in warmer years, Cabernet Sauvignon ripens well and is a wine for laying down.

Zinfandel, a long season grape,

seldom ripens properly in Oregon, but in choice years, when the grape does ripen, the wine can be very good. Hillcrest, in very small quantities, is one of the few Northwest wineries producing a Zinfandel, and in those rare good years, it is a most worthy wine.

To achieve high yield, good ripening, and well defined varietal character, Oregon vines need more leaf area exposed to the sun than warmer climate vines. To this end, Sommer has trained most of his vines into a tall divided canopy. When viewed down the vine row, the vines are shaped like a "U." Open in the center, each vine's double canopy form the sides of the "U." Developed independently, Sommer's vine training method closely parallels the "Open-Lyre" or "U" system developed by Carbonneau in France, a system that has garnered much attention even in tradition-bound France.

Most winegrowers are anxious to show off their winery or wines. Sommer steers an inquisitive visitor to his vineyard. A man of the seasons and the soil, after some three decades, Sommer's life is deeply rooted in his Hillcrest vineyard—so, too, the Oregon wine industry.

Hinman Vineyards

Hinman Vineyards began as a partnership of Doyle Hinman and David Smith. The enterprise grew immensely when Boardman Farms, a large-scale grape grower in eastern Oregon, became a major investor in Hinman Vineyards.

The Columbia Valley, Washington state's major grape growing region, also reaches into north-

eastern Oregon. Boardman Farms is Oregon's first major grape grower in the Columbia Valley. Although Hinman Vineyards is at the southern end of the Willamette Valley in western Oregon, the Columbia Valley in eastern Oregon is its major source of grapes.

Doyle Hinman, winery founder, once worked and studied at the Geisenheim Institute in Germany. While most Oregon winegrowers look primarily to France's Burgundy district for perspective on their own winemaking methods and styles, Hinman's Geisenheim experience significantly influences his own approach to winemaking. German wines can generally be characterized as flavorful but delicate, low in alcohol, and fairly high in acid. The white wines are almost always made with some residual sugar, which in combination with the higher acidity, gives German wines their characteristic piquancy.

Hinman Vineyards

27012 Briggs Hill Road
Eugene, Oregon 97405
(503) 345-1945

Owners
Doyle Hinman & David Smith

Winemaker
Doyle Hinman

Wine Production
80,000 gallons

Vineyard Acreage
20 acres

Year First Planted
1972

First Vintage
1979

Wines Produced
Riesling, White Pinot Noir,
Blush Riesling, Gewurztraminer,
Chardonnay, Tior White,
Tior Blush, Tior Red,
Cabernet Sauvignon, Pinot Noir

Hinman produces a moderately priced line of table wines under the Tior designation, a proprietary name that means "deer" in Old High German. Many Oregon wineries make a white wine from Pinot Noir grapes, usually finishing it with a slight amount of residual sweetness. Often wineries make this kind of wine when a vintage is too cool for a good red wine, or when the skins and pulp are needed for addition to other Pinot Noir to make a sturdier, more darkly colored red wine, or, if the market calls for more white wine. Unlike most Oregon wineries, Hinman's White Pinot Noir is a winery mainstay.

Hinman offers a line of wine for the restaurant trade. The selections come in 18 liter bag-in-a-box packages. Most bag-in-a-box wines are, at best, indifferent "jug" wines. Hinman's bag-in-a-box offerings are made from premium varietals. Moderately priced wines from premium varietals is the winery's speciality.

Not just a production facility, Hinman's winery grounds and buildings are attractively designed with visitors in mind. Picnicking is encouraged, and, during the summer months, the winery occasionally hosts jazz and classical music festivals in an outdoor amphitheater.

Honeywood Winery

The historic Honeywood Winery traces its roots to Repeal of Prohibition. Founded by Ron Honeyman and John Wood in 1934, Honeywood has a 50 year history of fruit and berry winemaking.

In 1973, Paul Gallick, a Minnesota bank manager, purchased what was, and still is, Oregon's oldest continuously operating winery. With an eye to business and marketing, Gallick refurbished the winery and added a large and popular gift shop.

Honeywood is changing with the changing interests of con-

Honeywood Winery

1350 Hines Street S.E.
Salem, Oregon 97302
(503) 362-4111

Tasting Room:
30 S.E. Highway 101
Lincoln City, Oregon 97367
(503) 944-2755

Owner
Paul Gallick

Winemaker
Bill Wrey

Grape Wine Production
12,000 gallons

Fruit & Berry Wine Production
12,000 gallons

Vineyard Acreage
none

First Vintage
1934

Wines Produced
Pinot Noir Blanc, Chardonnay, Riesling, Gewurztraminer, Pinot Noir, Muller-Thurgau; Rieslings in combination with various fruits and berries; Loganberry, Blackberry, Raspberry, Strawberry, Apricot, Currant, Apple

---

sumers. Inexpensive fruit and berry wines have long been the winery's mainstay, but Honeywood began producing vinifera grape wines in 1982. Twin Harvest is a more recent addition to Honeywood's line of wines, a combination of Riesling with two percent fruit or berry juices. The Twin Harvest line is tailored to bridge the gap between Honeywood's traditional customers and current consumer trends toward grape wines.

Hood River Vineyards

Hood River Vineyards was the first Oregon vinifera grape winery in the modern era to be located somewhere other than west of the Cascade Mountain Range—but that is not to say Hood River is east of the Cascades. The winery and vineyards are nestled in a unique growing climate at the intersection of the Cascade Range and the Columbia River.

At this intersection, the opposite climates of eastern and western Oregon collide to form a climatic habitat quite different than either. The summers are warmer and the winters colder than those of western Oregon's Willamette Valley, and rainfall is less. The unirrigated vines are cane pruned as is the predominant practice in western Oregon. Hood River's estate vineyards are on shallow two-foot soils with an underlying layer of friable volcanic basalt. A constant wind blows through the Columbia Gorge, bending the vines and modifying the climate.

Owned and operated by Cliff and Eileen Blanchette, the Blanchettes started making fruit wine from some of the eight acres of pears on their farm. Becoming enthused with Oregon's grape wines, the Blanchettes planted an experimental acre of Riesling in 1974, and increased their grape acreage to the present twelve. Additional grapes are purchased from other growers along the Columbia Gorge.

The Hood River area is warmer than the Willamette Valley, and Cabernet Sauvignon is a more viable variety, especially in warmer years. Hood River once produced an outstanding Gewurztraminer in the dry Alsatian style

■ **Cliff Blanchette**

(Blanchette's grandfather was born in the Alsace region of France). Regrettably, popular taste seems to demand residual sweetness in Gewurztraminer, so Blanchette's is now slightly sweet. The Columbia Gorge remains the Northwest's best growing area for this fine, but rather out of fashion grape varietal.

Hood River continues to make small quantities of fruit wines, in-

Hood River Vineyards

4693 Westwood Drive
Hood River, Oregon 97031
(503) 386-3772

Owners
Cliff & Eileen Blanchette

Winemaker
Cliff Blanchette

Wine Production
6,000 gallons

Vineyard Acreage
12 acres

Year First Planted
1974

First Vintage
1981

Wines Produced
Cabernet Sauvignon, Zinfandel,
Chardonnay, Gewurztraminer,
Niagara, Pinot Noir,
Sauvignon Blanc, Riesling, Pear,
Raspberry

cluding Perry, a pear wine, and an intensely flavored raspberry wine made with very minimal water amelioration. Grape wines, however, are the major focus. Unusual for the Northwest, Blanchette produces a Zinfandel from grapes he buys from an old, resuscitated, Columbia Gorge vineyard.

Because of limited acreage, the Columbia Gorge will never be a large grape growing region, but Blanchette is successfully exploring the potential of this unique growing climate.

Knudsen Erath Winery

I first met (or actually didn't meet) Dick Erath more than a decade ago. Cameras and notebook in hand, I asked the tasting room staff about seeing him. It was during the latter stages of a long and difficult harvest, and I was advised that it would be best to perhaps take a photo or two, but not to engage him in a long conversation.

Quite naive at the time, I had not fully realized that harvest meant weeks of extremely strenuous mental and physical activity with very little sleep. Understandably, in the second or third week of this fun, winemakers are not always thrilled at the prospect of whiling away an hour or two with idle conversation about the romance of winemaking.

After seeing Erath's imposing frame and searing eyes, I decided that a telephoto lens was a good choice for pictures that day. It was only on a later occasion in his home, over fine food and wines of that very same harvest, that I had the opportunity to enjoy his wit and insight.

Erath is another of the genuine pioneers of the Oregon wine in-

dustry, one of the early few who came to Oregon in the 1960s to make wine. A home winegrower and electronics engineer from California, Erath became interested in starting a commercial winery. On a trip through Oregon in 1967, Erath bought some grapes and made them into wine. Impressed with the quality, Erath and his family purchased vine-

Knudsen Erath Winery

17000 N.E. Knudsen Lane
Dundee, OR 97115
(503) 538-3318

Owner
Dick Erath

Winemaker
Dick Erath

Wine Production
75,000 gallons

Vineyard Acreage
45 acres

Year First Planted
1972

First Vintage
1972

Wines Produced
Pinot Noir,
Pinot Noir Vintage Select,
Chardonnay, Riesling,
Gewurztraminer,
Cabernet Sauvignon,
Pacific Mist, Coastal Mist

yard acreage in the Chehalem foothills in Oregon's northern Willamette Valley and, moved from California to start their new winery.

Later, in 1972, Erath developed a vineyard for Cal Knudsen in the picturesque Red Hills, near the town of Dundee. Erath and Knudsen each wanted to have their own separate wineries, but share the cost and use of expensive winemaking equipment. Legal restrictions prevented them from carrying out their plans, and, instead, the two men joined in partnership in 1975 and formed the

Knudsen Erath Winery.

For a time, the wines were sold under separate as well as joint labels, but beginning in 1980,

■ **Dick Erath**

Knudsen Erath adopted a single uniform label for all their wines. In 1988, Erath acquired sole ownership of the winery. In Oregon, small wineries are the rule, but Knudsen Erath ranks as America's second largest premium Pinot Noir producer.

Erath is one of the Oregon wine industry's genuine pioneers— one of the early few who came to Oregon in the 1960s to make wine.

Pinot Noir is Knudsen Erath's best wine. In the late 60s, when Riesling was still the "safe" grape to grow in this new and uncertain winegrowing region, Dick Erath was among the first to emphasize Pinot Noir, and in the early and mid 70's, when Oregon Pinot Noir was not yet consistently good, Erath developed a reputation for producing some of the best.

Knudsen Erath Pinots are usually full-bodied, full-flavored, and rather extracted.

Knudsen Erath's Pinot Noir is primarily the Pommard clone. Erath believes that Pommard may offer a bit more on the palate than other clones, though perhaps with less nose than the Wadenswil clone, but he emphasizes that microclimate, viticultural and winemaking practices, and year to year variation have far more effect than any clonal differences.

Erath ferments his Pinot Noir in closed, 3,000 gallon stainless steel tanks, and macerates the rising cap of skins and pulp by pumping the must over and through it under high pressure. Erath believes that the closed tank keeps the volatile flavor constituents from escaping, condensing them back into the must.

Erath inoculates the must to undergo malolactic fermentation concurrently with the alcohol fermentation. It has been Erath's experience that the troublesome haze sometimes associated with malolactic fermentation is not present when the fermentations are run concurrently. A further advantage, the winemaker need not delay adding sulfur dioxide while waiting for the bacterial malolactic fermentation, thereby insuring more immediate stability against contamination.

Erath allows the must to reach 90 degrees, and at the height of fermentation, pumps the must over the cap every two hours. Fermentation is usually completed in five days. At seven days, the wine cools to about 65 degrees, the cap is nearly sunk, malolactic fermentation is complete, and the wine is pressed and racked into French oak where it ages for a minimum of 11 months. Twenty percent of the barrels are renewed each year.

Chardonnay, Riesling, and Pinot Noir are Knudsen Erath's major wines. Smaller quantities of other varieties are also produced, including, in some years, Oregon Cabernet Sauvignon. The best wines from the best years are given the designation "Vintage Select."

Kramer Vineyards

The grape harvest is never a relaxing time. For the Kramers, it was even less so. Their commercial bond to make wine came just five hours before the first grapes arrived. The Kramers were also in the process of

---

Kramer Vineyards

26830 N.W. Olson Road
Gaston, Oregon 97119
(503) 662-4545

Owners
Keith & Trudy Kramer

Winemaker
Trudy Kramer

Grape Wine Production
2,500 gallons

Fruit & Berry Wine Production
1,000 gallons

Vineyard Acreage
12 acres

Year First Planted
1984

First Vintage
1989

Wines Produced
Pinot Noir, Chardonnay, Riesling, Muller-Thurgau, Gewurztraminer, Pinot Gris, Raspberry, Boysenberry, Blackberry, Red Currant

---

moving into their new house— from a 720 square foot converted barn that served as their home for a lucky 13 months. The previous year, they had sold their 2,700 square foot home in anticipation of buying a house that was for sale near their vineyard—but the deal fell through.

Keith Kramer is a pharmacist. Trudy is mother, winemaker, and accountant. The Kramers grew lots of berries at their former residence. Not knowing what else to do with a growing excess of berries, Trudy made wine from them. This quickly diminished the excess, and garnered a best of show prize at the state fair.

Winemaking interest evolved into grape wines and a vineyard. The vineyard soils are Willakenzie and Peavine, both soil types of sedimentary origin. The Kramers are continuing to make berry wines, primarily for the casual winery visitor, as well as grape wines.

Lange Winery

A writer and musician, Don Lange got his start in the wine business by working at several wineries in California's Santa Ynez Valley, north of Santa Barbara. Like many before them, Don and Wendy Lange became enamored with the prospect of

Lange Winery

18380 N.E. Buena Vista
Dundee, Oregon 97115
(503) 538-6476

Owners
Don & Wendy Lange

Winemaker
Don Lange

Wine Production
5,000 gallons

Vineyard Acreage
6 acres

Year First Planted
1988

First Vintage
1987

Wines Produced
Pinot Gris, Pinot Noir, Chardonnay

Oregon Pinot Noir and moved to Oregon. The Langes purchased property in the northern Willamette Valley's Red Hills of Dundee, the heart of Oregon Pinot Noir country.

Most of the Lange's land has not yet been planted, and grapes are purchased from other Willamette Valley vineyards. Pinot Noir, Chardonnay, and Pinot Gris are the winery's major focus.

Lange's Pinot Gris breaks with the Oregon tradition of fermenting the grape in stainless steel and bottling without it ever touching oak. Lange both ferments and ages his Pinot Gris in French oak. Unlike Chardonnay which seems incomplete without oak, Pinot Gris works well on its own—but it seems to work well with oak as well. Lange's version displays some of the richer, rounder, vanilla elements typical of a wine that has seen the oak barrel.

Laurel Ridge Winery

The Laurel Ridge Winery comes with a long history. In the late 1800s, Fredrick Reuter emigrated from Westphalia, Germany, established a homestead, and planted vineyards on a hillside near the community of Forest Grove, the second of eight wineries on what was to become known as Wine Hill.

In an article for the Oregon State Legislature's horticultural publication for the years 1905 and 1906, Ernest Reuter, Fredrick Reuter's son, wrote, "Contrary to general expectation, Oregon, the land of rain, is capable of producing some of the choicest vines." Just prior to the article's publication, Reuter's Riesling won a gold medal at the St. Louis World's Fair.

Prohibition caused dissolution of the winery and vineyards. The Reuter vineyard, and all of Wine Hill, lay viticulturally dormant until 1966, when Charles Coury, one of the new Oregon wine pioneers, moved into the old farmhouse and began cultivating the vineyard and making wine. The Coury winery later became Reuter's Hill winery until it, too, closed.

The site's newest winery, Laurel Ridge, promises to be more

Laurel Ridge Winery

Route 1, Box 255, David Hill Road
Forest Grove, Oregon 97116
(503) 359-5436

Owners
Partnership of the Teppola, Dowsett, & Wetzel families

Winemaker
Rich Cushman

Wine Production
22,000 gallons

Vineyard Acreage
74 acres

Year First Planted
1966

First Vintage
1986

Wines Produced
Gewurztraminer, Sauvignon Blanc, Pinot Noir, Sparkling, Laurel Blanc

successful and enduring than the two previous recent efforts. The Teppolas, partners in the operation, are owners of a large vineyard near Carlton, Oregon. Their vineyard, along with the estate vineyard, will provide all the grapes for the winery. Another partner, Mike Dowsett, is the City Attorney for Beaverton. He and his family moved into the original Reuter farmhouse, a landmark home built in 1883.

Winemaker Rich Cushman is a native of Oregon. Cushman has a

Masters degree in enology from U.C. Davis, and has worked at wineries in California, Germany, and Oregon. Cushman made one of Oregon's early best efforts with sparkling wine at the Chateau Benoit winery before coming to Laurel Ridge.

Not coincidentally, Laurel Ridge is making a major effort with bottle fermented sparkling wines. To date, premium Oregon sparkling wines have been made on a small scale, usually as an aside, rather than as a major offering. Laurel Ridge is one of the new Oregon wineries focusing in a major way on premium sparkling wine. The Brut is made from Pinot Noir, a Cuvee Blanc from Riesling. Barrel fermented Sauvignon Blanc is another winery speciality.

Laurel Ridge's philosophical direction differs from the Willamette Valley norm. Its successful variance is welcome, enriching the world of Oregon wine, and echoing the winery's pioneering origins.

Lookingglass Winery

In the Umpqua Valley, not far from the small community of Lookingglass, is a winery of the same name. Gerald and Margie Rizza bought their 47 acre piece of property in the mid- seventies, after consulting with Richard Sommer, the proverbial founding father of today's Oregon wine industry.

The Rizzas planted grapes, but had to be away from their property for a period of time, leaving the tender new vines to the gustatory whims of the local deer population. The Rizzas began planting vines again in 1988, at a rate of two acres a year. The soil is a Josephine clay loam. Until the

Rizzas' vineyard is in full production, the couple will buy grapes from neighboring Umpqua Valley vineyards, focusing on Chardonnay, Cabernet Sauvignon, and Pinot Noir.

The winery is built of slumpstone, a large, eleven inch thick brick, with a blue tile roof and

Lookingglass Winery

6561 Lookingglass Road
Roseburg, Oregon 97470
(503) 679-8198

Owners
Gerald & Margie Rizza

Winemaker
Gerald Rizza

Wine Production
2,000 gallons

Vineyard Acreage
4 acres

First Vintage
1988

Wines Produced
Riesling,
Cabernet Sauvignon Blanc,
Chardonnay, Pinot Noir

stained glass windows. Although wine production is presently quite modest, the winery and tasting room are large. The tasting room itself is some 1,400 square feet. An underground cellar affords the wine a stable temperature. For those seeking an eclectic experience, Lookingglass Winery houses a gift and antique shop as well.

Marquam Hill Vineyards Winery

Marylee and Joe Dobbes spent their honeymoon in California's Alexander Valley. Dobbes had been a home winemaker for more than two dozen years, and the honeymoon visit to California wine country stirred his

interest in winegrowing. The following year, the Dobbes planted cuttings on their Willamette Valley property, and the year after, 1984, planted the rooted cuttings in their vineyard.

The soil is Woodburne #1, with patches of Amity loam and clay. Most Oregon vineyards are situated on hillsides in the center of the Willamette Valley, or on its western slopes. Marquam Hill is one of the new wineries exploring the foothills of the Cascades, on the valley's eastern slopes. The vines are trained on a Geneva Double Curtain system. Dobbes keeps grass planted between the vine rows to reduce vine vigor.

Not unexpectedly for a Willamette Valley winery, Pinot Noir is a major focus for Marquam Hill. Less expectedly these days, Marquam Hill's Riesling, rather than

Marquam Hill Vineyards Winery

35803 S. Highway 213
Molalla, Oregon 97038
(503) 829-6677

Owners
Joe & Marylee Dobbes

Winemaker
Joe Dobbes

Wine Production
4,500 gallons

Vineyard Acreage
23 acres

Year First Planted
1984

First Vintage
1988

Wines Produced
Riesling, Gewurztraminer,
Pinot Noir, Chardonnay,
Muller-Thurgau

Chardonnay, is the white grape that enthuses Dobbes the most. Dobbes likes Riesling, and particularly likes the Riesling from his vineyard.

The Dobbes will keep Marquam Hill a small family winery, producing no more than 6,000 gallons a year. The portion of the grape crop that exceeds their needs will be sold to other wineries.

McKinlay Vineyard

As is the norm in the Willamette Valley, Pinot Noir and Chardonnay are McKinlay's leading wines. In a slight variance

McKinlay Vineyard
10610 N.W. St. Helens Road Portland, Oregon 97231 (503) 285-3896
Owners Matt Kinne, Selma Annala, Holly Kinne, Mike Kinne
Winemaker Matt Kinne
Wine Production 6,000 gallons
Vineyard Acreage 6 acres
Year First Planted 1988
First Vintage 1987
Wines Produced Chardonnay, Pinot Noir, Table Wines under Paulee label

from the central path, however, Chardonnay, not Pinot Noir, is the winery's flagship.

Why Chardonnay and not Pinot Noir? According to Kinne, there are many top quality Oregon Pinot Noirs, but fewer top quality Oregon Chardonnays. Kinne wants to fill that niche. Kinne is also planting a new vineyard. Pinot Noir is particularly sensitive to vine age, producing the best fruit when the vines are older. Kinne expects to make fine Pinot Noir, but he wants an even playing field for his leading wine, and a new Pinot Noir vineyard would not give him one.

On the other hand, Kinne does not quite want an even playing field. He is planting the Draper clone of Chardonnay rather than the more common 108 clone. The Draper clone tends to produce smaller clusters, smaller crops, and ripen better and earlier. The 108 clone tends to be overly vigorous in its growth habits, wants to throw large crops, and ripens later, with higher acids.

"Unlike some people, I don't necessarily think the 108 clone is awful by any means, and we'll probably use some from select

---

"The developer couldn't get a variance to grow houses and the land price dropped a lot. Now we'll grow grapes instead."

---

growing sites in our Chardonnays, but I prefer the flavors of the Draper clone. The 108 clone tends toward citrus and green apple flavors, where the Draper clone has more tropical fruit flavors."

Kinne feels that McKinlay's 32 acre vineyard site, located on Ladd Hill between Wilsonville and Newberg, is particularly well suited to the Draper clone of Chardonnay. The Jory and Nekia soils are well drained, but moderately rich.

Kinne looked at some 100 vineyard sites over a period of two years before buying the land. It had been too expensive, selling first to a land developer. "The developer couldn't get a variance to grow houses," says Kinne, "and the land price dropped a lot. Now

we'll grow grapes instead."

Prior to starting his own winery, Kinne worked for two years at the Adams winery where McKinlay's first two vintages were made. Sparkling wine from Pinot Noir and Chardonnay is on the agenda for future vintages.

Mirassou Cellars of Oregon

Pellier may not be a familiar wine name, but Mirassou probably is. Mitch Mirassou is the fifth generation of American winemaking Mirassous. California's Mirassou Vineyards is the family's most visible presence, but other branches of the family are in the business as well.

In 1854, in California's Santa Clara Valley, Mitch Mirassou's great great grandfather, Pierre

Mirassou Cellars of Oregon
6785 Spring Valley Road N.W. Salem, Oregon 97304 (503) 371-3001
Owners Mitch & Beverly Mirassou
Winemaker Mitch Mirassou
Wine Production 25,000 gallons
Vineyard Acreage 45 acres
Year First Planted 1982
First Vintage 1985
Wines Produced Riesling, Gewurztraminer, Pinot Noir, Cabernet Sauvignon, Chardonnay

Pellier, planted vine cuttings he brought from France. Pellier's oldest daughter, Henrietta, married a neighboring winemaker, Pierre Mirassou, and the three sons from that marriage carried on the family's winemaking business—and the Mirassou name.

The Mirassou winery survived phylloxera, Prohibition, and urban encroachment, but the lean years, and the increasing size of the family, spread the newer generations into other wineries and businesses. A California grape grower and winemaker, Mitch Mirassou traded some of his California land for 90 acres in Oregon's Willamette Valley. In 1981, Mirassou and his family moved to their land in the Willamette Valley's Eola Hills and planted wine grapes.

Mirassou is trying an unusual vine training system for Oregon. Known as head training or goblet training, the vines are pruned to short, individual bushes without trellising wires.

Except for a few Riesling grapes, all of Mirassou's wines are made from grapes grown in the Eola Hills, one of the Willamette Valley's emerging new winegrowing areas. A fifth generation American winegrower, Mitch Mirassou begins a new generational cycle of Oregon winegrowers.

Montinore Vineyards

Montinore is not your conventional Oregon winery. In terms of scale, financing, and outlook, Montinore's operation more closely resembles a high end California winery operation than anything else in Oregon. Montinore represents serious, major money invested in a major vineyard and winery enterprise. In a state where 40 acres is considered a fairly large vineyard, Montinore's 465 acres seems im-

mense—though, by California standards, a 465 acre premium winery is hardly out of the norm.

The Montinore name is a contraction of Montana-in- Oregon.

■ **Jeff Lamy**

The name is not a recent invention. In 1905, John Forbis, an attorney for Montana's Anaconda Copper Company assembled 361 acres of land from five land claims and named it Montinore Ranch. In the intervening years, the property, adjacent to Dilley Road, was known as The Dilley Farm. Leo and Jane Graham bought the property in 1965, subsequently adding additional contiguous parcels to bring the total to 588 acres. The site's original name, Montinore, evoked a European flavor that seemed ideal for a winery name.

The Grahams secured the services of Jeff Lamy, a real estate and business consultant involved with the Oregon wine industry since the 1970s, to evaluate and develop the land. Lamy recommended a major vineyard and winery for the site. The Grahams accepted Lamy's recommendations and retained him as general manager for the project. In 1987, Lamy was also named winemaker. Expanding wine produc-

tion subsequently prompted the hiring of additional winemakers. In an operational restructuring, Lamy was named "chief winemaker," overseeing all winemaking operations.

The vineyard ranges in elevation from 200 to 750 feet. Forty percent of the vineyard is in Laurelwood, a mixed soil of volcanic and sedimentary origins. The other soils include Cornelius and Woodburn. Most of 150 acres of Pinot Noir are planted on east facing slopes. Riesling, Chenin Blanc, and Sauvignon Blanc are planted on southwest slopes, and Chardonnay on southern slopes. Some of the Pinot Noir and Chardonnay intended for sparkling wines are planted on slopes with slight northern exposures.

A complex and varied growing site, the estate vineyard has many

Montinore Vineyards

Route 3, Box 193W
Dilley Road
P.O. Box 560
Forest Grove, Oregon 97116
(503) 359-5012

Owners
Montinore Vineyards Limited

Winemakers
Jeff Lamy, chief winemaker;
Paul Gates, enologist

Wine Production
130,000 gallons

Vineyard Acreage
465 acres

Year First Planted
1983

First Vintage
1987

Wines Produced
Pinot Noir, Chardonnay, Riesling,
Dry Riesling,
Late Harvest Riesling,
Riesling Ice Wine, Muller-Thurgau,
Pinot Gris, Gewurztraminer,
Chenin Blanc, Sauvignon Blanc,
Cascade Blanc,
Sparkling Riesling, Sparkling Brut,
Sparkling Blanc de Noir

combinations of exposures and soil types. Lamy's intent is to match the varying combinations to the most suitable grape varieties. Lamy is also evaluating a variety of trellising methods on the various vineyard parcels.

The 1905 mansion and elegant grounds are the focal point of the estate. The mansion now houses Montinore's business offices. The grounds overlook a pond and the many faceted slopes of the expansive vineyard.

Oak Knoll Winery

Each year, on the third weekend in May, Oak Knoll hosts the "Bacchus Goes Bluegrass Wine Festival," an event that draws thousands of visitors to a rural setting that was once the site of a dairy farm. The Vuylsteke family, natives of Oregon, have

Oak Knoll Winery

29700 S.W. Burkhalter Road
Hillsboro, Oregon 97123
(503) 648-8198

Tasting Room
Shipwreck Cellars
3524 S.W. Highway 101
Lincoln City, Oregon 97367

Owners
Vuylsteke Family

Winemaker
Ron Vuylsteke

Grape Wine Production
70,000 gallons

Fruit & Berry Wine Production
5,000 gallons

Vineyard Acreage
none

Year First Planted
1971

Wines Produced
Pinot Noir, Chardonnay, Riesling, Gewurztraminer, Pinot Noir Blanc, Twilight Blush, Niagara, Raspberry, Loganberry, Rhubarb, Blackberry

seen their winery grow from one gallon of homemade blackberry wine to an annual production of more than 70,000 gallons of fruit, berry, and grape wine.

An electronics engineer, Ron Vuylsteke quit his job at Tektronix to start a commercial winery. In

> **The Vuylsteke family have seen their winery grow from one gallon of homemade blackberry wine to an annual production of more than 70,000 gallons of fruit, berry, and grape wine.**

1970, the Vuylsteke family moved to the Willamette Valley countryside and produced their first commercial vintage, 3,000 gallons of fruit and berry wine. By 1978, Oak Knoll was producing a third of all Oregon wine sold within the state. Still relatively small by most standards, Oak Knoll remains one of Oregon's larger wineries.

Oak Knoll began as a fruit and berry winery, but has shifted its emphasis to premium grape wines. Grape wines now comprise more than 90 percent of Oak Knoll's production. The old dairy barn that seemed much too large for the Oak Knoll winery in 1970, became much too small, and the Vuylstekes built a second building to house the tasting room, office, bottling, and storage facilities.

The Vuylstekes own no vinifera vineyards of their own, relying on independent growers for their grapes. This arrangement offers less direct control over the grapes, and less assurance of continuity from year to year, but there are also advantages. Less capital is tied up in land and vines, more

grapes can be purchased in better years and fewer in less favorable years, and Oak Knoll is not tied to a single growing area or a fixed range of grape varieties. Oak Knoll describes itself as a market driven winery, making what the consumer wants, and changing as consumer tastes change.

Some of the winemaking philosophies developed with the fruit and berry wines are carried over to grape winemaking. The Vuylstekes believe that the fruity qualities of the grape should be preserved and emphasized. Oregon Pinot Noir is often fermented in open top containers, but the Vuylstekes prefer closed stainless steel fermenters. In their view, the closed fermenters trap volatile flavor constituents that would normally escape into the air, and condense them back into the wine.

After fermentation, the white wines are centrifuged and pumped into barrels or tanks. At one time, the red wines were also centrifuged, but the Vuylstekes found that some of the flavoring constituents were stripped away, and the practice was discontinued.

Oak Knoll's Pinot Noir earned the acclaim of Andre Tchelistcheff, America's most distinguished winemaker. Of Oak Knoll's 1980 Vintage Select Pinot Noir, Tchelistcheff told the Vuylstekes, "I have spent the last fifty years of my life searching for the world's finest Pinot Noirs, and yours is among the greatest I have ever tasted."

Oregon Cellars Winery

A partnership of two vineyard owners, Oregon Cellars Winery and its vineyards are situated in the southern Willamette Valley, in the foothills of the Coast Range Mountains. The vineyard soils are Bellpine and Jory. The vines have a southern exposure at an elevation of between 650 and 850 feet.

Oregon Cellars Winery releases wine under two labels, sparkling wines under the Northern Silk label, still wines under the Rain

Oregon Cellars Winery

92989 Templeton
Cheshire, Oregon 97419
(503) 998-1786

Owners
Mike & Merry Fix, Gary Carpenter

Winemakers
Mike Fix & Gary Carpenter

Wine Production
2,000 gallons

Vineyard Acreage
18 acres

Year First Planted
1982

First Vintage
1988

Wines Produced
Pinot Noir, Chardonnay,
Sparkling Wine

Song label. Pinot Noir and Chardonnay are the only still wines, fermented in small lots of two to four tons, then aged in French oak cooperage. The first sparkling wine was made from Riesling. Future sparkling wines include a blend of Riesling and Gewurztraminer, at a moderate price, released with only brief time in the bottle. A more expensive sparkler made from Chardonnay and Pinot Noir spends more time on the yeast before disgorging and release.

Panther Creek Cellars

In McMinnville, at the far end of a small triangular area zoned for commercial wineries, is Panther Creek Cellars. The winery is housed in an attractively renovated building that traces its origins back to 1910 and the dairy industry. Ken and Corby Wright are the owners and operators. For two years, Corby Wright was director of McMinnville's outstanding International Pinot Noir Celebration. Ken Wright is Panther Creek's winemaker. Partners Steve and Martha Lind help with marketing and sales.

Pinot Noir is virtually Panther Creek's sole focus—no off dry Riesling for cash flow and the casual wine consumer, nor even Chardonnay, the white Burgundian companion to Pinot Noir. Other than Pinot Noir, only a small amount of Melon sees the inside of the winery. For decades, American Melon has been mislabeled Pinot Blanc. Panther Creek is making a dry white wine from Melon—and marketing it under its correct name.

Some people get into the wine business with a generalized enthusiasm about wine, but no particular vision or philosophy. Such is not the case with Ken Wright. Wright worked for 10 years at California wineries before coming to Oregon to make Pinot Noir. Wright brought with him not only a singular commitment to Pinot Noir, but a commitment to a distinctive winemaking approach as well.

Wright greatly dislikes what the wine industry refers to as MOG— material other than grapes. During harvesting, leaves and other stray materials inevitably end up in the grape bins. When the grapes come in, Wright runs

them through a conveyor line to sort out the MOG, as well as grape clusters that are overripe, underripe, infected by rot, or otherwise undesirable. "Our production is small," says Wright, "but by the end of the day, we're shin deep in the junk we sort out."

Wright dislikes stems. "They narrow the wine," he says, "they contribute non-fruit flavors, and make the wine less supple, and somewhat bitter, a similar effect to not sorting out the leaves." Wright never includes stems in his Pinot. The grapes are lightly crushed, and most are put into 400 gallon fermentation bins.

The small fermentation containers allow Wright to use up to seven yeast strains. According to

■ **Ken Wright**

Wright, each strain contributes different flavor characteristics and adds complexity to the final blend. In some years, certain strains are emphasized. For example, in 1987, an extremely warm year, Wright heavily used a Bordeaux red yeast strain which he feels preserves the perception of acidity. Because the Bordeaux strain produces wines with less of the fruity characteristics of the grape, he uses far less of it in more normal vintages.

Most Oregon winemakers press the wine off the skins as soon as fermentation has finished. Wright, however, leaves the wine

---

Panther Creek Cellars

1501 East 14th Street
McMinnville, Oregon 97128
(503) 472-8080

Owners
Ken & Corby Wright,
Steve & Martha Lind

Winemaker
Ken Wright

Wine Production
8,000 gallons

Vineyard Acreage
none

First Vintage
1986

Wines Produced
Pinot Noir, Melon

---

to macerate on the skins and pulp for up to six days after fermentation has finished. The must is covered with the heavy neutral gas Argon to prevent spoilage. With the wine fully fermented at this stage, the alcohol extracts more tannins and color, as well as aromatics that differ from those extracted during the earlier stages of fermentation.

Wright likes a measure of tannin in his Pinots, and the extended maceration extracts them, though, interestingly, the wines are less tannic and softer than one might expect. During the maceration, the tannins polymerize, forming longer chain tannins which have a less aggressive mouth feel. Additionally, the larger tannin molecules begin to precipitate out of the wine as the process continues.

With extended maceration, the

wine first becomes increasingly tannic, then progressively less so as the tannins polymerize and drop out of the wine. The key is to halt the maceration at the optimal point in the progression.

Most of Wright's grapes come from the Eola Hills, an area he feels produces wines with the best structure and character. He also likes blending in Dundee Hills fruit which he feels has a more fleshy component. His grape contracts specify a maximum yield of three tons or less per acre.

Panther Creek's Pinots are aged primarily in Vosges oak, a tight grained French oak. In Wright's view, Vosges is less resinous than other French oaks and marries better with the wine. According to Wright, Vosges also has more complex sugars in the wood which contribute richness and texture to the wine. The lees are stirred to prevent off flavors from forming, but wine is not racked until time for bottling.

Panther Creek's regular bottling, previously called "early release" includes a higher percentage of the Wadenswil clone and is aged in older cooperage. The reserve bottling has a higher percentage of the Pommard clone and is aged in newer oak.

Because of the extended maceration, Panther Creek's wines are somewhat controversial. Winemakers in both Oregon and Burgundy are increasingly emphasizing the fruity characteristics of the grape. Panther Creek's approach is more toward an older style Cote de Nuits sort of wine. I personally enjoy a diversity of wine styles, and I'm glad that the Panther Creek approach to Pinot Noir has such a committed and effective advocate.

Ponderosa Vineyards

The Looney family's 75 acre property is home to a variety of crops and an array of farm animals. Unusual in most of the Willamette Valley, Ponderosa Pines are present in abundance, hence the winery's name. The Looneys' ancestors settled in the Willamette Valley in 1843, after crossing the Rocky Mountains on the Applegate Wagon Train.

The Looneys' began planting their vineyard in 1978, training the vines to stakes. Although the vineyard is on sloping land, the prop-

---

Ponderosa Vineyards

39538 Griggs Drive
Lebanon, Oregon 97355
(503) 259-3845

Owners
Bill & Judy Looney

Winemaker
Bill Looney

Wine Production
4,000 gallons

Vineyard Acreage
12 acres

Year First Planted
1978

First Vintage
1987

Wines Produced
Sauvignon Blanc, Pinot Noir,
Vin Rose, Satisfaction Plus,
Sweet Dessert Wine

---

erty is generally on low land rather than hillside slopes, and frost can be a threat in difficult seasons. The total grape harvest for the 12 acre vineyard has ranged between 2 1/2 and 3 tons per year, but the vines are being converted to a wire trellis system, and yields should increase.

Wine free of added sulfites is Ponderosa's speciality. Ponderosa is the only Oregon winery that excludes sulfites and any other preservative from the winemaking process. Most people do not react to sulfites, but, for those who do, wine without added sulfites is a significant boon.

Ponzi Vineyards

Dick and Nancy Ponzi are among the early Oregon wine industry pioneers who came to the Willamette Valley in the late 1960s and early 1970s. At that time, it was far from certain that growing wine grapes in Oregon was anything other than a foolish idea. Courage and a venturesome spirit were requisites for those who laid the groundwork for the many who would later follow. Now, Oregon is recognized as

■ **Dick Ponzi**

one of America's stellar wine-growing regions.

On Oregon wine, and, particularly, the star wine grape, Pinot Noir, Dick Ponzi says, "The vineyards have matured, and the winemakers have matured, too, over these last 15 to 20 years. America, as a country, makes Pinot Noir much differently now, realizing that it is a complex but

delicate wine, and needs a much different treatment than Cabernet Sauvignon. I think Oregon has contributed much to this understanding."

Approached from the many back roads that interlace the northern Willamette Valley, a new visitor would never imagine that Ponzi Vineyards' idyllic rural setting is only a short distance from Portland's suburban sprawl. Located in protected farmlands 15 miles southwest of Portland, and only a few miles from one of the northwest's largest shopping centers, Ponzi Vineyards remains well shielded from the urban milieu.

The vineyard's microclimate and soil are different from others in the Willamette Valley. Though most vineyards are planted up to a 1,000 feet above sea level on sloping hillsides, the Ponzi vineyard is planted in sandy benchland at an elevation of 250 feet. Nearby soil is quite claylike and less well suited to grape growing because of its poorer drainage characteristics. Ponzi's sandier soil may be attributable to geologic changes in the course of the nearby Tualatin River.

A family owned winery, Dick and Nancy Ponzi have made their home on the 17 acre estate for more than two decades. Supplementing their own grapes, the Ponzis purchase grapes on long-term contracts from two other vineyards, Five Mountain Vineyard near Hillsboro and Medici Vineyard near Newberg, both within ten miles of the winery.

Ponzi's estate vineyard was planted on a 7 x 9 foot spacing. Denser vine spacing is regarded as beneficial, and the vineyard has been subsequently interplanted to a 3 1/2 x 9 foot spacing. "We knew about tight spacing in the

early years," says Ponzi, "but even what we did then was pretty radical when you consider that California was up to 12 x 12 foot spacing. And then, too, we didn't

Ponzi Vineyards

Vandermost Road
Route 1, Box 842
Beaverton, Oregon 97007
(503) 628-1227

Owners
Dick & Nancy Ponzi

Winemaker
Dick Ponzi

Wine Production
15,000 gallons

Vineyard Acreage
12 acres

Year First Planted
1970

First Vintage
1974

Wines Produced
Pinot Noir, Pinot Noir Reserve,
Chardonnay, Pinot Gris,
Dry Riesling

have access to the machinery to work with the tight row spacings they have in France. I just knew I had a six foot tractor and needed room to get it down the rows."

Ponzi's estate Pinot Noir vines consist of two clones—Pommard, and a clone obtained from California's Mirassou winery. According to Ponzi, the Mirassou clone is easier to train and produces a darker wine, but also ripens later than the Pommard clone.

Ponzi believes that a long "hang-time" is key to wine quality, especially with Pinot Noir. A long, warm, fall season that gives the grapes the most time on the vines is ideal. In hot years, when the grapes ripen quickly, many wine-growers pick early to preserve the acids. Ponzi, in keeping with his views on hang-time, allows the grapes to remain on the vine longer, making acid adjustments to the juice as necessary. Ponzi's 1985 Pinot Noir, a rich, Cote de Nuits-like wine, was one of his best, and among Oregon's best in that exceptional Pinot Noir vintage.

Ponzi was among the first Oregon wineries to work with Pinot Gris, a grape variety with origins in Alsace and northern

---

"You can't just look for some magical formula, or assume that what everybody else is doing at a given time is the way to go. You have to try things on your own, make your own decisions, and find your own path."

Italy. As yet, very little Pinot Gris is planted in Oregon, but the grape, a genetic relative of Pinot Noir, promises to play a significant role in the state's wine industry. Ideally suited to the Willamette Valley growing climate, Pinot Gris produces a premium white table wine, and offers yet another choice for matching food and wine.

Most Riesling is made with some residual sweetness, but Ponzi's is made in a dry style to accompany food. Fermented at about 50 degrees, the wine sometimes requires up to four months to complete fermentation. Even for those who do not usually care for Rieslings, Ponzi's is worthy of interest.

Ponzi's attractive winery building successfully marries modern and traditional building materials. The roof is made of an expensive,

highly durable material designed to oxidize with exposure to the elements, forming a protective barrier, and a rustic patina that changes color with the weather. Heavy timber, and stone from a nearby quarry complete the solid, rustic appearance. A spacious lawn provides a setting for informal picnics, festivals, and a summer jazz concert series.

What lessons has Ponzi learned in two decades of Willamette Valley winegrowing? "You can't just look for some magical formula, or assume that what everybody else is doing at a given time is the way to go. You have to try things on your own, make your own decisions, and find your own path."

Rex Hill Vineyards

States Paul Hart, owner of Rex Hill Vineyards, "If I had my choice I would make nothing but Pinot Noir." Fortuitously, Hart chose 1983, one of Oregon's most

---

Rex Hill Vineyards

30835 North Highway 99W
Newberg, OR 97132
(503) 538-0666

Owners
Corporation—
Paul Hart, Chairman;
Jan Jacobsen, President

Winemaker
Lynn Penner-Ash

Wine Production
30,000 gallons

Vineyard Acreage
22 acres

Year First Planted
1982

First Vintage
1983

Wines Produced
Pinot Noir,
vineyard designated Pinot Noir,
Chardonnay, Pinot Gris,
Symphony, Riesling

---

publicized vintages, to start his winery and to pursue his commitment to Pinot Noir. An insurance actuary by profession, Hart sold his business in 1981 and established his winery and vineyard in the northern Willamette Valley on Rex Hill, a foothill of the Chehalem Mountains.

Hart's profound affection for great French Burgundies, and his long-term perspectives as an actuary, structure his philosophy on the wine business. Great Burgundies show the character of the individual vineyard site and microclimate, and the best are kept unblended. Similarly, Hart may bottle as many as seven different vineyard designated Pinots, plus two blended Pinots. In less good years, Hart bottles fewer vineyard designated Pinots and puts more of the wines into a second label, Kings Ridge.

Great Burgundies achieve excellence with time in the cellar. Hart releases only a portion of his new wines, holding back a major portion for future release at inevitably higher prices, an actuarially oriented approach, and one more typical of traditional European thinking than the modern American norm of quick cash flow and rapid product turnover. Rex Hill's Pinots from the best vintages are not cheap, but, laudably, Hart sells lesser wines from lesser vintages at lower prices.

Rex Hill is situated on the site of an old prune and nut drying facility. Hart rebuilt and added to the old building, while retaining much of its character, including the original wooden beams and decking. The modified drying tunnels are now barrel aging tunnels and vaults for a portion of Rex Hill's wine library. Rustic yet refined, Alsatian wallpaper and intricate wood carving by a local

■ **Paul Hart**

artist help set the tone for the winery.

Of the white wines, Chardonnay, another Burgundian variety, is Rex Hill's specialty. Both the Pinot Noir and Chardonnay from the best vintages are packed in wooden cases. Pinot Gris is a more recent addition to Rex Hill's line of wines. Unlike most Oregon Pinot Gris, Rex Hill's is aged in oak. Approximately half of Rex Hill's production is devoted to red wine, a higher percentage than most Oregon wineries, reflecting Hart's commitment to Pinot Noir.

Rex Hill is one of the closest wineries to the Portland metropolitan area. Located along Highway 99 West, a major route to the Oregon beaches, Rex Hill is a popular stop for the wine traveler.

Rogue River Vineyards

Rogue River Vineyards is a group of four families, all former employees of a large winery in California's San Joaquin Valley. For several years, the group worked weekends to build their small Oregon enterprise, returning during the week to their jobs at the California winery. By 1986, all four families had moved to southern Oregon.

The winery and small vineyard are situated near Grants Pass, along the Redwood Highway to the California Coast. Under the Rogue River Vineyards label, the winery releases a line of wines that includes Cabernet Sauvignon, but emphasizes light, fruity wines such as Pinot Noir Blanc, Cabernet Blanc, Riesling, and Gewurztraminer.

Oriented toward creating new markets with new product concepts, Rogue River produces wine coolers as well as a line of flavored wines called Lumiere Vineyards. For these wines, Rogue River buys white wine from California and flavors it with fruit juices.

The families' business interests include restaurants and woodworking craft. The wines are a secondary concern. Rogue River has large contracts with major California wineries to supply wine display racks. The wine racks, as well as finely designed and crafted gift boxes, are available at the winery tasting room.

Rogue River Vineyards

3145 Helms Road
Grants Pass, Oregon 97527
(503) 476-1051

Owners
Corporation

Winemaker
Bill Jiron

Wine Production
8,000 gallons

Vineyard Acreage
5 acres

Year First Planted
1981

First Vintage
1983

Wines Produced
Riesling, Pinot Noir,
Gewurztraminer, Chardonnay,
Pinot Noir Blanc, Cabernet Blanc,
White Table Wine, Red Table Wine,
Blush, Apri Blanc, Coolers

Saga Vineyards

Austrian citizens and residents for most of their lives, Richard and Juliana Pixner vacationed in the Northwest and became enamored with the region, particularly Oregon's Willamette Valley. The Pixners bought a piece of land, and later sold their business in Austria to retire in the tiny community of

---

Saga Vineyards

30815 South Wall Street
Colton, Oregon 97017
(503) 824-4600

Owners
Richard & Juliana Pixner

Winemaker
Richard Pixner

Wine Production
2,000 gallons

Vineyard Acreage
3 acres

Year First Planted
1985

First Vintage
1989

Wines Produced
Chardonnay, Pinot Noir, Riesling

Colton, at the northeastern end of the Willamette Valley.

As a part-time retirement business, Pixner began importing Austrian and Yugoslavian oak barrels, and started a tiny vineyard and winery to serve as a demonstrative vehicle for his barrel business. All the wines, including the Riesling, are fermented or aged in wood vats or barrels.

St. Innocent Winery

St. Innocent focuses on wine from Pinot Noir and Chardonnay grapes. The Chardonnay is barrel fermented and aged in small oak cooperage. The Pinot Noir is fermented in small lots and aged in oak for at least 16 months. Most of the wines carry vineyard designations. The winery was formed by a small group of stockholders in 1988.

Mark Vlossak began his experience with wine at the family

St. Innocent Winery

2701 22nd Street S.E.
Salem, Oregon 97302
(503) 378-1526

Owners
Corporation

Winemaker
Mark Vlossak

Wine Production
4,000 gallons

Vineyard Acreage
none

First Vintage
1988

Wines Produced
Pinot Noir, Chardonnay,
Sparkling Wine

---

dinner table when he was seven years old. Wine was always an integral part of a good meal. Vlossak moved to Oregon in 1980, and began preparing for winemaking by taking U.C. Davis short courses, apprenticing for six weeks at The Wine Lab in Napa, California, and working at another Oregon winery in 1987 and 1988.

Vlossak's father, John Innocent Vlossak, director of sales for the winery, has been active in the wine business for thirty years. The winery name, St. Innocent, was derived from his middle name.

The winery's production is pre-dominantly still wine, but bottle fermented sparkling wine is St. Innocent's principal purpose. Many

> ## "I'm looking for the richer, chocolatey, toasty style of sparkling wine."

New World sparkling wines see only a short time on the yeast, but Vlossak is a believer in lengthy yeast contact, and has the French Champagne houses as his model.

St. Innocent's Brut will rest on the yeast for three years before disgorging. The cuvee is Chardonnay and Pinot Noir, with Pinot Noir the largest proportion. Says Vlossak, "I'm looking for the richer, chocolatey, toasty style of sparkling wine." Eventually, Vlossak wants to produce a range of sparkling wines, including a vintage version with five to six years on the yeast.

Half of St. Innocent's wine goes to restaurants, a ratio that Vlossak wants to continue even as the winery's production expands.

St. Joseph's Weinkeller

In 1981, Josef and Lilli Fleischmann planted a small vineyard near Canby, in Oregon's northern Willamette Valley. The winery and vineyard are situated on bench-land between the Molalla and Pudding Rivers.

A baker by profession, Fleischmann retired from his former occupation and turned to wine—another product of yeast. For wine, Fleischmann often shuns commercial yeast strains in favor of the naturally occurring yeasts harvested with the grapes.

The wine yeasts present in European vineyards have been idealized over the centuries through natural selection processes. Although the wild yeasts present in New World vineyards are often quite different from those of European vineyards, Fleischmann is nevertheless satisfied with the effects of his vineyard's wild yeasts. A Hungarian raised in Germany, Fleischmann is returning to the winemaking craft practiced by his forebears.

The winery, complete with a Gothic script rendering of the winery name, suggests a Germanic flavor. Riesling is one of St. Josef's Weinkeller's principal wines, but some of the other wines are often quite different from a Germanic style. Fleischmann makes a Cabernet Sauvignon from Oregon grapes, and a late harvest Zinfandel from California grapes, a wine that sometimes tips the scale at more than 15 percent alcohol.

St. Joseph's Weinkeller

28836 South Barlow Road
Canby, Oregon 97013
(503) 651-3190

Owners
Josef & Lilli Fleischmann

Winemaker
Josef Fleischmann

Wine Production
14,000 gallons

Vineyard Acreage
11 acres

Year First Planted
1981

First Vintage
1983

Wines Produced
Chardonnay, Gewurztraminer,
Riesling, Cabernet Sauvignon,
White Cabernet, Pinot Noir,
Zinfandel

Schwarzenberg Vineyards

Schwarzenberg Vineyards is situated in a small cluster of hills between the Coast Range that forms the western border of the

---

Schwarzenberg Vineyards

11975 Smithfield Road
Dallas, Oregon 97338
(503) 623-6420

Owners
Helmut & Helga Schwarz

Winemaker
Norbert Fiebig

Wine Production
25,000 gallons

Vineyard Acreage
50 acres

Year First Planted
1982

First Vintage
1986

Wines Produced
Chardonnay, Pinot Noir, Riesling

Willamette Valley, and the Eola Hills, near the center of the valley.

The slopes of the Schwarzenberg vineyard form one of the boundaries of an ancient lake, and overlook the 2,500 acre Basket Slough National Wildlife Refuge that now covers the expanse of the ancient lakebed. Schwarzenberg's label depicts the Canadian Goose, featured resident of the more than 200 species of wildlife inhabiting the refuge.

Helmut and Helga Schwarz purchased the 150 acre site in 1981 and began planting grapes in 1982. Until the spring of 1989, the Schwarzs lived and worked in Washington, D.C., awaiting the time when they would return to the property to live and operate their winery.

Instead of the usual stainless steel tanks, visitors to the winery will see a new sight on the Northwest wine scene, bright, white, polyethylene tanks made in Pasco, Washington. The Chardonnay spends time on the lees in these tanks before a portion of it is put into French oak barrels.

A stylistic trademark, Schwarzenberg wines are toward the restrained, delicate end of the spectrum, with minimal oak. Schwarzenberg is continuing to refine this stylistic theme. The most recent releases are the best yet, and speak positively of things to come.

Serendipity Cellars Winery

The Longshores are the sort of people that I immediately enjoy—well educated and thoughtful, but with an easygoing folksy informality. I also enjoy their wines, reflections of the people that made them. Serendipity is one of the few wineries in the Willamette Valley not making Pinot Noir (although a Serendipity Pinot was made in earlier years). Unusual for Oregon, Marechal Foch and Muller-Thurgau are the winery's flagship wines. "Because we are small," say the Longshores, "it is advantageous for us to feature wines that are unique, and we make a conscious effort to do so."

The Muller-Thurgau, a Riesling-like wine, is released with about two percent residual sweetness. Usually, Muller-Thurgau is a rather characterless wine without great distinction, but if grown properly in the right site and made with appropriate winemaking attention, Muller-Thurgau has a distinctive and pleasing character.

Glen Longshore makes one of the Northwest's better Muller-Thurgaus. He mentions, however, that a judge at one competition once downrated his Muller-Thur-

---

Serendipity's line of wines offers welcome variety and enriches the world of Northwest wine.

---

gau for having too much character. Hopefully, Longshore will continue to resist the temptation to make simplistic sugar water for the sake of pleasing the lowest common denominator.

Serendipity's real star, and real surprise, is Marechal Foch. French-American hybrid wines, like Marechal Foch, are prevalent in the eastern United States, but uncommon on the west coast.

Serendipity Cellars Winery

15275 Dunn Forest Road
Monmouth, Oregon 97361
(503) 838-4284

Owners
Glen & Cheryl Longshore

Winemaker
Glen Longshore

Wine Production
4,500 gallons

Vineyard Acreage
3 acres

Year First Planted
1980

First Vintage
1981

Wines Produced
Marechal Foch, Chardonnay, Chenin Blanc, Muller-Thurgau, Cabernet Sauvignon, Zinfandel

---

Marechal Foch has less than a stellar reputation in the eastern United States, but its key to success in Oregon may be the higher level of ripeness it achieves. Like any grape, Marechal Foch only shows its best if growing conditions are just right—and Longshore seems to have found the "just right" environment.

Serendipity's Marechal Foch is a deeply colored, sturdily structured red wine with little, and, sometimes none, of the hybrid taste. The Serendipity Marechal Foch is usually picked at 23 degrees or more Brix. The grape is inherently high in malic acid, and Longshore puts the wine through a major malolactic fermentation to reduce the acidity to desired levels.

The Marechal Foch vines are cropped to 6 tons an acre. Longshore pays his grower based on a formula tied to the bottle price of the wine. A good vintage of Serendipity's Marechal Foch is a delightful wine, and a welcome change of pace from the more typical Northwest wine varietals. Except for a small experimental vineyard, all of Serendipity's grapes are purchased under long-term contracts from other growers in Oregon's Umpqua and Willamette Valleys.

The word serendipity carries the meaning of a pleasant surprise. It is fitting that Marechal Foch is Serendipity's main wine. Chenin Blanc and Zinfandel are among the winery's other offerings. The unique nature of Serendipity's line of wines offers welcome variety and enriches the world of Northwest wine.

Seven Hills Winery

Seven Hills is Oregon's first winery in the Walla Walla Valley viticultural area, an appellation that encompasses parts of both Oregon and Washington. The valley has little in common with western Oregon, the center of Oregon's wine industry, famed for Pinot Noir. The Walla Walla Valley, however, seems destined to become known for Cabernet Sauvignon.

Seven Hills Winery

235 East Broadway
Milton-Freewater, Oregon 97862
(509) 529-3943

Owners
James & Casey McClellan
families, principal owners

Winemaker
Casey McClellan

Wine Production
5,000 gallons

Vineyard Acreage
30 acres

Year First Planted
1982

First Vintage
1987

Wines Produced
Cabernet Sauvignon, Merlot,
Chardonnay, Sauvignon Blanc,
Riesling

The Seven Hills Winery is an outgrowth of Seven Hills Vineyards. Located between Milton-Freewater and Umapine, in northeastern Oregon, the vine-

---

Seven Hills is Oregon's first winery in the Walla Walla Valley

---

yard garnered attention when its grapes showed up in the wines of two highly regarded Washington Cabernet producers, Woodward Canyon and Leonetti. Differing from other vineyards in Washington's Columbia Valley, the soils are a deep silt loam.

The enterprise is a joint effort of two doctors, Herbert Hendricks and James Mcclellan, and their families. The Hendricks are primarily in charge of the vineyards, the McClellans are more involved in the winery side of the business. Casey McClellan, son of James McClellan, is winemaker.

After receiving a degree in pharmacy from the University of Washington, McClellan went to U.C. Davis for a masters degree in enology, then to Portugal for research and teaching prior to returning to the Northwest. McClellan now works part time at the hospital pharmacy in Walla Walla, and makes wine at the Seven Hills Winery in nearby Milton-Freewater.

The Waterbrook winery in Washington made the first wines for Seven Hills. Seven Hills own first crush, in 1989, was modest. Warm January temperatures sent springtime signs to the vines, followed by a hard freeze in February. Winter damage was severe.

Ironically, Cabernet Sauvignon, a variety sensitive to winter cold, came through in the best shape. A late budding varietal, the Cabernet was not as vulnerable in the February freeze. Hendricks continues to explore various methods of reducing the vines' vulnerability to winter cold, including using four main trunks for each vine, a variation on the classic fan training system.

Seven Hills is somewhat at the mercy of the irrigation canals. Grapes are not a major crop in the area, and sometimes the water is shutoff as early as the first of July. Though sometimes a problem, the early water shutoff, as well as the growing climate, may be part of the reason for vineyard's intense Cabernet Sauvignons. Reduced leaf canopy and judicious water stress benefit grape and wine quality.

Seven Hills will continue to sell grapes to other wineries, but most will go into Seven Hills own estate bottled wines. Until 1989, Walla Walla Valley wineries have always been on the Washington side of the appellation, though the valley's largest vineyard has always been in Oregon. Now, the valley's largest vineyard also has its own winery—both in Oregon.

Shafer Vineyard Cellars

In 1973, the Shafer family planted their first vines. For a time, the vineyard supplied local

---

Shafer Vineyard Cellars

Star Route, Box 269
Forest Grove, Oregon 97116
(503) 357-6604

Owner
Harvey Shafer

Winemaker
Harvey Shafer

Wine Production
20,000 gallons

Vineyard Acreage
20 acres

Year First Planted
1973

First Vintage
1978

Wines Produced
Chardonnay, Pinot Noir Blanc,
Pinot Noir, Riesling,
Gewurztraminer, Sauvignon Blanc

---

wineries with grapes, but the Shafers' desire to make their own wine from the fruit of their own land became overwhelming. Harvey Shafer believes that 80 percent of a wine's quality comes from the vineyard. As winemaker, Shafer now furnishes the other 20

percent.

Nearly all the grapes for Shafer's wines come from the Shafer estate, located in the narrow Gales Creek Valley, at an average elevation of 450 feet. Shafer speaks of localized climates and vineyard interrelationships, emphasizing the importance of grape growing to winemaking. Across the narrow valley, the exposures are more northerly and the hillsides often shrouded in fog. Even sites with southern exposures on the "good side" of the Gales Creek and Tualatin River Valleys can vary markedly. Vineyards within six miles of each other ripen as much as three weeks apart.

Some Oregon winemakers emphasize the delicate fruit flavors of the grape. Others prefer a style that emphasizes the transformation of these ethereal flavors and scents into more rounded, fuller flavors, with less fruit of the grape, but more complex character. Although such dichotomies are inevitably oversimplified, Shafer largely falls into the latter category.

The difference in style is evident in Shafer's Chardonnay. Shafer ferments the Chardonnay in oak barrels rather than stainless steel. He uses Montrachet yeast, a strain that has a reputation for extracting fuller flavors, but at the risk of an undesirable hydrogen sulfide byproduct. Guarding against hydrogen sulfide, Shafer applies no sulfur after July, and racks the wine (removes it from the remaining grape solids) immediately after fermentation is complete. Shafer's Chardonnays display the positive aspects of Montrachet yeast without its undesirable byproducts.

In addition to Pinot Noir, Riesling, and Chardonnay, Shafer was

among the first to produce Oregon Sauvignon Blanc. According to viticultural texts, the grape ripens late, and thus would not be ideally suited to the Willamette Valley climate. In Shafer's experience, however, the grape ripens as early as Pinot Noir. In cool years, like other varieties, it suffers from lack of ripeness, but unlike some varieties, varietal flavors begin to show early. The grape, particularly at lower levels of ripeness, has a pronounced grassy-herbaceous character. Shafer produces Sauvignon Blanc only in small quantities. The winery's specialty remains Pinot Noir and Chardonnay.

Silver Falls Winery

Most Willamette Valley vineyards are located on the western foothills of the Coast Range, or on the hills in the western center of the valley. Silver Falls Winery, and the vineyards of its owners, are on the lower slopes of the Cascade foothills, on

---

Silver Falls Winery

4972 Cascade Hwy S.E.
Sublimity, Oregon 97385
(503) 769-9463

Owners
Jim Palmquist, Ralph Schmidt,
John Schmidt, and Steve DeShaw

Winemaker
Jim Palmquist

Wine Production
6,000 gallons

Vineyard Acreage
15 acres

Year First Planted
1974

First Vintage
1983

Wines Produced
Pinot Noir, Chardonnay, Pinot Gris,
Riesling

---

the eastern side of the Willamette Valley, at elevations of 650 to 750 feet.

Because of its location, Silver Falls' vineyards typically ripen slightly later than other parts of the valley. Although this may present difficulties in cool years, it can be a benefit in the hot years when other parts of the valley are suffering from too much heat.

Jim Palmquist started the winery in 1983. After a period of inactivity while additional financing was obtained, Silver Falls resumed operations again with partners Ralph Schmidt, John Schmidt, and Steve DeShaw.

Palmquist's vineyard, adjacent to the winery, is trained to bilateral cordons, once an unusual vineyard practice in the Willamette Valley, but now a more common occurrence. Before they are filled with summer foliage, the 15 year old vines present a striking sight as the rows of thick-trunked "T" shaped vines sweep up the hillside in the sunlight.

Located between Salem and Silver Falls State Park, the winery takes its name from the nearby Silver Creek Falls, a series of scenic falls that form as the north and south forks of Silver Creek tumble out of the Cascade foothills and join within the park's boundaries.

Siskiyou Vineyards

The Illinois Valley is a grape growing region of increasing note. Although the valley is located only a few miles from the California border, it is significantly influenced by cooling coastal marine air. Suzi David's Siskiyou Vineyards was the first winery in the modern era to pioneer the Illinois Valley.

A few old vines, remnants of the winegrowing era prior to Prohibition, still remain, but the Illinois Valley lay viticulturally stagnant until Charles Coury, of

---

Suzi David's Siskiyou Vineyards was the first winery in the modern era to pioneer the Illinois Valley.

---

the now defunct Charles Coury winery in the northern Willamette Valley, came to Rogue Community College in 1972, and taught a course on enology and viticulture. As a result of the course, several area residents got cuttings from

Siskiyou Vineyards

6220 Caves Highway
Cave Junction, Oregon 97523
(503) 592-3727

Owner
Suzi David

Winemaker
Donna Devine

Wine Production
12,000 gallons

Vineyard Acreage
12 acres

Year First Planted
1974

First Vintage
1978

Wines Produced
Cabernet Sauvignon, Pinot Noir,
Chardonnay, Riesling,
Sauvignon Blanc, Gewurztraminer,
Muller-Thurgau,
Cabernet Sauvignon Blanc,
Pinot Noir Blanc,
The Rose of Cabernet,
La Cave Rouge, La Cave Blanc,
Zinfandel, Merlot

Coury and later planted vineyards.

Most of the first plantings were modest, a few vines for a hobby,

but the outcome was predictable and inevitable. The previous owner of David's property had attended the lectures and started a few vines. After acquiring the property, David planted a vineyard large enough for a commercial winery.

The soil, a Josephine loam, runs only three to five feet deep. Since the soil holds little water, irrigation is a necessity. Cool air drains from the steep hillsides surrounding the vineyard, and spring and fall frosts can be a problem. Siskiyou's overhead sprinkler systems not only provide irrigation for the vineyards during summer, but also protection against the frosts.

The attractive winery and grounds are just off the highway to the famous Oregon Caves National Monument, offering a convenient side stop for visitors. The tasting room is finished in redwood, and features the work of local artists. Each June, Siskiyou holds an art, music, and wine festival at the winery's two acre trout lake.

Sokol Blosser Winery

In 1974, Bill and Susan Blosser sold the first grapes from their vineyard to neighboring wineries. By 1977, plans for a winery took shape. The Blossers formed a limited partnership consisting of Bill and Susan Blosser as general partners, and members of Susan Sokol Blosser's family as limited partners. The Blossers built a winery, hired a winemaker, and crushed their first vintage.

At a time in the Oregon wine industry when most wineries were very small, marginally financed operations, Sokol Blosser was different, one of the first to start with a modern, well-financed operation. Instead of a garage or expediently built shed to serve as a winery, the Blossers built their winery of prestressed concrete, set into a rocky knoll. For their winemaker, they hired Bob McRitchie, then chief chemist for Franciscan Vineyards.

Instead of a makeshift table to serve as a tasting room, the Blossers hired John Storrs, a noted architect, to design an attractive, modern winetasting and visitors building adjacent to the winery. Equipped with a kitchen, the building is available for dinners and receptions. Sokol Blosser is one of Oregon's most popular wineries for touring.

■ **Sokol Blosser Winery**

Sokol Blosser Winery

5000 Sokol Blosser Lane
P.O. Box 399
Dundee, Oregon 97115
(503) 864-2282

Owners
Bill & Susan Blosser,
Hyland Vineyards,
Durant Vineyards

Winemakers
John Haw, Bill Blosser

Wine Production
55,000 gallons

Vineyard Acreage
135 acres

Year First Planted
1971

First Vintage
1977

Wines Produced
Pinot Noir Yamhill County,
Pinot Noir Redland,
Pinot Noir Redland Reserve,
Chardonnay, Riesling,
Muller-Thurgau, Sauvignon Blanc

Sokol Blosser is participating in several research projects. Four acres of Chardonnay are trellised by two different methods. Half the vines are trained on a single wire five feet high, the other half on a complex Geneva Double Curtain system. Balancing complexity, cost, maintenance, and support for the vine and grape crop is always a trade off. Sokol Blosser's experiment with two of the many trellising systems will help determine which systems are best for Oregon.

In conjunction with Oregon State University, Sokol Blosser is also experimenting with several pruning techniques to determine their effect on the size and quality of the grape crop. Outside the visitors' building, Sokol Blosser's test plot contains various clones of Pinot Noir, Chardonnay, and other varieties.

With the evolution of the Oregon wine industry, Sokol Blosser, too, has changed and evolved. McRitchie left to pursue other winemaking and consulting activities. In addition to their own estate grapes, Sokol Blosser had been purchasing grapes from two major sources, Hyland and Durant vineyards. In 1987, the two vineyards strengthened their association with the winery by buying out the interest of the Sokol family and joining with Bill and Susan Blosser to form a new company, Sokol Blosser, Ltd.

The Sokol Blosser and Durant vineyards are next to each other in the Dundee Hills. Hyland Vine-

yards, is about 15 miles southwest of the winery, near the town of Sheridan. With the change in business structure, the wine designations changed as well. Formerly, the higher end releases were vineyard designated. Since 1987, the premium wines have been given a proprietary name, and are a blend of vineyards. The most affordable, ready to drink Pinot Noir, for example, is designated Yamhill County. Next up the scale is the proprietary name, Redland, then the Redland Reserve.

The Sokol Blosser and Durant vineyards are planted in a volcanic clay loam soil known as Jory. Distinctive in appearance, the red soil provides a colorful backdrop for the vineyard's lush green foliage. Some growers in the area say grapes from this soil produce more robust, fuller flavored wines than grapes from more delicate soils found elsewhere in the Willamette Valley. In spite of the temptation offered by

> **Distinctive in appearance, the red volcanic soil provides a colorful backdrop for the vineyard's lush green foliage.**

their distinctive soil, the Blossers do not subscribe to this view, believing that soil character does not affect the taste of the wine.

Of the white wines, Chardonnay is Sokol Blosser's best. Popular taste runs toward lower acid wines. When such wines are consumed alone, they have a certain appeal, but when consumed with food, as most wine is meant to be, lower acid wines grow dull and cloying as the meal progresses, failing to cleanse and refresh the palate. Oregon wines are inherently higher in acid, but there is a tendency to release wines at lower acid levels to satisfy popular taste. Sokol Blosser's Chardonnay bucks this trend. Typically, the wine is tightly structured, and has sufficient acid to age well and marry well with food. Selected Chardonnays are released as reserve bottlings in some years.

Spring Hill Cellars

Interest in Oregon vineyard land has been in an upward growth pattern for years, but the recent intense interest and big money from European and California investors has dramatically accelerated the market. Mike

---

Spring Hill Cellars

2920 N.W. Scenic Drive
Albany, Oregon 97321
(503) 928-1009

Owner
Partnership

Winemakers
Mike McLain, Gary Budd

Wine Production
3,000 gallons

Vineyard Acreage
17 acres

Year First Planted
1978

First Vintage
1988

Wines Produced
Pinot Noir, Chardonnay, Riesling, Blush

McLain, a real estate broker specializing in vineyard property, has been more than a spectator in the industry's evolution.

McLain, has also had a small vineyard of his own for more than a decade. In conjunction with other partners, McLain decided to further participate in Oregon's wine scene by opening Spring Hill Cellars, a small commercial winery.

McLain's winery and vineyard are on Spring Hill, in the middle of the Willamette Valley. The soil type is a Veneta variant, a sedimentary soil similar to Willakenzie, with sandstone and soapstone components. West facing, the vineyard is somewhat more marine influenced and slightly cooler than many of the traditional growing sites in the northern Willamette. The vineyard is north of the corridor that runs from Corvallis to Newport on the coast, however, and is sheltered from the direct flow of marine air.

McLain likes the grapes from the vineyard, and is planting additional Pinot Noir and Pinot Gris at the site. A small winery, Spring Hill Cellars is attuned to local markets, and produces a relatively large proportion of Riesling and White Pinot. "Those wines will help us make a financial go of it," says McLain, a practical realist, "but my heart and mental energies are in the Pinot Noir."

Tempest Vineyards

Keith Orr works for the city of Portland fixing traffic signals, and makes wine on the side—or, as Orr puts it, his job goes "from red lights to red wine." A jovial and gregarious individual, Orr's commitment to fine wine is nevertheless studied and serious.

Orr and his wife, Patty Thomas, own 35 acres of vineyard property on the Amity end of the Eola Hills. Twenty acres are suitable for vineyards, though immediate plans call for only a token planting of

---

Tempest Vineyards

Mailing Address
9342 N.E. Hancock Drive
Portland, Oregon 97220
(503) 538-2733

Owners
Small Corporation:
Patricia Thomas & Keith Orr
majority owners

Winemaker
Keith Orr

Wine Production
3,000 gallons

Vineyard Acreage
none

First Vintage
1988

Wines Produced
Pinot Noir, Chardonnay,
Cabernet Sauvignon,
Gewurztraminer

---

two acres. Grapes for Orr's wines come primarily from the Eola Hills, with small amounts from the Chehalem Mountains and Dundee Hills.

The Tempest winery is presently located in an old garage on the property of Harry and Judy Peterson-Nedry. Judy is a noted Northwest wine authority and wine writer. Prior to opening a commercial winery, Orr made a series of small experimental wine batches with Judy's husband Harry. For several years, up to eighteen separate batches were made in a vintage, systematically varying fermentation factors on each batch.

Preferring delicate, aromatic Pinot Noir, Orr has settled on the general approach of removing the stems, very lightly crushing the berries, and fermenting at a moderate peak temperature in the 80s. Tempest's Chardonnay is barrel fermented. Orr also produces tiny batches of sweet Gewurztraminer dessert wine by freezing the grapes, then pressing them while still frozen. The juice is rich and intensely sweet, making a fine dessert wine.

Three Rivers Winery

The Columbia River Gorge cuts a path through the Cascade Range, the solid wall of mountains that runs north and

```
┌─────────────────────────────────┐
│        Three Rivers Winery       │
├─────────────────────────────────┤
│       275 Country Club Road      │
│      Hood River, Oregon  97031   │
│          (503) 386-5453          │
│                                  │
│             Owners               │
│         Bill & Ann Swain         │
│                                  │
│            Winemaker             │
│            Bill Swain            │
│                                  │
│         Wine Production          │
│          7,500 gallons           │
│                                  │
│        Vineyard Acreage          │
│             6 acres              │
│                                  │
│          First Vintage           │
│              1986                │
│                                  │
│         Wines Produced           │
│       Riesling, Chardonnay,      │
│   Gewurztraminer, Pinot Noir Rose,│
│            Pinot Noir            │
└─────────────────────────────────┘
```

south through Washington and Oregon. Three Rivers Winery is named for the convergence of three rivers at the heart of the gorge. The White Salmon River drainage flows from the slopes of Mt. Adams, the 12,000 foot glaciated volcanic cone on the Washington side of the gorge. On the Oregon side, the Hood River flows from the slopes of Mt. Hood, another glaciated volcanic cone. Both rivers join the Columbia River at one of the Northwest's most localized microclimates.

Bill Swain came to the gorge after a decade of winemaking experience at the Charles Krug and Cresta Blanca wineries in California. Swain likes Riesling. Enthused about the potential of Riesling grown in the gorge, Swain made Riesling a focus for his winery. The vineyards are on the Washington side of the gorge. The Oregon side offers better marketing opportunities, however, so Swain opened his winery and tasting room in the "Copper House," a turn-of-the-century home in the Oregon community of Hood River.

Tualatin Vineyards

When wine is discussed, conversation often turns to the growing climate that produced the grapes, sometimes to the specialized climate of the vineyard itself. At the Tualatin vineyard, theoretical abstractions are grounded in a grassroots reality.

The vineyard is one of the warmer growing sites in the area. Local residents remember a time when strawberry picking always began earliest at the Spangler farm. The children who worked for Spangler were often let out of school early to pick the already ripe berries. The Spangler farm is now the Tualatin vineyard. Now grapes instead of strawberries ripen earlier. In cooler, rainier years, Tualatin's warmer climate has a decided advantage.

In the early 1970's Bill Fuller and Bill Malkmus completed their search for a viticultural region suited to cooler climate, earlier maturing varieties of vinifera grapes, and founded Tualatin Vineyards. The two have different but complementary backgrounds. Malkmus is a graduate of Stanford University and Harvard Business School. Formerly an investment banker in San Francisco, Malkmus

```
┌─────────────────────────────────┐
│       Tualatin Vineyards         │
├─────────────────────────────────┤
│         Route 1, Box 339         │
│     Forest Grove, Oregon  97116  │
│          (503) 357-5005          │
│                                  │
│             Owners               │
│     Bill Malkmus & Bill Fuller   │
│                                  │
│            Winemaker             │
│            Bill Fuller           │
│                                  │
│         Wine Production          │
│          50,000 gallons          │
│                                  │
│        Vineyard Acreage          │
│             85 acres             │
│                                  │
│        Year First Planted        │
│              1973                │
│                                  │
│          First Vintage           │
│              1973                │
│                                  │
│         Wines Produced           │
│     Riesling, Gewurztraminer,    │
│       Chardonnay, Pinot Noir,    │
│    Oregon Rose, Muller-Thurgau,  │
│      Flora, Sauvignon Blanc      │
└─────────────────────────────────┘
```

is in charge of business operations and marketing, working out of Tualatin's California office.

Fuller holds an M.S. in Enology from the University of California at Davis and has long been involved with the wine industry. From 1964 to 1973, he was chief chemist and wine production manager with California's Louis M. Martini winery. Fuller, in charge of winemaking and vineyard operations, lives on the picturesque Tualatin estate with his wife, Virginia.

From his nine years at Louis M. Martini, Fuller brings to Oregon much of the style and philosophy of a larger California winery. A centrifuge and other modern technology are regarded as basic to the winery operation. Instead of planting vineyards and waiting for them to bear fruit, Fuller broke

115

an unwritten rule, and immediately began making wine from Washington grapes. The practice was subsequently adopted by most other northern Willamette Valley winemakers, though it is now largely a past practice as

> **Strawberry picking always began earliest at the Spangler farm. Children who worked for Spangler were let out of school early to pick the already ripe berries. Spangler farm is now the Tualatin vineyard, and now grapes instead of strawberries ripen early.**

Oregon grape production readily meets the needs of Oregon winemakers.

From the beginning, Tualatin emphasized cooler climate, white wine grapes. Eighty percent of the vineyard is planted to white wine varieties. More acreage is planted to Riesling than any other grape. Tualatin specializes in white wines in a Germanic style, low alcohol with some residual sweetness. Riesling is the principal wine in this style. Gewurztraminer, planted more heavily than at most Oregon vineyards, is another major variety for Tualatin made in the Germanic style.

Fuller is also working with Flora, a vinifera cross between Gewurztraminer and Semillon developed at the University of California at Davis. The Burgundian grape varieties, Chardonnay and Pinot Noir, are receiving increasing emphasis, and Tualatin's most recent vineyard expansion was devoted entirely to these two grapes.

Tualatin's wines reflect the relative warmth of the growing climate. The Pinot Noir has a riper, fuller-bodied quality, sometimes showing better in moderately cooler vintages. Chardonnay is perhaps Tualatin's best wine, made in a rich, ripe, complex style. The Germanic-style wines, too, often have a riper character than their counterparts from other Willamette Valley vineyards.

Tyee Wine Cellars

A partnership of two couples, Dave and Margy Buchanan, and Barney Watson and Nola Mosier, Tyee Wine Cellars is among Oregon's more noteworthy wineries—not in terms of scale, because Tyee is and will remain quite small, but in terms of quality and the direction of the Oregon wine industry.

Barney Watson, one of the part-

■ **Tyee winery**

ners, and Tyee's winemaker, is the enologist at Oregon State University's Department of Food Science and Technology. Watson is a leading figure in Oregon wine research and development.

Oregon State University is

bringing in and testing new clones and grape varieties from European research stations. Watson is charged with chemically analyzing the grapes and juice, making experimental batches of wine, and conducting sensory evaluations of the wines. As good as Oregon wine already is, the new clones and varieties promise even more.

Most of Oregon's current grape varieties and clones were brought in from California, and are not necessarily the best selections for the Oregon climate. The Davis 108 clone of Chardonnay, for example, Oregon's most widely planted clone of the grape, ripens mid to late season with relatively high acidity—ideal for California, but not always the best for Oregon. As the new clones become commercially available, Tyee will work with those that seem most promising.

The Buchanans constitute the other half of the partnership. Dave Buchanan, a fisheries biologist, returned to the Willamette Valley in the 1970s to manage the family farm. The Buchanans are the fourth generation on the farm. Dave Buchanan's interest in homemade wine, and his consultations with Watson, evolved into the joint winery venture. The farm, vineyard, and winery are located south of Corvallis, on the lower foothills of the Coast Range.

Grape growing is only a tiny part of the Buchanans' 460 acre farm. Land use has varied over the generations. Sheep, dairy cattle, and hazelnuts are part of the land's history. Farther back still, the confluence of two streams on the property was once the site of an Indian campground. As a child, Dave Buchanan milked cows in the barn that is now part of the Tyee winery.

The Buchanans have a genuineness about them that seems to grow out of their connection to the land and their reverence for it. Winegrowing is a natural direction for them. Fine wine, perhaps, is the most sublime expression of the land.

South of Corvallis, the Coast Range forms a crescent that shelters the area from the damp coastal air. Part of the crescent is shaped by Marys Peak, the highest mountain in the Coast Range. The Buchanan farm rests in the bowl of the crescent. Tyee's soils are relatively rich, but the grape clusters are thinned to reduce the crop. Pinot Noir is thinned to approximately two tons an acre.

Watson is a great fan of Gewurztraminer, and the varietal is something of a speciality for the winery, as is Pinot Gris. Pinot Noir and Chardonnay are the principal varietals. Beginning with the 1987 vintage, Tyee wines truly hit their stride, reflecting the quality of the people and effort behind them. Tyee's Chardonnay is particularly notable. Chardonnay is not always an easy grape in Oregon, but Tyee's Chardonnays are often among the state's best.

Umpqua River Vineyards

Greg and Debbie Denino and their family came to Oregon's Umpqua Valley from California. Greg Denino worked in California's vineyards and carried with him an ongoing interest in wine and winemaking. After a period of making wine at home, Denino planted his own vineyard on a 26 acre parcel of land and started his own commercial winery.

Umpqua River Vineyards

451 Hess
Roseburg, Oregon 97470
(503) 673-1975

Owners
Greg & Debbie Denino

Winemaker
Greg Denino

Wine Production
3,000 gallons

Vineyard Acreage
17 acres

First Vintage
1988

Wines Produced
Semillon, Cabernet Sauvignon, Rose

The Deninos' vineyard is situated on river bottom soil along the main trunk of the Umpqua River, in an area known as Garden Valley. The vines, in California fashion, are cordon rather than cane pruned, and trained to be free-standing without trellis wires. The vineyard is primarily Cabernet Sauvignon, with Semillon, Chenin Blanc, and the French-American hybrid, Baco Noir, among the other varieties. Denino likes red wine, and the Cabernet Sauvignon is the focus of his attention.

Valley View Vineyard

In 1972, the Wisnovsky family planted grapes in the Applegate Valley in southwest Oregon, marking the rediscovery of one of the Northwest's earliest viticul-

> **Sheltered from coastal marine air by the Klamath and Siskiyou Mountains, the Applegate Valley is among the sunniest, warmest, and driest winegrowing climates in western Oregon.**

tural regions. Western Oregon is known for its year-round temperate climate, richly foliaged landscapes, cloudy skies, and wet weather. Although this conception is substantially true for much of western Oregon, it does not apply to the Applegate Valley, a climatic region in the Jacksonville area of southwest Oregon.

Not far from the California border, and sheltered from coastal marine air by the Klamath Mountains and Siskiyou Mountains, the Applegate Valley is among the sunniest, warmest, and driest winegrowing climates in western Oregon. Grasses, long needle pines, and the absence of ubiquitous foliage demonstrate that this is indeed a much different climate.

Valley View Vineyard is situated in the Applegate Valley, at an elevation of 1,500 feet, an area known as Sunshine Village. The soil in the 26 acre vineyard varies, but is predominantly a Ruch sandy loam. Most areas in the

---

Valley View Vineyard

1000 Applegate Road
Jacksonville, Oregon 97530
(503) 899-8468

Tasting Rooms
690 North 5th Street
Jacksonville, Oregon 97530

52 E. Main
Ashland, Oregon 97520

Owners
Wisnovsky Family

Winemaker
John Guerrero

Wine Production
22,000 gallons

Vineyard Acreage
26 acres

Year First Planted
1972

First Vintage
1976

Wines Produced
Cabernet Sauvignon, Chardonnay,
Merlot, Sauvignon Blanc

Applegate Valley, including the Valley View vineyard site, are too warm for Gewurztraminer, Riesling, and Pinot Noir. Valley View's focus is on Cabernet Sauvignon, Merlot, and Chardonnay, the premium varieties best suited to the climate.

In their youth, the Valley View Cabernet Sauvignons have been rough and tannic, requiring lengthy cellar age, and a race between remaining tannin and remaining fruit. The wines of the current winemaker, U.C. Davis

trained John Guerrero, promise a more ideal balance, wines that are more supple in youth, yet capable of aging.

Veritas Vineyard

Traveling Highway 99 West, from the Portland metropolitan area toward Oregon's famed coastal beaches, Veritas Vineyard is one of the first of many estate wineries along the northern Willamette Valley wine route.

John Howieson, a physician at a Portland area medical school, wanted to have a vineyard as a retirement project. The Howiesons planned to plant near the Sokol Blosser winery, and have Sokol Blosser make the wine for their winery label. When a house and 40 acre parcel of vineyard land closer to Portland became available, the Howiesons bought the land, and planted their first vines in 1983. Sokol Blosser made the wines for Veritas's first vintage, but since 1984, Howieson has made all the wines at Veritas.

Pinot Noir and Chardonnay are Veritas's leading wines. Howieson ferments his Pinot Noir in temperature controlled stainless steel tanks, as well as the totes that are part of the Oregon winemaking tradition. Veritas's early Pinot Noirs were darker, more tannic, and more extracted than the Oregon norm, but the recent vintages are less tannic with more forward fruit. The Chardonnay is all barrel fermented.

The Veritas estate vineyard follows the multiple curvatures of Rex Hill. Only a small portion of the vineyard is visible from the

winery. The soil, a Laurelwood silt loam, is of volcanic and sedimentary origins, slightly richer and more water retentive than the purely volcanic Jory soils found in many other northern Willamette Valley vineyards.

Planting grape vines to run up and down the hillsides is easiest for cultivation, but topsoil runoff

■ **John Howieson**

is a growing concern. Veritas is one of the newer vineyards with drainage terraces and vines planted to run across the slope. In the newest portion of the vine-

---

Veritas Vineyard

31190 N.E. Veritas Lane
Newberg, Oregon 97132
(503) 538-1470

Owners
John & Diane Howieson

Winemaker
John Howieson;
John R. Eliassen,
Associate Winemaker

Wine Production
15,000 gallons

Vineyard Acreage
26 acres

Year First Planted
1983

First Vintage
1983

Wines Produced
Chardonnay, Muller-Thurgau,
Pinot Gris, Pinot Noir, Riesling,
Dry Riesling

---

yard, the vine rows actually follow the contour lines of the hillside. Aesthetics as well as soil conservation benefit. The artistic curvatures of the vine rows, integrated with the natural flow of the land, echo the spirit and essence of the Oregon winegrowing experience.

Wasson Brothers Winery

A partnership of twin brothers, Jim and John Wasson, Wasson Brothers Winery grew out of

Wasson Brothers Winery
41901 Highway 26 Sandy, Oregon 97055 (503) 668-3124
Owners Jim & John Wasson
Winemaker Jim Wasson
Grape Wine Production 4,300 gallons
Fruit & Berry Wine Production 2,300 gallons
Vineyard Acreage 7 acres
Year First Planted 1978
First Vintage 1982
Wines Produced Pinot Noir, Chardonnay, Riesling, Gewurztraminer, Early Muscat, Raspberry, Loganberry, Blackberry, Boysenberry, Strawberry, Rhubarb, Apricot

the success of the brothers' homemade fruit and berry wines in judgings at the Oregon State Fair. The two planted a small vineyard in Clackamas County near Oregon City and opened a winery.

Restrictive local regulations prevented the Wassons from having an active tasting and sales room, so the two moved their winery to the town of Sandy. Almost immediately, a shopping center development forced yet another move to a location on the other side of town.

Most Willamette Valley vineyards and wineries are in the western part of the valley. Wasson Brothers Winery and vineyard is one of the few east of the Willamette River, in Clackamas County. Situated outside the mainstream of Willamette Valley wine country, Wasson's average winery visitor prefers the fruit and berry offerings to the grape wines. With an eye to their winemaking roots and their customers, more than half of the Wassons' wine production is fruit and berry wine.

Winemaking expertise, however, is not limited only to fruit and berry wines. Unlike a number of other fruit and berry wineries, Wasson Brothers is quite adept at vinifera grape wines as well.

Weisinger's

The Weisinger winery and vineyard are located near the California border, not far from where the Siskiyou Mountains and Cascade Foothills converge. The winery parking area is decoratively bordered by large rocks and boulders dredged from the soil during the construction of the winery. The orangish-red sandstone rocks, imprinted with the fossilized remnants of shellfish, sharks teeth, and other sea life, bespeak the region's geologic origins.

John Weisinger, a minister, counselor, and human resources

Weisinger's
3150 Siskiyou Ashland, Oregon 97520 (503) 488-5989
Owners John & Sherita Weisinger
Winemaker John Weisinger & Donna Devine
Wine Production 10,000 gallons
Vineyard Acreage 4 1/2 acres
First Vintage 1988
Wines Produced Gewurztraminer, Cabernet Sauvignon Blanc, Mescolare, Chardonnay, Cabernet Sauvignon, Late Harvest Gewurztraminer

specialist, has been making homemade wine for several decades. His longstanding interest in wine, and contacts with the new pioneer winegrowers in southwest Oregon, led him to plant grapes on his hillside property, in the Bear Creek Valley, on the outskirts of Ashland.

The Bear Creek Valley, a tributary of the Rogue River, is becom-

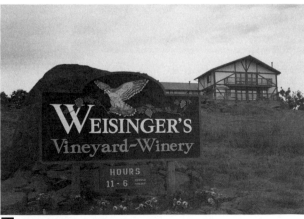

■ **Weisinger's winery**

ing a noteworthy Oregon winegrowing region. Farthest inland of the southwest Oregon grape growing valleys, Bear Creek Valley is sheltered from coastal marine air by both the Klamath and Siskiyou Mountains. It is one of the warmest climates in western Oregon.

Northern Italy is the model for Weisinger's winery. The winery architecture is patterned after the styles the Weisingers saw during a trip to Italy. Most of Weisinger's own vineyard is planted to Gewurztraminer, but he is budding over some of the vines to the Italian variety Nebbiolo. New plantings of Sangiovese and Cabernet Franc are also in his plans.

Commercial wine production is a new venture for Weisinger, but the first wines show fine promise. Weisinger produces a proprietary wine called Mescolare, a blend of approximately 80 percent Cabernet Sauvignon, 20 percent Pinot Noir, and fractions of another, unstated, grape variety.

The possibility of good Oregon Nebbiolo and Sangiovese, as well as Cabernet and the other more conventional varieties, stirs the interest of the enthusiastic enophile. Succeeding vintages will prove the merits of the enterprise.

Willamette Valley Vineyards

Winery founder and president, Jim Bernau, quickly and proudly proclaims that Willamette Valley Vineyards is the Northwest's first consumer owned winery, and one of the few in America so owned. An Oregon native, born and raised near Roseburg, Bernau's enterprise offered shares in the winery at $1.70 per share, with a minimum purchase of 600 shares.

Willamette Valley Vineyards sold the stock direct to the public, without going through a broker. The legal strictures on the category under which the stock was offered limited total sales to

Willamette Valley Vineyards

8800 Enchanted Way S.E.
Turner, Oregon 97392
(503) 588-9463
or
1-800-344-9463

Owners
Corporation, Jim Bernau, president

Winemaker
Bob McRitchie

Wine Production
40,000 gallons

Vineyard Acreage
25 acres

First Vintage
1989

Wines Produced
Pinot Noir, Chardonnay, Riesling, Pinot Noir Blanc

$1,500,000. The stock offering was highly successful, raising $1,870,000. The limit exceeded, more than a third of a million dollars had to be returned to would be investors.

"We didn't need to have a stock offering to raise money," says Bernau. I wanted a winery that was owned by wine enthusiasts, a consumer owned winery. There are more Oregon owners of Willamette Valley Vineyards than there are Oregon owners of all the other Oregon wineries combined. About 850 families own the winery."

Willamette Valley Vineyards is only two miles from the southern extremity of the Salem city limits. Situated in the South Salem Hills, the winery is readily visible to passers by along the Interstate 5 freeway. The land, in fact, extends down to the freeway. About 56 of

the 76 acres are plantable. The soils are Nekia and Jory. For trellising the vines, the Geneva Double Curtain training system is used exclusively.

Winemaker is Bob McRitchie, formerly of Oregon's Sokol Blosser winery. "We wanted to have the finest, state of the art equipment," says Bernau. "Bob was like a kid in a candy store. He just told us what he wanted, and we bought it."

Willamette Valley Vineyards is focusing on Oregon's traditional three major grapes, Pinot Noir, Chardonnay, and Riesling, in that order of priority. Most of the Chardonnay is fermented and aged in new Nevers French oak. The rest of the wines are fermented in stainless steel tanks—the Pinot Noir in tanks no larger than 2,500 gallons.

Designed for a maximum capacity of 160,000 gallons, the winery is constructed in a Northwest architectural style. Comprehensive visitor facilities are a major feature of the winery.

"There are more Oregon owners of Willamette Valley Vineyards than there are Oregon owners of all the other Oregon wineries combined."

"I want Willamette Valley Vineyards to be the highest quality possible," says Bernau, "a consumer owned and oriented winery that serves as a highly visible symbol for the Oregon wine industry. By our third year, we hope to exceed 100,000 visitors a year to the winery. Right now, the

Tillamook Cheese factory is the biggest commercial tourist attraction in Oregon. Enchanted Village, very close by to us, is number three. I want to see Willamette Valley Vineyards in the top ten."

Windy Ridge Winery

Windy Ridge Winery is part of Cuvee Northwest, Inc., a custom processing and bottling facility serving wineries and

Windy Ridge Winery

9816 S.W. Tigard Avenue
Tigard, Oregon 97223
(206) 684-2952

Owners
Robert Stone & other investors

Winemaker
Robert Leo

Wine Production
25,000 gallons

Vineyard Acreage
none

First Vintage
1988

Wines Produced

Windy Ridge: Sparkling Wine, Cabernet Sauvignon, Riesling

Alder Creek: Riesling, Red Table

Northwest Cuvee: Sparkling Wine

breweries throughout the Northwest. The facility produces a number of products including still table wines, Charmat process sparkling wines, bottled beers, and hard ciders. The winery acts as a negociant, buying wines in bulk from other Northwest wineries, then finishing and blending them at the winery.

The Charmat process can offer good quality, moderately priced sparkling wines. Although Charmat process sparkling wine is less costly to produce than bottle fer-

mented sparkling wines, the specialized tanks and equipment are very expensive. Windy Ridge is one of only two wineries in the Northwest with Charmat processing equipment.

The sparkling wines are generally made with Riesling or Chenin Blanc, but Chardonnay is occasionally used as well. Windy Ridge produces sparkling wine for other Northwest wineries as well as their own labels. The specialized bottling equipment has also been a boon to Oregon microbreweries, allowing them to sell bottled beer and ale rather than the draft product only.

Witness Tree Vineyard

The Witness Tree Vineyard takes its name from an ancient oak tree that stands on the hillside above the vineyards. The "witness tree," a native Oregon oak, is a protected survey marker, and now, with the passing decades, a stately historical marker bespeaking the pioneering history of the valley.

Witness Tree Vineyard is owned by Doug Gentzkow, a retired airforce meteorologist and now airline pilot. In 1987, Gentzkow bonded a winery of his own, and began making wine with a small portion of his grapes. In 1988, Gentzkow hired Rick Nunes, a PhD plant physiologist and biochemist, to make the wines and manage the vineyard. Prior to coming to Witness Tree, Nunes was cellarmaster at Knudsen Erath Winery. Nunes had been teaching at Linfield College in McMinnville when he was stricken with the wine bug and drawn away from his profession into the wine world.

Nunes brings some of the

methods from Knudsen Erath to Witness Tree. The Pinot Noir is fermented in a closed 3,000 gallon tank. Nunes takes this opportunity to keep the Pinot Noir macerating on the skins and pulp after fermentation has finished. Nunes likes the effect of extended maceration for color stability and the softer tannins that form as the tannins polymerize.

Witness Tree vineyard was originally cordoned pruned and trained, but the vines are being converted to a cane system for better and more consistent crops. Only half the suitable land for vineyards is in vine. The remaining portion will likely be planted to the new, recently released clones of Pinot Noir and Chardonnay.

Wine production remains small. More rapid expansion had been planned, but intervening

Witness Tree Vineyard

P.O. Box 5203
7111 Spring Valley Road N.W.
Salem, Oregon 97304
(503) 585-7874

Owner
Douglas Gentzkow

Winemaker
Rick Nunes

Wine Production
3,000 gallons

Vineyard Acreage
35 acres

First Vintage
1987

Wines Produced
Chardonnay, Pinot Noir

factors, including California wineries paying substantial prices for the vineyard's grapes, have delayed expansion. The good grape prices, however, will help finance the winery's growth.

Yamhill Valley Vineyards

In the fall of 1982, Denis Burger and his wife Elaine casually went looking at vineyard property. Within a week, they owned 34 acres of vineyard land. Joined by David and Terry Hinrichs, the partners now own 600 acres southwest of McMinnville, in the northern Willamette Valley. Nestled against the foothills of the Coast Range, the vineyard is sheltered from the onshore flow of Pacific marine air. Rain clouds tend to pass by on either side of the vineyard, and the site is slightly warmer and drier than many others in the northern Willamette Valley.

Unusual for Oregon, the vines are cordon pruned rather than

Yamhill Valley Vineyards

16250 S.W. Oldsville Road
McMinnville, Oregon 97128
(503) 843-3100

Owners
Denis Burger, Elaine McCall,
David & Terry Hinrichs

Winemaker
Denis Burger

Wine Production
20,000 gallons

Vineyard Acreage
100 acres

Year First Planted
1982

First Vintage
1983

Wines Produced
Pinot Noir, Chardonnay, Pinot Gris,
Riesling

---

cane pruned. Short spurs are left on permanent lateral arms (cordons), and the season's growth emerges from the buds on the short spurs. Oregon's cool, cloudy, early season climate can cause cropping problems with this method, but cordon pruning has advantages too, requiring less time to maintain each of the many thousands of vines, and allowing less experienced workers to do the pruning. So far, cordon training has proven well suited to the vineyard's growing climate.

Half of the winery's production is dedicated to Pinot Noir. The Pinots are made in a big style with ample amounts of tannin, extract, acid, and color. Sometimes big-style Pinot Noirs suffer from an overripe, pruney, or port-like character. Such is not the case with Yamhill Valley Vineyard's Pinots. The "bigness" comes not from overripe grapes, but from the winemaking methods applied to quality fruit.

Denis Burger ferments his Pinot Noir in stainless steel tanks at very warm fermentation temperatures, peaking at 90 degrees or above, to extract more body and extract from the grape. Hot fermentation temperatures run the risk of spoilage problems, but Burger, a microbiologist, counters this concern by fermenting in the enclosed stainless steel tanks, a method he favors over the smaller, open topped containers that had been the traditional norm for most of Oregon's winemakers.

Yamhill Valley Vineyard's recent Pinot Noir vintages are less overtly tannic, and show a stylistic evolution and refinement, while still retaining the full-bodied, extracted style that is the winery's hallmark. Burger's wines are excellent examples of Oregon Pinot Noir in this range of the stylistic spectrum.

Yamhill Valley Vineyards produces three white wines, Chardonnay, Pinot Gris, and Riesling. Burger's Chardonnay is fermented and aged in French oak

barrels. The Riesling is finished toward the drier end of the spectrum.

The attractive concrete winery building and tasting room was designed by Denis Burger's brother, Ed Burger, a San Francisco architect. Bob Burger, another brother, designed the label and named the winery.

■ **David Hinrichs**

A visit to the winery is an excellent encapsulation of the Oregon wine experience. The road to Yamhill Valley Vineyards passes among the vines and drops down a hill to the winery surrounded by elegant oak trees. The landing before entering the tasting room looks down to the working winery and oak barrels below. Sweeping limbs from old oak trees overhang the rear deck of the tasting room. The rear deck affords yet another view of the vineyards and the beauty of the surrounding countryside.

Washington's Wine Industry

Visionaries, entrepreneurs, & agriculturists join forces in one of America's most dynamic wine industries

Except for California, Washington produces more premium *Vitis vinifera* wine grapes than any state in America. Wine grapes have been grown in Washington since the 1800s, but until the state's wine renaissance in the late 1960s, the Washington wine industry had little interest in premium wines or wine grapes.

Washington had long been a large producer of grapes, but these were mostly *Vitis labrusca* varieties, principally Concord, used for grape juice products or for making indifferent, often fortified, wines.

Since the early 1800s, grapes have been planted at various locations both east and west of the Cascade Mountains. The first grapes were mostly non-vinifera varieties, often serving the multiple purposes of juice, jelly, table grapes, and sometimes wine. The early industry was primarily located in the wet, temperate, Puget Sound area of western Washington. As irrigation projects opened agricultural land in the Columbia Valley, east of the Cascades, grape growing shifted away from western Washington to the Columbia Valley, and the grape of choice shifted from Island Belle, a local variant of Campbell Early, to Concord.

Prior to Prohibition, Washington had an active grape growing industry, but no wine industry, as such. The Repeal of Prohibition and favorable state laws instantly created one. By 1937, 42 wineries were operating in the state. Wine quality, however, was poor. Most of the wines were made from Concord or other labrusca grape varieties. Protectionist state laws kept competition away.

In the Yakima Valley, east of the Cascade Mountains, William B.

Washington

Wine Grape Acreage
11,000 acres

Winegrowing Regions
Columbia Valley, Yakima Valley,
Walla Walla Valley, Columbia Gorge,
Southwest Washington, Puget Sound

Predominant Grape Varieties
Riesling, Chardonnay, Chenin Blanc,
Cabernet Sauvignon, Sauvignon Blanc, Merlot,
Semillon, Gewurztraminer

Catalysts for the Washington wine renaissance were an unlikely combination of a wine writer, some amateur winemakers, and the removal of protectionist state wine laws at the urging of wine retailers who were openly hostile to the state's wine industry.

Bridgman made a careful study of winegrowing climates, planted and purchased vinifera grapes, hired a German winemaker, and attempted to produce premium vinifera wines. Unfortunately, as wine authority Leon D. Adams reports, from personal experience, the wines were poorly made and were withdrawn from sale. Other accounts indicate that the wine market at the time would not support quality table wines, and that the Bridgman winery, trying to straddle the disjunction between quality wines and the demands of the marketplace, was doomed to failure.

Grape growers continued to cultivate a few vinifera grapes, only to have winemakers blend them with labrusca varieties. A viable premium wine industry was still decades away. After the initial flurry of winegrowing activity following Repeal of Prohibition, the industry sank into a long decline. The number of wineries steadily decreased. Wines were still made mostly from labrusca grapes, with some occasional vinifera thrown into the blend for good measure.

The rebirth of the Washington wine industry, based solely on premium *Vitis vinifera* grape varieties, did not come until the late 1960s. Catalysts for the Washington wine renaissance were an unlikely combination of a wine writer, some amateur winemakers, and the removal of protectionist state wine laws at the urging of wine retailers who were openly hostile to the state's wine industry and had little interest in premium wines from the state.

To abbreviate what is a rather elaborate story, a group of amateur winemakers began, in the late 1950s, purchasing vinifera grapes from Columbia Valley grape growers, rescuing them from fortified blends with *Vitis labrusca* grapes. In 1962, to insure a steady supply of grapes, the group purchased vineyard acreage and became a bonded winery, Associated Vintners. In 1966, Leon D. Adams, the noted authority on American wines, visited Associated Vintners. Impressed with some of their early efforts, Adams suggested that they become a commercial enterprise. In 1967, Associated Vintners produced their first commercial vintage. Though much transformed, Associated Vintners continues to operate, now under the name Columbia Winery.

With the expected removal of protectionist wine laws, another winery, American Wine Growers, one of the state's largest, and the corporate predecessor of Chateau Ste. Michelle, was becoming interested in developing premium table wines. At the suggestion of Adams, Andre Tchelistcheff, the legendary California winemaker, visited the state, tasted the wines, and ultimately became consultant to American Wine Growers.

In 1967, the same year that Associated Vintners went public, American Wine Growers, under the label Ste. Michelle, produced their first vintage of a new line of *Vitis vinifera* wine. Today, Chateau Ste. Michelle and its sister winery, Columbia Crest, under the corporate umbrella of Stimson Lane, dominate the Northwest wine scene. Stimson Lane is one of the 25 largest wine producers in

America. As a secondary effect of Stimson Lane's marketing acumen and market presence throughout the country, Chateau Ste. Michelle and Columbia Crest have opened new markets and stimulated consumer interest in other wines and wineries from the Northwest.

In the early years, the Washington wine industry was a paradox, having a relatively large quantity of grapes, but very few wineries, and at first, most of the state's winemaking was located in the urban areas west of the Cascades, far from the source of the grapes. By mid 1970s, the industry began shifting toward a better balance. More wineries began opening to give the grapes a home. Estate wineries became more common.

The Wallace family established Hinzerling Vineyards, a small vineyard and winery in Washington's Yakima Valley. Along the Columbia River Gorge, the Hendersons, with other partners, founded Bingen Wine Cellars (Mont Elise Vineyards). Near Pasco, on a much larger scale, the Prestons founded Preston Wine Cellars.

By the mid 1980s, the Washington wine industry finally became truly diversified. Western Washington wines joined Columbia Valley wines on the merchant's wine shelves. The largest wineries grew still larger. Many small and medium size wineries began operation. Numerous vineyards and estate wineries stretched from one end of the Yakima Valley to the other. New and distinct growing regions entered the scene, and wineries were opening all across the state.

Chateau Ste. Michelle expanded operations with a 26 million dollar winery and planted a single vineyard that stretched, literally, for miles, and the state's wine industry attracted its first foreign money with partial German financing of the F. W. Langguth Winery. For the first time since the years immediately following Repeal of Prohibition, the number of wineries exceeded 42, and this time around, the wine industry was based entirely on premium vinifera wine grapes—more than 10,000 acres of them.

The decades preceding the wine renaissance were not entirely wasted. Many of the first vinifera grapes were not good wine varieties or were poorly suited to the growing climate, but frosts and winter freezes offered winegrowers important lessons on cultivation practices, winegrowing sites, and the hardiness of various vinifera grape varieties.

In the late 1930s, Dr. Walter Clore, Washington State University horticulturist, among his other duties, began grape research at the Irrigated Agricultural Research and Extension Center at Prosser, in the Yakima Valley. In the coming decades, Clore helped refine grape growing practices, identified grape varieties best suited to the growing climates, and developed experimental vineyard test sites in selected growing areas. Nearly 50 years after he began his research, Clore, professor emeritus, working as a private consultant, submitted a petition to the BATF for the Columbia Valley viticultural area. On December 13, 1984, the BATF approved the petition, and the 18,000 square mile Columbia Valley viticultural area, the North-

Today, Chateau Ste. Michelle and its sister winery, Columbia Crest, under the corporate umbrella of Stimson Lane, dominate the Northwest wine scene. Stimson Lane is one of the 25 largest wine producers in America.

> **Washington's best wines
> are the red Bordeaux
> varieties and dry whites,
> not Riesling.
> A shift, already in progress,
> toward dry whites and reds
> is healthy for the industry,
> and a boon
> to the wine aficionado.**

west's largest, became a reality.

Riesling has been and still is the backbone of the Washington wine industry. Riesling is the most cold hardy of all the major vinifera varieties. Consumer demand for white wines, and for crisp, semi-sweet white wines in particular, made Riesling readily marketable. No other American winegrowing region can so easily produce quality Riesling on such a scale, and the grape fits the perception that Riesling would be one of the best grapes for one of America's northernmost states. For all these reasons, Washington grape growers planted heavily to Riesling—too heavily.

Demand is shifting toward the traditionally dry white varieties such as Chardonnay and Sauvignon Blanc, and more recently, Semillon. Red wine grapes, principally Cabernet Sauvignon and Merlot, are increasingly in demand as consumers and winegrowers become more aware that Washington is not just a Riesling or white wine state. Arguably, Washington's best wines are the red Bordeaux varieties and dry whites, not Riesling. A shift, already in progress, toward dry whites and reds is healthy for the industry, and a boon to the wine aficionado.

This shift, however, has neither been smooth nor predictable, nor has the overall size of grape harvests been easily predictable. Frosts and winter freezes periodically strike the industry. Riesling typically comes through in the best shape, with closer to normal crop levels, but the dry white and red varieties are more tender, and in some cases, their harvests are substantially reduced. In some years, winery capacity has not been able to handle the grape supply, and grapes, particularly Riesling, have been left hanging on the vine. Some growers, particularly those who had gotten into wine grapes as a new cash crop, began pulling up vines, particularly Riesling.

The Washington wine industry is in the midst of major growth and transition, and the frosts and freezes have come at a difficult times. On the one hand, vineyard expansion had been extraordinarily rapid. New vineyards reached maturity at about the same time, and spikes in grape production threatened to overwhelm the industry, producing far more grapes than could possibly be absorbed by existing wineries.

At the same time, the curse and salvation of a series of frosts and freezes reduced grape crops. In some vintages, the industry was overwhelmed with excess grapes, only to be followed by a vintage where grapes, particularly the dry white and red varieties, were in short supply.

The most recent years, however, have been relatively stable, with a welcome shift away from Riesling toward dry white and dry red varieties. Other states, including California, and foreign countries, including Japan, are now markets for Washington wine and Washington wine grapes.

Large-scale agricultural interests and family-owned farms and ranches are the economic backbone of the Columbia Valley. When it became clear that premium wine grapes were fast becoming an important crop, local farmers and ranchers were quick to respond. Unlike western Oregon, Washington has all the prerequisites for rapid and large-scale expansion. The 18,000 square mile Columbia Valley, the state's principal grape growing area, is not densely populated. Choice vineyard land competes less with residential sprawl. Land is relatively cheap, and vast acreage is available and suitable for grape growing.

The industry's major expansion of the 1980s is tiny compared to the state's capacity for expansion. Cabernet Sauvignon, Merlot, Chardonnay, and Semillon are destined to play a much greater role in the future of the Washington wine industry. It will be primarily from these grapes that the state will make its reputation for excellence.

Washington Winegrowing Regions

Intense & refined wines from a dramatic primordial terrain

Washington state is divided into two distinct and radically different climates, the major grape growing climate east of the Cascade Mountain Range in the vast drainage basin of the Columbia River Valley, and the much cooler and wetter climate west of the Cascade Range. In the Northwest's three state grape growing region, the Columbia Valley's growing climate is the sunniest and warmest. Western Washington's is the cloudiest and coolest.

Because of the climate and economics, very little acreage is devoted to wine grapes in western Washington. By contrast, Columbia Valley grapes and wines dominate not only Washington, but the entire Northwest wine industry. More than 99 percent of Washington wine is made from Columbia Valley grapes. More premium wine grapes are grown in the Columbia Valley than in all other grape growing areas of the Northwest combined. The Columbia Valley is second in quantity only to California in the production of premium vinifera grape wines. Within its boundaries, the expansive Columbia Valley encompasses many grape growing regions, including the Yakima Valley and Walla Walla Valley.

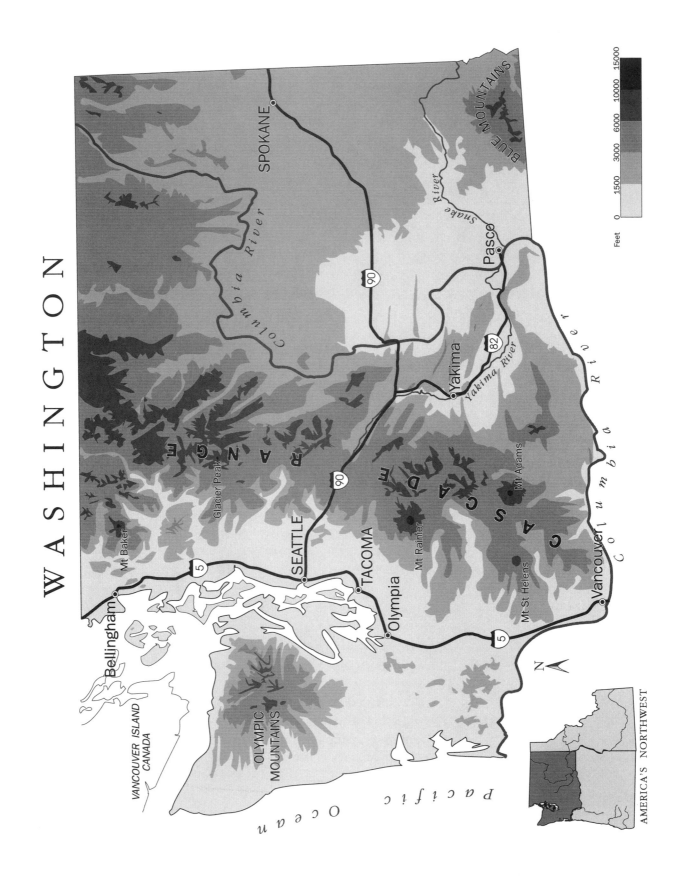

WASHINGTON

Bellingham

Mt Baker

Glacier Peak

SPOKANE

Columbia River

Snake River

BLUE MOUNTAINS

Pasco

90

Yakima

82

Yakima River

C A S C A D E

Mt Adams

R A N G E

90

SEATTLE

TACOMA

Olympia

5

Mt Rainier

Mt St Helens

Columbia River

Vancouver

5

OLYMPIC MOUNTAINS

Pacific Ocean

VANCOUVER ISLAND CANADA

N

Feet

15000
10000
6000
3000
1500
0

AMERICA'S NORTHWEST

Columbia Valley

More premium wine
grapes are grown in the
Columbia Valley
than in all other grape
growing areas of the
Northwest combined.
The Columbia Valley is
second in quantity
only to California in the
production of premium
vinifera grape wines.

In December of 1984, the Bureau of Alcohol, Tobacco, and Firearms (BATF) formally recognized the Columbia Valley as an American viticultural area. One hundred and eighty-five miles wide and 200 miles long, the Columbia Valley covers approximately 23,000 square miles. Except for a portion of land between Banks Lake and the Snake River Valley which has a growing season too short for wine grapes, all of the Columbia Valley is included in the designated viticultural area. Encompassing 18,000 square miles, the Columbia Valley viticultural area is by far the Northwest's largest, covering a nearly a third the land mass of Washington.

The open, gently undulating terrain is bordered on the west by the foothills of the Cascade Mountain Range, on the north by the Okanogan Highlands that extend into Canada, on the east by the rolling hills of the Palouse, and on the south, in Oregon, by the Blue Mountains and their foothills, and the foothills of the Cascade Range. Most of the Columbia Valley's land and nearly all its grape growing is in Washington, but some of the land and grape growing activity extends into Oregon as well. Within its boundaries, the Columbia Valley includes two other viticultural areas, the Yakima Valley and Walla Walla Valley.

As a winegrowing climate, the Columbia Valley is unique. A short distance from the Pacific Ocean, the towering peaks of the Cascade Range thrust more than 12,000 feet above sea level. The Cascade Range runs north to south through Washington and Oregon, forming a nearly continuous wall of mountains, blocking the flow of Pacific marine air, and creating a giant rain shadow extending across the Columbia Valley for hundreds of miles. The rain shadow renders the vast Columbia Valley a near desert. Much of the valley receives less than ten inches of rain a year. Except near rivers and streams, the land is naturally treeless. Grasses and sagebrush are the most common natural vegetation, but the famed Columbia River and its tributaries provide ample irrigation water, transforming the Columbia Valley into a rich agricultural region.

The growing season ranges from a low of 150 days, to a high of just over 200 days. Contrary to expectations for this northerly American winegrowing region, cool climate wine grapes are not the only suitable grape varieties. Measured in terms of heat summation units, the Columbia Valley encompasses the full range of the University of California's climatic regions, from the coolest Region I through the warmest Region V. All Columbia Valley vineyards, however, are on growing sites classified as Region I, II, or III, most are in Regions I and II.

The U. C. Davis climate classification system is only a rough guide, and far from adequately captures the unique nature of the Columbia Valley's grape growing environments and their effect on the grapes and wine. The classification system, however, begins to illustrate how the Columbia Valley, often associated with Riesling, can con-

Columbia Valley
Columbia Slopes

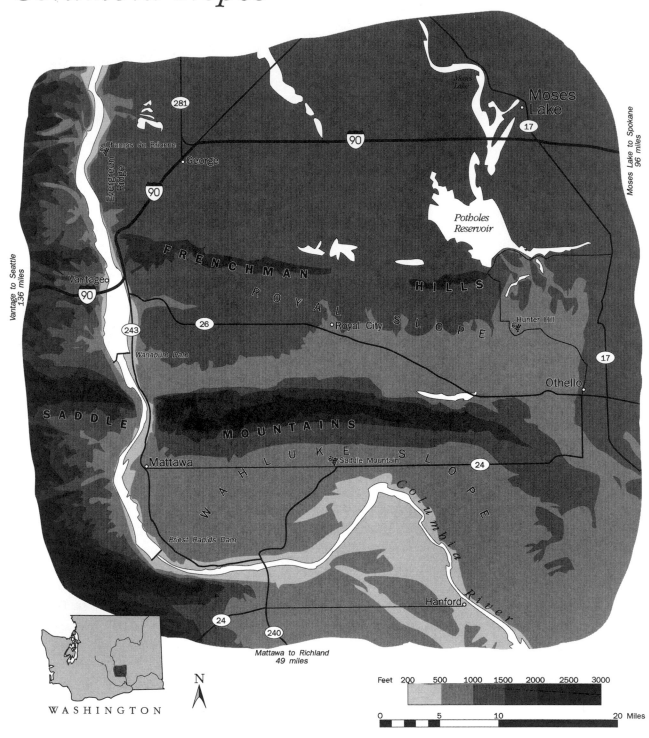

Moses Lake

Moses Lake to Spokane 96 miles

281

Champs de Brionne

George

90

90

Potholes Reservoir

17

FRENCHMAN

ROYAL

HILLS

SLOPE

Evergreen Ridge

Vantage

Vantage to Seattle 136 miles

90

243

26

Royal City

Hunter Hill

17

Wanapum Dam

SADDLE

Othello

MOUNTAINS

WAHLUKE SLOPE

Saddle Mountain

Mattawa

24

Columbia River

Priest Rapids Dam

Hanford

24

240

Mattawa to Richland 49 miles

WASHINGTON

N

Feet 200 500 1000 1500 2000 2500 3000

0 5 10 20 Miles

Columbia Valley
Pasco Basin

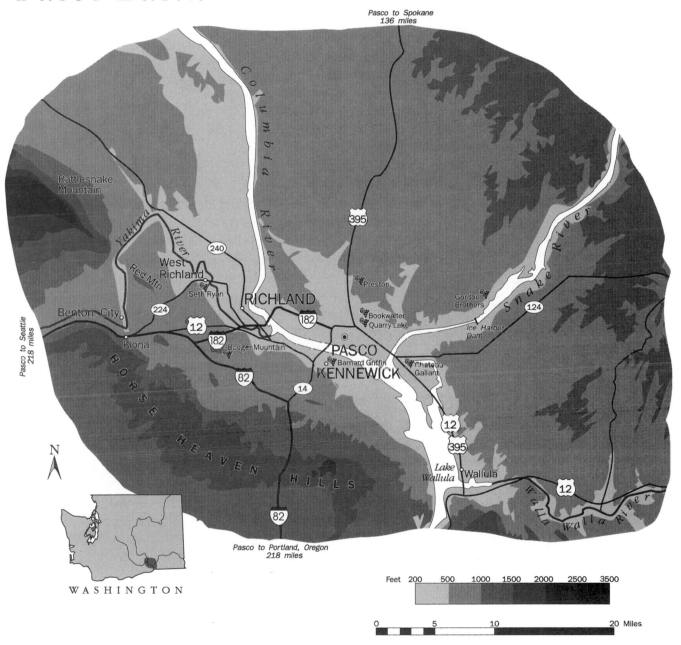

Pasco to Spokane
136 miles

Columbia River

Pasco to Seattle
218 miles

Rattlesnake Mountain

Yakima River

Red Mtn

West Richland

240

Seth Ryan

RICHLAND

395

Preston

Bookwalter

Quarry Lake

Gordon Brothers

Snake River

124

Ice Harbor Dam

Benton City

224

182

12

Kiona

182

Badger Mountain

82

PASCO

Barnard Griffin

KENNEWICK

Chateau Gallant

14

12

395

HORSE HEAVEN HILLS

Lake Wallula

Wallula

82

Pasco to Portland, Oregon
218 miles

12

Walla Walla River

N

WASHINGTON

Feet 200 500 1000 1500 2000 2500 3500

0 5 10 20 Miles

sistently produce excellent wines from warmer climate varieties such as Cabernet Sauvignon and Semillon.

In many respects, the Columbia Valley growing climate is ideal. Under cloudless skies, warm sunny days are followed by cool clear nights. Because of the northerly latitude, day length is longer during the growing season. Rain during harvest is rare. Winter freezing presents the only major critical problem for grape growers, but better viticultural practices have greatly lessened the danger.

The growing season is relatively short and intense. At midsummer, during the height of the grape vine's vegetative period, the Columbia Valley averages two more hours sunlight than the Napa Valley. Temperatures remain in a range ideal for photosynthesis and vine growth, and grape sugars rise rapidly. As fall and the final grape ripening approaches, day length rapidly decreases and the intense heat of the summer gives way to rapidly moderating temperatures. Because the final ripening of the grapes does not take place under conditions of intense heat, the grape's volatile aromatics and flavoring components are preserved.

In the cloudless, near desert climate, nighttime temperatures are relatively cool, even in the middle of summer. Nighttime coolness becomes increasingly pronounced as fall approaches. Because acid reduction is mostly dependent on warm temperatures, but increases in grape sugar depend on both warm temperatures and sunlight, the combination of cool nights and warm sunny days produces grapes that retain adequate acidity even at relatively high sugar levels. The Columbia Valley can produce grapes with higher sugar levels usually associated with more southerly growing climates, but because of the Columbia Valley's unique climate, adequate acids, and complex fruit flavors and aromatics are preserved.

Every winegrowing region has characteristics that are both problems and opportunities for the winegrower. In Europe's premium winegrowing regions, winegrowers work with grapes that tend to be low in sugar and high in acid, Californians with grapes that tend to be high in sugar and low in acid. Columbia Valley winegrowers work with grapes that can be abundant in both sugar and acid. Although one of the Columbia Valley's assets, this is sometimes too much of a good thing. One of the challenges for the Washington wine industry has been to develop viticultural practices that insure the grapes will not be simultaneously overripe with too high an acid content, and to develop winemaking practices to handle grapes with these tendencies.

Frost and winter cold present the only serious problem for Columbia Valley winegrowers. Not totally an inland climate, some marine air still reaches the Columbia Valley to moderate temperature extremes. The Columbia River Gorge, cutting through the Cascade Range, provides a pathway for the marine air to reach the inland valleys. The marine influence is enough to allow the grape vines to

The combination of cool nights and warm sunny days produces grapes that retain adequate acidity even at relatively high sugar levels. Because of the Columbia Valley's unique climate, adequate acids, and complex fruit flavors and aromatics are preserved.

Columbia Valley

Horse Heaven Hills

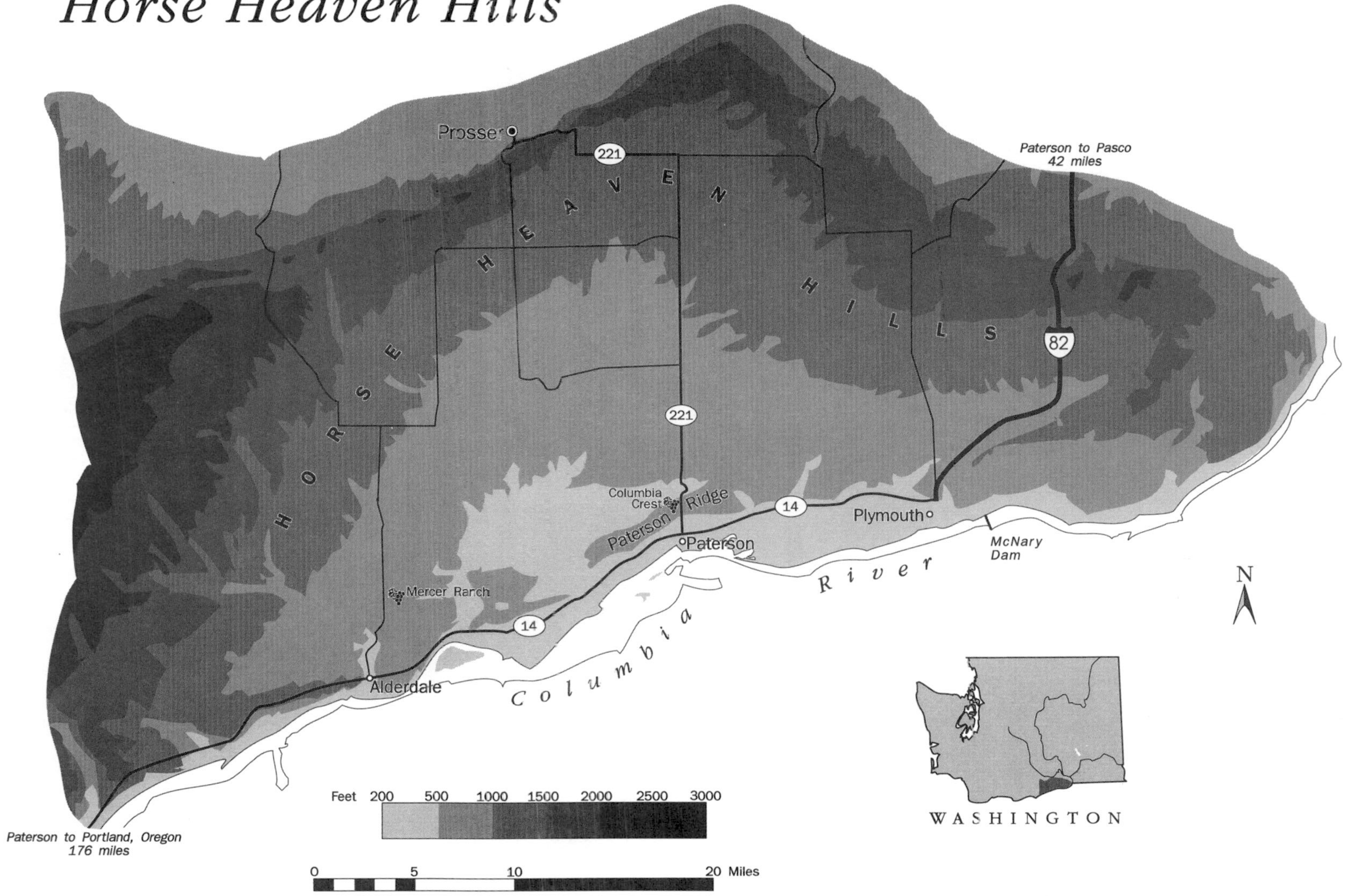

Paterson to Pasco
42 miles

82

N

McNary
Dam

Plymouth

River

14

WASHINGTON

Columbia Crest
Ridge

221

Paterson

Paterson

Columbia

221

221

Prosser

14

Mercer Ranch

Alderdale

H O R S E

H E A V E N

H I L L S

Paterson to Portland, Oregon
176 miles

| Feet | 200 | 500 | 1000 | 1500 | 2000 | 2500 | 3000 |

0 5 10 20 Miles

survive the winter cold, but not enough to totally free the wine-grower from the concerns of frosts and winter freezes.

The same Cascade Mountains that block the onshore flow of marine air and help create ideal grape growing conditions during the summer months, also block the moderating marine influences in winter. The rain shadow of summer becomes the snow shadow of winter, and the frequent lack of insulating snow cover leaves the vines more vulnerable to cold. Spring and fall frosts can also be a problem, damaging the newly budded vines, shortening the growing season, and preventing the vines from hardening their wood for the winter cold. In winter, cold temperatures can freeze the nascent buds, vine trunks, and even kill the vines at their roots.

Improved grape growing practices have greatly lessened the threat and severity of winter damage. Winegrowers can expect some vine damage or crop reduction several times a decade in most growing sites, but total vine kill is rare, and for most winegrowers following proper cultural practices, frosts or severe winters mean little more than a temporary reduction in the crop level. An unusual series of frosts and freezes in the mid '80s damaged vines and reduced the grape crop, but, at the same time, further proved that winegrowing in the Columbia Valley is viticulturally and economically viable. The continuing survival of vines from the last century, remnants of an earlier winegrowing era, offer the weight of history to the Columbia Valley winegrowing enterprise.

The Columbia Valley is the Northwest's most versatile winegrowing region. More varieties grow well in the Columbia Valley than in any other Northwest climate. With proper site selection, virtually all the major grape varieties will ripen, develop good varietal flavors, and maintain desired acid levels. And as a bonus, warm days of sunshine, nighttime cooling, and the control of moisture through irrigation provide an excellent climatic environment for sweet botrytised wines.

Vineyards can be pruned for modest yields for premium wines, yet because the climate allows high yields while maintaining good acid balance and varietal definition, the region lends itself well to the production of premium "jug" wines. The large blocks of land available for cultivation and the typically gentle slopes make mechanical harvesting easily feasible. Premium wines, however, gave birth to Washington's modern wine industry, and premium wines continue to be the industry's foundation as well as its glory.

Columbia Valley growing areas include the Yakima Valley; Walla Walla Valley; Horse Heaven Hills, near the Columbia River and Oregon border; Pasco Basin, in the wide "U" of land formed by the confluence of the Columbia and Snake Rivers; and further north along the Columbia River, Cold Creek Valley; and the Wahluke and Royal Slopes.

In the last ten million years, the northward movement of coastal land masses folded and buckled the western portion of the Colum-

> **The Columbia Valley is the Northwest's most versatile winegrowing region. More varieties grow well in the Columbia Valley than in any other Northwest climate.**

bia Valley, creating a series of high ridges. Running east to west, the ridges act as barriers to the winter arctic air from the north, and many of their lower slopes offer ideal vineyard sites with extended south facing exposures and good air drainage. Examples of these ridges are the Saddle Mountains, Rattlesnake Hills, Ahtanum Ridge, and Frenchman Hills.

Some of the ridges already figure prominently in viticultural activity. Most Yakima Valley vineyards, for example, are situated on the lower slopes of the Rattlesnake Hills. The Wahluke Slope, near the town of Mattawa, on lower southern slope of the Saddle Mountains, has only recently seen viticultural development, but is already recognized as a major grape growing area. Other sites, such as the Royal Slope on the lower reaches of the Frenchman Hills, are promising, but have had little development.

For all the many thousands of square miles in the Columbia Valley viticultural area, only a very small portion has been developed for grape growing. The climate is so unique and the region so diverse that the Columbia Valley's full potential as a winegrowing region is scarcely known, and may not really be understood for decades.

Yakima Valley

The Yakima Valley is shaped not so much by the course of the river itself, but by ridges formed from basaltic uplifts millions of years ago.

In May of 1983, the Yakima Valley became the Northwest's first viticultural area recognized by the BATF. Wholly contained within the more encompassing Columbia Valley appellation, the Yakima Valley is the most intensely developed agricultural region in the Columbia Valley. Nearly 75 miles long and 22 miles wide at broadest point, the Yakima Valley encompasses slightly more than 1,000 square miles.

One of the Columbia River's major tributaries, the Yakima River emerges from the Northwest in the Cascade Mountains, meeting the Columbia River near the southern border of the state, just before the Columbia angles abruptly westward toward the Pacific Ocean. The Yakima Valley is the most geographically distinct of the Columbia Valley's major grape growing areas. The Yakima Valley is shaped not so much by the course of the river itself, but by ridges formed from basaltic uplifts in the terrain millions of years ago. Running in a generally east to west direction, the ridges define the shape of the valley.

Just south of the city of Yakima, the Ahtanum Ridge and Rattlesnake Hills define the Yakima Valley's northern boundary. The Toppenish Ridge and Horse Heaven Hills form the southern boundary, and the foothills of the Cascade Mountains form the western boundary. On the east, the southeastern extension of the Rattlesnake Hills, Red Mountain, and Badger Mountain separate the Yakima Valley viticultural area from the rest of the vast Columbia Valley. Most of the valley's vineyards are located on gently sloping

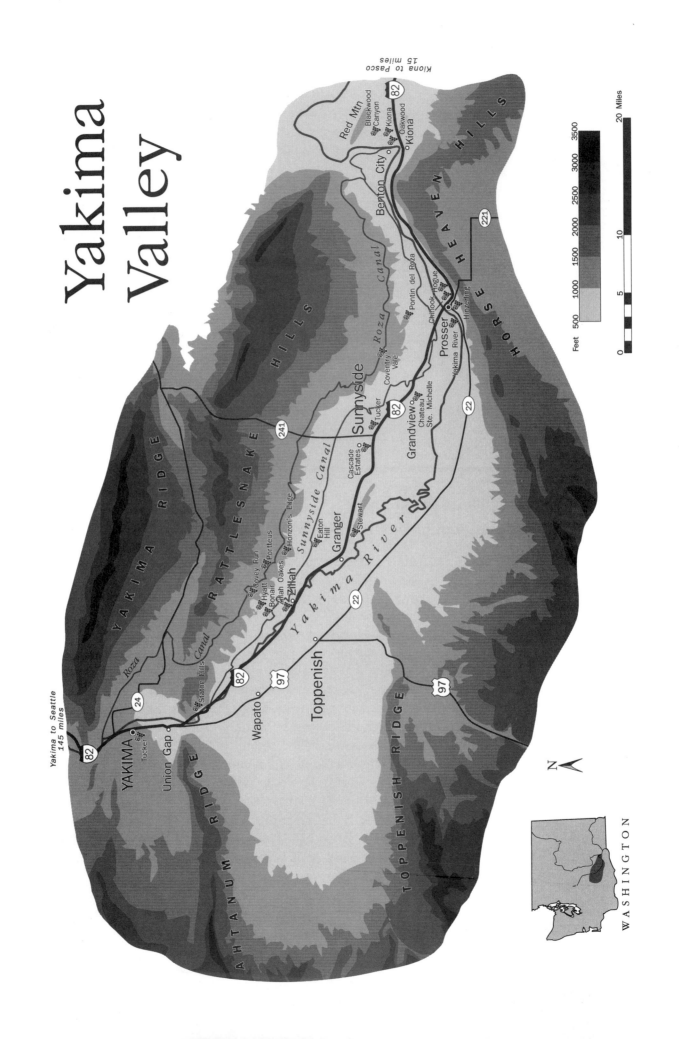

sites on the eastern side of the Yakima River, on the lower slopes of the Rattlesnake Hills.

Much of the Columbia Valley is desolate, but the Yakima Valley is dotted with many small cities and towns. The terrain is dry and naturally treeless. Sagebrush and grasses cover the higher slopes of the golden brown hills, but since the early 1900s, irrigation canal systems have opened up much of the land for intense agricultural development. The irrigation systems turned the Yakima Valley into an agricultural center, home for a wide range of crops, including many tree fruits, vegetables, hops, mint—and grapes.

Native American grape varieties, mostly Concord, predominate, planted not for wine, but for grape juice. The native American varieties have been widely cultivated since the early 1900s, but vinifera wine grapes did not become an important crop until the 1970s. Native American grape varieties still greatly outnumber wine grapes, but they play no role in the Yakima Valley wine industry.

In terms of the grape growing climate classification system developed at U. C. Davis, most of the Yakima Valley is classified as Region II. The growing season averages approximately 190 days. An outstanding wine producing region, the Yakima Valley is slightly cooler than most of the Columbia Valley's other major grape growing areas. The Yakima Valley winegrowing climate varies significantly among different growing sites, however, and a wide range of grape varieties can be matched to the varying locations. Frost and winter cold damage can be problems, so careful selection of vineyard sites is key to wine quality and consistent crop yields.

Although the cooler climate or earlier ripening varieties such as Riesling and Gewurztraminer are especially well suited to many growing sites, the Yakima Valley has earned an excellent reputation for warmer climate varieties such as Cabernet Sauvignon.

Walla Walla Valley
Washington

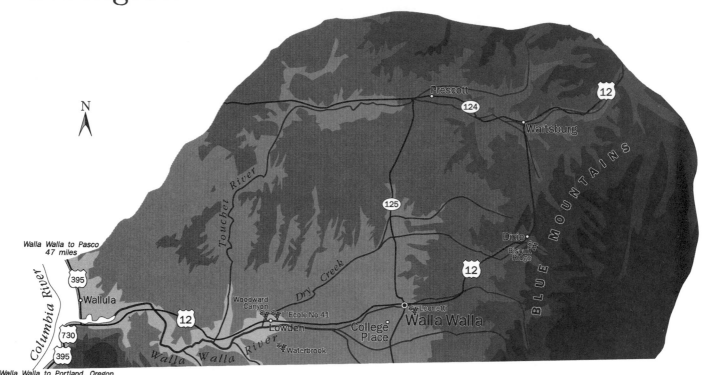

N

Walla Walla to Pasco
47 miles

Columbia River

395

Wallula

730

395

Walla Walla to Portland, Oregon
262 miles

Touchet River

Dry Creek

Woodward
Canyon

L'Ecole No 41

Lowden

Waterbrook

Walla Walla River

12

College
Place

Walla Walla

Leonetti

125

12

Dixie

Biscuit
Ridge

Prescott

124

Waitsburg

12

BLUE MOUNTAINS

WASHINGTON

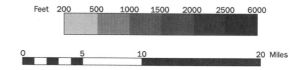

Feet 200 500 1000 1500 2000 2500 6000

0 5 10 20 Miles

Walla Walla Valley

In March of 1984, the Walla Walla Valley became a BATF viticultural area. Part of the more encompassing Columbia Valley appellation, the Walla Walla Valley, like the Columbia Valley, includes land in both Washington and Oregon. Also like the Columbia Valley, most Walla Walla winegrowing is centered on the Washington side of the border, in the southeast portion of the state. A dormant wine industry awaiting rebirth, some of Washington's first grapes for wine were grown in the Walla Walla Valley during the last century.

The Walla Walla Valley viticultural area is relatively small, encompassing approximately 280 square miles. Slightly moister than most of the Columbia Valley, a variety of grasses share space with the Columbia Valley's ever present sagebrush. Damaging winter freezes can sometimes prove severe. Several wineries are located in the Walla Walla Valley, but as yet few acres are planted to wine grapes. Walla Walla winegrowing climates are quite varied. So far, Cabernet Sauvignon has shown fine promise. Early indications suggest that the Walla Walla Valley will become an important source for quality wine grapes.

Columbia Gorge

Along the narrow Gorge, the radically different climates of the hot, dry Columbia Valley and the moist temperate western marine climate converge and collide.

The confluence of the Columbia and Klickitat Rivers near the town of The Dalles marks the eastern boundary of the Columbia Valley. To the west, the Columbia River courses through the Columbia River Gorge, a geologically and climatically dramatic area. Here the Columbia River cuts through the otherwise unbreachable barrier of the Cascade Mountain Range. Along the narrow Gorge, the radically different climates of the hot, dry Columbia Valley and the moist temperate western marine climate converge and collide. Winds race incessantly through the Gorge, and major climatic differences occur within short distances.

Land suitable for vineyards is limited, but both the Washington and Oregon side of the border are home for wineries and vineyards. Grenache grows well in the warmest growing sites in the eastern part of the Gorge. Further west, a number of varieties, including Cabernet Sauvignon, Pinot Noir, Gewurztraminer, and Chardonnay grow successfully. Gewurztraminer from the Bingen and Hood River areas is particularly notable.

Columbia Gorge
Washington

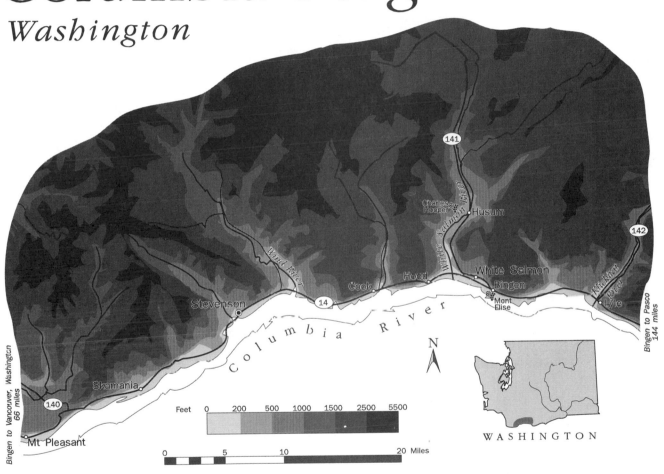

141

142

Charles
Hooper

Husum

White Salmon River

Wind River

Cook

Hood

White Salmon

Bingen

Mont
Elise

Klickitat River

Lyle

Stevenson

14

Skamania

140

Columbia River

Mt Pleasant

Bingen to Vancouver, Washington
66 miles

Bingen to Pasco
144 miles

N

Feet	0	200	500	1000	1500	2500	5500

0	5	10	20 Miles

WASHINGTON

Southwest Washington—Willamette Trough

The southwest corner of Washington is an exception to the general rule that western Washington is significantly cooler and moister than western Oregon. Here the land juts southward behind the northern reaches of Oregon's coastal mountains. This portion of southwest Washington is climatically and geologically associated with Oregon's Willamette Valley.

The area, principally in Clark County, is slightly cooler, but very similar to Oregon's Willamette Valley climate. Grape varieties such as Pinot Noir and Chardonnay predominate, rather than the Puget Sound varieties such as Madeleine Angevine and Muller-Thurgau. For more information on southwest Washington's grape growing climate, refer to the Oregon sections in this book pertaining to the Willamette Valley.

Southwest Washington
Willamette Trough

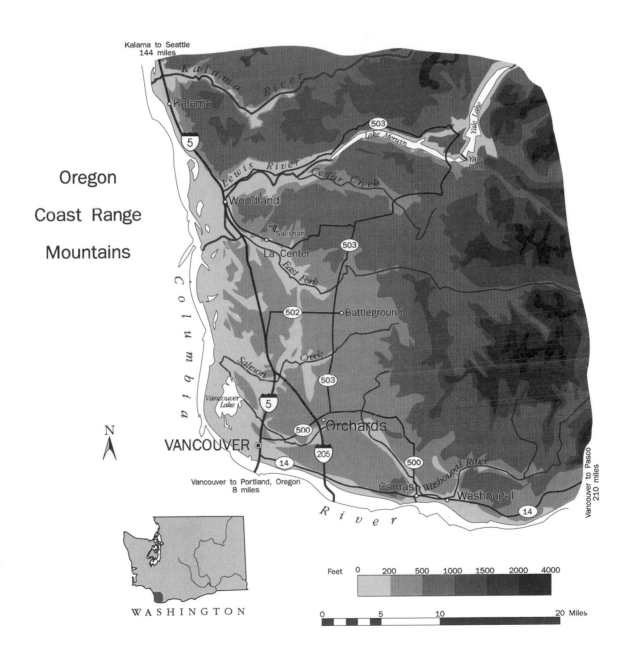

Oregon

Coast Range

Mountains

Kalama to Seattle
144 miles

Kalama River

Kalama

5

Lewis River

Cedar Creek

503

Lake Merwin

Yale Lake

Yale Dam

Woodland

Salishan

La Center

503

East Fork

502

Battleground

Salmon

Creek

503

Vancouver Lake

5

500

Orchards

N

VANCOUVER

205

500

14

Washougal River

Vancouver to Pasco
210 miles

Camas

Washougal

14

Columbia

River

Vancouver to Portland, Oregon
8 miles

WASHINGTON

Feet	0	200	500	1000	1500	2000	4000

0   5   10   20 Miles

Western Washington—Puget Sound

In Washington, unlike Oregon, few wine grapes are grown in the western part of the state. Most of the wineries located in western Washington make wine from Columbia Valley grapes, not from western Washington grapes. The amount of wine made from western Washington grapes is insignificant compared with the volume of wine produced by all of Washington's wineries from Columbia Valley grapes.

Western Washington winegrowing is significant not because of its impact on the marketplace, but for the uniqueness of its wines. Western Washington has the coolest winegrowing climate in America. Most of the wine grapes grown in western Washington are vinifera—usually not the more familiar vinifera varieties such as Cabernet Sauvignon and Riesling, but less familiar varieties more suited to the long but very cool growing season—varieties such as Madeleine Angevine, or the somewhat more familiar Muller-Thurgau.

Oregon's major winegrowing region is situated in western Oregon between a coastal mountain range and the Cascade Range. The Coast Range partially interrupts the direct flow of marine air, rendering most of western Oregon warmer, sunnier, and drier than most of western Washington. In Washington, the Olympic Mountain Range and Canada's Vancouver Island help temper the onshore flow of air from the Pacific Ocean, but western Washington does not have Oregon's continuous coastal barrier to the marine air. Consequently, most of western Washington is cooler, less sunny, and more moist than western Oregon.

In general, western Washington's warmest growing sites are located further away from the coast, on the slopes of Cascade foothills. The warmest sites, however, are also rainier and have shorter growing seasons. The best growing sites are situated where these conflicting tendencies are balanced, or in localized climates offering special advantage. Grapes are grown on selected sites all along western Washington from the Canadian to Oregon border. Vineyards are typically very small. The principal Puget Sound grape growing areas include the Nooksack, Puyallup, and Carbon River Valleys, and Bainbridge Island in Puget Sound.

Seattle Metropolitan Area

WASHINGTON
Other Washington Wineries

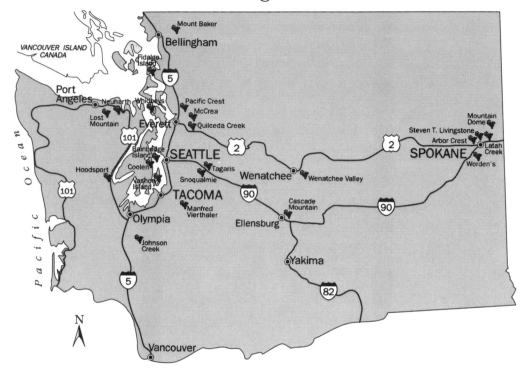

Washington Wineries

Diversity is the rule, sized from tiny to tremendous

Arbor Crest Winery

For three generations, the Mielke family has grown and processed fruit near the city of Spokane. David Mielke continued operating the family business, while brother Harold Mielke pursued a medical career, becoming director of the Institute of Cancer Research at San Francisco's Pacific Medical Center.

In the late 1970s, the brothers started a joint project centered around Harold's interest in wine and David's interest in fruit growing. The Mielkes planted forty different kinds of vinifera, native American, and French-American hybrid grapes in a small six acre experimental vineyard on the family farm.

Interest in grape growing stimulated interest in a winery, and in 1982, the Mielkes hired Scott Harris, a U. C. Davis graduate in enology, then assistant winemaker at California's Davis Bynum winery. The Mielkes sold their cherry processing equipment and moved in winemaking equipment.

The experimental vineyard showed them that the Spokane area was not suitable for premium vinifera wine grapes, the kind of grapes they wanted for Arbor Crest's wines. Arbor Crest buys grapes from several growers throughout the Columbia Valley.

Arbor Crest Winery

North 4705 Fruithill Road
Spokane, Washington 99207
(509) 927-9463

Owners
David & Harold Mielke

Winemaker
Scott Harris

Wine Production
80,000 gallons

Vineyard Acreage
88 acres

Year First Planted
1982

First Vintage
1982

Wines Produced
Chardonnay, Sauvignon Blanc, Riesling, Dry Riesling, Merlot, Cabernet Sauvignon, Muscat Canelli, Jardin des Fleurs Blush, Late Harvest Gewurztraminer, Select Late Harvest Riesling

---

The Mielkes also joined a grape growing partnership and planted a vineyard on the Wahluke Slope, one of Washington's most promising new grape growing areas.

What does Scott Harris, a U. C. Davis graduate and California winemaker for five years, think of Washington grapes and Washington wine? "What amazes me so much," says Harris, "is that the grapes are damn near perfect. The acids and sugars need little or no correction."

In California, the grapes are usually very warm when they come into the winery, and the winery, unless cooled, is warm as well. "I was unprepared for my first crush at Arbor Crest," says Harris. "The grapes were cool, and we had a cellar temperature of 48 degrees. In California, for the white wines, we always had to chill the must before we could ferment. Here, we just start making the wine."

For most medium-size and larger Washington wineries, Riesling is the predominant wine, and Riesling is the first wine shipped to out-of-state markets. At Arbor Crest, the approach is different.

White wines comprise 80 percent of Arbor Crest's production, but Chardonnay and Sauvignon Blanc, not Riesling, account for nearly half the winery's production. "Instead of Riesling," says Harris, "we use Chardonnay to put us into new markets."

Only French oak is used for barrel aging. In typical Washington style, the white wines emphasize crisp acidity and the fruit of the grape. But within this style, Arbor Crest's whites have a fuller, more textural quality. Arbor Crest's Sauvignon Blanc and Chardonnay are finished with a slight amount of residual sugar, contributing a more full-bodied, softer impression. Purists may not favor this style, but the wines have been exceptionally popular regionally and nationally.

The original winery was well equipped, but the corrugated steel, one-time cherry processing building was not the last word in esthetics. For the winery's new home, the Mielkes purchased Spokane's historic Riblet mansion and estate. Renamed the Arbor Crest Cliff House, the mansion is located on a basalt outcropping 450 feet above the winding Spokane River. The Cliff House, a national historic landmark, houses Arbor Crest's tasting room and visitors' center.

Badger Mountain Vineyard

Badger Mountain Vineyard is the largest fully organic vineyard in the Northwest. Is this a nouveau marketing gimmick, or a starry-eyed business venture by a group radical environmentalists fleeing the urban milieu?

It is neither. From an environmental perspective, organic

farming is intrinsically good, but Bill Powers efforts have long roots and an authenticity that make his organic viticulture all the more meaningful. Powers has been a farmer and orchardist since the 1950s, and a wine grape grower

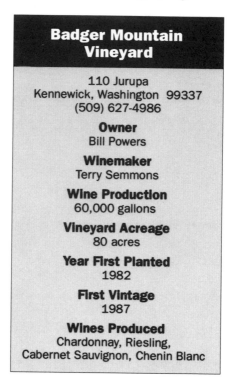

Badger Mountain Vineyard

110 Jurupa
Kennewick, Washington 99337
(509) 627-4986

Owner
Bill Powers

Winemaker
Terry Semmons

Wine Production
60,000 gallons

Vineyard Acreage
80 acres

Year First Planted
1982

First Vintage
1987

Wines Produced
Chardonnay, Riesling,
Cabernet Sauvignon, Chenin Blanc

since 1982. Why, in 1989, did he suddenly go to fully organic farming?

"I finally just got sick of dumping on all that stuff," says Powers. "In later years, they were telling us not to go back in for seven days after we put on some of the stuff. In the 1950s and 1960s, we wouldn't even cover up when we put it on. It wasn't supposed to be a problem. Either people were not telling us the truth, or they were ignorant.

"What they let you put on now isn't as bad, and there are more precautions, but it's still no good, and maybe we're still not getting the truth, and maybe people still don't know what all the effects are. Our vineyard is pretty close to Kennewick, and we have people riding horseback and jogging by.

I just didn't want to put the damn stuff on any more."

Powers could not find anyone in the state with information on how to manage an organic vineyard, so he talked to people in California. There are a few organic wine grape vineyards in California, but Powers found his best help from table grape growers near Delano.

A special soap replaces conventional insecticides, killing insects without poisoning them. Blood meal is the fertilizer. Powers reports that blood meal costs four to five times as much as conventional fertilizers, and is only 15 percent nitrogen, but it contributes a broad spectrum of other minerals. If a fungicide is necessary, mined sulfur is applied. Powers is highly pleased with the results.

Powers is straightforward about his reasons for getting into the wine business. Grape prices in 1987 were very poor, and some varieties were nearly unsalable. He started the winery to have more control over the return on his labors and investment, processing juice and making wine in bulk for later resale to other wineries.

Now, Powers operates a custom crush facility, processing grapes into juice and wine for other vineyards and wineries. Most is sold in bulk, but a small portion is released under the Badger Mountain label. All Badger Mountain Chardonnays are barrel fermented. In 1989, Powers shipped his first container of wine to Japan.

Bainbridge Island Winery

Bainbridge Island Vineyards and Winery is a 30 minute ferryboat ride from Seattle's picturesque waterfront. Located a quarter mile from the Bainbridge Island ferry terminal, JoAnn and Gerard Bentryns' winery is dedicated to the production of premium vinifera wines from western Washington grapes.

The first vines were planted in 1978. The Bentryns grow about 20 tons of grapes each year on their

---

Bainbridge Island Winery

682 State Highway 305 N.E.
Bainbridge Island, Washington
98110
(206) 842-9463

Owners
Gerard & JoAnn Bentryn

Winemaker
Gerard Bentryn

Wine Production
5,000 gallons

Vineyard Acreage
5 1/2 acres

Year First Planted
1978

First Vintage
1981

Wines Produced
Muller-Thurgau,
Dry Muller-Thurgau,
Late Harvest Siegerrebe,
Ferryboat White, Strawberry

---

own estate vineyard. Some additional grapes are purchased from other growers in western Washington's Puget Sound area.

Western Washington, particularly the Puget Sound area, is a very cool, moist, growing climate, and the grape varieties and wine styles are quite different from those grown east of the Cascade Mountains in Washington's Columbia Valley. Most of the

Bentryns' grapes are of German origin, and the wines are Germanic in style, low alcohol, crisp, dry to slightly sweet white wines, emphasizing delicate fruit flavors and fragrances.

Muller-Thurgau is the principal variety, but Bentryn is also working with other cool climate vinifera varieties such as Siegerrebe, Pinot Noir, and Pinot Gris, and relatively unknown varieties of French origin such as Madeleine Sylvaner and Madeleine Angevine, both now popularly grown in England as wine grapes. Siegerrebe itself is a cross of Madeleine Angevine and Gewurztraminer.

The Puget Sound growing climate has similarities to both Germany and England, but is not quite the same as either, being cooler and less sunny than Germany, but warmer and drier than England. The Bentryns believe that the cool Puget Sound growing area is ideal for preserving floral intensity and the delicate fruit esters of grapes carefully chosen for the climate.

In the Bentryns' view, Muller-Thurgau does not have the reputation it deserves because it is usually grossly overcropped, and grown where it is too warm and the varietal character is burned out of the grape. The Bentryns crop their vines to a moderate 4 1/2 tons an acre, using labor intensive pruning and training techniques to maximize heat and sunlight for the grape clusters. Grown in this way the Muller-Thurgau has a pronounced varietal character with a distinct musky flavor. Those accustomed to the modestly flavored sugar water usually labeled Muller-Thurgau will be quite surprised at the intense scent and flavors of Bainbridge Island Winery's rendi-

tion of the grape.

Ferryboat White, a varying nonvintage blend of western Washington grapes is Bainbridge Island Winery's least expensive wine. It often displays more interest than the ubiquitous and sometimes overly insistent Columbia Valley Rieslings.

Ardent supporters of the vertically integrated, small, family winery, the Bentryns quit their other jobs to operate all aspects of their enterprise, from grape growing to winemaking to marketing. Nearly all the wine is sold directly from the winery. An attractive winery and tasting room, small wine museum, picnic grounds, and fragrance garden adjoin the vineyard.

Barnard Griffin Wines

Rob Griffin is winemaker and general manager for The Hogue Cellars, one of the Yakima

---

Barnard Griffin Wines

1707 West 8th Place
Kennewick, Washington 99336

Owners
Rob Griffin & Deborah Barnard

Winemaker
Rob Griffin

Wine Production
2,000 gallons

Vineyard Acreage
none

First Vintage
1983

Wines Produced
Cabernet Sauvignon, Chardonnay,
Fume Blanc, Riesling

Valley's leading wineries. In partnership with his wife, Deborah Barnard, Griffin also makes wine for their own, small Barnard Griffin Winery.

The Chardonnay and Sauvignon Blanc are fermented in small French oak barrels. The fermentation temperatures start at about 50 degrees, and peak at about 68 degrees. Griffin does need to control the temperature so that it does not reach any higher than about 68 degrees, however. "I couldn't have fermented the wines this way in California without refrigeration," says Griffin, formerly a California winemaker. "In Washington, when I want to cool down the fermentation temperature in the barrels, I just open the winery doors to the cold October night."

The Chardonnay and Sauvignon Blanc are given extended lees contact. The wine is left in the barrel on the lees (the sediment of dead yeast cells and grape solids) and stirred once a month. The Chardonnay is left on the lees for nearly a year, and goes through a malolactic fermentation.

Biscuit Ridge Winery

A winery situated in the northeastern end of the Walla Walla Valley would be unique enough, but Jack Durham is also specializing in Gewurztraminer—and not just Gewurztraminer, but dry Gewurztraminer, an almost extinct creature in the Northwest.

What about the vineyard climate for growing Gewurztraminer? The Biscuit Ridge vineyard, located in the foothills of the Blue Mountains, is different than other grape growing areas in the Walla Walla Valley. According to Durham, marine air comes up the Columbia and finds a path through the Pendleton, Oregon area, hitting the Blue Mountains, then following their contour into the Washington part of the Walla

Walla Valley.

Durham reports that his vineyard gets 24 inches of rain a year, much more rain than other parts

Biscuit Ridge Winery

Route 1, Box 132
Waitsburg, Washington 99361
(509) 529-4986

Owners
Jack & Helen Durham

Winemaker
Jack Durham

Wine Production
3,000 gallons

Vineyard Acreage
10 acres

Year First Planted
1983

First Vintage
1987

Wines Produced
Gewurztraminer, Pinot Noir

of the valley. Rainfall increases an inch per mile as you travel east into the foothills of the Blue Mountains. According to Durham, the Dixie area, where his vineyard is located, is ten degrees cooler than the city of Walla Walla in the summer. High temperatures virtually never reach the 100 degree mark, and the nights are cool.

Because of the moderate climate, Durham is also pursuing Pinot Noir. Durham planted his first Pinot Noir vines on a 10 foot by 3 foot spacing in the spring of 1989. In the future, Durham may plant the Gamay Beaujolais clone of Pinot Noir for a fruity, early drinking wine.

Prior to release, Durham's Gewurztraminer is aged for two to three years, mostly in stainless steel, but for a brief period in American oak barrels. Durham puts the wine in barrels to round it out, not to achieve a pronounced oak character. The

Gewurztraminers are finished virtually dry, with crisp acidity to age well and go well with food.

Biscuit Ridge is named for a road of the same name that runs past the winery, to an early settlement area in the Blue Mountains called Biscuit Ridge.

Blackwood Canyon Vintners

If you're looking for a nice, simple, commercial wine—a wine designed neither to impress nor offend, Blackwood Canyon is not your winery. If you're looking for a winery visit greeted by personnel with a saccharine smile, memorized platitudes, and a whatever you like is wonderful approach, Blackwood Canyon is not your winery either.

Blackwood Canyon is a radical, take-no-prisoners, anti- commercialistic, extremism in the pursuit of excellence is no vice kind of a winery. Mike Moore is Blackwood Canyon's winemaker, vineyard manager, and iconoclastic radical.

In Moore's view (and to a large extent, at least with respect to the recent past, I agree with him), it's

If you're looking for a nice, simple, commercial wine— a wine designed neither to impress nor offend, Blackwood Canyon is not your winery.

not so much that he's so radical as it is that Washington winemaking has been so U. C. Davis textbook conservative. At a time when many Washington wines, particularly the whites, had evolved into a stylistic formula, Blackwood Canyon's wines had been, and are, distinctly different.

The predominant, Washington, dry, white, wine style has empha-

■ M. Taylor Moore

sized the crisp fresh fruit flavors of the grape, employing such methods as fermentation in temperature controlled stainless steel tanks, "clean," cool fermentations, the absence of a secondary malolactic fermentation, perhaps brief aging in new oak, and, occasionally, bottling "dry" wines with slight residual sugar.

While few Washington wineries match this formula exactly, these have been the elements of an overriding theme. The style is valid and successful, and yet, the style sacrifices too much of the enduring complexities and nuances for overly insistent, simple, fresh fruit flavors.

Moore's wines make no such sacrifice. His winemaking methods combine the techniques of traditional European winemaking practices with approaches of some California boutique wineries, backed by U. C. Davis science. Moore's white wines are fermented in small oak barrels.

The wine is not racked off the lees (grape solids and sediment) for up to two years, often undergoing a gradual malolactic fermentation in the barrel. Different barrels are fermented with as many as seven different yeast strains for added complexity before being blended together for bottling.

Moore likes to ferment his Chardonnay with about 10 to 15 percent solids in the must. To achieve this, he sometimes scrapes out the grape remnants in the crushing tank to add to the barrels. Moore believes that the fear of off flavors from lengthy contact with the lees evolves out of poor vineyard practices and problems arising out of the reductive (starved for oxygen) effects of keeping wines in stainless steel tanks. All Moore's dry white wines are barrel fermented.

Moore's red wines are also made in a unique style. Moore leaves the wine on the skins for up to six or more weeks after the fermentation has completed. Alcohol and water extract different flavors from the grape, and Moore likes the character obtained from the alcohol extractions that predominate after the fermentation has finished. Ironically, the wine is not more tannic for its additional time on the skins. The tannins polymerize and fall out as sediment, reducing the overall tannin to moderate levels. The fermentation temperature is a warm 85 to 90 degrees. To avoid excessive oak flavors, the Cabernet is aged in older oak barrels.

Moore's methods do not fit the Washington norm, but the complex flavors of his wines validate his approach. A graduate in enology from U. C. Davis, with additional training in viticulture, Moore worked with several California wineries before coming to

the Northwest in search of a cooler growing climate to start his own winery.

After a lengthy search, Moore settled on the Red Mountain area and founded Blackwood Canyon Vintners. At the far eastern end of the Yakima Valley, just before merging with the Columbia River, the Yakima River runs into Red Mountain, taking an abrupt turn northward before turning back south to join the Columbia. Situated on the grass and sagebrush covered slopes of Red Mountain, the Blackwood Canyon winery and vineyards overlook the Yakima River, and the long view westward up the valley. The Red Mountain area is one of the warm-

Blackwood Canyon Vintners

Route 2, Box 2169H
Kiona, Washington 99320
(509) 588-6249

Owner
M. Taylor Moore

Winemaker
M. Taylor Moore

Wine Production
90,000 gallons

Vineyard Acreage
51 acres

Year First Planted
1984

First Vintage
1982

Wines Produced
Chardonnay, Semillon,
Dry Riesling, Dry Chenin Blanc,
Cabernet Sauvignon, Merlot,
Late Harvest Wines

est growing areas in the Yakima Valley, and one of the premier sites for Cabernet Sauvignon.

Only a part of Moore's 180 acre site is in vine. The undulating land is comprised of several vineyard areas. Chardonnay is planted on a slight north slope, Cabernet Sauvignon on a warmer, south facing slope. Moore practices what he terms flavor farming, manipulating vine stress to yield the flavors and concentration he desires. The Red Mountain soil is similar in at least certain respects to some of Europe's premium vineyard soils in that it contains a large portion of calcium carbonate, and is a high 8.2 pH.

A tragic fire in October 1985 fire burned Moore's home and winery to the ground, destroying most of Blackwood Canyon's unreleased wines, and setting back the winery's plans. Neighboring wineries helped with the remainder of the year's crush, and Moore rebuilt. At one time, in Washington state, Moore was virtually alone in his approach to winemaking, though now, more wineries are moving in a similar direction, albeit in a more tempered fashion.

Moore is specializing in Cabernet Sauvignon, Chardonnay, Semillon, and late harvest desert wines from several grape varieties. His Cabernet Sauvignon, the best still unreleased, and the late harvest botrytised wines rank among the Northwest's finest. Moore is among those who believe that Semillon is one of Washington's outstanding wine grapes, and he is giving it the winemaking attention it deserves.

At Blackwood Canyon, the unusual is the norm. Moore has made dry Riesling and Chenin Blanc in the style of a barrel fermented Chardonnay, complete with ample lees contact. The Riesling was unusual and surprisingly good. The best of the Chenin Blancs tasted like it was meant to be made that way all along.

Bonair Winery

With Bonair's first commercial vintage, Gail Puryear established Chardonnay as the winery speciality. Although he had made wines at home for a decade, Puryear had never before

■ **Shirley & Gail Puryear**

worked on a commercial scale, so he secured the services of a highly regarded consultant for his first commercial crush.

At the time, few Washington winemakers were putting Chardonnay through malolactic fermentation. The consultant advised against the practice, but Puryear tried it anyway. The results? Puryear's first Chardonnay was among the best in the state, and Puryear's consultant began working with malolactic fermentation in his own wines.

Gail and Shirley Puryear are both Yakima Valley natives. After ten years pursuing their careers in California, the two returned to the Yakima Valley. Gail is a school principal in Toppenish. Shirley, a social worker and teacher, now works full time at the winery. Shirley provides an exuberant and gregarious welcome for winery visitors. Although, refreshingly,

the two don't seem to take themselves too seriously, they take quality winemaking quite seriously indeed.

Many Washington grape growers treat wine grapes just like any other agricultural crop. Lush vigorous foliage, big berries, and a heavy crop are regarded as positives. Unfortunately, for wine grapes, these are significant negatives.

Puryear takes a radically opposite approach to grape growing. His own vineyard has never been fertilized, receives very limited irrigation, and is leaf stripped to reduce and open up the leaf canopy. Puryear also buys grapes from other growers. He steadfastly avoids lush verdant vineyards. "I look for vineyards that look like hell," he says, exaggerating only slightly. Puryear wants grapes that are physiologically ripe at relatively low sugars, not immature grapes with a high malic acid content that are merely high in sugar.

Bonair releases several bot-

Bonair Winery

500 S. Bonair Road
Zillah, WA 98953
(509) 829-6027

Owners
Gail & Shirley Puryear

Winemaker
Gail Puryear

Wine Production
9,000 gallons

Vineyard Acreage
5 acres

Year First Planted
1980

First Vintage
1985

Wines Produced
Chardonnay, Cabernet Sauvignon,
Sunset, Riesling,
Barrel Fermented Dry Riesling,
Nouveau Rouge

tlings of Chardonnay. Some of the Chardonnays are barrel fermented and given extensive lees contact. Puryear's first Chardonnays received only a partial

---

**Lush foliage,
big berries,
and a heavy crop
are not what you want
for quality wine grapes.
"I look for vineyards
that look like hell,"
says Puryear,
exaggerating only
slightly.**

---

malolactic fermentation, but Puryear has refined his techniques so that complete malolactic fermentation is readily achievable.

Although Bonair established its reputation on Chardonnay, upcoming releases of Cabernet Sauvignon may steal the crown. Cabernets from the Puryear and Morrison vineyards have distinctively different characteristics, but both show excellent concentration of fruit, moderate tannins, good structure, and the absence of herbaceous flavors. Bonair's forthcoming releases of Cabernet Sauvignon promise to be among the state's best.

Bookwalter Winery

From 1976 to 1983, Jerry Bookwalter managed Sagemoor Farms, the Northwest's largest, independent, wine grape, vineyard operation. In 1983, Bookwalter left Sagemoor to start his own grape and wine marketing services—and to start his own winery. Additionally, in 1988,

Bookwalter joined forces with viticulturalist Tom Thorsen and began Thorsen, Bookwalter, and Associates to manage vineyard properties.

Bookwalter has no vineyards of his own, and prefers it that way. In Bookwalter's view, buying grapes on the open market allows for much greater flexibility. Knowing grape growing areas, vineyards, and grapes is an intrinsic part of Bookwalter's consulting and brokerage services—an advantage when it comes to choosing and buying grapes for his own winery.

Bookwalter buys grapes from many parts of Washington's vast Columbia Valley, including the Royal Slope, one of the state's newer and more northerly growing areas. The Royal Slope is located on the lower reaches of the Frenchman Hills, east of the community of Vantage. The Wahluke

---

Bookwalter Winery

2708 Commercial Avenue
Pasco, Washington 99301
(509) 547-8571

Owners
Jerry & Jean Bookwalter

Winemaker
Jerry Bookwalter

Wine Production
12,000 gallons

Vineyard Acreage
none

Year First Planted
1983

Wines Produced
Chardonnay, Cabernet Sauvignon,
Chenin Blanc, Muscat Blanc,
Riesling, Sparkling Wine,
Red Table Wine,
Late Harvest Riesling

---

slope, just south of the Royal Slope, is one of Washington's most promising new grape growing areas.

"I think that great wine is made in the vineyard," says Bookwalter. "There is high art to winemaking, but a winemaker can't create quality that isn't in the grapes. The best he can do is capture 100 percent of what the grapes offer. We try to locate pockets of greatness in the vineyards, and turn them into the best wines possible." Bookwalter sees his winery as very consumer oriented. He prefers to make high quality, popularly styled, user friendly wines.

Cascade Estates

Although Cascade Estates is one of Washington's newer, larger wineries, its key personnel are far from newcomers to the Washington wine scene. Winery founder, Toby Halbert, is a Washington native. Halbert held several engineering and personnel management positions during his 20 years at Boeing. Halbert migrated to Chateau Ste. Michelle, in 1977, as Vice President of Operations, before leaving to start Cascade Estates.

Joining Halbert is horticulturist Bob Fay, General Manager of the Sunnyside Land Group, a 250 acre Yakima Valley vineyard operation. Fay spent 11 years as a viticultural research specialist, at the Washington State experimental station in Prosser, prior to his commercial ventures.

The Sunnyside Land Group is the principal grape supplier for Cascade Estates. Although the initial wine releases were either purchased from other sources or made elsewhere, the winery's style and merit will ultimately be demonstrated by winemaker Christopher Smith. Smith comes to Cascade Estates from California's Jordan Winery, where he

Cascade Estates

111 East Lincoln Ave.
Sunnyside, Washington 98944
(509) 839-9463

13649 N.E. 126th Place, #104
Kirkland, Washington 98034

Owners
Corporation—principal
stockholders include Toby Halbert,
Bob Fay, William Pierson, &
Stanley Zeitz

Winemaker
Christopher Smith

Wine Production
300,000 gallons

Vineyard Acreage
none

First Vintage
1987

Wines Produced
Cabernet Sauvignon, Merlot,
Chardonnay, Sauvignon Blanc,
Gewurztraminer, Riesling,
Chenin Blanc, Semillon,
Muscat Canelli, Blush

was Assistant Enologist.

Cascade Estates has a tasting room and small winemaking facility in Kirkland, a suburb of Seattle, but the principal production facility is in the Yakima Valley, near the source of the grapes. A refurbished, former, Carnation Dairy plant in Sunnyside offered a readily available winery for Cascade Estate's rapid start-up. Cascade Estates is specializing in what are termed "fighting varietals," premium grape wines finished in a popular style and sold at a moderate price.

Cascade Mountain Cellars

Born and raised in Germany, Juergen Grieb studied winemaking at the Enology Institute in Trier, then worked for several German wineries. Grieb was employed with the giant German winemaking firm, F. W. Langguth, when he was sent to Langguth's newly founded outpost in Washington state.

At Langguth's Mattawa, Washington winery, Grieb met his wife-to-be, Julia. The two left Langguth to start their own winery in Ellensburg, Washington. The Griebs' winery is housed in the old, historic, Northern Pacific train depot. The rich woodwork, 18 foot high ceilings, and terrazzo floors set the Cascade Mountain Cellars

Cascade Mountain Cellars

606 West Third
Ellensburg, Washington 98926
(509) 925-2998

Owners
Juergen & Julia Grieb

Winemaker
Juergen Grieb

Wine Production
8,000 gallons

Vineyard Acreage
none

First Vintage
1987

Wines Produced
Chardonnay, "Vouvray," Merlot,
Sunset Blush, Chenin Blanc

winery apart from the ordinary. The old ticket window now serves as the winery's tasting bar.

Grieb is specializing in wines made "in the German style," light and fruity, with moderate alcohol, and, usually, some residual sweetness. Although the Northwest has gotten away from naming wines after European place names such as "Burgundy" and "Chablis," Grieb has chosen to name one of his Chenin Blancs "Vouvray," a French wine of the Loire Valley made from the Chenin Blanc grape.

Cavatappi Winery

The Cavatappi Winery is an outgrowth of Peter Dow's Cafe Juanita, a restaurant specializing in northern Italian cuisine and known for its fine food and cordial atmosphere. At Cafe Juanita, the emphasis is on the food, and a comfortable ambiance, rather than the ritualistic pomp and puffery that mars many "fine dining" experiences. If you like valet parking and stiff-necked waiters, look elsewhere.

The winery is in the expanded basement of the restaurant. Production is small, and most of the wine is sold only at the restaurant to accompany the food. Recently, the wines have become available on a very limited basis through a few Seattle area wine merchants. Dow is a thoroughly irreverent individual with a thorough reverence for fine food and fine wine.

Cavatappi Winery

9702 N.E. 120th Place
Kirkland Washington 98034
(206) 823-6533

Owner
Peter Dow

Winemaker
Peter Dow

Wine Production
1,500 gallons

Vineyard Acreage
none

First Vintage
1985

Wines Produced
Maddalena (Nebbiolo),
Sauvignon Blanc,
Cabernet Sauvignon

The restaurant wine list offers a broad selection of Italian wines, as well as Dow's own.

Most notable is Dow's work with the great Italian wine grape, Nebbiolo, the grape of Italian

Barolo and Barbaresco. In cooperation with superb grape grower, Mike Sauer, of Red Willow Vineyards, Dow is producing the Northwest's only Nebbiolo. Nebbiolo is an exceptional but highly fickle grape, and Dow and Sauer are working hard to develop its potential in Washington state.

Nebbiolo grape clusters are massive. Even with radical pruning, the first crop from the vines was very large, and the wine was good, but a bit diffuse. Subsequent vintages have begun to demonstrate the excellence of the grape, and Washington's potential for fine Nebbiolo wine.

Dow has made pilgrimages to Italy, working the Nebbiolo crush with the famed Angelo Gaja. The distinguished Gaja returned the visit, and ventured to the Red Willow Vineyard in the Yakima Valley with Dow. In a "me too" world of ubiquitous Cabernet and Chardonnay, Dow's work with Nebbiolo is most welcome.

Champs de Brionne

On a high bank, overlooking the Columbia River and the massive basalt cliffs cut by its course, the Champs de Brionne estate embraces one of the most scenic views in Washington's wine country—but the site was not chosen merely for the view. Several trips to Europe and a conviction in the excellence of Washington winegrowing climates prompted Vince and Carol Bryan to travel Washington seeking a site for their vineyards.

From their studies, the Bryans made a list of eleven key characteristics for their vineyard site. Their European travels led them to give more than usual emphasis

to soil type. Working with soil test reports prepared by the Army Corps of Engineers for the Grand Coulee Dam project, their quest took them outside the already established growing areas to the center of the state, and a vineyard site near Quincy Washington. Champs de Brionne's soil is high in calcium carbonate with a pH of 7.8.

Situated on Evergreen Ridge, 900 feet above the Columbia River, the vineyard's soils are not the only factor that makes the site special for growing grapes. Tempered by the nearby Columbia, Champs de Brionne has a 195 day growing season.

Comparing the growing climate with the Yakima Valley, for example, a more established growing region, bud break (the seasons new growth) is two weeks later, and spring frosts are not a threat as they are in the Yakima Valley. At 2,800 heat units,

---

On a high bank, overlooking the Columbia River and the massive basalt cliffs cut by its course, the Champs de Brionne estate embraces one of the more scenic views in Washington's wine country.

---

the growing climate has a greater heat accumulation than many Yakima growing sites, but the greater accumulations occur in the summer, during the grapevine's vegetative period.

In the fall, during the final ripening of the grapes, when overly warm temperatures can burn out

---

Champs de Brionne

98 Road West N.W.
Quincy, WA 98848
(509) 785-6685

Owners
Partnership:
Vince & Carol Bryan,
Managing Partners

Winemaker
Kevin McGuire

Wine Production
90,000 gallons

Vineyard Acreage
130 acres

Year First Planted
1980

First Vintage
1983

Wines Produced
Cabernet Sauvignon, Merlot, Pinot Noir, Pinot Noir Blush, Sauvignon Blanc, Chenin Blanc, Semillon, Chardonnay, Riesling

---

delicate flavors, the temperatures are actually cooler than many sites in the Yakima Valley. Chilling late fall temperatures come abruptly, however, making fall frosts, and the vine's final energy gathering period before winter, all the more critical. The final ripening of the grapes typically takes place some two weeks later at Champs de Brionne.

Prompted by similarities in soil and climate with France's Burgundy district, the Bryan's had been most enthusiastic about the prospects of Pinot Noir and Chardonnay. As the vineyards mature, however, Cabernet Sauvignon and Merlot, the Bordeaux grape varieties, are looking more and more like the ideal red grapes for the site.

Semillon is another variety that is emerging as a winery specialty. In California, Sauvignon Blanc predominates, a more herbaceous variety capable of standing up to the heat. In Europe, Sauvignon Blanc is not as highly regarded, and Semillon has a much more important role. Semillon is proving very successful in Washington's Columbia Valley. Champ de Brionne's style of Semillon has a restrained, grassy, varietal character touched with French oak.

Champs de Brionne is a partnership comprised of 35 limited partners with Vince and Carol Bryan as the general partners and principal owners. A neurosurgeon by profession, Vince Bryan's enthusiasm and commitment to the winery is genuine and profound, extending from the technical aspects of grape growing to the esthetic experience of the natural setting.

"Do you like the smell of sage?" asks Bryan, picking a sprig from a nearby bush. "I love the smell. When we first came here and walked the fields, I slept with my shoes by my pillow." Just past the north facing Pinot Noir vineyard, a natural amphitheater is set into a bluff overlooking the Columbia and its basalt cliffs, cut by the river into the ancient volcanic basalt. The acoustics and view are unsurpassed. Spring and summer concerts by internationally known musicians draw huge crowds to this remote and beautiful part of Washington.

Chateau Gallant

In 1972, before the meteoric Washington wine revolution was off the ground, David Gallant planted an acre of wine grapes on his farmland to satisfy a curiosity about Washington wine grape growing. His curiosity was piqued rather than satisfied, however, and the vineyard grew to 25 acres. Then, after years of selling grapes to other wineries, the next step was a winery of his own.

The first wines were made or purchased elsewhere, but beginning with the 1988 vintage, all the wines have been made at the estate winery from Gallant grapes. Mike Wallace of Hinzerling Vineyards is winemaker. Wallace is one of the Washington wine pioneers that helped start the modern Washington wine industry.

The Gallant family has diverse business interests in real estate, insurance, and accounting, as well as agricultural crops. David

Chateau Gallant

South 1355 Gallant Road
Pasco, Washington 99301
(509) 545-9570

Owners
Gallant Family

Winemaker
Mike Wallace

Wine Production
1,200 gallons

Vineyard Acreage
25 acres

Year First Planted
1972

First Vintage
1988

Wines Produced
Chardonnay, Riesling,
Sauvignon Blanc, Gewurztraminer

Gallant got into the grape and wine business not just because it was another agricultural crop, but because of his interest in wine. As daughter Theresa Gallant, Chateau Gallant's Seattle area marketing agent, puts it, "With respect to wine grapes and wine, my father is interested in the cultural as well as the agricultural."

The winery and vineyard are located east of Burbank near Pasco, on the Burbank Sloughs that are fed by the Columbia River. The site overlooks the McNary National Wildlife Refuge, home

and stopping place for many species of waterfowl. The pastoral setting and continuous flights of birds are notable features of a visit to Chateau Gallant.

Chateau Ste. Michelle

In many parts of the country, Chateau Ste. Michelle carries the torch for premium Washington wine. For thousands of Americans, Chateau Ste. Michelle offers their first experience with the wines of Washington state.

A relatively unknown wine region is often dismissed or ignored. The Washington wine industry can be thankful that Chateau Ste. Michelle has been such an effective torch bearer. Not only Chateau Ste. Michelle's wines, but also its personnel and corporate culture, convey a sense of competence and professionalism—a sense that this winery and this winegrowing region are to be taken seriously.

The lengthy roots of Chateau Ste. Michelle reach back to the era immediately following Prohibition, when two companies, Nawico and Pommerelle, began producing wines from hybrids, and native American grape varieties such as Concord. In 1954, the companies merged to form American Wine Growers. In 1967, under the direction of Victor Allison, American Wine Growers made Semillon, Cabernet Sauvignon, Pinot Noir, and Grenache Rose, the winery's first systematic pursuit of premium vinifera grape wines—and the first wines to bear the Ste. Michelle name.

In 1973, a group of local investors headed by Wallace Opdycke purchased American Wine Growers. The following year, Ste. Michelle became a wholly owned subsidiary of the United States Tobacco Company. Within a decade, the massive infusion of capital by the winery's parent company transformed Chateau Ste. Michelle into one of America's major premium wineries.

In 1976, Chateau Ste. Michelle built a modern showcase winery near the community of Woodinville, not far from the city of Seattle. Situated on an 87 acre estate once owned by Seattle lumberman Fred Stimson, the attractive chateau-style building houses corporate offices and visitor facilities. Scarcely visible from the winery grounds, the 140,000 square foot production facility is set on a lower plane, maintaining the estate's pastoral ambience.

The grounds have been carefully preserved, designed in the early 1900s by the Olmstead brothers of Boston, designers of New York's Central Park and Seattle's Arboretum. The Stimson home, a National Historical Monument, is available to groups for wine tastings. Approximately 150,000 people visit Chateau Ste. Michelle's Woodinville winery every year.

Chateau Ste. Michelle's red wines are fermented at the small, original Nawico facility at Grandview, in the Yakima Valley. Refinished and refurbished, the Grandview winery's open top tanks proved ideal for fermenting red wines. More old fashion and utilitarian than the Woodinville winery, the Grandview winery is nevertheless rich with authenticity, bespeaking the historical roots of Chateau Ste. Michelle and the Washington wine industry.

Until the late 1970s, all Chateau Ste. Michelle's Cabernet Sauvignon and Merlot were aged in

■ **Chateau Ste. Michelle's Woodinville winery**

American oak. In 1978, Chateau Ste. Michelle released its second reserve bottling of Cabernet Sauvignon, their first red wine aged entirely in French oak. The French

---

Chateau Ste. Michelle

One Stimson Lane
P.O. Box 1976
Woodinville, Washington 98072
(206) 488-1133

205 West 5th
Grandview, Washington 98930
(509) 882-3928

Owner
Stimson Lane Wine & Spirits, Ltd.

Winemakers
Cheryl Barber, Head Winemaker;
Gordy Hill, Red Winemaker

Wine Production
1,400,000 gallons

Vineyard Acreage
2,000 acres

Year First Planted
1942

First Vintage
1967

Wines Produced
Cabernet Sauvignon,
Cabernet Blanc, Cabernet Rose,
Chardonnay, Chenin Blanc,
Fume Blanc, Gewurztraminer,
Riesling, Merlot, Muscat Canelli,
Pinot Noir, Sauvignon Blanc,
Semillon, Semillon Blanc,
Riesling, Sparkling Blanc de Noir,
Sparkling Domaine Brut,
Sparkling Blanc de Blanc,
Sparkling Non-Vintage

---

oak favorably enhanced the character of the wine, and in 1981, Ste. Michelle began putting some of its "regular" Cabernet and Merlot in French oak. With each successive year, French oak comprises an increasing percentage of the cooperage.

For Washington, and for Chateau Ste. Michelle, consistent success with red wine was long in coming, but by the late 70s, much had been learned about growing the grapes and making the wine. Selecting the right growing site is particularly critical for Cabernet Sauvignon. The site needs to be warm, yet the grapes must maintain good acidity and low pH. Chateau Ste. Michelle's best Cabernet grapes routinely come from their Cold Creek Vineyard in the Rattlesnake Hills. The vineyard has a very slight 5 degree southerly slope and receives an average 3,300 heat units during its 210 day growing season.

Development of the red wines dates back to Ste Michelle's inception. In 1967, Andre Tchelistcheff, the legendary California winemaker, visited American Wine Growers, the corporate predecessor to Chateau Ste. Michelle, to discuss Washington's future in the premium wine industry. Tchelistcheff agreed to act as special consultant.

From the beginning, as he had in California, Tchelistcheff advocated malolactic fermentation for Ste. Michelle's red wines. This secondary bacterial fermentation converts malic acid to less acidic lactic acid, softening and rounding the wine, and contributing to its complexity. In 1974, Chateau Ste. Michelle achieved their first complete malolactic fermentation, marking an important turning point in the quality of their red wines.

Merlot, another Bordeaux grape variety, had been planted in 1972 to soften the Cabernet's higher acidity and harshness, but by the time the Merlot was ready

---

Not everyone is aware that America has a premium wine producing state named "Washington" in its upper left corner. Ste. Michelle's Bob Betz tells the story of giving an extensive presentation on the east coast, detailing the unique features of the Washington winegrowing region, only to be asked at the end, "On what side of the Potomac do you grow the grapes?"

---

for its first harvest in 1976, it was no longer needed for the Cabernet. Washington Merlot has proven to be an excellent wine on its own, and Chateau Ste. Michelle sells its Merlot as a 100 percent varietal bottling.

Although Chateau Ste. Michelle's early successes with red wines had been notable in the context of pioneering efforts, the winery achieved a major leap in quality in the early 1980s, with the arrival of red winemaker Doug Gore, and a better understanding of grape growing and winemak-

ing practices. Although Gore has subsequently moved to Chateau Ste. Michelle's sister winery, Columbia Crest, success with red wine continues.

The white wines have been Chateau Ste. Michelle's most successful. Riesling, finished with some residual sweetness, is by far Chateau Ste. Michelle's most popular wine. While other grape varieties took some learning and development, Chateau Ste. Michelle's Rieslings were very good from the start, and immediately appealing to a broad spectrum of consumers. Riesling continues to play a major role at Chateau Ste. Michelle.

For the wine aficionado, Chateau Ste. Michelle's dry white wines are becoming increasingly noteworthy. Both the Chardonnay and Fume Blanc are partially fermented in French oak tanks or barrels, then aged briefly in oak prior to bottling. Although the 1978 vintage of Chardonnay was put through a malolactic fermentation, subsequent vintages were prevented from undergoing the process, a common, but often less than optimum practice for Washington Chardonnay.

In 1986, Chateau Ste. Michelle again began incorporating malolactic fermentation in some of its Chardonnays. The degree of malolactic fermentation varies from year to year and from vineyard to vineyard, but it is again part of the winemakers repertoire. The warm Cold Creek Chardonnay is less likely to get malolactic fermentation, while the cooler River

Ridge vineyard may see 100 percent malolactic fermentation. The Chardonnays also receive some, though not lengthy, lees contact. Chateau Ste. Michelle Chardonnays are not overblown wines. The new versions are restrained, yet manifest sufficient complexity and character for aging.

Chateau Ste. Michelle, in conjunction with its sister winery, Columbia Crest, is one of America's largest premium wineries, but growth in production has not meant a decrease in wine quality. The current wines are, by far, the best they have made. Chateau Ste. Michelle views itself as a premier American winery, a leader and innovator in grape growing and winemaking at the frontier of a new and important wine region— as a winery not constrained by its large size, but all the more capable because its resources. In many respects, this corporate perception of itself rings true.

Chateau Ste. Michelle is a dynamic enterprise, constantly changing itself to meet its own changing needs. In 1983, Chateau Ste. Michelle president Wallace Opdycke, one of the early organizers of the enterprise, resigned his post to pursue other business interests. A specialist in finance, Opdycke played the

■ **Wine aging in oak barrels**

principal role in acquiring a faltering winery in Seattle's industrial district, and within a decade, transforming the winery into the dominant showcase for Northwest wine.

Allen Shoup is Chateau Ste. Michelle's current president. The winery's tremendous expansion, coming at a time when the American wine market is experiencing

---

**Expanded production
has not meant
a decrease in
wine quality.
The current wines
are, by far, the best
Ste. Michelle has made.**

---

a flat growth period, requires consummate marketing acumen. Shoup's credentials are impressive. After receiving a bachelor's degree in marketing and a master's degree in psychology, Shoup became marketing manager for the Ernest and Julio Gallo winery, then a director of marketing for Max Factor in the highly competitive cosmetics industry.

The battle for recognition, both for Chateau Ste. Michelle and the Washington wine industry in general, is not easy. Not everyone seems aware that there is a state in the upper left corner of America named "Washington," and that it produces fine wines. Bob Betz, Chateau Ste. Michelle's Vice President of Corporate Communications, tells the story of conducting an extensive presentation and winetasting on the east coast, detailing the unique features and excellence of the Washington winegrowing region, only to be

asked, at the end of the presentation, "On what side of the Potomac do you grow the grapes?"

Chateau Ste. Michelle and the Washington wine industry have made considerable headway since that presentation, but not without considerable effort. In a restructuring move, U.S. Tobacco's wine and spirits interests are now under the umbrella company, Stimson Lane Wine and Spirits, Ltd. Chateau Ste. Michelle is the company's flagship winery, spinning off the River Ridge winery into a separate entity, Columbia Crest, as well as the historic Whidbey Island port and liqueur operation, under the name of Whidbeys. Helping to feed the product line and support a national marketing force of some 50 persons, Stimson Lane now owns two California wineries and operates a wine and spirit importing branch.

Chateau Ste. Michelle has come far from its modest production of 15,000 gallons of premium wine in 1967. For Chateau Ste. Michelle, and its parent company, Stimson Lane Wine and Spirits, Ltd., failure is not an issue, only the magnitude of success. Washington is at last becoming firmly established in the American wine scene, and Chateau Ste. Michelle has done much to pave the way.

Chinook Wines

Kay Simon and Clay Mackey, both U. C. Davis trained, worked for several large wineries in California and Washington before they left their positions to start their own wine consulting businesses, get married, and open their own winery. "We wanted to do something that was entirely our own," says Mackey. "At

Chinook, we do everything from renovating the winery building to winemaking and marketing."

Mackey and Simon have since discontinued their consulting and lab work to focus attention on Chinook, but their widespread influence and expertise has made its mark on the Washington wine industry. Consummate technicians, Simon and Mackey are also warm, genuine, open people, a tone that carries through to their winery as well.

Situated near a freeway exit, the Chinook winery, a converted pri-

---

Chinook Wines

Wine Country Road
at Wittkopf Road

P.O. Box 387
Prosser, Washington 99350
(509) 786-2725

Owners
Kay Simon & Clay Mackey

Winemakers
Kay Simon & Clay Mackey

Wine Production
4,000 gallons

Vineyard Acreage
none

First Vintage
1983

Wines Produced
Chardonnay, Sauvignon Blanc,
Semillon, Topaz, Merlot,
Sparkling Riesling

---

vate residence, still manages to convey a rustic atmosphere. A pathway from the house to the garage is covered by an arbor of craggy, old, thick-trunked Concord and Black Monukka vines. The backyard is now a picnic area for visitors, and the tasting room is the living and dining area of the old house.

Chinook wines are made in a dry, crisp, fruity style. Recent vintages have seen an increase in oak in the white wines, with partial malolactic fermentation and lees contact for some of the Chardonnays. The ubiquitous semi-sweet Riesling is missing from the Chinook line of wines, as is Chenin Blanc. Unlike most Washington wineries, Chinook produces no semi-sweet wine to broaden its marketing base.

The term "food wine," heavily overworked and claimed by all, is quite apt for Chinook's wines. The absence of residual sweetness coupled with crisp acidity match the wines well with food. Sauvignon Blanc, Chardonnay, and Topaz, a proprietary blend of Semillon and sometimes Sauvignon Blanc, are fermented in stainless steel (except for occasional experimental or reserve batches) and aged in French oak barrels or tanks. The Sauvignon Blanc is blended with about 25 percent Semillon to tone down the Sauvignon herbaceousness and contribute fruitiness and the typical Semillon fresh cut grass character.

Produced in very limited quantities, Chinook pioneered a new Washington wine style, now emulated by other wineries. Chinook's bottle fermented sparkling Riesling is left on the yeast only briefly, approximately six months, so that the fruit is emphasized rather than the yeast. The strong, varietal, Riesling character is muted, however, and the wine is nicely balanced with no single flavor predominating.

Merlot, Chinook's only red wine, carries through the winery's stylistic theme, emphasizing the fruit of the grape with sufficient acidity to age and marry well with food. For all its popularity, Merlot sometimes makes a rather dull wine on its own. Chinook's Merlot nicely overcomes this syndrome, and is one of Washington's best

renderings of the grape.

Columbia Crest Winery

By far the Northwest's largest winery, Columbia Crest began life as Chateau Ste. Michelle's River Ridge winery, at Paterson, Washington. The

---

Columbia Crest Winery

P.O. Box 231
Paterson, Washington 99345
(206) 875-2061

Owner
Stimson Lane Wine & Spirits, Ltd.

Winemakers
Doug Gore, Winemaker;
Joy Anderson,
Assistant Winemaker

Wine Production
1,200,000 gallons

Vineyard Acreage
1,100 acres

Year First Planted
1979

First Vintage
1984

Wines Produced
Columbia Crest: Riesling,
Chenin Blanc, Gewurztraminer,
Sauvignon Blanc,
Dry White Grenache,
Cabernet Sauvignon, Merlot,
Semillon, White, Blush

Allison Combs: Chenin Blanc,
Riesling, White Grenache,
Cabernet Sauvignon,
Sauvignon Blanc

Farron Ridge: White, Red, Blush,
Blanc de Blanc, Riesling,
White Grenache

Columbia Crest label was originally a marketing initiative for a line of moderately priced, elegantly packaged wines. The Columbia Crest name also marked Chateau Ste. Michelle's successful efforts in getting official approval for the Columbia Valley viticultural appellation.

The concept worked, and the

Paterson facility became the Columbia Crest winery. After an organizational restructuring necessitated by the corporation's expanding commitment to wine and spirits, Chateau Ste. Michelle and Columbia Crest became separate wineries under the ownership umbrella of Stimson Lane Wine & Spirits, Ltd.

As large as the Chateau Ste. Michelle's Woodinville winery must have seemed when it was first built, rapid expansion rapidly outgrew the winery's capacity. In 1983, Chateau Ste. Michelle completed construction of what is now Columbia Crest, a modern, 26 million dollar winery overlooking the Columbia River.

The Columbia Crest winery and vineyards were major and bold moves for the corporation. Nearly three times the size of the Woodinville winery, Columbia Crest symbolized the corporation's commitment to Washington wine, confidence in the success of the enterprise, and, more broadly, an affirmation of the importance of Washington wine on the future of the American wine scene.

Columbia Crest is surrounded by its own 1,780 acre vineyard, situated on Paterson Ridge, on the lower reaches of the Horse Heaven Hills, just above the Columbia River. These several square miles of vines represent nearly a fifth of all the wine grape vineyard land in Washington.

The site had been planted in corn, and irrigated, in Columbia Valley agricultural fashion, with huge center-pivot irrigation systems. Initially, some of the vineyard was planted in circular sections of roughly 100 acres each, watered by center-pivot irrigation. The irrigation pipe was suspended above the vines on mobile towers on wheels, and,

■ **Columbia Crest Winery**

like the hands on a clock, the irrigation pipe and its sprinkler heads swept across the circular vineyard, irrigating the vines as it passed.

It was a striking sight in the vineyard, and a handy viewing perch, as I recall, having climbed up on one to photograph the winery behind me and the Columbia River below. Unfortunately, it was a less than optimum system for the vines, so, at considerable expense, Columbia Crest replaced the central pivots with a drip irrigation system.

Nearly 90 percent of the Columbia Crest winery is underground, optimizing control of temperature and humidity. The impressive facility has five laboratories for wine, soil, vine, and packaging analysis. Spectacularly massive 80,000 gallon stainless steel tanks are used for blending, but the fermenting tanks range in size from 3,000 to 12,000 gallons. For such a large winery, the relatively small tanks offer the opportunity to make different blends from the separate lots, or keep aside distinctive batches for special handling. The finely furnished visitor's building is designed in the manner of a rustic country estate.

Columbia Crest wines are, in marketspeak, "fighting varietals," premium wines made from premium grape varieties, moderately priced, with appeal to a broad spectrum of consumers. The wines succeed admirably at their assigned task. It is no surprise that the white wines have done so well, but the reds are particularly noteworthy. Red wine is arguably the best the state has to offer, but, in Washington, it is more of a challenge to get the right fruit and make moderately priced, quality red wines on a large scale. The initial releases of Columbia Crest's Cabernet Sauvignon and Merlot show that it can be done.

Columbia Winery

In 1984, Washington's oldest, continuously operating, premium, grape winery changed its name from Associated Vintners to Columbia Winery. In its more than two decades of existence, the winery has gone through many changes. Its beginnings are now legendary.

In the early 1950s, Lloyd Woodburne, then a professor of psychology at the University of Washington, began making homemade wine. Interest spread among Woodburne's colleagues, and before long, a number of the University's faculty were buying grapes and making wine. The

group purchased a grape crusher that Woodburne kept in his garage. To comply with legal restrictions, the winemakers formed a corporation and bonded a winery. In 1962, the association of vintners became Associated Vintners.

In 1966, the noted wine authority, Leon Adams, tasted one of Woodburne's Grenache roses, found it excellent, and suggested that Associated Vintners should become a commercial winery. In 1967, the most famous and respected of all American winemakers, Andre Tchelistcheff, tasted a Gewurztraminer made by Phil Church, another home winemaker in the group, describing it as the best Gewurztraminer made in the United States.

Spurred by this enthusiastic response, the group moved the crusher from Woodburne's garage to a small 40' by 40' facility in Kirkland, Washington, a suburb of Seattle. In 1967, Associated Vintners produced their first commercial vintage.

Phil Church, a meteorologist, and one of the original ten shareholders, made early studies of Washington's climates, showing, among other things, that parts of Washington east of the Cascades have virtually the same heat units as parts of France's Burgundy region. Although it is now recognized that heat unit measurements are only a partial indication of viticultural comparability, Church's early studies provided much of the impetus for vinifera grape growing in Washington. Woodburne credits Church, now deceased, for pioneering work that helped launch Washington's rapidly growing wine industry.

In 1976, the winery moved from its small building in Kirkland

■ **David Lake**

to a much larger, more modern facility in nearby Redmond. Master of Wine, David Lake, arrived in 1979 and assumed winemaking responsibilities. By 1980, production had increased to more than 10,000 cases a year, and it became increasingly apparent that Associated Vintners was outgrowing itself.

The time had come for a transformation to preserve and enhance the vitality of the original enterprise without compromising its fundamental and sustaining spirit. The winery generated new capital by selling its vineyards and increasing the number of shareholders to 30. Included in the new group were key members with business and marketing expertise.

In 1981, Associated Vintners moved to the adjacent community of Bellevue, to a building three times the size of the Redmond facility. In 1984, under the direction of president and majority investor, Dan Baty, Associated Vintners changed its operating name to Columbia Winery, reflecting the winery's transformation, and echoing its ties with the Columbia Valley, Washington's most important winegrowing region. The winery's expansion called for additional personnel,

and Columbia hired Swiss winemaker, Max Zellweger, most recently from Washington's Langguth winery, as operations manager.

By 1989, Columbia was again outgrowing its space. Search for a new facility ended when the building designed for the Haviland winery became available. Columbia's newest winery offers greatly expanded production space and much needed visitor facilities.

When a winery sells its vineyards, takes on new investors, greatly increases production, emphasizes business and marketing concerns, and changes its iden-

Columbia Winery

14030 N.E. 145th
Woodinville, Washington 98072
(206) 488-2776

Owners
Corporation—privately held &
locally owned corporation

Winemaker
David Lake

Wine Production
220,000 gallons

Vineyard Acreage
none

First Vintage
1967

Wines Produced
Cabernet Sauvignon;
Cabernet Sauvignon, Red Willow
Vineyard, David Lake Signature;
Cabernet Sauvignon, Otis
Vineyard, David Lake Signature;
Cabernet Sauvignon, Sagemoor
Vineyard, David Lake Signature;
Merlot; Merlot, Milestone, Red
Willow Vineyard; Syrah, Red Willow
Vineyard; Pinot Noir, Woodburne
Collection; Chardonnay;
Chardonnay, Woodburne
Collection; Chardonnay, David
Lake Signature; Semillon;
Riesling; Riesling, Cellarmasters
Reserve; Riesling, Red Willow
Vineyard, Late Harvest;
Gewurztraminer;
Dry Gewurztraminer, Woodburne
Collection; Chenin Blanc

tity, decline in quality and commitment to excellence is a certainty—almost a certainty. For Columbia Winery, the effect was quite the opposite.

David Lake, Columbia's winemaker and vice-president, played a key role in the winery's transformation. Lake holds what is undoubtedly the wine world's most distinguished title—Master of Wine from Britain's Institute of Masters of Wine. Although the institute has been in existence for some 35 years, only about 140 Masters of Wine have been certified.

A Canadian by birth, Lake came to the United States after ten years in the British wine trade. He studied for a year at the University of California at Davis, and worked for a time with David Lett at Eyrie Vineyards in Oregon, who subsequently recommended him to Woodburne.

Matching current market interests and perceptions is the safest business path. Leading the market and shaping it through a commitment to the best is much riskier. Columbia Winery is not blind to current market trends, but neither is it a blind follower of those trends.

"The conventional wisdom," said Lake, when I talked with him in the early 1980s, "is that this is a white wine region. We obviously have potential for very good white wines, but red, I think, will be even more exceptional. My own feeling is that in ten years time, or twenty years time at least, we are going to see that this is an even more outstanding region for red wine." Recent widespread acclaim has already begun to validate Lake's assessment.

Columbia's red wines offer convincing evidence of Lake's commitment to red wines. In

1979, his first vintage as winemaker, Lake produced a Cabernet Sauvignon that set a benchmark. Of the wine, the great American winemaker Andre Tchelistcheff said, "This is one of the best Cabernets I have ever tasted. It is a wonderful wine, deep, with a velvety texture, enormously complex, very much in the style of a

> **Of the wine, the great American winemaker Andre Tchelistcheff said, "This is one of the best Cabernets I have ever tasted. It is a wonderful wine… enormously complex, very much in the style of a classic Medoc… artistically complete, balanced, and perfect."**

classic Medoc—a lovely wine, perfect in every way; not one single flaw that I could find; artistically complete, balanced and perfect."

The 1979 vintage was exceptional, and Columbia had decided to release the Cabernet with a special designation, "Millennium," a wine to be laid down until its twenty-first birthday, in the year 2000. Lake asked Tchelistcheff if he thought Columbia was justified in its claim that the wine would continue to develop in the bottle until the arrival of the new century. Tchelistcheff's reply was succinct, "Of course, without any doubt."

Columbia Winery produces a higher proportion of red wine than any other Washington winery of its size, and Lake hopes

to increase the proportion even further. Lake systematically searches out and enters into extended contracts with some of Washington's best red wine vineyards. Three of the Cabernet vineyards are routinely released as separate reserve bottlings under the David Lake Signature series.

From fan trained vines, three decades old, the Otis Vineyard produces a rather atypical Cabernet, displaying distinctive weedy and berrylike flavors. In recent vintages, refinements in the vineyard and more new oak in the winery have brought the Otis wines closer to the mainstream. Diehard Otis fans may be disappointed, but I heartily welcome the refinements to what is probably Washington's best structured Cabernet.

From a warmer growing area in the Columbia Valley's Pasco Basin, the Sagemoor fruit yields full-bodied Cabernets with a richer, denser, more textural profile. Sagemoor is one of Washington's oldest major vineyards.

Mike Sauer's Red Willow Vineyard is Columbia's star. The vineyard is the most steeply sloped in the Yakima Valley. Situated on the slopes of Ahtanum Ridge, it is the northwesternmost vineyard in the valley. It is an exceptional site for red wine grapes. Red Willow Cabernets offer refined, complex flavors. In their youth they are typically restrained and closed-in. With bottle age, Red Willow Cabernets develop flavors reminiscent of traditionally styled Bordeaux.

At a blind tasting of Cabernets, a well-known Bordeaux principal identified the "ringer" Bordeaux in the group—the wine, however, was not the "ringer" Bordeaux, but a Columbia Red Willow Cabernet. Ironically, but not surpris-

ingly, other Columbia Cabernets often show better at wine judgings. Less voluptuous and forward in youth, the young Red Willow Cabernets do not have the organoleptic voice that is most readily heard in the context of a typical wine judging. Time in the cellar is the true test for great red wines, however, and here the Red Willow Cabernet leaves no doubt as to its status.

Except for Nebbiolo grapes that go to the Cavatappi Winery, Columbia has an exclusive contract for Red Willow grapes. Lake and Sauer work closely together. Merlot, Cabernet Franc, and Syrah are among Red Willow's more recent additions. Columbia's Milestone, a proprietary wine, is a blend of Red Willow Merlot and Cabernet Franc. Even in their first vintages, the Merlot and Cabernet Franc showed fine fruit character and the trademark Red Willow style.

In 1985, in cooperation with Lake and Columbia Winery, Sauer planted Washington's first commercial vineyard of Syrah, the great Rhone red wine grape. The

> **An increasingly popular Washington varietal, Columbia was one of the first wineries to recognize Semillon's potential.**

vine has taken well to the growing site, and early results have been very encouraging.

Washington Cabernets are inherently rough and tannic in their youth, but Lake does not purposely soften the single vineyard wines for early drinkability. On the other hand, Lake does not produce immensely tannic, high alcohol, low acid, overripe beasts. Such wines promise a long life, but their lack of acidity and balance prevents them from developing well with age.

Lake's Cabernets are tightly structured wines with concentrated flavors, low pH, and good acidity—a structure not unlike traditionally made Bordeaux, though sometimes with a riper quality befitting Washington's growing climate. In recent vintages, Lake has taken steps to moderate the tannins, making the wines more graceful in youth as well as excellent candidates for lengthy cellaring.

In addition to the three Cabernet vineyards featured in the Signature wines, Lake works with several other vineyards, most notably Brookside in southwest Washington. Here, in an area known geologically as the Willamette Trough, the climate and grapes resemble those of Oregon's Willamette Valley. From Brookside, Lake buys Pinot Noir and Chardonnay.

Lake was admittedly uncomfortable with the sale of the winery's vineyards, and the loss of immediate and direct control over the grapes. In retrospect, the decision was a good one. Columbia is not locked into a single growing area for all their wines. Different grape varieties are purchased from the vineyards that grow them best.

Lake works closely with Columbia's grape growers throughout the season. As harvest approaches, Lake visits the vineyards at least once a week, looking at the condition of the vines, and tasting the grapes. Sugar, acid, and pH readings do not tell the whole story, and tasting the grapes gives important indica-tions of ripeness, quality, and character.

Gewurztraminer is not an easy wine to make well, but Columbia has justly earned a reputation for this variety, made in a dry Alsatian style. Although it has been a winery specialty since the first days of Associated Vintners,

■ **David Lake & Red Willow Vineyards' Mike Sauer**

Gewurztraminer, especially dry Gewurztraminer, is a tough sell in the market, so Columbia's production is limited. Columbia's dry Gewurztraminer is now sold under the Woodburne label.

Chardonnay, Semillon, and a sweet Riesling called Cellarmaster's Reserve are Columbia's major white wines. In recent vintages, a move toward more barrel fermentation, lees contact, and oak have greatly benefited the Columbia Chardonnays. The current wines are the best ever to come out of the winery.

Columbia's focus on Semillon as a major variety is especially noteworthy. Largely ignored in America in favor of Sauvignon Blanc, Semillon holds a superior position in Bordeaux, where it is regarded as having a more refined character and the ability to age and develop far better than Sauvignon Blanc. In the best white Bordeaux, destined for a long life, Semillon predominates. Sauvignon Blanc may be the best variety for California's warmer growing climate, but in Washington, Semillon demonstrates its superiority.

Increasingly popular as a Washington varietal, Columbia was one of the first wineries to recognize Semillon's potential. In Lake's opinion, nowhere else in the world does Semillon produce such a distinctive and flavorful wine of such high quality. Lake's Semillon is made in an intensely varietal rendition of the grape, with a pronounced, crisp, grassy aroma and taste, but without the aggressive herbaceous edge of a Sauvignon Blanc. Columbia's Semillons see no oak.

For a winegrowing region most commonly known for its Rieslings, Columbia's focus and success with Cabernet Sauvignon, Merlot, Cabernet Franc, and Semillon, Bordeaux grape varieties, defines an important direction for premium Washington wine.

Nearly three decades ago, a

> **Though much has changed, Columbia Winery successfully preserves the pioneering, innovative, and independent spirit of the original founders.**

loose association of amateur vintners banded together, formed a winery, and became instrumental in the birth of Washington's premium wine industry. Much has changed, but the transformed Columbia Winery successfully preserves the pioneering, innovative, and independent spirit of the original founders. Now, just as then, Columbia Winery remains a leader in Washington's premium wine industry.

Coolen Wine Cellar

On the Kitsap Peninsula, jutting into Puget Sound, Dick Coolen has planted a half acre of Madeleine Angevine and Siegerrebe on his 10 acre property of farm and woods. Coolen, a masonry contractor, has the goal of expanding his vineyard and producing sparkling wines from western Washington grape varieties.

Most of Coolen's wines are presently made from California grapes. Coolen produces a dry red, an off-dry red, and a rose. The wines are made without the addition of sulfites.

Coolen Wine Cellar

5759 Banner Road S.E.
Port Orchard, Washington 98366

P.O. Box 4031
South Colby, Washington 98384
(206) 871-0567

Owners
Dick & Linda Coolen

Winemaker
Dick Coolen

Wine Production
800 gallons

First Vintage
1986

Wines Produced
Proprietary blends from
California & Washington grapes

Coventry Vale Winery

Coventry Vale is one of the Northwest's larger wineries, yet, especially until recently, hardly anyone outside the wine industry even knew it existed. Coventry Vale is what is known as a "custom crush facility." It is a winery for other wineries.

Who uses Coventry Vale? Typical customers include new wineries without complete winemaking facility of their own, wineries in need of expanded capacity, and grape growers who need to turn their grapes into

---

Coventry Vale Winery

Wilgus & Evans Roads
P.O. Box 249
Grandview, Washington 98930
(206) 882-4100

Owners
David Wyckoff & Donald Toci

Winemaker
Bill Bagge

Wine Production
undisclosed

Vineyard Acreage
undisclosed

First Vintage
1983

Wines Produced
Riesling, Chenin Blanc,
Muscat Canelli, Chardonnay,
Blush, Sparkling Wine

---

wine for marketing reasons.

Coventry Vale was founded by David Wyckoff, a former Seattle attorney who returned to the Yakima Valley to manage his family's vineyards and other agricultural interests. Wyckoff started Coventry Vale at a time of rapid growth in the Washington wine industry. Many of the grapes from the record crop years made a trip through Coventry Vale on their way to the wine bottle.

The tumultuous growth of the Washington wine industry created varying periods of excesses and shortages of grapes and wine. Grape growers without a ready market for their grapes can buy time by turning the grapes into wine at Coventry Vale. Since wine keeps longer than grapes on a vine, the grower can then search out markets for his product.

Vineyard owner Donald Toci subsequently joined forces with Wyckoff, further expanding Coventry Vale's production capacity. Coventry Vale remains primarily a custom crush facility, but now releases wines under its own labels as well. The winery sells a line of sparkling wines under the Coventry Vale label, and a line of table wines under the Washington Discovery label, offering the consumer a range of good quality, moderately priced wines.

Covey Run

Covey Run started business at a time when most Yakima Valley wineries were bare bones facilities with all the architectural elegance of a machine shed. The Covey Run winery was clearly something quite different.

The beautifully designed concrete and cedar winery is nestled just below the Roza Canal, high on the lower slopes of the Rattlesnake Hills, offering a broad view of the valley and distant mountains. A partnership of 20 owners, Covey Run was the first well-financed, showcase, estate winery in the Yakima Valley.

In 1987, Covey Run opened a small satellite winery in the downtown waterfront community of Kirkland, a fashionable suburb of Seattle. Unlike Oregon, which permits additional tasting rooms separate from wineries, Washington law permits only winery tasting rooms. Covey Run at Moss Bay is not much of a production facility, but it satisfies the technical requirements of the law, and offers access to Covey Run wines in a popular metropolitan location.

Most of Covey Run's grapes come from vineyards owned by two of the winery's partners. Covey Run also buys grapes from other Yakima Valley growers to supplement production from its own vineyards. Washington's larger wineries have traditionally developed their vineyards outside the Yakima Valley. Covey Run was the first winery of its size to produce wines solely from Yakima Valley grapes. One of Washington's most important grape growing regions, the Yakima Valley is generally cooler than the other major growing areas in Washington's vast Columbia Valley.

A beautifully designed concrete and cedar structure, Covey Run was the first well-financed, showcase, estate winery in the Yakima Valley.

Most of Covey Run's wines are the conventional Washington varietals, but small quantities of more unusual grape varieties are a winery hallmark. Covey Run adds variety to the Washington wine scene by producing small quanti-

ties of wine from several lesser known grapes, Aligote, Morio Muskat, and Lemberger.

Aligote is a high yielding, white, Burgundian grape, somewhat similar to the more refined

■ **Covey Run Winery**

and aristocratic Chardonnay variety. Covey Run sometimes blends Chardonnay with Aligote, then ages the wine briefly in French oak. Covey Run's Aligote

Covey Run

1500 Vintage Road
Zillah, Washington 98953
(509) 829-6235

107 Central Way
Kirkland, Washington 98033
(206) 828-3848

Owners
General Partnership

Winemaker
Dave Crippen

Wine Production
90,000 gallons

Vineyard Acreage
180 acres

Year First Planted
1980

First Vintage
1982

Wines Produced
Chardonnay, La Caille de Fume,
Aligote, Morio Muskat, Riesling,
Late Harvest Riesling,
Riesling Ice Wine,
Cabernet Sauvignon, Merlot,
Lemberger

is a less expensive alternative to Chardonnay.

Morio Muskat was developed in Germany from a cross of Sylvaner and Pinot Blanc. The linalool component of the Sylvaner is greatly emphasized in the crossing, yielding an appealing wine with a pronounced muscat character.

Lemberger is the more prominent of the three lesser known grape varieties. A German red wine grape, Lemberger holds fine promise for Washington state. The variety yields relatively high quantities of darkly colored, low pH, fruity wine. Dr. Walter Clore, a Washington State University horticulturist, advocated Lemberger even before Washington's premium wine industry was born. Covey Run was among the first few Washington wineries to produce the wine commercially.

Lemberger lends itself to a wide variety of styles. After trying several styles, Covey Run settled on a less conventional approach for a red wine. To emphasize the variety's fresh, berrylike flavors, the Lemberger is fermented and aged in stainless steel, then bottled without wood aging, and without a malolactic fermentation. The wine is intensely colored, fruity, and berrylike. Crisp, relatively high acidity contributes to the wine's fresh fruity character.

Covey Run's La Caille de Fume is a proprietary blend of Semillon and Sauvignon Blanc. Washington produces excellent Semillon grapes. In the tradition of white Bordeaux, Covey Run blends Semillon with Sauvignon Blanc. The La Caille de Fume blend combines the refined grassy-citrusy character of Semillon with the more herbaceous intensity of Sauvignon Blanc. The two grapes complement each other well.

With the arrival of Dave Crippen in 1988, Covey Run's style is evolving away from emphasis on the simple fruity flavors of the grape, to a more complexly flavored wine style. Barrel aging, lees contact, and malolactic fermentation have a more prominent role than before in the Chardonnay, Aligote, and Le Caille de Fume. This stylistic evolution is all to the good, and parallels a broader stylistic evolution in Washington wine.

Most of Covey Run's wines are made from traditional grape varieties such as Chardonnay, Riesling, Chenin Blanc, and Cabernet Sauvignon. The less common grape varieties like Morio Muskat, Lemberger, and Aligote, and special blended wines such as the La Caille de Fume, offer additional interest for the wine consumer, while exploring some of the dimensions and directions of the Washington winegrowing industry. Covey Run has earned a well-deserved reputation for both its traditional and less common wine varieties.

Eaton Hill Winery

The Yakima Valley is layered with the history of pioneering generations settling in the valley to work the land. In 1984, Edwin and JoAnn Stear set about capturing and preserving a small piece of Yakima Valley's history. The Stears' purchased the old Eaton Homestead and transformed the historic home, built in 1905, into a bed and breakfast for Yakima Valley travelers.

Eaton's daughter married Floyd Rinehold, and built the adjacent Rinehold cannery in 1925. For years, the cannery produced fruits and vegetables under the Yakima Farmer label. The cannery, house, and adjacent land had subsequently fallen into the hands of separate owners. The Stears purchased the cannery and adjacent property and "assembled" the original homestead.

Edwin Stear holds a PhD in electrical engineering. He has been both a teacher in academia and a consultant for private industry. Stear is restoring the historic cannery building and turning it into the Eaton Hill Winery. Although the 12,000 square foot building provides ample space for a relatively large winery, the size of Stear's winery is and will remain very small.

Stear has no singular focus in mind for the winery. Plans call for a range of wines, including a few made from fruits and berries. Stear is doing most of the restoration work on his own, no small task, as the cannery required removal and replacement of 350 window panes, and the rebuilding of the individual window frames.

Eaton Hill Winery

530 Gurley Road
Granger, Washington 98932
(509) 854-2508

Owners
Edwin & JoAnn Stear

Winemaker
Edwin Stear

Wine Production
2,000 gallons

Vineyard Acreage
7 acres

First Vintage
1988

Wines Produced
Riesling, Semillon

Facelli Winery

Lou Facelli is one of the more popular figures in the Northwest wine industry. Facelli moved to Idaho from California in 1973

Facelli Winery

12335 134th Court N.E., #100
Redmond, Washington 98052
(206) 823-9466

Owners
Lou & Sandy Facelli

Winemaker
Lou Facelli

Wine Production
7,000 gallons

Vineyard Acreage
none

First Vintage
1988

Wines Produced
Chardonnay, Fume Blanc, Semillon, Dry Riesling, Merlot, Cabernet Sauvignon

and began making wine, first on a home scale, then for commercial release. His first wines did exceptionally well in wine judgings, but when people came beating on his door for wine, he had little to sell.

Looking to expand the winery and make it into a full-time, self-sustaining concern, Facelli took on two local farmers as majority investors. Most regrettably, the investors soon sold their majority share in the winery and vineyard, and suddenly there was no Facelli winery.

Moving to Washington, Facelli worked briefly at the Salmon Bay and Haviland wineries before gathering the resources to start his own winery again. This time, Facelli will avoid the disheartenment and lost time by steadfastly retaining control of his winery, and growing to no more than 15,000 gallons.

Facelli's wines see no American

oak. Chardonnay is his leading wine. The Chardonnay is barrel fermented in French oak, and aged on the lees. The wine undergoes either partial or full malolactic fermentation. Facelli does not like the overly fat Chardonnays, but wants, instead, to produce wine that compliments food and ages well.

In a world that often seems lost in a sea of expediencies and superficialities, Facelli's friendly, genuine manner, and commitment to personal ideals, is refreshing.

Facelli's mustache, beret, and suspenders have been a personal trademark since he was twenty. In a world that often seems lost in a sea of expediencies and superficialities, Facelli's friendly, genuine manner, and commitment to personal ideals, is refreshing. A meticulous craftsman, it is good to see Facelli back in business again.

Fidalgo Island Winery

Wine without sulfites is Fidalgo Island Winery's principal claim to notoriety. Charles Dawsey, himself allergic to sulfites, has dedicated his efforts to the production of sulfite free wine.

During the winemaking process, nearly all commercial wineries add sulfites as a protective agent. Without sulfites, wines are in jeopardy of spoilage or the

---

Fidalgo Island Winery

5303 Doon Way
Anacortes, Washington 98221
(206) 293-4342

Owner
Charles Dawsey

Winemaker
Charles Dawsey

Wine Production
3,000 gallons

Vineyard Acreage
none

First Vintage
1986

Wines Produced
Riesling, Chardonnay,
Cabernet Sauvignon

---

development of undesirable flavors. Good wine can be made without sulfites, but it is not an easy proposition. Dawsey's first efforts were sulfite free, but the aroma and flavors were in need of refinement. Dawsey wants to expand Fidalgo Island Winery, but, for now, the wines are made in his garage. Some of the wines receive oak flavors from extracts made from oak chips.

E.B. Foote Winery

A small family operation, the E. B. Foote winery is headed by Gene Foote, a senior engineer at Boeing. The winery is a natural outgrowth of Foote's interest in wines and winemaking, a pursuit that started innocently enough with a batch of blackberry wine. Foote quickly became interested in making fine wines from premium grapes. A small commercial winery followed some 10 years later.

Foote's first winery facility was located in an industrial park in south Seattle. In 1983, Foote moved to a new location. Only eight blocks away from the old

winery, the setting is greatly different. Foote's new winery is on part of the Joe Desimone farm, an island of agriculture in the industrial milieu.

The Southpark area once supplied fresh produce to nearby Seattle. The Desimone farm still does. Foote's winery is surrounded by fields of lettuce, basil, and pansies. Joe Desimone Sr. came to the area in 1916, and became one of the founders and directors of Seattle's famous Pike Place Market. Desimone's son still farms part of the original property.

Foote makes all his wines to go with food. With rare exception,

---

E.B.Foote Winery

9354 4th Avenue South
Seattle, Washington 98126
(206) 763-9928

Owner
Eugene Foote

Winemaker
Eugene Foote

Wine Production
2,000 gallons

Vineyard Acreage
none

First Vintage
1978

Wines Produced
Riesling, Chenin Blanc,
Chardonnay,
Late Harvest Riesling, Pinot Noir,
Cabernet Sauvignon

---

the wines are made in a completely dry style. Foote's wines are rarely fined or filtered. They are available primarily from the winery.

French Creek Cellars

For years, an informal group of home winemakers got together to buy grapes and exchange ideas about making wine. After a decade, a few in the group decided to start a commercial winery—French Creek Cellars. The partners have changed over the years, some leaving, some joining. At present, French Creek is owned and operated by seven partners.

French Creek Cellars

17721 132nd Avenue N.E.
Woodinville, Washington 98072
(206) 486-1900

Owners
Partnership

Winemaker
Richard Winter

Wine Production
12,000 gallons

Vineyard Acreage
none

First Vintage
1983

Wines Produced
Chardonnay, Sauvignon Blanc,
Riesling, Muscat Canelli,
Semillon, White Lemberger,
Lemberger, Cabernet Sauvignon,
Merlot, Chenin Blanc,
Gewurztraminer, Pinot Noir,
Morio Muscat, Petite Sirah

Serious red wines, specifically, Cabernet Sauvignon, were at the heart of the winery's original purpose. Cabernet Sauvignon and Merlot remain French Creek's leading wines. French Creek also makes Pinot Noir, sometimes from Oregon grapes, and a small amount of Lemberger, a promising Washington red grape variety that is beginning to play a role similar to that of Zinfandel in California.

Winemaker Richard Winter first made Lemberger in 1976 from a small experimental planting at Sagemoor Farms in the Columbia Valley. French Creek's Lemberger is made in varying styles, from a fruity and Beaujolais-like quaffer to a full-bodied, French oak aged wine meant for bottle age.

With changes in partners, winemakers, and winemaking direction, French Creek's wines have had a varying nature. But now, the operation seems to be stabilizing. French Creek's move from the former Redmond industrial park to a much more attractive location in Woodinville sets a positive tone. Shaded picnic facilities overlooking Bear Creek offer a welcome refuge from the suburban milieu.

Gordon Brothers Cellars

Some of the sights in the near-desert environment of eastern Washington have a raw primal beauty and grandeur of the sort not offered in the more lushly vegetated parts of the state. The Gordon Brothers vineyard, located a dozen miles northeast of Pasco, on the bluffs overlooking the Snake River, offers such a vista. The vineyard is two miles upstream of Ice Harbor Dam, overlooking Levey Park.

The nearby Snake River moderates the climate, and the sloping terrain keeps the air from pooling. The site is more temperate than many other grape growing areas in the Columbia Valley. The vineyard is cooler in summer, frosts less in spring and fall, and freezes less in winter.

At one time, Jeff Gordon managed a potato farm on what is now part of Chateau Ste. Michelle's and Columbia Crest's large Paterson vineyard. Jeff and Bill Gordon also had their own potato farming operation. When they decided to expand their farming interests into other crops, wine grapes were a natural choice. Part of their land is rocky

---

Gordon Brothers Cellars

531 Levey Road
Pasco, Washington 99301
(509) 547-6224

Owners
Jeff & Bill Gordon

Winemaker
Jeff Gordon

Wine Production
6,000 gallons

Vineyard Acreage
80 acres

Year First Planted
1980

First Vintage
1983

Wines Produced
Merlot, Chardonnay,
Cabernet Sauvignon, Riesling,
Chenin Blanc, Sauvignon Blanc

---

and sloping, not the best for growing potatoes, but good for tree fruits, and especially excellent for wine grapes.

The vineyard vista in the near-desert environment of eastern Washington has a raw primal beauty and grandeur of the sort not offered in the more lushly vegetated parts of the state.

With their first crop, the Gordons experienced some of the trials of the Washington winegrowing industry—rapid, tumultuous growth, with supply and demand for wine grapes fluctuating widely and seldom in balance. Their first harvest was in a year when the supply of grapes exceeded demand.

Although the Gordon Brothers' winery was born in a year of grape oversupply and the need to do something with the grapes, the winery is far more than a conduit for excess Riesling. Riesling, in fact, is not even planted in the Gordon Brothers' vineyard. The vineyard has become a prime red wine grape growing site. Ninety percent of the Gordon brothers' grapes are sold to other wineries, but Jeff Gordon has also made a name for his grapes and winery with his Merlot. It is often among the best Merlots in the Northwest.

Focusing on red wines, the Gordon brothers have replaced their Chenin Blanc with more Cabernet Sauvignon and Merlot. Thanks to a temporary oversupply of grapes one year, Washington now has another excellent red wine vineyard and red wine winery.

Hinzerling Vineyards

One of the true pioneers of the Washington wine renaissance, Mike Wallace and his family left the metropolitan lifestyle of Seattle to establish a vineyard and winery in Washington's Yakima Valley. The first vines were planted in 1972. That first winter, a severe freeze killed many of the tender young vines. Others who planted grapes that year did not replant. The Wallaces replanted and persevered.

Hinzerling was among the first Washington winegrowers to work with botrytised wines. *Botrytis cinerea* is a fungus that, under the right conditions, concentrates the juice of the grapes by reducing their water content, and, at the same time, contributes glycerol and flavors of its own to yield an intense, richly sweet wine.

Hinzerling's botrytised wines are made from Riesling and

Hinzerling Vineyards

1520 Sheridan Avenue
Prosser, Washington 99350
(509) 786-2163

Owners
Wallace Family

Winemaker
Mike Wallace

Wine Production
2,500 gallons

Vineyard Acreage
none

First Vintage
1976

Wines Produced
Limberger, Merlot,
Cabernet Sauvignon, Die Sonne,
Vintage Port, Tawny Port

Gewurztraminer. According to Wallace, Gewurztraminer is more resistant to Botrytis than Riesling, but just enough so that it is more easily manageable.

Hinzerling's most heavily botrytised Gewurztraminer is called Die Sonne, a wine made by picking selected bunches of botrytised grapes and laying them in trays behind the winery. Bees and nighttime condensation help spread the botrytis, further desiccating the grapes and concentrating their essences. The grapes are not crushed until the sugars rise to nearly 40 degrees Brix. Hinzerling's most heavily botrytised Riesling is made from individual, hand-selected, botrytised berries. The botrytised wines are not made every year, but only when conditions are favorable.

Cabernet Sauvignon has not been the easiest grape for Wash-

ington to tame. In the early years, with the exception of some sporadic successes, talk of potential was more prevalent than the actuality. Wallace was among the first to succeed with the grape. Early Hinzerling's Cabernets were "big" wines, very rough and tannic in their youth, requiring years of bottle aging to smooth their edges and show their best. More recently, Wallace modified his winemaking methods so that the Cabernets are not only more accessible when young, but will have more finesse with age.

In France, Cabernet Sauvignon, Bordeaux's premier grape, is almost always blended with other related varieties. Merlot is the best known of these, but there are others. Wallace has experimented with Cabernet Franc as well as Malbec.

Cabernet Franc, Wallace reports, is quite similar to Cabernet Sauvignon, though not as intense and flavorful. Malbec, on the other hand, is distinctive, combining pleasant herbaceous flavors with scents of violets and lavender. Malbec berries are large, and the clusters are straggly, a result of the variety's typically un-

---

Without the commitment of Mike Wallace and the other winegrowing pioneers, the Washington wine industry might not exist today.

---

even berry set. Malbec is naturally high in malic acid. Wallace's experimental blends with Malbec have been very successful, but few grapes are yet available to provide more than a tiny percentage of a blend in a commercial release.

After more than a decade and a half in the Washington winegrowing business, the Wallaces sold the winery and vineyard in 1988. The purchasers failed to fulfill the terms of the sale, however, so the Wallaces again assumed ownership. Although the vineyard was subsequently sold, Wallace continues to operate the winery, and is a winemaking and marketing consultant for a number of small wineries.

With more than 10,000 acres now in vine, and international interest and acclaim for Washington wine, it is difficult to imagine the obstacles faced by those who were in the industry's vanguard. When the Wallaces first planted grapes in 1972, many were skeptical that a viable Washington wine industry was possible, and skeptical, even, that wine grapes could be reliably grown in Washington. The Washington wine industry, and we as consumers, owe much to Mike Wallace and the other winegrowing pioneers. Without their commitment, the Washington wine industry might not exist today.

The Hogue Cellars

In 1949, the Hogue family planted 40 acres of hops in Washington's Yakima Valley. The Hogues still harvest hops from the towering hop trellises, and still process them at their own hop plant, where the moist, sticky, fragrant, hop buds are dried in a traditional hop kiln, then packed into bales.

Hops remain an important crop, satisfying the needs of the brewing industry, but Hogue Ranches also raises cattle, and grows a variety of crops, including spearmint, asparagus, potatoes—and grapes. For decades, the Hogues grew Concord grapes for the valley's grape juice processing plants. In the 1970s, the Hogues planted their first premium, vinifera, wine grapes.

The winery has expanded rapidly since its inception. Gary Hogue returned from other busi-

The Hogue Cellars

Wine Country Road
P.O. Box 31
Prosser, Washington 99350
(509) 786-4557

Owner
Mike Hogue

Winemakers
Rob Griffin & David Forsyth

Wine Production
400,000 gallons

Vineyard Acreage
300 acres

Year First Planted
1975

First Vintage
1982

Wines Produced
Chenin Blanc, Riesling,
Dry Riesling,
Reserve Dry Riesling,
Late Harvest Riesling,
Fume Blanc, Semillon,
Chardonnay, Reserve Chardonnay,
Merlot, Reserve Merlot,
Cabernet Sauvignon,
Reserve Cabernet Sauvignon,
Blush, Brut Sparkling Wine,
Harvest White,
Harvest Blanc de Blanc,
Harvest Blush, Harvest Red

ness interests to become winery president. Winemaker Rob Griffin assumed additional duties as general manager. David Forsyth was hired to be assistant winemaker in charge of day-to-day winemaking operations. In 1989, Hogue built a new 1.3 million dol-

lar, 30,000 square foot winery. Hogue has expanded its market to Japan, selling both wine and grapes.

Hogue was a leader in what is now the predominant Washington style for Chenin Blanc and Riesling. The two grapes, both delicate, floral/fruity varieties, respond well to the Yakima Valley climate. Hogue emphasizes the delicate, fruity quality of the grapes by keeping the alcohol content to a low 10 to 11 percent, fermenting at cool temperatures, and releasing the wines with crisp acidity to balance the residual sweetness. Chenin Blanc and Riesling comprise the majority of Hogue's production.

Chenin Blanc and Riesling led the way into the marketplace for Hogue, but as Hogue's vineyards mature, other varieties are playing an increasingly important role. The Chardonnay and Semillon are aged in French oak. For Sauvignon Blanc, Griffin likes American oak. The more aggressive American oak flavors act as an effective foil for the aggressive herbaceous character of the Sauvignon Blanc grape.

Similarly, Cabernet Sauvignon, an aggressively flavored red wine variety, is aged in air dried, fire bent, American oak barrels. Hogue's first Cabernet Sauvignon release, the 1983 Reserve, created a sensation at the Atlanta International Wine Festival. An intense wine with a highly pronounced American oak character, Hogue's Cabernet was awarded "Best of Show" out of 1,667 entries. For a region that was then best known for its Rieslings, Hogue's Cabernet Sauvignon was a revelation.

After Griffin made a successful test batch of bottle fermented sparkling Riesling, Hogue decided to produce the wine on a commercial scale. Griffin's sparkling Riesling is left only a short time on the yeast, emphasizing the fruit of the grape rather than the yeasty character.

"We've always had a lot of pride in what we produce, but its identity always got lost as soon as we brought in the crop and sold it. Wine is different. It's our wine. Our pride is in it, and our label is on it."

Griffin also makes wine for his own small winery. Drawing on the methods he explored at his winery, Griffin decided to make a barrel fermented Semillon Reserve at Hogue. After the barrel fermentation is complete, Griffin leaves the Hogue Semillon Reserve in contact with the lees (the sediment of yeast cells and pulp). This method makes a less fruity wine, but one with more rounded, more complex flavors.

In California, most Semillon is relatively dull and undistinguished. Sauvignon Blanc is considered easily superior. Washington produces excellent, distinctive Semillons, wines that live up to the grape's European reputation. It can be argued that Washington Semillon is superior to Sauvignon Blanc. Griffin makes wine from both grapes, and likes them both.

"They are really complementary grapes," says Griffin. "I don't think one should be ranked above the other. Fermented cool, Semil-

lon is not too different from a Chenin Blanc. At higher temperatures, Semillon shows a fuller character. Some Semillon, depending on where and how the grapes are grown and how the wine is made, can be even more herbaceous than Sauvignon Blanc. From a winemaking standpoint, Washington Semillon is a versatile grape."

For the Hogue family, the winery is a special part of their enterprise. Says Mike Hogue, "We've always had a lot of pride in what we produce, but its identity always got lost as soon as we brought in the crop and sold it. Some of the gum you chew has our Scotch spearmint in it, but its not all our mint, and the gum says Wrigley's, not Hogue. Wine is different. It's our wine. Our pride is in it, and our label is on it."

Hoodsport Winery

On western Washington's Olympic Peninsula, along the Hood Canal, Dick and Peggy Patterson operate a fruit, berry, and grape winery. Most of the grape wines are made from grapes grown in Washington's Columbia Valley, east of the Cas-

■ **Dick Patterson**

cade Mountain Range, but, from an historical perspective, Hoodsport's most interesting wine is Island Belle, a light red wine made from a non-vinifera, native American variety.

In the late 1800s, Adam Eckert came to Puget Sound's Stretch Is-

---

Hoodsport Winery

N. 23501 Highway 101
Hoodsport, Washington 98548
(206) 877-9894

Owners
Dick & Peggy Patterson

Winemaker
Dick Patterson

Grape Wine Production
20,000 gallons

Fruit & Berry Wine Production
20,000 gallons

Vineyard Acreage
5 acres

Year First Planted
1872 (historic vineyard)

First Vintage
1980

Wines Produced
Chardonnay, Chenin Blanc, Gewurztraminer, Riesling, Muller-Thurgau, White Cap, Merlot, Lemberger, Island Belle, Rhubarb, Raspberry, Loganberry, Gooseberry

---

land from New York and established a fruit and grape nursery. Eckert developed a grape he called Island Belle, a local variant of the grape Campbell Early. Very little Campbell Early is planted in America, but it is one of Japan's major grape varieties.

Island Belle enjoyed early commercial success as a table, jelly, and wine grape, before Concord from Washington's Columbia Valley gained popularity and took its place. With lack of interest and support, Island Belle, and Eckert's vineyard, fell to neglect. In 1975, Harry and Mary Branch and Bonnie Hanson purchased Eckert's Stretch Island vineyard. The new owners resuscitated the old vines and began selling the grapes on a "U-pick" basis to visitors and local residents.

In 1981, the Pattersons discovered the grapes, and Hoodsport made its first Island Belle wine. The vineyard owners have since become shareholders in the Hoodsport winery, and Island Belle, one of Washington's oldest grape varieties from one of Washington's oldest vineyards, is a Hoodsport specialty.

Although fruit and berry wines still predominate, the Pattersons have shifted the winery's emphasis to include a significant portion of vinifera grape wines. Raspberry is Hoodsport's most notable fruit wine. The Raspberry is a component in the winery's raspberry-chocolate truffles, a feature of the tasting room.

Charles Hooper Family Winery

For more than twenty years, Charles and Beverlee Hooper lived overseas in England, France, and Germany, working for the Department of Defense school system. During their last assignment, the Hoopers found time to work in the Mosel vineyards near Trier, Germany.

Returning to the states after their children were grown, the Hoopers settled in the Columbia Gorge, near the small community of Husum, and planted wine grapes. Situated on a very steep south facing slope, the Hooper vineyard looks out across the Columbia River to Oregon's Mount Hood, one of the Cascade Mountains' towering, snow covered, volcanic cones.

In the extremely steep vine-

Charles Hooper Family Winery

196 Spring Creek Road
Husum, Washington 98623
(509) 493-2324

Owners
Charles & Beverlee Hooper

Winemaker
Charles Hooper

Wine Production
2,400 gallons

Vineyard Acreage
6 acres

Year First Planted
1979

First Vintage
1984

Wines Produced
Riesling, Gewurztraminer,
Chardonnay, Pinot Noir Blanc

---

yards of the Mosel, conventional wire trellising is impossible, and the vines are trained on individual stakes. Following the German practice, the Hoopers train their vines on stakes, an unusual practice in America. Hooper usually leaves two canes on each vine, arcing them upward, and tying them to the stake.

Also in the German tradition, all Hooper's wines are white, and the focus is on Riesling. The Hoopers purchase a few grapes, but all come from Columbia Gorge vineyards.

Horizon's Edge Winery

In the mid 1970s, Tom Campbell graduated from the University of Montana with a degree in Zoology. At the time, career opportunities in his field were limited. Interested in agribusiness, Campbell went to U. C. Davis for more training. The subjects in the department of enology and viticulture sounded appealing. A year later, Campbell left,

---

having completed the course work in enology and viticulture.

In 1979, while working for a California winery, Campbell returned briefly to his native Montana and planted an experimental vineyard near Flathead Lake, in the western part of the state. In the early 1980s, Campbell left California for Washington, working as a consultant and winemaker for several Yakima Valley wineries.

In 1985, Campbell and his wife Hema Shah bonded their own winery. After coming to Washington from England, Hema worked as a pharmacist for the Yakima Valley Farm Workers Clinic. The Horizon's Edge vineyard is planted to several varieties, including Pinot Noir. Campbell believes that his north facing Pinot Noir growing site will be sufficiently cool to make a quality

---

Horizon's Edge Winery

4530 East Zillah Drive
Zillah, Washington 98953
(509) 829-6401

Owners
Tom Campbell & Hema Shah

Winemaker
Tom Campbell

Wine Production
4,000 gallons

Vineyard Acreage
16 acres

Year First Planted
1985

First Vintage
1984

Wines Produced
Chardonnay, Muscat Canelli,
Pinot Noir, Cabernet Sauvignon,
Sparkling Wine

---

wine. As necessary, on hot days, Campbell cools the Pinot Noir with an overhead sprinkler system.

Chardonnay from estate grown grapes is Campbell's flagship

wine. A late harvest Muscat Canelli, released as a nouveau wine, one month after the vintage, is a Horizon's Edge speciality.

Along with his parents, Campbell started a second winery, Mission Mountain in Montana. Although most of Mission Mountain's wines are made at Horizon's Edge from Washington grapes, Campbell makes sparkling wines from Pinot Noir grapes grown along Montana's Flathead Lake. The moderating climate of the large lake makes vinifera wines a limited but real possibility.

Hunter Hill Vineyards

Within the last 10 million years, the northward movement of the Northwest's coastal land mass buckled the Columbia Valley's basalt lava flows and formed folded high ridges. The ridges run in a generally east to west direction, offering shelter from the cold of the north—and sunny south facing slopes for grape growing.

Hunter Hill Vineyards is the first winery on one of the Columbia Valley's more northerly folded

> **Hunter Hill Vineyards is the first winery on the Royal Slope, one of the Columbia Valley's most northerly basalt ridges.**

ridges, the Royal Slope, a grape growing area just north of the more familiar Wahluke Slope. In 1977, Airline pilot, Art Byron, bought a 233 acre farm at the far eastern end of the Royal Slope and turned part of it into a vineyard and winery. The vineyard spans the Adams and Grant county line. The winery itself is just off Highway 12 in Adams county, the county's first winery.

A Washington State University research farm is within a mile of the vineyard, but little is known about Royal Slope grape growing. So far, Byron reports that the grapes ripen about eight to ten days later than the Yakima Valley. The heat during the summer months is more intense than other parts of the Columbia Valley, but the growing season is slightly shorter and more compressed.

Byron consulted with noted Washington horticulturist, Walter Clore, before planting his vineyard to Riesling, Merlot, and Gewurztraminer. Byron subsequently expanded his vineyard with Chardonnay and more Merlot.

European winegrowing has evolved over the course of some 2,000 years, but only within the last two decades have winegrowers begun systematically exploring Washington's highly unique winegrowing climates. The Royal Slope is one of the Columbia Valley's newest grape growing regions. Byron is one of the state's new pioneers.

Hyatt Vineyards

Hyatt Vineyards

2020 Gilbert Road
Zillah, Washington 98953
(509) 829-6333

Owners
Leland & Lynda Hyatt

Winemaker
Stan Clarke

Wine Production
10,000 gallons

Vineyard Acreage
73 acres

Year First Planted
1983

First Vintage
1987

Wines Produced
Chardonnay, Dry Chenin Blanc,
Sauvignon Blanc, Riesling,
Cabernet Sauvignon, Merlot,
Late Harvest Riesling,
Riesling Ice Wine

Between the Sunnyside and Roza Irrigation Canals, on the lower slopes of the Rattlesnake Hills, Hyatt Vineyards overlooks the Yakima Valley, with views of Mount Adams and Mount Rainier, the towering, perpetually snow covered, ancient volcanic cones.

Principally involved in grape growing and other business interests, Leland and Lynda Hyatt decided to open a winery to have better control over widely fluctuating prices and demand for their wine grapes. To launch their winery enterprise, the Hyatts se-

Hunter Hill Vineyards

2752 West McMannaman Road
Othello, Washington 99344
(509) 346-2607

Owners
H. H. V., Inc.

Winemaker
Art Byron

Wine Production
10,000 gallons

Vineyard Acreage
28 acres

Year First Planted
1981

First Vintage
1984

Wines Produced
Riesling, Dry Riesling,
Select Riesling,
Cabernet Sauvignon, Merlot,
Chardonnay, Petite Rouge Blush,
Peach, Plum

cured the services of two highly regarded figures in the Washington wine scene. Noted viticulturalist Wade Wolfe set up the winery and made the first wines. Stan Clarke, formerly viticulturalist and general manager at Covey Run, replaced Wolfe in 1989.

Hyatt produces only a limited amount of Riesling. The winery focus will be on more "serious" varietals such as Chardonnay, Sauvignon Blanc, Cabernet Sauvignon, and Merlot.

The Hyatt winery and vineyards are located only a few miles from Zillah, a town that is rapidly becoming a center for some of Yakima Valley's finer wineries and vineyard sites. Wade Wolfe got the winery off to a fine start. Stan Clarke's viticultural skills and winery management acumen should insure a strong future.

Johnson Creek Winery

In the Skookumchuck Valley, 26 miles southeast of the state capitol of Olympia, Vince and

Johnson Creek Winery

19248 Johnson Creek Road S.E.
Tenino, Washington 98589
(206) 264-2100

Owners
Vince & Ann de Bellis

Winemaker
Vince de Bellis

Wine Production
4,000 gallons

Vineyard Acreage
3 acres

Year First Planted
1985

First Vintage
1984

Wines Produced
Pink Riesling, Chenin Blanc,
Muller-Thurgau, Chardonnay,
Cabernet Sauvignon, Merlot

Ann de Bellis own and operate Alice's Restaurant. Converted from a rural farmhouse, Alice's Restaurant features a six course, two hour dinner, Wednesday through Sunday. Fresh rainbow trout and fresh bread are served with every meal.

An outgrowth of the restaurant, the de Bellis's planted a small vineyard and a started their own winery, Johnson Creek. The family owns 33 acres of land on Johnson Creek, but only three acres on the valley floor are suitable for vineyards.

Western Washington is a very cool grape growing climate. De Bellis planted his vineyard at a very dense spacing of five feet between each row and four feet between each vine within the rows. The dense spacing is typical of cool climate winegrowing, reducing the load on each vine for a better quality crop. His vine trellises are seven feet tall to catch the sunshine, a precious commodity in western Washington.

De Bellis is one of the few winegrowers working with grapes grown west of the Cascade Mountains. He has planted some experimental vines, but most of the vineyard is planted to Muller-Thurgau, a Riesling-like grape suitable to very cool climates like western Washington. De Bellis buys more grapes from other western Washington grape growers, but two-thirds of his grapes come from the Columbia Valley, east of the Cascade Mountains. De Bellis stems and crushes the grapes in the vineyard, bringing only the juice back to the winery to ferment.

De Bellis prefers Muller-Thurgau to the other typical western Washington grape varieties such as Madeleine Angevine and Madeleine Sylvaner, and he is fo-

cusing on this variety for his western Washington wines. Most of Johnson Creek's wines are sold directly from the winery. They are also available to accompany Alice's Restaurant's hearty dinners.

Kiona Vineyards

Before merging with the Columbia, the Yakima River runs up against a short but determinant block of hills, and takes a

Kiona Vineyards

Route 2, Box 2169E
Sunset Road
Benton City, Washington 99320
(206) 588-6716

Owners
Jim & Pat Holmes,
John & Ann Williams

Winemaker
Jim Holmes

Wine Production
20,000 gallons

Vineyard Acreage
30 acres

Year First Planted
1975

First Vintage
1980

Wines Produced
Lemberger, Cabernet Sauvignon,
Merlot, Chardonnay,
Chenin Blanc, Riesling,
Dry Riesling,
Late Harvest Riesling,
Merlot Rose,
Muscat Canelli,
Late Harvest Gewurztraminer

brief, radical turn northward. One of the warmest and driest parts of the Yakima Valley, this area, on the northward turn of the river, at the far eastern end of the Yakima Valley, was nearly left to sagebrush when the Kennewick Irrigation District abandoned plans for an irrigation canal.

In 1974, however, the partnership that would later become Kiona Vineyards drilled a well 550 feet deep to a major aquifer, the first deep well water in the area. The following year, the Kiona partners planted their vineyard on the lower slopes of Red Mountain,

Kiona's pioneering success brought other grape growers and wineries to the area, and Red Mountain has emerged as an important sub-region of the Yakima Valley.

near the town of Kiona. Their pioneering success brought other grape growers and wineries to the area, and Red Mountain has emerged as an important sub-region of the Yakima Valley.

Kiona Vineyards is a partnership of two families, Jim and Pat Holmes , and John and Ann Williams. Since 1961, Holmes and Williams have worked together as engineers. Holmes, a native of San Francisco, and long time home winemaker, describes the Kiona winery as a hobby that got out of hand. Kiona sold its first grapes to other wineries, but in 1979, the partners bonded their winery, and, in 1980, Holmes crushed Kiona's first commercial vintage in the crowded confines of his garage. Since then, the winery has moved to a newly constructed facility at the vineyard site.

The soil is a Hezel silt loam, running 25 feet down to a 60 to 80 foot layer of sand and gravel. Clumps of calcium carbonate dot the soil. At 8.4, the soil's pH is one of the highest in the Northwest, a desired characteristic for growing grapes.

Some of Washington's early vinifera grape plantings were fan trained. On a fan trained vine, several trunks emerge from the vine's base and spread upward forming a tall fan. In eastern European countries, soil is plowed over the base of the fan trained trunks to protect the vine from winter cold, or else the trunks themselves are bent to the

■ **Jim Holmes & one of Kiona's classic fan trained vines**

ground and buried. In the early years of Washington winegrowing, fan training was a recommended method of winter protection.

The training method has since been abandoned as unnecessary for winter protection, but, at Kiona, most of the vines are still fan trained—not for winter protection, but because Holmes and Williams see other advantages. In their view, the vines have fewer mildew problems, sunlight more evenly strikes the leaves near the grape clusters, and the grapes ripen earlier. For the winery visitor, fan trained vines are a pleasing esthetic difference, and an

encapsulated glimpse at Washington winegrowing history.

Chenin Blanc and Riesling are the winery's staples, both made in dry and slightly sweet renditions. Kiona's Chardonnay, fermented in French oak and aged on the lees, is the premier white wine. Kiona makes and sells Cabernet Sauvignon under their own label, and also sells Cabernet Sauvignon grapes to other select wineries. Kiona is emerging as one of Washington's leading Cabernet Sauvignon vineyards. The Kiona grapes yield Cabernets with concentrated varietal fruit, moderate herbal characteristics, and a fine textural richness.

Kiona's speciality wine is Lemberger, a little know red wine grape recommended by Dr. Walter Clore, professor emeritus at Washington State University. Kiona's Lemberger was planted in 1976, the oldest commercial planting in the state. Kiona was also the first Washington winery to release Lemberger as a varietal wine. The vintage was 1980.

Lemberger's berry and vanilla flavors are rather simple and direct, but good, and especially tasty when young, when the fruit of the grape shows prominently. Kiona ages Lemberger in American oak for added texture and flavor complexity. Lemberger offers a pleasant change of pace from the more conventional varieties. Kiona's Lembergers are routinely some of the best.

L'Ecole No 41

L'Ecole No 41 was founded by Baker and Jean Ferguson, a vibrant, silver-haired couple with a wry wit and self-effacing humor. As a retirement adventure, the Fergusons bought a large frame building that once housed the classrooms and offices for Lowden's School District No 41—thus the winery name. L'Ecole No 41 specializes in two Bordeaux grape varieties, Merlot and Semillon, and, more recently, a Chenin Blanc, whimsically named Walla Voila, pronounced (in case you don't speak Northwest French) Walla Walla.

L'Ecole No 41's label is the result of a contest among the Fergusons young nieces, nephews, and cousins. The winning design, a child's drawing of the schoolhouse, effectively captures the winery's theme.

The extensively and artistically remodeled schoolhouse includes the winery on the cellar floor, a tasting room and public area on the second floor, and living quarters on the third floor. Special events are catered in an elegant dining area for groups of 10 to 30 by Barbara Mastin, formerly owner and chef of a highly acclaimed restaurant in California's wine country. Mastin's catering is available for groups by prior arrangement by calling (509) 529-1159.

Recently, the Fergusons turned the winery's day-to-day operations over to other members of the family. The Fergusons' daughter Megan and her husband Marty Clubb left their jobs in San Francisco for the rural Walla Walla Valley lifestyle. Marty, an MBA with a chemical engineering background, began making the wine at L'Ecole No 41 in 1989.

Much of the winery's tradition continues. The Fergusons remain involved, and a visit to the winery will just as likely find them there. Baker Ferguson is a rich-voiced, articulate, folksy orator with a deep sense of history, and a sense of his roots in the Walla Walla Val-

ley. His great-grandfather, a Washington pioneer, founded the oldest bank in Washington, the Baker Boyer National Bank in Walla Walla.

■ **Baker & Jean Ferguson**

In the modern era, winegrowing in the Walla Walla Valley is only just beginning, but Ferguson's research shows that the Walla Walla Valley was among the

L'Ecole No 41

41 Lowden School Road
P.O. Box 111
Lowden, Washington 99360
(509) 525-0940

Owners
Marty & Megan Clubb

Winemaker
Marty Clubb

Wine Production
7,000 gallons

Vineyard Acreage
none

First Vintage
1983

Wines Produced
Merlot, Semillon, Chenin Blanc

earliest winegrowing areas in the Northwest. According to Ferguson, winegrowing in the Walla Walla Valley may have predated winegrowing in California's Napa Valley.

Like other early winegrowing efforts in the Northwest, grape

cultural practices, winemaking, and timing did little to insure the continuance of the industry. Ferguson hopes the time is now right. The Fergusons and the rest of the new wave of upstart Walla Walla winemakers are at the beginning of a winegrowing renaissance. The Walla Walla vine has lengthy roots and a promising future.

Latah Creek Wine Cellars

Mike Conway, an experienced California winemaker, came to Spokane in 1980 to make wine for Worden's Washington Winery, Spokane's first winery in the modern era. After two years at Worden's, Conway left to become winemaker for Hogue Cellars. That same year, under arrangement with Hogue, Conway opened a winery of his own in Spokane, Latah Creek Wine Cellars. After an agreed transitional period, Conway left his winemaking role at Hogue to concentrate his efforts full-time at Latah Creek.

Unlike many new winemakers coming to Washington, Conway is a microbiologist, and not a winemaking graduate of U. C. Davis. While attending school, Conway worked nights as a lab technician for California's Gallo Winery. After graduating, he went to work for Franzia, and soon became directly interested in winemaking. In 1977, Conway left Franzia to become assistant winemaker at Parducci.

One of Latah Creek's specialties is a direct result of Conway's association with Parducci. Joe Monostori, Parducci's cellarmaster, learned winemaking in Hungary from his grandfather. In the spring, to celebrate the planting of

■ Mike Conway

new crops, the local Hungarian winemakers made May Wine, a light, sweet, fragrant wine flavored with woodruff and strawberries. At Parducci, Monostori made small quantities for sale only at the winery. Conway learned the recipe from Monostori, and May Wine is now a Latah Creek speciality, released each spring to coincide with Spokane's Lilac Festival. The wine is intensely flavored and semi-sweet, with crisp balancing acidity.

Crisp acidity and fresh fruitiness are the mark of Washington's predominant white wine style. The very nature of the winegrowing region lends itself to this wine style, and no one exemplifies and demonstrates it more than Conway. Conway's wines are very fruity, fresh and clean, and apparently low in phenols. The wines, especially Chenin Blanc and Riesling, are low in alcohol, with residual sweetness balanced by fairly high acidity.

Conway's Chenin Blanc is especially notable. Normally a wine of modest interest, Chenin Blanc suffered greatly from its reputation as an indifferent jug wine grape in California's warm growing regions. Although Washington had produced good Chenin Blanc for more than a de-

cade, Conway's dedication to the grape carried the wine an additional qualitative step further. Different than the Chenin Blanc of France's Loire district, Conway's Chenin Blanc is in a fruitier style, similar in profile, if not in taste, to a Washington Riesling.

Riesling and Chenin Blanc are Latah Creek's major wines. Both are fermented slowly at cool temperatures to preserve their fresh fruity qualities. Different yeast strains

Latah Creek Wine Cellars

13030 East Indiana Avenue
Spokane, Washington 99216
(509) 926-0164

Owners
Mike & Ellena Conway

Winemaker
Mike Conway

Wine Production
32,000 gallons

Vineyard Acreage
none

First Vintage
1982

Wines Produced
Chardonnay, Feather Chardonnay, Semillon, Sauvignon Blanc, Riesling, Chenin Blanc, Muscat Canelli, Merlot, Cabernet Sauvignon, May Wine, Spokane Blush

behave in different ways. Some yeast strains "stick" at low temperatures and cannot be readily restarted, causing many problems for the winemaker. Conway, especially for his delicate white varietals, prefers the Steinberg strain. Steinberg ferments slowly and reliably at low temperatures, yet can be easily stopped when the desired sweetness is reached. Most comes from

California as a liquid culture, but Conway's is a German dry culture he obtains from Canada via the barter system, trading some of his grape juice for the yeast.

Conway likes to keep his delicate white wines cool from the onset of fermentation through the bottling process. Keeping the wine continuously cool traps carbon dioxide and makes the wine slightly "spritzy" when the bottle is opened and the wine is served. The slight effervescence from the release of the trapped gas contributes to the wine's fresh taste.

Chardonnay, Muscat Canelli, Semillon, Merlot and Cabernet Sauvignon round out Latah Creek's line of wines. Conway is gradually shifting his emphasis toward Merlot and Chardonnay. All carry through the Latah Creek style. Even the red wines emphasize the fresh fruity character of the grape, Conway's trademark. Conway is one of an increasing number of Washington winemakers enthused about Semillon. Conway's Semillon is released with moderately high acid and slight residual sugar. The wine tastes almost, but not quite, dry.

Conway has definite ideas about the kind of wine he wants to make. Taking a cue from Parducci, a winery that has long had a reputation for good wine at a reasonable price, Conway is not emphasizing expensive specialty wines, but good wines at moderate prices.

Leonetti Cellar

Leonetti Cellar is one of Washington's easternmost winegrowing estates. Owned and operated by Gary and Nancy Figgins, Leonetti Cellar has a lengthy heritage. Figgins' grandfather, an Italian immigrant, settled in the Walla Walla Valley, growing grapes and making wine for family use. In the modern winegrowing era, Figgins opened the first winery in the Walla Walla Valley.

For a time, Figgins made wine from grapes grown on the original vineyard site, supplemented by grapes grown elsewhere in the Columbia Valley. The historic family vineyard is no longer a source of grapes, but Figgins tends a tiny one acre Merlot vineyard adjacent to his winery, relying on select growers in the Walla Walla and Columbia Valleys for most of his

Figgins once made a Riesling, since discontinued, in favor of his fundamental mission—red wine. Figgins released Leonetti's first

■ **Gary & Nancy Figgins**

Cabernet from the 1978 vintage, and immediately gained recognition in major regional and national wine judgings. Leonetti's other red grape, Merlot, has had similar success. The wines are made in a ripe, oaky, relatively low acid style, with lengthy vatting to extract the most from the grape, and lengthy aging in a high percentage of new French and American oak barrels to pick up additional tannins and complexity.

Figgins works with grapes from a variety of sources, including the Seven Hills Vineyard, a vineyard that is not actually in Washington, but just across the border, in the Oregon portion of the Walla Walla Valley. Figgins has bottled the Seven Hills Cabernet separately, but most of his wines are blends of more than one vineyard—and more than one grape variety, as well. A little Cabernet is usually blended into the Merlot, and vice versa.

Leonetti's first wines were made in a small shed behind the family home, but in 1985, Figgins completed construction of an underground cellar to protect his

wines from the Walla Walla Valley's temperature extremes. Except for the yearly September release of new wines, Leonetti is not open to the public. The wines are only available locally and in select markets.

Steven T. Livingstone Wines

Steve Livingstone did not enter the wine business along any typical, predictable, or linear path. Livingstone was a chemistry student at Purdue University when he dropped out of college to join a carnival. After nearly a decade of carnival life, Livingstone returned to Spokane in 1978, settled down, and started several businesses.

Livingstone's interest in wine prompted him to start one more business, a business that would have a special appeal—a winery. Mike Scott, formerly of the Latah Creek winery, is operations manager. Prior to bonding his own facility, Livingstone's first

---

Leonetti Cellar

1321 School Avenue
Walla Walla, Washington 99362
(509) 525-1428

Owners
Gary & Nancy Figgins

Winemaker
Gary Figgins

Wine Production
6,000 gallons

Vineyard Acreage
1 acre

Year First Planted
1978

First Vintage
1978

Wines Produced
Cabernet Sauvignon,
Cabernet Sauvignon Reserve,
Merlot

---

grape supply. Recently, his father, Berle Figgins, planted five acres of Cabernet Sauvignon and Cabernet Franc on the Snake River, near Windust, all destined for Leonetti wines.

Steven T. Livingstone Wines

East 14 Mission
Spokane, Washington 99202
(509) 328-5069

Owners
Steve & Debbie Livingstone

Winemaker
Steve Livingstone

Wine Production
10,000 gallons

Vineyard Acreage
none

First Vintage
1988

Wines Produced
Chardonnay, Chardonnay Reserve,
Sauvignon Blanc, Riesling,
Dry Riesling, Muscat Canelli,
Cabernet Sauvignon, Merlot,
Petite Sirah

---

wines were made at Latah Creek. The Livingstone winery is in an old Spokane bakery. Scott cautions that visitors should not be deterred by the less than elegant exterior. The interior is warm and welcoming, offering a mahogany tasting bar and the refurbished brick of the old bakery.

Sauvignon Blanc and Chardonnay comprise a third of Livingstone's production. Livingstone offers two bottlings of Chardonnay, one fermented in stainless steel, and another fermented in 160 gallon oak puncheons, put through malolactic fermentation, and aged in Allier oak barrels. The Sauvignon Blanc and one of the Rieslings are also aged in oak. Both are finished nearly dry, at .5 milligrams residual sugar. Future releases will see an increasing emphasis on red wines, including a small amount of Petite Sirah. The warm Red Mountain area of the Yakima Valley is the source for most of Livingstone's grapes.

Lost Mountain Winery

A research chemist, Romeo Conca revived his Italian family tradition and began making homemade wine, a practice learned as a child from his father. Upon retirement, Conca

---

**The dry Muscat Alexandria was a bit like a Gewurztraminer from hell.
I bought a case.**

---

started his own tiny commercial winery near the town of Sequim, on Washington's Olympic Peninsula. For those sensitive to

---

Lost Mountain Winery

730 Lost Mountain Road
Sequim, Washington 98382
(206) 683-5229

Owner
Romeo Conca

Winemaker
Romeo Conca

Wine Production
1,300 gallons

Vineyard Acreage
none

First Vintage
1981

Wines Produced
Cabernet Sauvignon, Merlot, Poesia, Pinot Noir, Zinfandel, Muscat Alexandria, Lost Mountain Red

---

sulfites, Conca uses no sulfiting agents in the winemaking process.

Lost Mountain's Cabernet Sauvignon and Merlot are made from Washington grapes. Conca brings in Zinfandel and Petite Sirah grapes from California for his blended wines as well as his single varietal bottlings. An unusual Lost Mountain Red wine is made from a blend of Zinfandel, Petite Syrah, and Muscat. All Lost Mountain's wines are make in a robust, high alcohol, full- bodied style.

Lost Mountain also releases wines in a special poetry series, named Poesia, the Italian word for poetry. Each is a blended red wine featuring a poem by a local poet. Since 1985, Poesia has been a 50/50 blend of Cabernet Sauvignon and Merlot. Most very small wineries have fairly primitive labels. Lost Mountain's Poesia was awarded the Best of Category prize at the Atlanta International Wine Competition. Its design and execution is befitting a wine whose theme is based on artistic expression.

With rare exception, Conca makes only red wines. Though only occasionally available, one of the rare exceptions is a dry Muscat Alexandria, a wine made from the world's most ancient vinifera wine grape. Conca's grapes come from an old "pre-wine- boom" vineyard in the Columbia Gorge. Even for a muscat, the Muscat Alexandria variety has a reputation for having rather crude and overbearing flavors. Conca's rendition is a bit like a Gewurztraminer-from-hell. I bought a case.

McCrea Winery

Doug McCrea attributes some of his winemaking interest and approach to his New Orleans upbringing, and to his mother who is part Creole. The French

---

McCrea Winery

12707 18th Street S.E.
Lake Stevens, Washington 98258
(206) 334-5248

Owners
Doug & Susan McCrea

Winemaker
Doug McCrea

Wine Production
1,200 gallons

Vineyard Acreage
none

First Vintage
1988

Wines Produced
Chardonnay, Mariah

---

and Creole influences infuse New Orleans culture with a taste for wine and an appreciation for diversity and a broad spectrum of flavors and flavor combinations.

McCrea makes two wines, Chardonnay, and a proprietary red wine featuring the grape varieties of France's Rhone region. McCrea is enthused about the prospects of Washington Syrah, Mourvedre, and Grenache.

Presently, McCrea only has access to Grenache from the Graves vineyard in the Columbia Gorge. He hopes to establish new plantings of Syrah and Mourvedre in several select Washington growing sites. "If we succeed," says McCrea, "we'll be blending a spicy red wine made entirely from Rhone grape varieties."

"It's an exciting time in Washington," says McCrea. "Even with the specialized focus I have, there are so many possibilities, so much to explore."

The proprietary red wine is called Mariah, a take-off on the Mistral winds of the Rhone Valley. The proprietary name is fitting for the Grenache from the Graves vineyard. The winds roar through the narrow Gorge where Pacific marine air and dry, near desert air of the inland Columbia Valley collide in a tumultuous mixing.

McCrea's first wine, a barrel fermented Chardonnay, drew immediate acclaim. The wine remained on the lees for ten months. Not until the fourth or fifth month, says McCrea, did the lees character start to show in the wine. McCrea puts his Chardonnay through a partial malolactic fermentation to achieve the balance of fruitiness and rounded malolactic fermentation flavors he prefers.

A new and tiny winery, McCrea has already earned a reputation for carefully crafted wines.

Mercer Ranch Vineyards

One of Washington's earliest commercial wine grape growers in the modern era, Don

---

Mercer Ranch Vineyards

522 Alderdale Road
Prosser, Washington 99350
(509) 894-4741

Owners
Don & Linda Mercer

Winemaker
Don Mercer

Wine Production
4,000 gallons

Vineyard Acreage
132 acres

Year First Planted
1972

First Vintage
1984

Wines Produced
Limberger (Lemberger),
Cabernet Sauvignon,
Muscat Canelli,
Sadie Louise Blush

---

and Linda Mercer opened their own winery after more than a decade of grape growing. The Mercers still sell most of their grapes to other wineries, reserving enough of the harvest for their own small winery.

Although the winery has a Prosser mailing address, Mercer Ranch is actually located outside the Yakima Valley, on the other side of the Horse Heaven Hills. The winery and vineyards are five miles north of the Columbia River, 18 miles west of the town of Paterson.

The Mercer family has deep roots in the region. Until 1952, the Mercers were sheep ranchers. The original ranch, started in the late 1800s by Don Mercer's grandfather, is located just east of the present site. For decades, the family moved the sheep by rail to their summer range in Montana, then back

again in the fall to the winter range along the Columbia River. For the long trip, the Mercers herded the sheep to the town of Whitcomb, on the Columbia River, loaded the sheep in stock cars, the wagons and trucks on flatcars, and the sheepherders and

---

Mercer's Cabernet fruit produces wines with a distinctive plum pit character.

---

range hands in an old coach car. The Mercer's sheep ranching heritage is depicted on the Mercer Ranch label.

Although Mercer produces a Blush wine called Sadie Louise, and an excellent Muscat Canelli, red wines, specifically, Cabernet Sauvignon and Limberger, are the focus. For a time, Mercer Ranch had the largest Limberger vine-

■ **Don & Linda Mercer**

yard in North America—12 acres. An uncommon grape variety, Limberger is becoming very popular in Washington. Acreage throughout the state promises to increase dramatically as planting wood becomes more readily available. Washington State University researchers Dr. Walter Clore and George Carter were early advocates of the grape. In the late 1960s, Mercer tasted some of their experimental wines and became an advocate as well.

Mercer's Cabernet comes from four vineyards located within a half mile of each other. Mercer blends some of the Cabernets from the different vineyards, and releases some as individual vineyard bottlings.

Mercer's vineyard location is unique, and the Cabernet Sauvignon fruit produces wines with a distinctive character that Mercer, rather accurately, describes as "plum pit." Mercer sells his grapes to a variety of wineries. In the past, some of his clients did not always show Mercer Ranch Cabernet Sauvignon at its best. In recent years, however, Mercer Ranch Cabernet Sauvignon has been showing up as an important component in the wines of some of Washington's best Cabernet Sauvignon artists. And now, with his own winery, Mercer can showcase his own Cabernet Sauvignon as well.

Mont Elise Vineyards

Charles Henderson has been involved with agronomy all his life, and for the past 20 years, has grown grapes in the Columbia River Gorge near the town of Bingen. In the early years of grape growing, Henderson worked closely with Dr. Clore and others from the Irrigated Agricultural Research and Extension Center at Prosser, Washington to evaluate the grape varieties best suited to the Bingen area.

From about 20 experimentally planted grape varieties, Pinot Noir and Gewurztraminer were

selected as the best, and in 1972, Henderson planted his vineyard to them. A total of 200 acres of Henderson's property are suitable for wine grapes. Henderson's first wines were marketed under the

Mont Elise Vineyards

315 West Steuben
Bingen, Washington 98605
(509) 493-3001

Owners
Henderson family

Winemaker
Chuck Henderson, Jr.

Wine Production
14,000 gallons

Vineyard Acreage
35 acres

Year First Planted
1972

First Vintage
1975

Wines Produced
Gewurztraminer, Riesling, Gamay Beaujolais, Chenin Blanc, Pinot Noir Blanc, Pinot Rose, Pinot Noir, Sauvignon Blanc, Sparkling

name Bingen Wine Cellars, but in late 1978, the Hendersons bought out the other winery partners and became sole owners, changing the winery's name to Mont Elise Vineyards.

The Cascade Mountains and the Columbia River Gorge are remarkable geologic phenomena, and their climatic influence is no less profound. The Mont Elise vineyards are just east of where the Columbia River Gorge cuts through the line of the Cascade Range. The Cascades block the easterly flow of marine air, making much of eastern Washington a desert while leaving western Washington moist, temperate, and lushly vegetated. The Columbia River Gorge is a passageway along which the two dramatically different climates converge and

collide. Understandably, radical climatic changes occur within relatively few miles. Parts of the gorge are characterized by this tempestuous mixing of climates.

In terms of the commonly used heat summation method of climate measurement, heat units at the Mont Elise vineyards range from 2,000 to 2,100 a year. A short distance west, and heat units measure 1,800 or less; a short distance east, and heat units measure 2,900 or higher. Thus, the Mont Elise growing climate is very tightly defined, one of the most highly localized grape growing climates in the Northwest. Climates, however, are much more complex than the measure of relative heat units. Henderson points out that Bingen receives slightly fewer heat units than growing areas in Oregon's Willamette Valley, yet Bingen grapes generally harvest one to two Brix higher in any given year.

In 1985, Henderson's son, Charles Jr., completed his studies in enology at U. C. Davis and returned to Mont Elise to assume the winemaking duties, allowing Charles Sr. to devote more attention to the expanded vineyard operations.

In accordance with market interest, Mont Elise is shifting emphasis more to white wines. Fully 90 percent of Mont Elise's production is now white. The principal red wine, Gamay Beaujolais, is made in a light, fruity style with slight residual sweetness. Largely replacing red Pinot Noir, a bottle fermented Brut-style sparkling Pinot Noir is Mont Elise's new flagship wine.

Mount Baker Vineyards

Washington has two distinct climates. West of the Cascade Mountain Range, the marine climate is characterized by temperate summers, moderate winters, and frequent clouds and rain. East of the Cascades, the climate is cooler in the winter and much warmer in the summer. The skies are frequently cloudless, and there is little rain.

Although the first premium grape wineries in the modern era were located in metropolitan areas west of the Cascade Mountains, virtually all the grapes were grown east of the Cascades, in Washington's vast Columbia Valley. The Columbia Valley will always remain the state's largest winegrowing region, but western Washington's cool, temperate, winegrowing climate insures a niche for a unique range of wines.

Al Stratton, founder of Mount Baker Vineyards, and Jim Hildt, horticulturist and partner in the winery, are major proponents of western Washington grape growing. A retired military physician, Stratton became involved with research projects at Washington State University's Research and Extension Unit at Mount Vernon, Washington. When time came to make wine from the experimentally grown grapes, the research center's horticulturist, Bob Norton, turned to Stratton. The Mount Vernon area, averaging about 1,300 heat units during the growing season, is far from the best growing climate in western Washington, but Stratton was impressed that good quality wine could be made even in this very cool area.

Many areas west of the Cascades are far better suited to growing grapes. The site of Mount Baker's own vineyards is in one such area. The vineyards are located a dozen miles east of Bellingham, Washington, in a localized climate a quarter mile wide and two miles long. Even though the vineyards are on the

---

The late harvest Madeleine Angevine successfully explores new ground. Mount Baker's wines add welcome diversity to the Northwest wine spectrum.

---

valley floor, nighttime thermal air currents keep the vines frost free during the growing season, a season that lasts from 210 to 240 days, longer than the growing season in most Columbia Valley vineyards.

Mount Baker's grape growing sites average approximately 2,200 heat units during the growing season. Heat units are by no means the only factor in choosing a grape growing area, but they are an important indicator. Mount Baker's sites are quite warm for western Washington. The heat units are almost as high as some of the Columbia Valley's cooler growing sites, though Stratton's site has more frequent cloud cover, warmer nights, and less intensely hot days.

Many of the grape varieties that grow best and produce the best wine in western Washington are not the same as Washington's Columbia Valley grape varieties. Mount Baker's major grapes are Madeleine Angevine, Muller-Thurgau, Okanogan Riesling, and Gewurztraminer. The vineyards

also have smaller plantings of Pinot Noir and Chardonnay. Grapes for some wines, notably the warmer climate varieties, are purchased from growers in the Columbia Valley.

Madeleine Angevine is a French vinifera variety bred in the Loire Valley in the 1850s. It is a cross of two older vinifera varieties, Precoce de Malingre and Madeleine Royale. A traditional Canadian wine grape, Okanogan Riesling was brought to the New World by Hungarian immigrants, and named after a Canadian val-

Mount Baker Vineyards

4298 Mount Baker Highway
Deming, Washington 98244
(206) 592-2300

Owners
The Stratton & Hildt Families

Winemaker
Jim Hildt, winemaker;
John Kelly, cellarmaster

Wine Production
20,000 gallons

Vineyard Acreage
25 acres

Year First Planted
1977

First Vintage
1982

Wines Produced
Madeleine Angevine,
Madeleine Angevine Limited
Reserve, Chardonnay,
Gewurztraminer,
Okanogan Riesling,
Muller-Thurgau,
Dry Muller-Thurgau,
Island Classic, Island Blush,
Tulip Blush, Crystal Rain Blanc,
Siegerrebe, Pinot Noir,
Cabernet Sauvignon, Merlot,
Royal Crimson Plum Wine

ley. A grape of mysterious origin, Okanogan Riesling is probably an interspecific hybrid and not a true vinifera variety. Muller-Thurgau is one of the most widely planted varieties in Germany.

As a table wine, Madeleine Angevine may be best when fermented totally dry rather than finished slightly sweet, but Mount Baker has explored new ground at the other end of the sweetness scale, with a highly successful, quite sweet, late harvest version.

Mountain Dome Winery

Most wineries produce at least one cash-flow wine, a wine that requires no expensive oak barrels, and little or no aging before it can be released and sold. Mountain Dome, however, produces only one wine, and it is the antithesis of a cash-flow wine.

Mountain Dome Winery
Route 2, Box 199M Spokane, Washington 99207 (509) 922-7408
Owners Michael & Patricia Manz
Winemakers Michael & Patricia Manz
Wine Production 3,200 gallons
Vineyard Acreage 1 acre
Year First Planted 1987
First Vintage 1984
Wines Produced Sparkling Brut

Mountain Dome makes only sparkling wine. Although it is possible to make a quick-sell sparkling wine, the best require expensive equipment, extensive hand labor, or both. Mountain Dome's sparkling wines are fermented in French oak barrels, put through a malolactic fermentation, and left on the lees in the bottle for four years prior to dis-

gorging. The cuvee consists of one-third Chardonnay and two-thirds Pinot Noir. A vineyard in the Columbia Valley's Pasco Basin supplies the grapes.

The Manzs' have a small experimental vineyard planted to Pinot Noir and Chardonnay. The Spokane area is not exactly a prime grape growing region, but grapes for sparkling wines are harvested at lower sugars, so there is at least the prospect of success. So far, the vines have handily survived the winters.

The Manzs' crushed only one ton of grapes in 1984, and continued on an experimental scale for several years. In 1988, the Manzs' crushed enough grapes to make a wine for commercial sale. Mountain Dome's first commercial release is a vintage dated sparkling wine scheduled to meet consumers in 1992.

Neuharth Winery

A retired grape grower from California's northern San Joaquin Valley, Eugene Neuharth and his wife Maria moved to Sequim, on Washington's Olympic Peninsula, in 1973. In 1979, the Neuharths planted 33 different grape varieties, mostly French-American hybrids, in two small experimental vineyards.

The Olympic Peninsula is Washington's rainiest region, but Sequim's unusual climate, situated in a localized rain shadow, is one of the driest in the western part of the state. Unfortunately, the Sequim area does not receive enough heat units to ripen most grape varieties properly. Except for the portions that go into Neuharth's proprietary Dungeness Red, White, and Rose table wines, all Neuharth's grapes come

Neuharth Winery
148 Still Road Sequim, Washington 98382 (206) 683-9652
Owners Gene & Maria Neuharth
Winemakers Gene Neuharth & Dan Caudill
Wine Production 5,000 gallons
Vineyard Acreage 1/2 acre
Year First Planted 1979
First Vintage 1979
Wines Produced Chardonnay, Merlot, Cabernet Sauvignon, Riesling, Dungeness White, Dungeness Rose, Dungeness Red

from east of the Cascade Mountains, in Washington's Columbia Valley.

Although Neuharth had little familiarity with winemaking or premium wine grapes prior to coming to Washington, he quickly learned the art and science of his new pursuit. At a time when most

■ Gene Neuharth

Washington Chardonnays were simplistic wines with little of the complexity and nuance that makes fine Chardonnay what it is, Neuharth was one of those demonstrating Washington's potential with the grape.

Neuharth also proved his facility with red wines, turning out fine examples of Cabernet Sauvignon and Merlot. Neuharth particularly likes Washington Merlot, preferring it, even, to Cabernet Sauvignon.

The red wines are aged in American oak from Missouri, the white wines in a combination of French and Yugoslavian oak. Neuharth does not like pumps in his winery. They can leak, suck in air, be hard to sterilize, and, perhaps most importantly, damage the wine by their shearing effect.

All Neuharth's wine is moved by gravity flow. The barrels and small custom tanks are elevated with a forklift for the process. Low ceilings are not a problem. The winery is a striking structure, a pole barn built in the 1930s. It is a finely preserved example of the area's and era's architecture.

Oakwood Cellars

Oakwood Cellars is located just above the Yakima River, in the Red Mountain area, at the far eastern end of the Yakima Valley. The estate vineyard consists of three acres of Riesling, but additional grapes are purchased from other valley growers.

A chemical engineer at the Hanford facility, Bob Skelton turned his wine interests into a small commercial winery. Oakwood Cellars' winemaking methods are evolving. In 1988, Skelton and McLain traveled to Europe to glean ideas about wine-

---

Oakwood Cellars

Route 2, Box 2321
Benton City, Washington 99320
(509) 588-5332

Owners
Bob Skelton & Evelyn McLain

Winemaker
Bob Skelton

Wine Production
5,000 gallons

Vineyard Acreage
3 acres

First Vintage
1986

Wines Produced
Riesling, Late Harvest Riesling, Semillon, Chardonnay, Cabernet Sauvignon, Merlot, Lemberger, Rose

---

making techniques from European winegrowers. The Oakwood Cellars Lemberger was one of the early best bets, made in a forward, oaky, fruity style.

Pacific Crest Wine Cellars

Most Washington wineries regard Riesling as a grape for cash-flow wine, a grape that can quickly be made into wine and released to the market. Gary Graves, Pacific Crest's owner and winemaker, releases his own Riesling soon after the vintage as well, but he regards the grape differently. Riesling is his principal wine.

Says Graves, "Most Washington wineries are not putting in the time and care to make the best possible Riesling. Other wines get a lot of attention, but because Riesling can be sold almost immediately after the vintage, it is regarded as a money maker, a wine to make cheaply and sell quickly."

When the grapes come in, Graves crushes and presses the grapes, then chills the juice for about five days to let the grape solids settle out. The Riesling is fermented with an Alsatian yeast noted for producing highly fruity qualities in the wine. With his floating lid tanks, air space can be

---

Pacific Crest Wine Cellars

1326 Sixth Street
Marysville, Washington 98270
(206) 653-3925

Owner
Gary Graves

Winemaker
Gary Graves

Wine Production
1,500 gallons

Vineyard Acreage
none

First Vintage
1985

Wines Produced
Riesling, Chardonnay, Gewurztraminer

---

adjusted to almost zero, so less sulfur dioxide is needed for protection. In addition to Riesling, Graves also makes Chardonnay and Gewurztraminer.

Pontin del Roza

In the 1920s, an Italian immigrant, Angelo Pontin, planted grapes in the Cottonwood Canyon area west of Yakima. In the 1950s, Angelo's son, Nesto, and daughter-in-law, Delores, started a farm in the Yakima Valley near the community of Prosser. In the 1980s, Nesto and Delores opened a winery, Pontin del Roza. Son Scott is winemaker and general manager.

The winery and vineyards are located along the Roza Canal, a major irrigation system that opened up much of the Yakima

Pontin del Roza

Route 4, Box 4735
Prosser, Washington 99350
(509) 786-4449

Owners
Pontin family

Winemaker
Scott Pontin

Wine Production
20,000 gallons

Vineyard Acreage
15 acres

Year First Planted
1979

First Vintage
1984

Wines Produced
Riesling, Chenin Blanc,
Chardonnay, Cabernet Sauvignon,
Fume Blanc, Merlot,
Roza Sunset Blush

Valley to farming. They are the Pontins of the Roza—in Italian, Pontin del Roza, the winery name.

The Pontins' farmlands include grasses, grains, potatoes, Concord grapes—and, the most recent addition, wine grapes. Their 15 acre vinifera vineyard is planted to Riesling. The Pontins supplement the production of their own vineyard with grapes of other varieties purchased from other vineyards.

The turn to wine grapes was prompted, in part, by a 1975 return to northern Italy and the original family vineyards that Scott's grandfather, Angelo, knew as a child. After visiting the Pontins of Italy, the Pontins of the Roza returned to a long family tradition—growing grapes and making wine.

Portteus Vineyards

Are you looking for an off-dry Riesling or an off-dry Chenin Blanc? Don't look to Portteus Vineyards. Not only does Portteus not make off-dry Riesling or Chenin Blanc, Portteus doesn't make any kind of Riesling or Chenin Blanc. There is no quick cash flow wine, and no sugary drink for the casual tasting room visitor. At Portteus, the focus is on serious wines for the serious wine enthusiast.

Nineteen acres of the Portteus vineyard are planted to Cabernet Sauvignon, 14 to Chardonnay, 8 to Merlot, 3 to Semillon, and 1 acre each to Cabernet Franc, Lemberger, and Zinfandel.

Portteus reports that the old-timers in the area had excellent results with Zinfandel, contrary to

> **At Portteus,
> there is no sugary drink
> for the casual
> tasting room visitor.
> The focus is on
> serious wines
> for the serious
> wine enthusiast.**

current thinking and experiences on the matter. Zinfandel, he believes, only needs a good vineyard site and appropriate viticultural practices to produce fine wine in Washington.

Any definitive statements on the matter would be premature, but tasting Zinfandel from Portteus's first two vintages is more than encouraging. The second vintage, 1989, is particularly notable, a deeply colored wine with fine fruit character. The wines came from only 40 vines, the first planted at the site. Production from the first vines is too small for a commercial release of Zinfandel. As the remainder of the acre begins to bear fruit, however, the Zinfandel will be available on a

limited basis by the early to mid 1990s.

The vineyard, on the upper reaches of Highland Drive, is high on the lower slopes of the Rattlesnake Hills. At an elevation of 1,400 feet, Portteus is higher than most nearby vineyards. According to Portteus, local area vineyards at elevations of 1,200 to 1,400 feet are the warmest and have excellent air drainage to protect against frost. After 1,600 feet, there is increased frost danger and a significant drop in temperature degree days.

Portteus's wines, notably the Cabernet Sauvignon, reflect the warmer climate, showing true fruit qualities and an absence of herbaceous characteristics. Con-

Portteus Vineyards

5201 Highland Drive
Zillah, Washington 98953
(509) 829-6970

Owners
Paul Portteus III &
Paul Portteus Jr.

Winemaker
Paul Portteus III

Wine Production
6,000 gallons

Vineyard Acreage
47 acres

Year First Planted
1982

First Vintage
1984

Wines Produced
Cabernet Sauvignon, Merlot,
Lemberger, Pinot Noir,
Chardonnay, Semillon, Zinfandel

tributing to the absence of herbaceousness is Portteus's practice of limiting irrigation to stress the vines and reduce the vigor of the vine canopy.

Portteus leaves the Cabernet on the skins and pulp for two to three weeks after fermentation has finished. Because the tannins polymerize and drop out of the wine, the Cabernet is intense without being overly tannic.

The Chardonnay is barrel fermented. Portteus started out using up to five different yeasts for fermentation, but has subsequently reduced the number to two, Montrachet for rich flavors and texture, and Bordeaux white for structure and backbone. Says Portteus, "Most Washington Chardonnay is made in a light fruity style. I'm on the other end of the spectrum. My Chardonnays are for that 20 percent of the wine consumers that like a richer, more complex wine."

Portteus's winemaking methods play an important role in the character of his wines, but he admonishes that the most important factor is the vineyard. Where the grapes are grown and how the vines are tended are the keys to excellence. Portteus's first wines hold the promise of an auspicious future.

Preston Wine Cellars

The Snake and Columbia Rivers converge in the southern Columbia Valley forming a broad V-shaped section of land, geographically defining one of the Columbia Valley's major grape growing areas. In the southern center of this V-shaped area of land, just five miles north of the city of Pasco, is Preston Wine Cellars, Washington's largest family-owned winery. Just off Highway 395, a large 48 foot sign marks the entrance to the winery estate. And Preston is a winery estate in the fullest sense, with the winery and family home set amidst the vines.

A moderately large winery, Preston retains a family-owned

flavor. Bill Preston's son Brent, winemaker and general manager, designed and built the tasting room bar and furniture. Daughter Cathy is public relations manager.

For those accustomed to the dramatic grandeur of lushly green mountains and snowcapped peaks, the southern Columbia Valley looks stark, empty, and desolate. But the vastness of the desert flatlands and rolling hills commands its own grandeur. In the more lushly green areas of the Northwest, so much visual stimuli continuously bombard the viewer that sometimes nothing really stands out—

■ **Bill Preston**

Preston Wine Cellars

502 East Vineyard Drive
Pasco, Washington 99301
(509) 545-1990

Owners
Preston Family

Winemakers
Brent Preston, Bill Preston, and Del Long

Wine Production
120,000 gallons

Vineyard Acreage
190 acres

Year First Planted
1972

First Vintage
1976

Wines Produced
Chardonnay, Fume Blanc,
Gewurztraminer, Riesling,
Riesling Select Harvest,
Chenin Blanc, Desert Gold,
Desert Mist, Pinot Noir Blanc,
Desert Blossom,
Gamay Beaujolais Rose,
Muscat of Alexandria, Ice Wine,
Merlot, Cabernet Sauvignon,
Extra Dry Champagne,
Cuvee du Chardonnay,
Late Harvest Wines

nothing is really seen. In the southern Columbia Valley, every sensory happening stands forth and commands attention. The furrowed desert fields are, to some, like a Zen garden on a vast scale.

But Bill Preston's cultural base is quite different. A native of the area, Preston is a self-made man in the American tradition. Preston retired from his irrigation and

> **A native of the area, and one of Washington's pioneer winegrowers, Preston is a self-made man in the American tradition.**

farm implement business to plant one of Washington's first commercial premium grape vineyards in the modern era, followed soon after by the Preston winery. Preston's vineyard estate is planted to 11 varieties: Chardonnay, Riesling, Cabernet Sauvignon, Pinot Noir, Sauvignon Blanc, Chenin Blanc, Gewurztraminer, Merlot, Gamay Beaujolais, Muscat of Alexandria, and Royalty.

The southern Columbia Valley is one of the warmer growing areas in the state. Preston is convinced that this area produces the finest wines in the Northwest. He characterizes the area as a huge natural greenhouse. The desert soil is too dry and sandy to support much natural vegetation, yet as a viticultural medium, it is highly receptive to the means and ends of winegrowing technology. Precise moisture control is achieved through irrigation; desired nutrient balance is maintained by adding fertilizers to the neutral sandy soil; and the warm sunny climate means there is little chance rain will fall at inopportune times.

This is not to say the area is without problems. Unlike a greenhouse, Preston's vineyards, as others in the Columbia Valley, have been subjected to frosts and winter freezing that severely damage the vines. A good portion of Preston's first plantings was destroyed the following winter. The cold is a problem most winters, but even in this context, Preston sees the advantages of the region. The growing climate fosters vigorous growth for replanted vines, and rapid recovery for those that are damaged.

Chardonnay and Fume Blanc, both fermented in stainless steel and aged in French oak, are Preston's leading wines. Gewurztraminer and Riesling predominate in Desert Gold, a popular, moderately sweet, proprietary blend. Preston also produces bottle fermented sparkling wine.

The Preston tasting room is directly over the winery. Its large windows and an open deck provide a panoramic view of the estate vineyard, small picnic park, gazebo, amphitheater for outdoor performances, and the expansive desert countryside. Some of Preston's specialty wines such as

botrytised Riesling and botrytised Sauvignon Blanc are available only at the tasting room. A self-guided tour allows visitors to look at various parts of the winery through viewing areas that overlook winery operations below. A collection of over 400 modern and antique corkscrews is also available for viewing.

Quarry Lake Vintners

In 1927, the Balcom family of Grandview and the Moe family of Ellensburg formed a farming

■ **Maury Balcom**

partnership. More than half a century and several generations later, the partnership, now a corporation, continues to prosper. In 1965, Balcom and Moe pioneered farming just north of Pasco, in of one of the last segments of the vast Columbia Basin Irrigation Project. Lush agricultural crops replaced the sagebrush. Balcom and Moe grow many crops on their 3,000 acre farm, including potatoes, cherries, apples—and wine grapes.

Maurice Balcom, one of the original founding partners,

believed that Balcom and Moe could produce fine premium wine grapes. In 1971, Balcom and Moe planted the first commercial

---

In 1971, Balcom and Moe planted the Pasco Basin's first commercial wine grape vineyard.

---

vinifera vineyard in the area. Maurice's son, Maury, went to Fresno State in California to study enology and viticulture. Maury received a degree in enology, and almost a degree in viticulture, save for the required courses on raisin and table grapes which he decided to forego.

Quarry Lake Vintners

2520 Commercial Avenue
Pasco, Washington 99301
(509) 547-7307

Owners
Balcom & Moe, Inc.

Winemaker
Maury Balcom

Wine Production
80,000 gallons

Vineyard Acreage
110 acres

Year First Planted
1971

First Vintage
1985

Wines Produced
Cabernet Sauvignon, Merlot,
Chardonnay, Riesling,
Chenin Blanc, Sauvignon Blanc,
Pinot Noir, Blush, Blanc de Blanc,
White Table Wine

Today, it seems difficult to believe, but scarcely more than a decade ago, the viability of Washington's wine industry was far from proven, only a few wineries existed, and few or none were interested in buying more grapes. For the first few years, Balcom and Moe had difficulty selling their grapes. The first grape crops were finally purchased by Oregon wineries.

Change came rapidly for Washington's wine industry, and Balcom and Moe's grapes were soon in much demand. From the beginning, Balcom and Moe had planned to open a winery. In 1985, the company fulfilled the original intent, and crushed Balcom and Moe's first commercial vintage. The Quarry Lake name is taken from a lake formed in a depleted gravel quarry located along highway 395, just north of Pasco. Balcom and Moe purchased the lake and property, and eventually plan to plant more vineyards and build a new winery on the site.

Balcom believes that their vineyard produces especially good Chardonnay, Cabernet Sauvignon, and Merlot, and he is focusing his efforts accordingly. Balcom and Moe has planted a new, small, Cabernet Sauvignon vineyard. The vines rows are on a conventional ten foot spacing, but only three feet apart between each vine within the row, instead of the usual six or more foot spacing. With 1,450 vines per acre, double or more the usual number of vines, each vine does not need to produce as much fruit to achieve the same yield per acre. With a denser vine spacing, Balcom hopes to achieve lower pH, more intensely flavored, better quality fruit—and better wines.

Balcom is also using new technology to better manage irrigation. Ideally, the soil is maintained at a consistent minimal moisture level near the roots, moderately stressing the vine and producing reduced vegetative growth and the best possible fruit.

For nearly a decade and a half, Balcom and Moe had waited for the "right time" to start a winery. Other wineries have been making fine wines from Balcom and Moe's grapes. Now Maury Balcom has his turn.

Quilceda Creek Vintners

Consulting enologist for the tiny Quilceda Creek Vintners is none other than Andre

■ Alex Golitzin

Tchelistcheff, the legendary California winemaker. It so happens that Alex Golitzin, Quilceda Creek's owner and winemaker, is Tchelistcheff's nephew. Since 1946, when Golitzin came to America from France, he remembers frequent visits with his uncle, and afternoons playing in the Beaulieu vineyards.

A chemical engineering graduate from the University of California at Berkeley, in 1972 Golitzin moved to Snohomish, a small community not far from Seattle. At about that time, Tchelistcheff was consulting regularly with nearby Chateau Ste. Mi-

chelle. At Tchelistcheff's encouragement, Golitzin experimented with winemaking, and, ultimately, started a small commercial winery of his own.

The association with Tchelistcheff is notable, but Golitzin is an excellent winemaker in his own right. After more than a decade of aging, Golitzin's early experimental Cabernets have developed exceptionally well, showing fine breed and complexity. Quilceda Creek is very small, but professionally operated.

Quilceda Creek's first Cabernets were made from grapes grown at Otis Vineyards in the Yakima Valley, one of the state's oldest commercial Cabernet Sauvignon vineyards. Although greatly minimized in Golitzin's wines, the Otis grapes have a pronounced herbal characteristic that clashes with conventional conceptions of classic Cabernet Sauvignon.

After several vintages of buying grapes from Kiona Vineyards as well as Otis, Golitzin made the switch to the Kiona grapes in 1983. Located at the warmer far eastern

After more than a decade of aging, Golitzin's early Cabernets have developed exceptionally well, showing fine breed and complexity.

end of the Yakima Valley, grapes from the Kiona Vineyard ripen sooner and yield wines with a fuller, less angular texture.

In 1986, Mercer Ranch Cabernet Sauvignon, from the Columbia Valley's Horse Heaven Hills, became a component in the blend. The Mercer Ranch Cabernet is tannic and meaty, with a distinctive plum pit characteristic. Both Kiona and Mercer Ranch Cabernet fruit rank among the

---

Quilceda Creek Vintners

5226 Machias Road
Snohomish, Washington 98290
(206) 568-2389

Owners
Alex & Jeannette Golitzin

Winemaker
Alex Golitzin

Wine Production
1,500 gallons

Vineyard Acreage
none

First Vintage
1979

Wines Produced
Cabernet Sauvignon

---

state's best, and the two work well together in a blend. Golitzin's first Cabernets were aged primarily in very old American oak barrels. With the 1981 vintage, Golitzin began phasing in French Nevers barrels.

Except for 1980, a lighter vintage by nature, Golitzin's Cabernets had always been aggressively tannic and hard in their youth. Inspired by his visits to Bordeaux, Golitzin modified his methods beginning with the 1986 vintage. His newer Cabernets are more approachable in youth, and display more forward fruit. Many recent Bordeaux wines have gone to unfortunate extremes along this path, rendering the wines overly soft and simple compared to years past, but Golitzin has skillfully applied some of the methods

without giving way to the extremes. Golitzin's newest wines are among his best.

Employed full time as a chemical engineer, and without a large volume of wine to market, Golitzin is not tied to the necessities of immediate cash flow and pushing product. "We are a bit perfectionist here," says Golitzin, "but if you start letting go of a small detail here and there, soon those small concessions add up and you find that a measure of quality has been lost."

Saddle Mountain Winery

Saddle Mountain Winery is named for its location on the lower slopes of the Saddle Mountains, an area called the Wahluke

---

Saddle Mountain Winery

2340 Winery Road
Mattawa, Washington 99344
(509) 932-4943

Owners
Snoqualmie Falls Holding Company

Winemaker
Mike Januik

Wine Production
250,000 gallons

Vineyard Acreage
none

First Vintage
1982

Wines Produced
Chardonnay, Cabernet Sauvignon,
Merlot, Fume Blanc,
Riesling, Chenin Blanc,
Gewurztraminer,
Blush White Riesling, White Table,
Blanc de Blanc, Cascade Blush

Slope, a relatively new, but excellent grape growing area in Washington's Columbia Valley.

In its initial incarnation, Saddle Mountain Winery began business as the five million dollar F. W.

Langguth Winery. Langguth was the first winery in the Northwest substantially financed by a foreign wine company. Its parent corporation was F. W. Langguth Erben, GMBH, a huge winemaking operation headquartered at Traben-Trarbach in Germany's Mosel region.

In the late 1970s, Langguth began looking around the world for a wine producing region to expand its operation. Such diverse areas as Brazil, North Africa, Australia, and California were considered, but on the advice of Dr. Helmut Becker, director of the famous German viticultural school at Geisenheim, Langguth chose Washington. Washington offered a climate suitable for growing Riesling, as well as local investment partners interested in the venture.

The owners of Snoqualmie Falls Winery purchased controlling interest in Langguth in 1986, and the facility is now well on its way to realizing its potential. The winery is a paragon of high-tech excellence. Saddle Mountain wines are made by Mike Januik, a winemaker who has earned a reputation for turning out quality wines on more than a boutique scale. A full line of moderately priced wines are marketed under the Saddle Mountain label.

Salishan Vineyards

Nowhere will you find a more genuine individual than Joan Wolverton. She is the kind of person that makes me glad I'm in the wine writing business. Candid and unassuming, with sparkling eyes and a gentle wit, Wolverton is the winemaker, vineyardist, and guiding spirit behind Salishan Vineyards.

The winery had its beginnings some two decades ago, when husband Linc Wolverton extensively researched meteorological data from Burgundy and Bordeaux. With the assistance of a computer, Wolverton generated climatic correlations with potential grape growing areas in the Northwest. This research led the Wolvertons to their present site.

In 1971, the Wolvertons planted 11 acres of grapes near the town of La Center, in southwest Washington, and became the first winegrowers in western Washington to focus on vinifera grapes. The first wines were released in 1976, but until 1982, when Joan Wolverton assumed winemaking duties, the wines were made for Salishan by other northwest wineries.

The early years were not easy. The Wolvertons now live at the vineyard site, and Joan devotes full time to the vineyard and winery, but at first, the couple both had full-time jobs in Seattle, Joan as a reporter for *The Seattle Times* and Linc as an economist for Boeing. Weekends were spent commuting to the vineyard for the back-breaking pleasure of tending 9,000 vines.

In the first six years, a third of the vines were lost to deer and rabbit. Closer to Mt. St. Helens than any other winery, one of the 1980 eruptions dropped ash on Salishan's vineyard, scouring away the pollen. Bloom and berry set were poor, reducing the 1980 grape crop, but making the wines more concentrated. In 1981, the destructive form of botrytis destroyed nearly all the crop.

Experience has brought accommodation and innovation. The Wolvertons put plastic mesh rabbit guards around the young vines, simultaneously protecting the vines and eliminating the need for stakes to keep them growing straight. The soil, a Hessom clay loam, retains more moisture than sandier soils, delaying growth in the spring, but to compensate, the Wolvertons cover the new vine rows with black plastic film.

The black plastic absorbs heat, keeps down weeds, and controls water evaporation. The space between the vine rows is left exposed, and the clay loam soil lets the moisture from rain disperse laterally underneath the black plastic. Irrigation for the young vines, otherwise a necessity, is rarely needed. According to Wolverton, new vines produce a good grape crop after only two years, instead of the usual four or five years.

The Salishan climate is neither like the hot, dry, Columbia Valley growing climate east of the Cascade Mountains, nor like the wet-

■ **Joan Wolverton**

Salishan Vineyards

Route 2, Box 8
La Center, Washington 98629
(206) 263-2713

Owners
Joan & Lincoln Wolverton

Winemaker
Joan Wolverton

Wine Production
6,000 gallons

Vineyard Acreage
12 acres

Year First Planted
1971

First Vintage
1976

Wines Produced
Pinot Noir, Chardonnay,
Dry Chenin Blanc, Dry Riesling,
Cabernet Sauvignon

---

ter, cooler, western Washington growing climates situated further north. Salishan's climate is most like that of Oregon's northern Willamette Valley, and, like the Willamette Valley, Pinot Noir is the leading grape variety.

With a growing climate slightly cooler than that of the northern Willamette, Salishan's Pinot Noir typically ripens a week later, a disadvantage in cooler years, but a qualitative advantage in warmer years. The climate is excellent for Pinot Noir, and Salishan is virtually the only Washington winery

---

Salishan's T-shirts whimsically, but pointedly, proclaim, "Washington's answer to Oregon Pinot Noir."

---

producing consistently successful wines from this difficult varietal. Salishan's T-shirts whimsically, but pointedly, proclaim, "Washington's answer to Oregon Pinot Noir."

In addition to Chardonnay, dry Chenin Blanc and dry Riesling are other Salishan specialities. In some years, the dry Chenin Blanc is particularly notable. Both the vineyard and winemaking are now hitting stride. Wolverton's recent wines (some still unreleased) are her best yet. The Wolvertons' pioneering effort has been a success. Others have planted grapes nearby, and Clark County now has more than 100 acres in vine.

Salmon Bay Winery

The Salmon Bay Winery came into being out of the conversations of Bruce Crabtree, then sommelier at Rosellini's Four-10, a

Salmon Bay Winery

13416 N.E. 177th Place
Woodinville, Washington 98072
(206) 483-9463

Owners
Kenneth Rogstad, Bobby Capps,
Bruce Crabtree

Winemaker
Bruce Crabtree

Wine Production
10,000 gallons

Vineyard Acreage
none

First Vintage
1982

Wines Produced
Chardonnay, Cabernet Sauvignon,
Merlot, Sauvignon Blanc, Riesling,
Copper River Blush,
Oyster Shell White (Semillon)

prominent Seattle restaurant, and patrons of the restaurant, Kenneth Rogstad and Bobby Capps. Crabtree's family has long been associated with the restaurant industry. At one time, the family owned 26 restaurants in the Pacific Northwest.

Drawing upon the close association with restaurants, the concepts of food wines and restaurant wines have been the winery's theme since its inception. Crabtree made the first wines. Subsequent vintages have

involved consulting winemakers as well as wines made at custom crush facilities in the Columbia Valley.

In 1989, the winery made a long-awaited move from its original facility in an industrial area of south Seattle to its new Woodinville home. After a long period of settling in, the winery should now be better poised to fulfill its original intent.

First known as Vernier Wines, after a patron saint of wine, the Salmon Bay name emerged from a realignment in the winery's focus and approach. Crabtree says of the name change and shift in focus, "We wanted a name that was identified with western Washington and with our local and regional cuisine. Salmon Bay captures that for us."

Seth Ryan Winery

While working as research scientists at Battelle Laboratories, Khris Olsen and Ron

Seth Ryan Winery

681 South 40th
West Richland, Washington
99352
(509) 375-0486 or 967-9204

Owners
Brodzinski & Olsen families

Winemakers
Khris Olsen & Ron Brodzinski

Wine Production
1,000 gallons

Vineyard Acreage
none

First Vintage
1985

Wines Produced
Riesling, Late Harvest Riesling,
Gewurztraminer, Chardonnay

Brodzinski became enthused with the prospect of having a vineyard

and winery. Their two families purchased vineyard land together on Red Mountain, at the easternmost end of the Yakima Valley. As yet, the vineyard has not been planted.

While awaiting evolution of their plans, the families started a small experimental winery in the Olsen garage. Oak aged sweet Rieslings and various fermentation methods are part of Seth Ryan's ongoing experimental exploration of the wide world of winemaking. Chardonnay, Gewurztraminer, and various Rieslings are currently available. Cabernet Sauvignon and Merlot are in the plans for the near future.

Silver Lake Winery

Silver Lake Winery is an outgrowth of Spire Mountain Ciders. Spire Mountain began operations by importing cider from Canada, then packaging and selling it under the Spire Mountain label. Company president, Sal Leone, became interested in making cider from Washington apples, and interested, too, in starting a winery.

Leone hired Brian Carter, a highly regarded Washington winemaker with experience making wine from fruit and berries, as well as grapes. The first wines released under the Silver Lake label were made elsewhere and purchased by the winery. The Chardonnay, made under Carter's direction at another facility, reflects Carter's trademark approach to the wine.

Silver Lake's regular bottling of Chardonnay is fermented in stainless steel and aged briefly in oak. The reserve is barrel fermented and left on the lees. Both go through a partial malolactic fer-

Silver Lake Winery

17616 15th Avenue S.E., 106B
Bothell, Washington 98012
(206) 485-2437

Owner
Corporation

Winemaker
Brian Carter

Wine Production
15,000 gallons

Vineyard Acreage
none

First Vintage
1988

Wines Produced
Chardonnay, Reserve Chardonnay,
Riesling, Cabernet Sauvignon,
Merlot, Sauvignon Blanc,
Spire Mountain Ciders

mentation. Carter prefers a partial malolactic so that some of the fruitiness of the Chardonnay is preserved, while the malolactic element contributes additional complexity and texture.

French oak is used exclusively for the white wines. The red wines, in accordance with Carter's preferences, are aged in American oak. A third of the winery's production is red wine, a higher percentage than average for a Washington winery.

Snoqualmie Winery

Snoqualmie Winery is located in a picturesque setting just outside the town of Snoqualmie, about a half hour drive from Seattle. The winery offers an impressive view of the Snoqualmie Valley, Mount Si, and the Cascade Foothills. One hundred and thirty-five acres of lawn and natural vegetation surround the winery, inviting picnicking and enjoyment of the view. Deer and occasional elk roam the nearby woods.

Snoqualmie Falls Winery was founded in 1983. Snoqualmie's first wines were made at Coventry Vale, a custom crush facility in the Yakima Valley. After a change in ownership, the new owners additionally purchased controlling interest in the Langguth Winery. Located on the Wahluke Slope, in Washington's Columbia Valley, the Langguth Winery, now called Saddle Mountain, is a paragon of technical excellence, one of the Northwest's best equipped wineries.

In 1987, Mike Januik was hired as winemaker for the Saddle Mountain facility, and is now winemaker for both the Snoqualmie and Saddle Mountain brands. Januik has earned a reputation for producing well-crafted wines with both substance and finesse. The Saddle Mountain

Snoqualmie Winery

1000 Winery Road
Snoqualmie, Washington 98065
(206) 888-4000

Owners
Snoqualmie Falls Holding Company

Winemaker
Mike Januik

Wine Production
150,000 gallons

Vineyard Acreage
none

First Vintage
1983

Wines Produced
Cabernet Sauvignon,
Merlot Reserve, Chardonnay,
Chardonnay Reserve, Fume Blanc,
Semillon, Lemberger,
Dry Chenin Blanc, Muscat Canelli,
Riesling, Dry Riesling,
Late Harvest Riesling,
Gewurztraminer

wines are more moderately priced and made in a more readily accessible style.

The Snoqualmie facility is a bonded winery, but virtually all the wines are produced at the Saddle Mountain winery in Mattawa. The Snoqualmie winery functions primarily as a visitor

> **About a half hour drive from Seattle, Snoqualmie winery offers an impressive view of the Snoqualmie Valley, Mount Si, and the Cascade Foothills.**

facility, a tasting room, and a place to go to escape the urban milieu. It is an integral part of the community's growing tourist attractions. Snoqualmie's historic train depot and the nearby Snoqualmie Falls are two other visitor attractions in the area. All can be reached by taking eastbound exit 27 off I-90.

Staton Hills Winery

Leaving the city of Yakima and traveling south and east on I-82, the road and the Yakima River immediately funnel through a narrow constriction formed by the convergence of the Rattlesnake Hills and the Ahtanum Ridge, emerging into the northwesternmost end of the Yakima Valley. The valley immediately opens broadly to the south and east, but the river and highway hug the lower slopes of the Rattlesnake Hills.

On this route, less than ten minutes from Yakima, is one of the Yakima Valley's showcase wineries. Surrounded by the estate vineyard, the winery looks out upon a distant snowcapped

■ **Staton Hills Winery**

Mt. Adams, a dormant volcanic dome just east of Mt. St. Helens.

An attorney, founder David Staton grew tired of Wall Street and New York and moved to San Francisco to become president of a large energy company. Weekend trips to the nearby Napa and Sonoma Valleys spurred Staton's interest in wine. In the early 1970s, seeing an article about the potential of premium wine in Washington state, Staton corresponded with Dr. Walter Clore, the dean of Washington viticulture.

Proceeding cautiously, Staton and his family purchased an apple orchard in the Yakima Valley, and moved to Washington in 1974. The Washington wine industry

---

Less than ten minutes from Yakima, Staton Hills is one of the valley's showcase wineries.

---

and Staton's own grape test plots were proving highly successful. In 1982, Staton purchased the land for his winery and vineyard.

Appointed by two state administrations to the Tree Fruit Re-

search Commission, Staton helped oversee extensive research programs. Staton's interest in research and innovation carry through to his own 16 acre vineyard which features three uncommon trellising systems.

Virtually all Washington grape vines are trained vertically along a

Staton Hills Winery

71 Gangl Road
Wapato, Washington 98951
(509) 877-2112

1910 Post Alley
Seattle, Washington 98101
(206) 443-8084

Owners
Staton Hills Winery Co., Ltd.;
David Staton, President/CEO

Winemaker
Rob Stuart

Wine Production
150,000 gallons

Vineyard Acreage
16 acres

Year First Planted
1982

First Vintage
1984

Wines Produced
Merlot, Cabernet Sauvignon,
Pinot Noir, Chardonnay,
Fume Blanc, Chenin Blanc,
Gewurztraminer,
Riesling, Pink Riesling,
Muscat de Cielo, Port,
Brut Sparkling Wine,
Brut Rose Sparkling Wine

single plane. With the traditional method, the upper foliage droops over the lower foliage, shading the grapes and lower leaves from the sun. With all three of Staton's trellising systems, Gable, Tartura, and a modified Double-Guyot, two trunks are trained into an open vertical V-shape with the lateral arms of the vines running along the wires in the vine row. With these systems, the grapes and vine canopy are better and more uniformly exposed to the sun.

All three systems have similarities to the Open Lyre system developed by Carbonneau, in the early 1970s, at the Viticultural Research Station in Bordeaux. Among the theoretical advantages, these systems should produce better quality grapes at higher and more consistent crop levels. Their advantages and disadvantages will emerge more clearly with succeeding vintages.

Staton's vines are planted relatively densely, at more than 1,000 vines per acre, reducing the load that each vine must produce. The closer spacing also crowds the root systems longitudinally, forcing the roots deeper into the soil, adding increased protection for the vine's winter survival. The irrigation pattern is also controlled to force the roots deeper.

Yakima Valley soils are usually shallow, but Staton's site, probably a turn in the Yakima River at one time, has soil 35 feet deep. The Staton Hills vineyard is set apart from most other Yakima Valley vineyards, in a localized warm belt. The site has proven warmer than ideal for Chardonnay, but excellent for red wines, so Staton replaced the Chardonnay vines with Cabernet Sauvignon.

Rob Stuart, formerly with Krug Champagnes in California and

Oregon's Valley View winery, is Staton's winemaker. Charles Ortman, friend and associate of Staton, is consulting enologist.

Staton Hills was one of the first Northwest wineries to sell wine in Asian markets. Staton's efforts were far from token. Among their visits, David and his wife Susanne Staton spent eight weeks in Pacific Rim countries developing and promoting their efforts. Noted artist Sebastian Titus was instrumental in developing wine labels and packaging targeted at Asian markets.

In 1989, Staton entered into a business venture with a large Japanese company, transforming the winery into an international corporation, and offering a major presence in Japan's growing premium wine market. At the same time, Staton Hills reduced production volume and number of varieties produced to focus on a narrower range of premium table wines and sparkling wine.

Most Yakima Valley wineries are not immediately visible from the main highway through the valley. But now, at the head of the valley, a few minutes from the city of Yakima, the prominence of the elegant Staton Hills winery, the estate vineyards, terraced landscape, and gabled trellises clearly announce that the traveler is entering premium wine country. For those in the Seattle metropolitan area, Staton Hills also has a satellite winery and tasting room in the city's historic Pike Place Market.

Stewart Vineyards

A vinifera grape grower since the late 1960s, Dr. George Stewart planted his first vineyard in the Yakima Valley, on Harrison Hill near Sunnyside. The Harrison

---

Stewart Vineyards

1711 Cherry Hill Road
Granger, Washington 98932
(509) 854-1882

Owners
George & Martha Stewart

Winemaker
Scott Benham

Wine Production
22,000 gallons

Vineyard Acreage
50 acres

Year First Planted
1968

First Vintage
1983

Wines Produced
Chardonnay, Chardonnay Reserve,
Cabernet Sauvignon,
Riesling, Dry Riesling,
Late Harvest Riesling,
Sauvignon Blanc, Gewurztraminer,
Muscat Canelli, Cherry Hill Blush

Hill site was once a part of the vineyards owned by William Bridgman, a pioneering vinifera winegrower of the 1930s and 1940s. The old vineyard was planted to less than desirable varieties, so Stewart tore out the old vines and planted the site to Cabernet Sauvignon and other premium grapes.

On recommendation from Dr. Walter Clore, Washington's most noted viticulturalist, Stewart later became the first grower to plant grapes on the Wahluke Slope. A warm, cold-protected growing site, the Wahluke Slope is one of the Columbia Valley's most promising winegrowing areas. Muscat Canelli, a grape that is easily damaged by cold, thrives on the Wahluke. In vintages following cold damage, Stewart is sometimes one of the few wineries able to produce Muscat Canelli wine. Stewart has 40 acres planted on the Wahluke, but he owns a total of 150 acres on the slope that are suitable for vineyards.

Seattle native and U.C. Davis enology graduate, Scott Benham, is Stewart's winemaker. After apprenticing at Hogue Cellars, Benham came to Stewart in 1987, replacing Mike Januik.

Stewart is best known for its Rieslings and Chardonnays. The Rieslings are rich and ripe, with peach and apricot flavors. Unlike some Washington Rieslings that are made in this richer style, Benham's retain a clean, fresh fruit quality. They are not particularly Germanic, but they show a Washington style at its best. The late harvest renditions are especially lush and rich. The Chardonnays, too, are made in a richer style, with the benefit of barrel fermentation to round the wines and add complexity.

Tagaris Winery

In 1904, when Peter Tagaris arrived in America, the officials at Ellis Island did not do the best job in the transliteration of his name. Grandson Michael is the third

---

Tagaris Winery

39202 Meadowbrook Way
Snoqualmie, Washington 98065
(206) 888-9400

Owner
Michael Taggares

Winemaker
Peter Bos

Wine Production
25,000 gallons

Vineyard Acreage
120 acres

Year First Planted
1982

First Vintage
1986

Wines Produced
Riesling, Chardonnay, Fume Blanc,
Chenin Blanc, Arete, Pinot Noir,
Cabernet Sauvignon

---

generation to carry the Ellis Is-landization of the family name, now spelled Taggares. Grape grower, and now winery owner, Michael Taggares is honoring his heritage in his winery's name—spelled Tagaris.

The family has a long connection with Columbia Valley agriculture and grape growing. In 1924, Peter Tagaris planted grapes, though they were not vinifera winegrapes. The family now owns the world's largest planting of Concord grapes. In the 1960s, the family planted an experimental vinifera vineyard on the Snake River, near Pasco. Cuttings from the vines helped start many of Washington's early vinifera vineyards.

The Taggares winegrape vineyard is located on the east end of the Wahluke Slope, a relatively new grape growing area in Washington's Columbia Valley. The eastern end of the Wahluke merges with the lower end of the Saddle Mountains. The Taggares vineyard embraces both sides of the slope's crest. Most of the vineyards face south, but a block of the heat shy Pinot Noir grape is planted over the crest of the slope, facing north.

Winemaker Peter Bos has had more than a decade of experience in various facets of the Washington wine industry, most recently, as assistant winemaker at Columbia Winery. Tagaris's first wines were made at several Washington winemaking facilities. The new winery at Snoqualmie will give Bos tighter control and focus with the wines. The first releases were primarily white wines, but Taggares and Bos have their keenist interest in the reds.

Paul Thomas Winery

On a wall in the Paul Thomas winery, in elegant calligraphy, is a poster with a quote by John Stuart Mill from "On Liberty." The quote reads, "Eccentricity has always abounded when and where strength of character has abounded. And the amount of eccentricity in a society has generally been proportional to the amount of genius, mental vigor, and moral courage it contained. That too few dare to be eccentric marks the chief danger of our time."

Paul Thomas Winery

1717 136th Place N.E.
Bellevue, Washington 98005
(206) 747-1008

Owners
Paul Thomas

Winemaker
Mark Cave

Wine Production
35,000 gallons

Vineyard Acreage
none

First Vintage
1979

Wines Produced
Crimson Rhubarb,
Dry Bartlett Pear, Chenin Blanc,
Riesling, Muscat Canelli,
Sauvignon Blanc, Chardonnay,
Chardonnay Reserve,
Cabernet Sauvignon

The quotation is no less than a rallying cry for Paul Thomas, a vinous call to arms. Something of a dichotomy has evolved, wherein serious wine drinkers always drink vinifera grape wines, and these wines are almost always dry. Non-serious wine drinkers drink fruit and berry wines, and these are always sweet. Paul Thomas wines militate against this dichotomy. Most Paul Thomas fruit wines have only moderate re-

sidual sweetness. They are wines meant to accompany food, wines, in Paul Thomas's view, for the serious wine drinker.

Paul Thomas also produces table wines from vinifera grapes as well as from fruit. The grape wines include Chardonnay, Riesling, Chenin Blanc, Muscat Canelli, Sauvignon Blanc, and Cabernet Sauvignon. In some years, the reserve Chardonnay has shown outstanding complexity and balance, ranking among the finest in the state.

Although most makers of premium grape wines would not think of defiling their product line with fruit wines, Thomas sees no inconsistency in his combined approach. Most grape wineries rely on wines with some residual sweetness, such as Riesling and Chenin Blanc, for a major portion of their production. Paul Thomas's fruit wines are finished in a similar style, with slight residual sweetness balanced by crisp acidity.

Crimson, a rhubarb blush wine, accounts for 40 percent of the winery's production. Although it has some residual sugar, the taste is relatively dry, and the wine goes well with food. In appearance and taste, it is not totally unlike the currently popular White Zinfandel wines, scoring well against them in competitions.

Federal regulations prohibit vintage dating of fruit and berry wines, but the lot numbers on Paul Thomas wines tell the story. Lot 786, for example, means that the fruit was crushed and fermented in July of 1986.

Paul Thomas became interested in wine on a trip to Paris in 1960, and has been studying and drinking wine ever since. He began making vinifera grape wine at home in 1968. A Wenatchee native, some of his friends from the area suggested he make wine from Bing cherries, and so began his interest in table wines made from fruits.

When the time came to open a commercial winery, Thomas decided it would be better to enter the market with a unique product, nearly dry, premium fruit wines, rather than trying to improve on and compete with the vinifera grape wines already on the market. Thomas is increasingly shifting more of his emphasis to grape wines, but the popularity of Crimson has proven the success of his original thesis—and there has been little competition.

Tucker Cellars

In the heart of the Yakima Valley, the small agricultural community of Sunnyside is moving apace with the rest of the world. Local motels host small fraternal conventions. A well- known fast food restaurant chain and other modern day artifacts affirm the certainty of change. Yet, some of the changes echo and reaffirm the community's unchanging historical roots. Founded in the 1980s amidst Washington state's winegrowing boom, Tucker Cellars traces its own roots to the very beginnings of Washington's vinifera wine industry.

Born in 1930, Dean Tucker has lived all his life on the family farmlands near Sunnyside. Dean's father, M. F. Tucker, was one of the original growers supplying grapes to Washington's first vinifera grape winery, the Upland Winery at Sunnyside. William B. Bridgman founded the Upland Winery shortly after repeal of Prohibition and brought in a winemaker from Europe to make the wines. The Tucker family's first vineyard included Malvoisie, Muscat, Riesling, and Semillon grapes. A large photograph of Dean Tucker as a boy in the family vineyards now hangs in the Tucker Cellar's tasting room.

The Upland Winery met with hard times and went into a decline leading to its eventual demise. With Upland gone, there was little demand for premium wine grapes. Tucker remembers that Riesling was bought as a sweetener for the less than noble fortified "Ports" of the day. With little market for the grapes, the Tuckers moved off their vineyard property, and, shortly thereafter, the vineyards were pulled up, and the land planted to sugar beets.

Dean Tucker has seen crops come and go as interests and needs wax and wane. After sugar beets came orchards, then con-

---

Tucker Cellars

Route 1, Box 1696
Sunnyside, Washington 98944
(509) 837-8701

5 North First Avenue
Yakima, Washington 98902
(509) 454-WINE

Owners
Dean & Rose Tucker

Winemaker
Randy Tucker

Wine Production
20,000 gallons

Vineyard Acreage
55 acres

Year First Planted
1979

First Vintage
1981

Wines Produced
Cabernet Sauvignon, Pinot Noir,
Chardonnay, Chenin Blanc,
Riesling, Gewurztraminer,
Muscat Canelli,
Indian Summer (White Pinot Noir),
Late Harvest Muscat Canelli,
Late Harvest Riesling

---

cord grapes and row crops, then sugar beets again. Then in 1980, on 22 acres of the Tucker family's 500 acre farm, the Tuckers again planted wine grapes. This time,

---

Though founded in the 1980s, amidst Washington state's winegrowing boom, Tucker Cellars traces its roots to the very beginnings of Washington's vinifera wine industry.

---

the Tuckers opened a winery of their own, adjacent to the family fruit and vegetable market on the outskirts of Sunnyside.

After several generations, the Tucker farm is still very much a family business. All of Tucker's four children help operate various aspects of the enterprise. Randy Tucker is winemaker and winery manager. The farm includes an 80 acre orchard, hay, and a variety of row crops. The diversification provides a steady year-round work cycle for the Tucker family and their employees. After the apples are picked, the grapes are ready for harvest and crush. Late fall and winter allow time for work in the winery. Spring brings on furious planting, and the main asparagus harvest.

Begun as a secondary element in the family's farm operations, the Tucker winery is emerging as an important focal point and flagship for the family business. The muted background mosaic for Tucker's wine label features symbols for some of the family's other food products, including honeycomb, peaches, cherries, and popcorn, echoing the gourmet food items under the Tucker label. Besides wine, a winery visit offers the opportunity to purchase specialty food items and fresh fruits and vegetables from the Tucker farm. In 1989, Tucker Cellars opened a satellite winery and tasting room in Yesterday's Village in downtown Yakima, one of the 150 different shops and businesses in the renovated Pacific Fruit Exchange Building.

Vashon Winery

The original Chalone winery in California was owned by ten shareholders, predominantly airline pilots. William Gerrior, a

---

Vashon Winery

12629 S.W. Cemetery Road
Vashon Island, Washington 98070
(206) 463-9092

Owners
William & Karen Gerrior

Winemaker
William & Karen Gerrior

Wine Production
3,000 gallons

Vineyard Acreage
none

First Vintage
1987

Wines Produced
Chardonnay, Semillon,
Cabernet Sauvignon

---

pilot for Delta Airlines, and Karen Peterson Gerrior were part of the original Chalone ownership. The Gerriors carried their interest in wines and wineries to the Northwest. They made experimental batches of wine from Yakima Valley grapes beginning in 1984, and had their first commercial crush in 1987.

The Gerrior home and winery is on 44 acres on Vashon Island, a short ferryboat ride from either Seattle or Tacoma. The Puget Sound island was once a major produce supplier for western Washington population centers. The Gerriors grow most of what they eat on their property. "Good food and good wine just fits together," says Karen Gerrior, "and what you grow is so much better than what you can buy in the store."

Grapes come from the Portteus vineyard near Zillah, in the Yakima Valley, a relatively new but highly promising vineyard. The Gerriors produce Chardonnay, Cabernet Sauvignon, and Semillon. The Chardonnay is barrel fermented, as is the Semillon, if barrel capacity permits. Lees contact, malolactic fermentation, and French oak are all part of the winemaking regime.

Manfred Vierthaler Winery

Built in a Bavarian architectural style, the Manfred Vierthaler winery and restaurant is located on El-Hi Hill overlooking the Puyallup River Valley. One of the few wineries making wine from western Washington grapes, Vierthaler's own vineyard is planted on the steep slope surrounding the winery, but most of the acreage is under contract with western Washington growers. Gutedel, Muller-Thurgau, and Riesling are the principal varieties.

Although Vierthaler produces wine from western Washington grapes, most of the wine is made from California grape juice. The wines from the California juice have the word "American" included on the label. Some of Vierthaler's generic wine names are unique and fanciful. They include Moselle, Rhine Rose, and Select Harvest Burgundy.

Though he has lived most of his life in America, Vierthaler was born in Germany, and, as described in the winery's literature, is a direct descendant of the Emperor Charlemagne, as well as some of the royal families of Bavaria. In discussing the criteria for labeling a wine "Late Harvest," Vierthaler refers to German wine laws, and speaks of sugar levels in terms of the German Oechsle scale. From Vierthaler's perspective, "Late Harvest" wines should be designated as such based solely on the sugar content of the grapes—or grape juice. From this point of view, most of the wines from California's hot Central Valley would be considered "Late Harvest"—or better.

In the same building as the winery and tasting room is the

Manfred Vierthaler Winery

17136 Highway 410
Sumner, Washington 98390
(206) 863-1633

Owner
Manfred Vierthaler

Winemaker
Manfred Vierthaler

Wine Production
6,000 gallons

Vineyard Acreage
1 acre

Year First Planted
1976

First Vintage
1976

Wines Produced
Banquet White, Chablis, Moselle,
Riesling, Select Harvest Riesling,
Gewurztraminer,
Select Harvest Gewurztraminer,
Barbecue Red, Rhine Rose,
Burgundy, Cabernet Sauvignon,
Select Harvest Burgundy,
Angelica, Cream Sherry, Port

Roofgarden restaurant, overlooking the Puyallup River Valley. Included on the menu are vineyard snails in herb butter, breaded wild boar filets, and hippopotamus roast, as well as more conventional German and American dishes.

Waterbrook Winery

Eric and Janet Rindal worked at the nearby L'Ecole 41 winery during its first crush. Inspired by the experience, the Rindals decided to start a winery of

---

Waterbrook Winery

Route 1, Box 46
McDonald Road
Lowden, Washington 99360
(509) 522-1918

Owners
Eric & Janet Rindal

Winemaker
Eric Rindal

Wine Production
18,000 gallons

Vineyard Acreage
32 acres

Year First Planted
1989

First Vintage
1984

Wines Produced
Chardonnay, Chardonnay Reserve,
Sauvignon Blanc,
Cabernet Sauvignon, Merlot

---

their own. Janet Rindal is a Walla Walla Valley native. A building on one of her family's farms housed the first winery. Expansion and new buildings soon followed. Though by no means a large winery, Waterbrook is the largest of the Walla Walla area wineries.

Most Washington wineries produce Riesling, Chenin Blanc, or other varieties typically finished with some residual sweetness.

Preferring "food wines" in a European style, the Rindals shun the grape varieties that are usually finished slightly sweet, in favor of grape varieties that traditionally make the best dry wines—Sauvignon Blanc, Chardonnay, Cabernet Sauvignon, and Merlot.

Waterbrook's white wines strike a balance between a highly fruity style and a style that trades the fruit of the grape for richer flavors and textures. Waterbrook's Chardonnay have been particularly successful. The moderately priced regular version is often a fine wine at a good price. The higher end reserve Chardonnays receive more barrel fermentation, barrel aging, and lees contact, and malolactic fermentation treatments.

Rindal does not put his Sauvignon Blanc through a malolactic fermentation, letting the grape's more angular profile and herbaceous character assert itself. If the Sauvignon Blanc needs any toning down, Rindal blends in a companion grape, Semillon.

To cut down on the grassy element typical of many Columbia Valley grapes, the juice for Rindal's white wines is left in contact with the skins only briefly prior to fermentation. If possible, Rindal avoids adding sulfur dioxide at crush which he believes causes the wine to pick up astringency and bitterness from the skins.

Waterbrook white wines were the first on the market, but Cabernet Sauvignon and Merlot are a major focus for the winery. Rindal believes in keeping the red wines a little "dirty" in the earlier stages of winemaking, not filtering the wine before it goes into the aging barrels, and letting the wine rest on the sediment longer before racking. Such practices tend to produce more complex flavors in the finished wine.

One of the Northwest's earliest winegrowing regions, the Walla Walla Valley is one of the newer regions to join the Washington wine renaissance. The small band of Walla Walla winemakers is a cohesive group, and the Rindals share its perspective in their dedication to traditional French grape varieties made into dry wines to complement food.

Wenatchee Valley Vineyards and Winery

Wenatchee Valley Vintners is the Columbia Valley's northernmost winery and vineyard. The enterprise, owned and operated by Mike and Debbie Hansen, is situated near east

---

Wenatchee Valley Vineyards and Winery

1111 South Vansickle
East Wenatchee, Washington
98802
(509) 884-8235

Owners
Mike & Debbie Hansen

Winemaker
Mike Hansen

Wine Production
30,000 gallons

Vineyard Acreage
18 acres

Year First Planted
1982

First Vintage
1986

Wines Produced
Riesling, Sauvignon Blanc,
Valley Blush, Cote de la Columbie,
Cabernet Sauvignon, Merlot

Wenatchee. The area is in the heart of Washington's prime apple orchard country, so fruit growing is hardly foreign to the area—nor, so it turns out, is grape growing.

According to Hansen, the nearby community of Malaga was named after the Malaga grape. In 1890, a German immigrant planted 200 acres of wine grapes in the area. A difficult grape market prompted the vines to be uprooted or fall into neglect, but still, a 100 years later, a few of the original vines remain.

Here the valley narrows, and in the summer months, the basalt cliffs act as a heat sink, further warming the vineyard.

The Hansen vineyard is at the 1000 foot elevation, about 400 feet above the Columbia River. The soils vary in the vineyard, but generally consist of a shallow layer of fertile loam over decomposed granite. The vines are planted more densely than the Washington norm, about 6 1/2 feet by 3 feet, some 2,100 vines per acre. Each vine has two main trunks that are trained to high cordons. The small vineyard tractor fits underneath the leaf canopy as it makes its way between the vine rows.

For now, not all the winery's grapes are from the Wenatchee area. Some come from other parts of the Columbia Valley, including his father's vineyard near Zillah, in the Yakima Valley.

The Columbia Valley appellation is quite narrow near Wenatchee. Hansen's vineyard is between the Columbia River's basalt cliffs. In the summer months, the cliffs act as a heat sink, further warming the narrowed valley. Hansen reports that the area is relatively cooler in the spring and fall than other Columbia Valley grape growing areas, but warmer in the summer months. The cool fall nights help preserve the acids and character of the fruit. Says Hansen, "Wenatchee apples sell for a dollar more a box than Yakima Valley apples. I think the same quality difference is there with the grapes as well."

In addition to the conventional selection of wines, Hansen is producing a proprietary red wine called "Cote de la Columbie," Hills of the Columbia. The wine is made from Cabernet Sauvignon, Merlot, Pinot Noir, Lemberger, and the white grape, Chardonnay. Hansen sees the style as similar to the French red Rhone wine, Chateauneuf-du-Pape, which is made from different grape varieties than his wine, but includes white wine grapes in the blend as well.

Whidbeys

Whidbeys is owned by Stimson Lane Wine & Spirits, Ltd., the parent company of Chateau Ste. Michelle and Columbia Crest. Whidbeys is a new name, but the winery comes with a long history. Whidbeys was originally Greenbank Farm, the single largest loganberry planting in America. Greenbank Farm supplied fruit for Nawico and Pommerelle, two post-Prohibition wineries that later merged to become American Wine Growers, and subsequently, Chateau Ste. Michelle.

Initially, loganberries had no role in Chateau Ste. Michelle's focus on premium Washington grape wines, and the property waned. If anything, loganberry wines were an image problem, a reminder of the dark days in the Washington wine industry when Washington wine was synonymous with cheap wines made from fruits, berries, and less than premium grapes.

Now, the merit of premium Washington grape wines is unquestioned and firmly established. Confident in its position, and looking to broaden its wine and spirits interests, Stimson Lane revived and revitalized Greenbank Farm. Whidbeys specializes

---

Whidbeys

Highway 525 at Wonn Road
P.O. Box AB
Greenbank, Washington 98253
(206) 678-7700

Owner
Stimson Lane Wine & Spirits, Ltd.

Winemakers
Cheryl Barber, Liqueur;
Gordy Hill, Port

Wine Production
6,000 gallons

Liqueur Production
6,000 gallons

Vineyard Acreage
40 acres

Fruit Acreage
35 acres of Loganberries

First Vintage
1984

Products Produced
Loganberry Liqueur, Vintage Port,
Loganberry Wine

---

in Port, Loganberry Liqueur, and, more recently, Loganberry wine.

The liqueur is made by infusing loganberries with neutral grain spirits. The flavors are simple and direct, capturing the fruit of the loganberry. The port is made from exceptionally ripe Cabernet Sauvignon grapes from Stimson Lane's Cold Creek vineyard. In port tradition, fermentation is stopped with the addition of brandy before the wine is fully fermented dry, then aged in oak barrels prior to release.

Whidbeys winery and tasting room are housed in a refurbished turn-of-the-century barn on Greenbank Farm. Whidbeys offers a slice of history, and a scenic, pastoral setting on Puget Sound's largest Island.

Whittlesey Mark Winery

For most Northwest wineries, sparkling wine is a secondary item, something to expand and

Whittlesey Mark Winery

5318 22 Avenue N.W.
Seattle, Washington 98107
(206) 789-6543

Owner
Oregon
Methode Champenoise, Inc.

Winemaker
Mark Newton

Wine Production
3,000 gallons

Vineyard Acreage
none

First Vintage
1984

Wines Produced
Oregon Brut,
Oregon Brut de Noir,
Oregon Blanc de Blanc,
DiStefano Chardonnay

add interest to a product line. For Mark Newton, sparkling wine is the reason for his winery, although he also produces a small amount of still wine—as a secondary item.

Made from Oregon grapes, Newton's 1985 Brut was easily one of the best sparkling wines to come out of the Northwest. The winery's name then was Newton and Newton, named for Mark Newton and his brother. Unfortunately, California's Newton Winery expressed a willingness to engage in one of America's most popular participatory sports, a law suit, to deny Newton the right to use his own name on his wines. It made little difference that Mark Newton would likely win the suit in the end. Without a sea of money and an army of lawyers at his disposal, Mark Newton changed the winery's name.

The new name, Whittlesey Mark, is comprised of Newton's middle and first names. The name may be a bit awkward, but the wines are not. Newton's sparkling wine is not his sole occupation, but it is his passion. In preparation for his winery, Newton studied with several California sparkling wine houses, including the French based Maison Deutz.

Why does a Washington winery use only Oregon grapes for sparkling wine? Because, in Newton's view, they are the best for sparkling wine. Newton looked at grape sources in California and Washington, but settled on Oregon's Willamette Valley. Newton has the grapes picked at 19 to 19 1/2 Brix. In Oregon, grapes are more physiologically ripe at lower sugar levels, a prerequisite for the best sparkling wine.

The grapes are crushed in Oregon, then the juice is brought to Washington for fermentation. The sparkling wines are put through a malolactic fermentation and spend a minimum of 12 months on the yeast before disgorging.

Barrel fermented Chardonnay is the base wine for the dosage. Newton also releases small quantities of the Chardonnay under the DiStefano label, his wife's maiden name. Newton originally intended to make sparkling wines primarily from Pinot Noir, but found that Oregon Chardonnay had more character for sparkling wine than Oregon Pinot Noir, so his principal grape is Chardonnay. Pinot Meunier, a traditional Champagne grape and relative of Pinot Noir, is also included in the blend.

Woodward Canyon Winery

In the tiny community of Lowden, in a converted agricultural shed, tucked behind grain elevators and a corrugated steel machine shop, is Woodward Canyon Winery, one of Washington's best wineries. New French oak cooperage fills much of the crowded space. This is a winery with a focus on substance rather than appearance.

Do you like simple, fruity, stainless steel fermented Chardonnay? If so, Woodward Canyon is not your winery. Long before Washington wineries began their gradual shift away from simplistic, fruity Chardon-

In a converted agricultural shed, tucked behind grain elevators and a corrugated steel machine shop, is one of Washington's best wineries.

nay, Rick Small was making rich, complex, barrel fermented Chardonnays, put through a malolactic fermentation, and aged on the lees in French oak.

Small's Cabernet Sauvignon is similarly uncompromising. Small buys new French oak every year, and all his red wine spends at least some time in new barrels. Typically, the Cabernet Sauvignons spend slightly more than a total of two years in barrel. Small's Cabernet fruit comes from several excellent grape sources, including the Seven Hills Vineyard in the Walla Walla Valley, Mercer Ranch in the Horse Heaven Hills, and the Charbonneau vineyard along the Snake River in Walla Walla County.

The latter vineyard is on shallow soils over basalt rock, and rarely produces more than a ton an acre. Merlot and Cabernet Sauvignon from the Charbonneau vineyard are blended into a proprietary wine of the same name. Small also makes a white Charbonneau in very small quantities. It is primarily Semillon with some

■ **Rick Small**

Sauvignon Blanc blended in for accent.

Semillon is one of Washington's finest wine grapes, and its most underrated. Most Washington Semillon is made in a simplistic fruity style, and is frequently insulted with a touch of residual sweetness. Small makes his Charbonneau in the style of great dry white bordeaux—barrel fermented and aged on the lees in French oak. In the tradition of the greatest white Bordeaux, Sauvignon Blanc plays only a minor and supporting role to Semillon. Small is one of the few winemakers genuinely exploring the potential of Washington Semillon.

All Woodward Canyon wines see a lot of French oak, occasionally to an extreme for some tastes, but this is a small point for wines that are already among the very best and aspire to even greater heights. If Washington wineries were ranked like Bordeaux, Woodward Canyon would easily be a first growth.

Small continues to refine and develop his methods. The wines in the barrel are almost always his best yet. And the wines age well in the bottle, developing complexity and nuance over time.

The Smalls played a key role in establishing the Walla Walla Valley viticultural area. Darcey Fugman-Small, a land use planner for Walla Walla County, and wife of winemaker Rick Small, successfully prepared the BATF petition. The Walla Walla Valley, extending across the state boundary into Oregon, does not have many acres in vines, but it is one of the Northwest's oldest grape growing areas.

Small is uncompromising in his approach to winemaking. French oak, quality fruit, and attention to detail are not cheap, and neither are Woodward Canyon wines. Yet, although the wallet may be wounded, the palate is rewarded handsomely.

Worden's Washington Winery

A native of Chelan, Jack Worden was looking to expand his apple orchards when he got caught up in the enthusiasm of Washington's wine boom. A transition from growing apples to growing grapes seemed like a logical course of action, but at the time, Washington had more than ample vineyard acreage and too few wineries, so Worden set aside the idea of grape growing to open Spokane's first commercial winery in the modern era. Most of Worden's grapes come from the 80 acre Charbonneau Vineyard near Pasco.

Worden's is a market driven winery. When the white wine boom was at its peak, Worden's produced very little red wine, focusing primarily on the white wines usually finished with some residual sweetness, such as Riesling, Chenin Blanc, and Gewürz-

---

Woodward Canyon Winery

Route 1, Box 387
Lowden, Washington 99360
(509) 525-4129

Owners
Rick & Darcey Small

Winemaker
Rick Small

Wine Production
11,000 gallons

Vineyard Acreage
10 acres

Year First Planted
1977

First Vintage
1981

Wines Produced
Cabernet Sauvignon, Merlot, Chardonnay, Riesling, Charbonneau Red (Cabernet Sauvignon and Merlot), Charbonneau White (Semillon and Sauvignon Blanc)

traminer. Consumer demand dictated this choice, but increasing consumer interest in red and the drier white wines from Washington dictated a swing in emphasis. At one time, nearly half of Worden's production was in Riesling. Riesling is still the major

Worden's Washington Winery

7217 West 45th
Spokane, Washington 99204
(509) 455-7835

Owners
Jack & Phyllis Worden

Winemaker
Jack Worden

Wine Production
40,000 gallons

Vineyard Acreage
none

First Vintage
1980

Wines Produced
Riesling, Chardonnay,
Chenin Blanc, Sauvignon Blanc,
Gewurztraminer,
Cabernet Sauvignon, Merlot

variety, but production of red wines and Chardonnay have increased.

Worden's Sauvignon Blanc is finished with a trace of residual sweetness, a currently popular style for Washington Sauvignon Blanc. The Sauvignon Blanc, Chardonnay, Cabernet Sauvignon, and Merlot are aged in small French oak barrels. In some vintages, Cabernet Sauvignon is blended with up to 50 percent Merlot for texture, and for the grape's inherent softening effect.

A specialty of the winery, Worden produces a Gamay Beaujolais Rose from the Gamay clone of Pinot Noir. The wine is made in a fresh, fruity style with slight residual sweetness. In 1987, Worden's became the first Washington winery to ship wine to Taiwan. The first shipment included the Gamay Beaujolais Rose, as well as Riesling, Nouveau Blush, and Gewurztraminer.

When conditions are right, Worden's produces special late harvest dessert wines. Riesling and Gewurztraminer are the major varieties for these rich sweet wines. The grapes for late harvest wines are often picked up to two months or more after the regular harvest.

Worden's tasting room is a log building nestled among pine trees just west of Spokane. The log building, trees, and picnic tables have a summer home in the woods atmosphere that invites a picnic.

Yakima River Winery

Former residents of New York, John Rauner and his wife, Louise, first encountered Washington grapes on a vacation trip through the state in 1974. A home winemaker for many years, Rauner purchased a few grapes and made two gallons of wine in their travel trailer. Rauner was impressed by the fruit. Even under the primitive conditions of the travel trailer, the wine was far superior to what he had made in New York. The following year, the Rauners moved to the Yakima Valley and began preparations for their winery.

Unlike many Washington wineries located on the east side of the Cascades, the Yakima River Winery relies on grapes purchased from independent growers. Arguments abound both for and against this arrangement. From his perspective, Rauner believes he could not do justice to both grape growing and wine-making—both highly demanding and time consuming activities.

Rauner believes that by not owning any vineyards, he can select grapes from vineyard sites best suited to a particular variety. "Some people ask," says Rauner, "if I don't feel at a disadvantage in not having my own vineyard. I say no—I would feel at a disadvantage if I did have my own vineyard." Nearly all of Yakima River's grapes come from the Yakima Valley.

A major fan of red wines,

Yakima River Winery

North River Road
Route 1, Box 1657
Prosser, Washington 99350
(509) 786-2805

Owners
John & Louise Rauner

Winemaker
John Rauner

Wine Production
20,000 gallons

Vineyard Acreage
none

First Vintage
1978

Wines Produced
Fume Blanc, Cabernet Sauvignon,
Merlot, Riesling, Blush Riesling,
Late Harvest Riesling,
Dry Berry Selection Riesling,
Riesling Ice Wine, Port,
Rendezvous

Rauner has gradually steered his winery toward a greater percentage of reds, now 85% of Yakima River's total wine production. Somewhat unusually, Rauner's Merlot and Cabernet Sauvignon are partially fermented in oak barrels. Pursuing a softer, more readily accessible red wine style, Rauner begins fermentation in stainless steel tanks, then at about 8 degrees Brix, takes the must off the pulp and tannic skins, and completes the fermentation in small French and American oak barrels. Made in a softer, earlier drinking style, restaurants are a major target market for Rauner's red wines.

Ice wine, although produced infrequently, is one of Yakima River's specialties. In 1980, Rauner produced his first ice wine. Gewurztraminer grapes were harvested December 5, frozen on the vine at 18 degrees Fahrenheit. At pressing, the grapes yielded highly concentrated juice, measuring 40.4 Brix sugar. The wine was finished at 17 percent residual sugar and .88 acid. The second opportunity did not come until 1984, when Rauner brought in botrytised Riesling grapes frozen on the vine at two degrees above zero. The must analysis measured 44.3 Brix with a good balancing acidity reading of 1.2. A third ice wine was made in 1988. Availability is limited, and the ice wines, not surprisingly, are very expensive.

In 1989, Yakima River released its first Port, a 1986, made from Merlot. Prior to release, the wine was aged for 34 months in American oak barrels.

Zillah Oakes Winery

Zillah Oakes is part of the same partnership that owns and runs the Covey Run winery. The Zillah Oakes winery specializes in moderately priced premium wines. The winery's origins came from Covey Run's desire to expand wine production for a second line of wines. At the time, the Covey Run winery was already near capacity. The partnership decided to keep the Covey Run winery dedicated to the upper scale of premium and speciality wines, and build a separate

Zillah Oakes Winery

Exit 52, Interstate 82
Zillah, Washington 98953
(509) 829-6235

Owners
General Partnership

Winemaker
Dave Crippen

First Vintage
1987

Wines Produced
Chardonnay, Muscat Canelli, Riesling, Late Harvest Riesling, Maywine, Zillah Blushed

winery for a more moderately priced line of wines.

You will not find any reserve Cabernets under the Zillah Oakes label, but the winery offers Chardonnay and Riesling at moderate prices, as well as blush wines and Maywine, a traditional wine flavored with woodruff.

The Zillah Oakes winery is conspicuously accessible, just off Interstate 82, near Zillah. The winery's name encapsulates a slice of Yakima Valley history. While surveying the townsite, Walter Granger became attracted by the charm of Zillah, the young daughter of Thomas Oakes, an official of the Northern Pacific Railway—hence, the town's name of Zillah, and the winery's name, Zillah Oakes.

Idaho's Wine Industry

Pioneering success in a state known more for potatoes, snow, & fly fishing

Idaho's modern day wine industry is less than two decades old, but its winegrowing roots are traceable to the last century, to the Clearwater River Valley, near the northwestern Idaho town of Lewiston. Winegrowing in the Clearwater Valley dates back to the 1860s. The last Clearwater Valley winery finally closed its doors in 1945.

After a long dormancy, Idaho's wine industry began anew in the 1970s. A winery in northwestern Idaho opened in 1971, making wine from hybrid grapes, but soon folded. At about the same time, Robert Wing, a weatherman and climate researcher, planted premium vinifera grape varieties in an experimental vineyard in the Clearwater Valley. In 1976, in the Snake River Valley of southwestern Idaho, Bill Broich crushed the first commercial vintage for Ste. Chapelle, then a tiny winery that would soon become one of the Northwest's largest wineries.

Wine aficionados outside the state did not immediately accept the idea that Idaho could have a good growing climate for premium vinifera grape wines. Idaho is usually perceived as mountainous, with a climate as rugged as the landscape, but parts of the state have a warm, relatively temperate climate. Doubts about Idaho winegrowing were rapidly dispelled in Ste. Chapelle's first few vintages. The winery's first Riesling release established Idaho as a viable winegrowing region.

It may not have been too difficult to accept that Idaho could make good Riesling. After all, it could be reasoned, German Rieslings are

Idaho
Wine Grape Acreage
750 acres
Winegrowing Regions
Snake River Valley, Clearwater Valley
Predominant Grape Varieties
Riesling, Chardonnay

grown in very cool growing regions, and it was not too farfetched that Idaho might succeed with the grape. Other grape varieties, most thought, would not fair nearly as well. Ste. Chapelle's first Chardonnay shattered most of the remaining misconceptions. The wine was not an austere, French Chablis style of Chardonnay, but a rich, buttery, high alcohol wine, not too far removed from the prevalent California style of the day. Idaho is capable of a range of Chardonnay styles, including the leaner, crisper renditions, but that first Chardonnay proved a point—many common conceptions about Idaho winegrowing did not apply.

Unlike earlier Idaho winegrowing efforts, virtually all of today's Idaho grape wines are made from *Vitis vinifera* grape varieties. Until the 1980s, Ste. Chapelle remained Idaho's only winery. Ste. Chapelle still dominates the state's wine industry, but each new Idaho winery broadens the scope of the industry, adding its own focus and style, and sometimes, new wine grapes to test Idaho's vinous horizons.

Frosts, winter cold, and a relatively short growing season are the state's only major limitations. Gewurztraminer, Chenin Blanc, Pinot Noir, Semillon, and Cabernet Sauvignon have since joined the list of Idaho wines, and other varieties, in smaller quantities, have been planted to vine.

Pinot Noir had been regarded as the most likely candidate for an Idaho red wine. Unlike Chardonnay, however, Pinot Noir is not a very flexible variety. Pinot Noir produces fine wines only if conditions are just right, and Idaho's hot days may prove too much for consistently good Pinot Noir. Surprisingly, testing its limits against the cold winters and short growing season, Cabernet Sauvignon may yet turn out to be Idaho's red wine grape.

The Oregon and Washington wine industries have had the support of their state governments. Located in a section of the state where anti-alcohol sentiments are common, Idaho's wine industry is not as fortunate. The agribusiness environment of the Snake River Valley, however, offers a significant source of land and financial resources. Most of Idaho's wineries are tied to local orchard and farming interests.

Recent severe winters have caused major damage in some vineyards, prompting a few growers to pull up grape vines and replace them with a more hardy crop. Yet, at the same time, more vineyards are being planted or expanded. The Idaho wine industry is still dominated by one winery, Ste. Chapelle, but new wineries and new winegrowing areas are bringing a healthy and much needed diversity to the wine industry.

Idaho is usually perceived as mountainous, with a climate as rugged as the landscape, but parts of the state have a warm, relatively temperate climate.

Idaho Winegrowing Regions

An intense climate, yielding wines of a similar nature

Idaho is usually associated with mountains, forests, snow, and potatoes. Wine, made from grapes grown in Idaho, shakes our usual vision of the state. More startling still, Idaho's wines are not made from native American varieties or hybrids, but from premium *Vitis vinifera* grape varieties such as Chardonnay and Riesling. The state is separated from the moderating marine influences of the Pacific Ocean by 300 miles and several mountain ranges. How can delicate vinifera grapes grow in such a northerly inland region?

Parts of Idaho are still directly affected by the Pacific marine air. Idaho's climate is linked to the Pacific Ocean by the Columbia River and its major tributary, the Snake River. Cutting through the mountain ranges, the Columbia River carves a climatic pathway through the Northwest landscape. Marine air travels through the Columbia River Gorge and into the Columbia Valley in Washington and Oregon. The Snake River merges with the Columbia in southwest Washington, and the marine air flows further inland up the Snake River, into the tributary river valleys that feed the Snake, through the narrow and rugged Snake River Canyon on the Oregon and Idaho border, and into the broad Snake River Valley in southwest Idaho.

After such a great distance along a convoluted path, the effect of the marine air is greatly reduced, but the remaining marine influence, and the sheltered, low elevation (for Idaho) valleys make winegrowing possible. The first fall frost is delayed, and winter temperatures are not as extreme as areas more separated from the marine influence. Because of the Pacific Ocean, the Columbia River and its tributaries, and the shape of the landscape, parts of Idaho

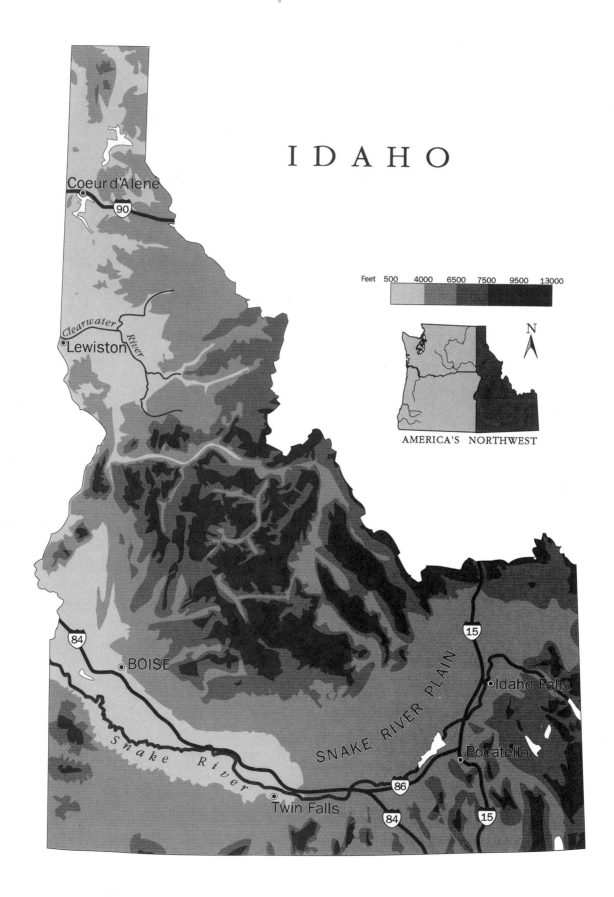

IDAHO

Feet 500 4000 6500 7500 9500 13000

AMERICA'S NORTHWEST

N

Coeur d'Alene

90

Clearwater River

Lewiston

84

BOISE

Idaho Falls

15

SNAKE RIVER PLAIN

Snake River

Pocatello

86

Twin Falls

84

15

have a growing season long enough for premium wine grapes, and winters mild enough not to kill the vines.

Several areas in Idaho are suitable for winegrowing, including the Clearwater Valley near the Washington border, site of some of Idaho's earliest vineyards. Robert Wing, an independent grape researcher with a two decade old experimental vineyard at Lewiston, has recorded 2,475 average yearly heat units with 177 frost free growing days. Further up the valley, Wing estimates that heat units exceed 2,600 with more than 180 growing days—conditions suited to a wide range of premium vinifera grape varieties. Wing estimates that some 1,000 acres in the Clearwater Valley are suitable for growing premium wine grapes. As yet, however, only the Snake River Valley in southwest Idaho has been developed in any major way.

Snake River Valley

The Snake River Valley cuts a broad crescent through southern Idaho. The eastern half is a very broad, flat, nearly featureless lava plain, bordered by mountains to the north, south, and east. Toward the west, the Snake River Valley narrows, and the landscape is featured with new and old lakebeds, terraces, small canyons, and open valleys created by the Boise River and other streams that feed into the Snake. Nearly all of Idaho's wine grapes are grown on the south facing slopes at the western end of the Snake River Valley. Traditional orchard land, vineyards now share the choice slopes with apples, peaches, and other tree fruits.

Most Northwest vineyards are planted at elevations of less than 1,000 feet. All Snake River Valley vineyards are planted above the 2,000 foot elevation mark, and partly because of this, the valley's growing season is one of the shortest in the Northwest. In many respects, the climate is very similar to the climate of Washington's Columbia Valley.

During the growing season, the days are sunny, dry, and hot. The nights are cool, and progressively more so during the final ripening of the grapes, as fall approaches and the growing season comes to a close. Like the Columbia Valley, Idaho grapes can achieve high sugar levels while retaining crisp acidity. The cool nights and moderating climate during the final ripening of the grapes preserves the acidity and the grape's delicate flavor nuances.

As might be expected, frosts and winter cold can damage the vines and reduce the grape crop in difficult years. Sun scalding is a greater threat in the Snake River Valley than in the Columbia Valley. Dominated by an interior high pressure cell in the winter, courtesy of the climatic influence of the northern Sierra Nevada Mountains to the southwest, the days are intensely bright and sunny, and the nights are cold. Bright sunlight reflecting off the snow cover can cause sun scalding as parts of the vines are warmed during the daytime, followed by a rapid temperature drop at nightfall. Any agricultural crop anywhere faces difficulties. Frosts, cold, and sun scalding are Idaho's blessings. These may be a threat to a year's grape harvest—but not Idaho's winegrowing industry.

Although the Snake River Valley climate is very similar to the Columbia Valley climate, the Snake's shorter growing season challenges the range of grape varieties. Cabernet Sauvignon, for example, a variety requiring a relatively long, warm growing season, is a major Columbia Valley variety. Recent efforts suggest that Cabernet Sauvignon may also be suited to the Snake River Valley, but not without an ongoing race with the length of the growing season. In terms of the usual perception of the Idaho climate, the Snake River Valley has proven quite versatile. Winegrowing is not merely limited to Riesling or other very cool climate varieties.

Chardonnay and Gewurztraminer, both short season varieties, do exceptionally well, and Chenin Blanc, though susceptible to the

> **Nearly all of Idaho's wine grapes are grown on the south facing slopes at the western end of the Snake River Valley. Traditional orchard land, vineyards now share choice slopes with apples, peaches, and other tree fruits.**

Snake River Valley
Western Snake River Valley

Caldwell to Portland, Oregon
405 miles

Nampa to Twin Falls
149 miles

IDAHO

OWYHEE MOUNTAINS

BOISE

Meridian

Nampa

Caldwell

Wilder

Homedale

Marsing

Weston

Ste. Chapelle

Hell's Canyon

Pintler

Lake Lowell

Kuna

Murphy

Mountain Home

New York Canal

Indian Creek

Mora Canal

Phyllis Canal

Boise River

Snake River

River

N

Feet 2000 2500 3000 3500 4000 5000 8000

0 5 10 20 Miles

winter cold, produces wines that exceed the American reputation for the grape. Other varieties, such as Semillon, show excellent promise, though Semillon is also quite susceptible to winter damage. Ironically, Riesling is a long season grape, but it yields distinctive wines under a wide range of conditions, from very low sugars in an underripe state, to high sugars with a riper, more muscat-like character. Idaho is capable of the latter style, but as in Washington, some winegrowers are beginning to tend toward a less ripe, more delicate, refined style.

So new are the Northwest's winegrowing regions, their potential is scarcely known. Historical winegrowing efforts notwithstanding, Idaho's Snake River Valley winegrowing region is by far the youngest in the Northwest. In its first decade, each new successful variety brought new surprises, broadening the Snake River Valley's winegrowing horizons still further. It seems safe to say that the future promises more surprises and continued extensions of the Snake River Valley's winegrowing horizons.

Snake River Valley
West Central Snake River Valley

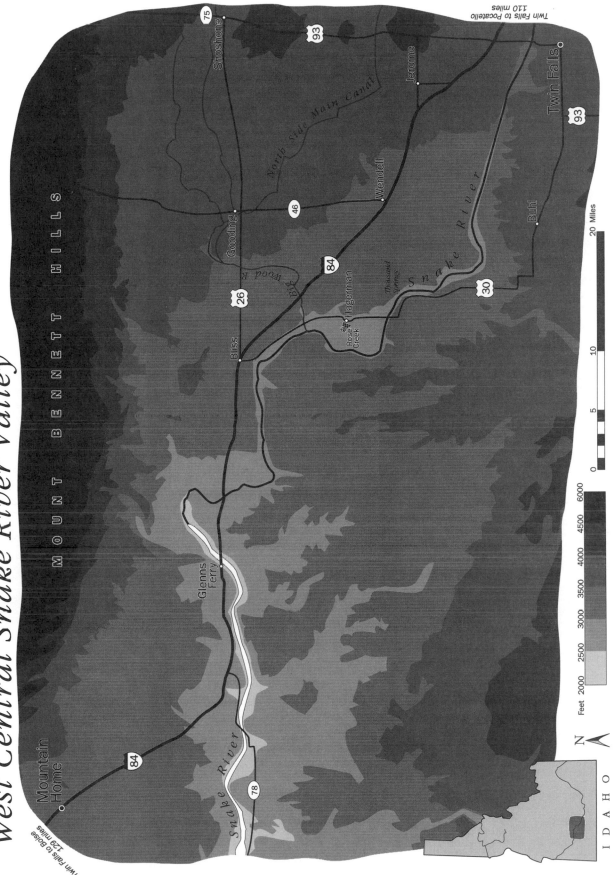

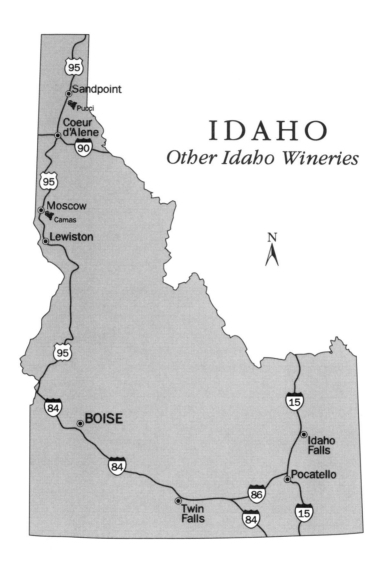

IDAHO
Other Idaho Wineries

Idaho Wineries

A single winery predominates, new wineries add diversity

Camas Winery

In the early 1970s, Stuart Scott worked in a retail wine shop, and lived within a short distance of several wineries in California's Santa Clara Valley. Talking with the winemakers and helping out with cellar work spurred his interest in home winemaking. Camas Winery is an outgrowth of Scott's hobbiest interests.

The winery once occupied a niche in the family home. In 1989, Camas opened a tasting room at its new location in downtown Moscow. Grapes come from the Columbia Valley in nearby Washington. A recent effort with a local beekeeper has added Mead, made from wildflower honey, to Camas's line of wines.

Scott likes his wines in a smoother, slightly lower acid style than the Northwest norm, and he makes his wines to fit this preference. The Chardonnay is finished with slight residual sugar, not so much for sweetness, as for the perception of smoothness and body.

Hog Heaven Red, a Camas speciality, is a proprietary blend of grape and cherry wine. Hog Heaven Red is slightly sweet, but does not taste strongly of cherries. Scott likens its character to Lambrusco. Complimenting Hog Heaven Red is Hog Heaven White, a more recent addition to Camas's line of wines, made entirely from Gewurztraminer.

Camas Winery

110 S. Main Street
Moscow, Idaho 83843
(208) 882-0214

Owners
Stuart & Susan Scott

Winemaker
Stuart Scott

Wine Production
3,000 gallons

Vineyard Acreage
none

First Vintage
1983

Wines Produced
Cabernet Sauvignon, Chardonnay, Riesling, Blush, Muscat, Hog Heaven Red, Hog Heaven White, Mead, Spiced Wine

Hell's Canyon Winery

At the corner of Chicken Dinner and Symms Road is the Robertsons' family residence, 40

Hell's Canyon Winery

18835 Symms Road
Caldwell, Idaho 83605
(208) 336-2277

Owners
Steve & Leslie Robertson

Winemaker
Steve Robertson

Wine Production
2,000 gallons

Vineyard Acreage
5 acres

Wines Produced
Chardonnay, Cabernet Sauvignon

acres of agricultural land, and Hell's Canyon Winery. The Snake River's Hell's Canyon is the deepest canyon in America, considerably deeper, even, than the Colorado River's Grand Canyon. Hell's Canyon Winery overlooks the winding Snake River upriver from the canyon, at a much broader and more placid part of the Snake River Valley.

President of the Idaho Grape Growers Association, Steve Robertson has been making small quantities of wine under the bonds of other wineries since 1981. The wines have done very well, garnering considerable acclaim in tastings in England. In 1989, Robertson bonded his own winery.

Robertson's speciality is Chardonnay, employing methods typi-

---

In spite of the short growing season, Robertson reports that his Cabernet ripens readily.

---

cal of a Burgundian approach to the grape—barrel fermentation, lees contact, and malolactic fermentation. Robertson has also experimented with whole berry pressing, different oaks, and a variety of yeasts.

The vineyard soil is a Truesdale sandy loam, running three to twelve feet deep to a layer of caliche. A rocky, lean soil, Robertson has had no problems controlling vine vigor. Robertson also grows and makes a small amount of Cabernet Sauvignon, a wine that enthuses him greatly. Although the short 160 day growing season is marginal for Cabernet Sauvignon, Robertson believes that a warm growing site and reduced vine canopy are keys to success. Robertson reports that his own Cabernet Sauvignon ripens readily.

"Most people associate Idaho with potatoes, clean air, and good fishing," says Robertson, "but not

with wine. We're gearing our own sales efforts partly to international markets. England has been very receptive. People in America, as well as abroad, will eventually associate Idaho with fine wine as well."

Indian Creek Winery

A retired Air Force officer, Bill Stowe became interested in wines while stationed in Germany. After retiring, Stowe took up farming in Idaho's Snake River Valley, growing, among other things, wine grapes.

Stowe's two vineyards are situated near Kuna Butte and the town of Kuna. Idaho's modern wine industry began in the Sunnyslope area, roughly 10 miles to the west. The Kuna area is less sloped, but the growing environment is otherwise similar. A layer of caliche underlies the relatively shallow soils. Once the caliche is ripped and broken up at planting,

Indian Creek Winery

Route 1, 1000 N. McDermott Road
Kuna, Idaho 83634
(208) 922-4791

Owners
Bill & Mike Stowe,
Richard Ostrogorsky

Winemaker
Bill Stowe

Wine Production
8,000 gallons

Vineyard Acreage
18 acres

Year First Planted
1982

First Vintage
1987

Wines Produced
Pinot Noir, Chardonnay, Riesling, Cabernet Sauvignon, Semillon, Chenin Blanc, Sauvignon Blanc, Lemberger, White Pinot Noir, Chelois, Interlaken

the underlying cracked lava rock provides good drainage for the vineyard.

Stowe grows Chardonnay, Pinot Noir, and Riesling. He is particularly enthused with Pinot Noir, though it has proven to be less winter hardy than Chardonnay. In the Northwest, Idaho's Snake River Valley is closest to Washington's Columbia Valley in growing climate. Although Columbia Valley Pinot Noir has not been very promising, Stowe believes the Snake River Valley's colder nights and slightly different growing environment are just the right conditions for the highly fickle Pinot Noir.

Stowe ferments the Pinot Noir in the low 70s, leaving a third of the grape clusters whole. The wine is not pressed off the skins until about two weeks after fermentation has finished, giving the wine an extended period of maceration. The Chardonnay is barrel fermented and left on the lees for at least a year prior to bottling.

Stowe produces small amounts of wine from the French-American hybrids Chelois (red wine) and Interlaken (white wine). Supplementing the Idaho grapes when a severe winter reduces the grape crop, Stowe also buys grapes from Washington's Columbia Valley, most recently, Sauvignon Blanc and Lemberger.

Pintler Winery

In a state known mostly for Riesling and Chardonnay, the Pintler Winery, and winegrower Brad Pintler, have succeeded in stretching the state's horizons with two Bordeaux wine grapes, Cabernet Sauvignon and Semillon—and not with marginally successful wines, but wines that show excellent promise for the two grape varieties in Idaho's Snake River Valley.

Semillon is the predominant grape in the great white Bordeaux wines. It is a grape with finesse, complexity, and the capacity for cellaring that sets it above the more common and overly insistent Sauvignon Blanc, though the two work well together in blends. Semillon performs superbly in Washington's Columbia Valley, though the winemaking seldom matches the grape's potential.

Idaho has been locked to Chardonnay as its only dry white wine grape. Semillon made from Pintler's grapes was Idaho's first commercial release of the variety. Pintler's first Semillon was fermented in stainless steel and saw no oak. Highly successful, Pintler decided to go further, and treat the grape like a serious white wine, with barrel fermentation, lees contact, and oak aging.

Regrettably, Semillon is sensitive to winter cold, and the severe winter freeze of 1989 killed the Semillon down to its roots, so Pintler made no Semillon from that vintage. Regrettably, too, consumers are not sufficiently attuned to the grape. "I like Semillon very much," says Pintler, "but I don't know if the market is there to make it one of my major grapes." Idaho winters and an uncertain market may be difficult for Semillon, but Pintler has shown the way for Semillon in Idaho's Snake River Valley.

Cabernet Sauvignon has a reputation for winter sensitivity, but, ironically, Pintler reports that his Cabernet made it through the 1989 winter even better than his Chardonnay, and better, even, than his Riesling, producing three tons of grapes from his solitary

Pintler Winery

13750 Surrey Lane
Nampa, Idaho 83686
(208) 467-1200

Owners
Pintler Family

Winemaker
Brad Pintler

Wine Production
4,000 gallons

Vineyard Acreage
13 acres

First Vintage
1987

Wines Produced
Chardonnay, Semillon, Riesling,
Chenin Blanc,
Cabernet Sauvignon,
Pinot Noir, Blush

acre of Cabernet.

Idaho has largely stayed away from Cabernet Sauvignon, partly, Pintler thinks, because of Ste. Chapelle's less than happy experience with the grape. "My Cabernet is the last maturing grape," says Pintler, "but it gets to 24 Brix and hardens off well for the winter." Pintler's excellent success in the vineyard and in the winery is sure to prompt further exploration of Idaho Cabernet Sauvignon.

Pintler's vineyard is on a sloped site fairly near the Snake River. The air drainage and moderating effect of the river help prevent frost. The shallow, one foot, silt, loam soil over volcanic red cinder gravel limits vegetative growth and helps the vines harden off for winter, a particularly important factor with the Cabernet, not only for the vine's health, but for the quality of the wine as well.

Pintler is focusing on Cabernet Sauvignon and Chardonnay. What about Pinot Noir? Pintler is very confident in Cabernet—not as confident in Pinot Noir. "I am working with Pinot Noir. It might

be a good grape for Idaho," says Pintler, "but we'll have to wait and see."

Pintler's Chardonnay is barrel fermented and left on the lees. A portion of the grapes are not crushed and destemmed, but pressed as whole clusters. His Chenin Blanc is made much like a Chardonnay, fermented in French oak, and finished completely dry. The local market prefers sweet wines, but Pintler will continue making the dry Chenin Blanc as long as there is a market for the style.

Less safe and less conventional than many Idaho wineries, Pintler is among those successfully testing the states winegrowing horizons.

Pucci Winery

Skip Pucci's grandfather emigrated from Italy to California's Sacramento Valley and began making Zinfandel for the family table. Skip Pucci and his children continue the family tradition, making Zinfandel, and other wines, for the home—and now for commercial release. The

Pucci Winery

1055 Garfield Bay Road
Sandpoint, Idaho 83864
(208) 263-5807

Owner
Skip Pucci

Winemaker
Skip Pucci

Wine Production
4,000 gallons

Vineyard Acreage
none

First Vintage
1982

Wines Produced
Cabernet Sauvignon, Riesling,
Chardonnay, Zinfandel

Northwest's growing seasons are generally too short and too cool for Zinfandel, so Pucci brings in Zinfandel grapes from California and makes red, rose, and white Zinfandel wine. Pucci also makes Cabernet Sauvignon, Riesling, and Chardonnay from Washington grapes.

All Pucci's wines are fermented dry, and all are fermented and aged in oak. Pucci buys old whiskey barrels, scrapes away the char, and treats the barrels with citric acid and soda ash to remove the whiskey taste. Says Pucci, "Its taken some practice, but I've gotten so I can take a barrel completely apart and reassemble it in seven minutes." Pucci's oak grape crusher is patterned after his father's.

For red wines, Pucci removes the end of a barrel and stands it on end to make an open-topped fermenter. When the wine is almost fermented dry, Pucci transfers it to oak barrels to finish fermentation and begin the aging process. All the white wines, including Riesling, are also fermented in oak barrels.

The winery evolved from a long family tradition of informal home winemaking, and the wines and winery reflect this approach. A construction superintendent by occupation, Pucci operates the winery in his spare time. Complete with picnic grounds, the winery overlooks Pend Oreille Lake, and the view on into Montana.

Rose Creek Vineyards

A hundred miles from Idaho's other Snake River Valley wineries, at the edge of the Snake River Lava Plain that sweeps across southern Idaho, Jamie and Susan Martin own and operate Rose Creek Vineyards. Why have a winery in such a viticulturally remote area? Jamie Martin grew

---

Rose Creek Vineyards is a hundred miles from Idaho's other Snake River Valley wineries, at the edge of the Snake River Lava Plain that sweeps across southern Idaho.

---

up in the locale. He and Susan became interested in wine, and wondered about the prospect of winemaking in the Hagerman area.

Known as the melon belt for its

Rose Creek Vineyards

111 West Hagerman
P.O. Box 356
Hagerman, Idaho 83332

Tasting Room
Capitol Terrace Plaza, 2nd Floor
8th and Bannock
Boise, Idaho

Owners
Jamie & Susan Martin,
& Stephanie Martin

Winemaker
Jamie Martin

Wine Production
12,000 gallons

Vineyard Acreage
30 acres

Year First Planted
1980

First Vintage
1984

Wines Produced
Chardonnay, Riesling,
Chenin Blanc, Pinot Noir,
Pinot Noir Vin Gris,
Cabernet Sauvignon,
Rose Creek Mist

warm climate and large melon crop, Hagerman looked like a good prospect for grape growing. At an elevation of 2,700 to 3,000 feet, winter freezing and frosts are a risk, and the growing season is shortened, but the proximity of the Snake River, and the sheltering, heat-reflectant basalt canyon walls temper the climate. Overhead sprinkler systems also help control frosts.

The Martins first sold their grapes to other Idaho wineries, but as acreage increased, and as other local growers began having grapes for sale, the Martins decided to open their own winery. Unlike some out-of-the-way winery enterprises where winegrowing is casual and unfocused, and the wines reflect that approach, the Martins' efforts show a serious dedication to quality.

The Hagerman area has about 40 acres of grapes planted in small parcels of two to ten acres each. Chardonnay and Riesling are proving well suited to the area. Martin also buys Cabernet Sauvignon grapes from Washington and Pinot Noir grapes from Oregon.

The Rose Creek winery is in an historic dry goods store built in 1887 to serve the needs of early settlers. The three foot thick walls of local lava stone help insulate the building from the heat of southern Idaho summers. A bank occupies the upper floor. The winery is in the building's cellar. When outside summer temperatures reach over 100 degrees, the cellar remains at a cool 55 degrees.

Ste. Chapelle Winery

Ste. Chapelle Vineyards is a remarkable success story. The first winery in a virtually untested new winegrowing region, Ste. Chapelle almost instantly became one of the Northwest's largest and best known wineries. Because of Ste. Chapelle's growth, Idaho winegrowing developed faster than in any other Northwest state.

Ste. Chapelle was founded by Bill Broich. Broich made his first wines, then formed a corporation with the Symms family, prominent fruit growers in Idaho's Snake River Valley. The Symms family provided necessary land and capital for Ste. Chapelle's meteoric growth. The Ste. Chapelle winery and estate vineyards are located on the Symms' property, in the Sunny Slope area near the Idaho communities of Nampa and Caldwell.

Ste. Chapelle crushed its first commercial vintage in 1976, from vines planted in the early 1970's. Bill Broich was Ste. Chapelle's winemaker until he left the corporation in 1985.

Mimi Mook, Broich's successor, is an excellently credentialed winemaker, formerly of California's J. Lohr winery. Her winemaking skills and technical acumen have brought added refinement to Ste. Chapelle's wines.

Ste. Chapelle began its existence in, what must have seemed to most, a financial and viticultural climate of great uncertainty. Many outside the state have the conception that potatoes and snow are Idaho's only viable crops, yet the Snake River Valley has long been noted for its orchards of cherries, pears, apples, peaches, and other fruits.

It is a rule of thumb that any area capable of growing peaches can also grow premium vinifera wine grapes. The overwhelming success of Ste. Chapelle's vineyards and wines do not contradict this maxim. At an elevation of 2,500 feet, the area is one of the highest major growing regions in the Northwest.

Not unexpectedly, Riesling was Ste. Chapelle's first wine from Idaho grapes, soon followed by Chardonnay, Gewurztraminer, and Pinot Noir. In 1986, Ste. Chapelle added another variety to its list of grapes, with a 25 acre planting of Sauvignon Blanc.

Many could accept the idea that Idaho was capable of producing Riesling, a cool climate grape that shows well even when underripe, but when Ste. Chapelle released a

Ste. Chapelle Winery

14068 Sunny Slope Road
Caldwell, Idaho 83605
(208) 459-7222 or 888-9463

Owners
Symms Family

Winemaker
Mimi Mook

Wine Production
240,000 gallons

Vineyard Acreage
190 acres

Year First Planted
1971

First Vintage
1976

Wines Produced
Riesling, Dry Riesling,
Special Harvest Riesling,
Chardonnay, Cabernet Sauvignon,
Merlot, Pinot Noir,
Pinot Noir Blanc, Gewurztraminer,
Chenin Blanc, Fume Blanc, Blush;
Charmat Process Sparkling
Riesling, Chardonnay, Pinot Noir;
Methode Champenoise Brut

successful Chardonnay, it was a revelation, a confirmation that Idaho is not just a winegrowing curiosity, but a broadly based winegrowing climate.

Ste. Chapelle can produce excellent Gewurztraminer. In some grape growing areas, Gewurztraminer makes wines with low

> **The first winery in a virtually untested new winegrowing region, Ste. Chapelle almost instantly became one of the Northwest's largest and best known wineries.**

acidity, some bitterness in the finish, and a bubble gum character. Idaho Gewurztraminers can show off the grape at its best, with the spiciness typical of the variety. Unfortunately, Gewurztraminer is not in high demand with the consumer, and much of Ste. Chapelle's Gewurztraminer goes into a proprietary blend with Riesling.

In northern European growing climates, and in Washington and Idaho, Chenin Blanc can make wines of some distinction. Ste. Chapelle's is made in the Northwest style—fresh and fruity, with crisp acidity and some residual sweetness. Unfortunately, Chenin Blanc is susceptible to winter damage, especially when the vines are allowed to produce large grape crops, a characteristic of the variety. Idaho growers are showing reluctance to plant more of the variety because of this danger.

Ste. Chapelle produces far more sparkling wine than any other Northwest winery, some 25,000 cases a year. Ste. Chapelle is taking an unusual approach to

■ **The old windmill presides over the Ste. Chapelle winery and vineyards**

sparkling wine. Most wineries make premium varietal sparkling wines by the bottle fermented process. Wines made by the Charmat process, fermenting sparkling wine in pressurized tanks, are usually made from inexpensive, nondescript grape varieties and are sold at cheap prices. There are some notable exceptions. German Sekt is one. Even the very best Sekts, made from Riesling grapes, are still made in tanks by the Charmat process.

Ste. Chapelle makes small quantities of bottle fermented sparkling wine, but most of its sparkling wines are made by the Charmat process, and all are made from premium grape varieties, Riesling, Chardonnay, and Pinot Noir.

The three sparkling wines emphasize the fruit of the varietals rather than a yeasty character. The Riesling is moderately sweet with pronounced Riesling flavors. The Chardonnay is drier, with a fresh, fruity character—different than most sparkling Chardonnays, but very successful. The wines are moderately priced, selling for less than bottle fermented wines made

from the same varieties.

Ste. Chapelle continues to explore and expand Idaho's wine-growing horizons. Some of Ste. Chapelle's new Pinot Noir vineyards are destined for a red wine, and Idaho Cabernet Sauvignon and Merlot are part of the winery's future. In 1985, for the first time, Ste. Chapelle had botrytis in some of their Riesling grapes, and Ste. Chapelle produced its first botrytised wine.

Ste. Chapelle's winery is distinctive and striking. Designed by architect Nat Adams from photographs of the Ste. Chapelle chapel in Paris, its octagonal roof reaches a peak 52 feet above the winery floor. Multiple windows, 24 feet high, allow a panoramic view of the vineyards and the broad, gently sloping valley below. The tasting room and reception area are finished in oak, and contribute to the winery's warm atmosphere.

Weston Winery

During his student days, Cheyne Weston worked with the now defunct Charles Coury winery in Oregon, then with California's Sebastiani winery. Not long after graduating from college, Weston left Sebastiani to pursue his career as a cinematographer. After six years of extensive traveling and absences from his family in Idaho, Weston gave up his career, returned full-time to his wife and children, and returned full-time to winemaking, in Idaho's Snake River Valley.

Formerly vineyard manager and crush foreman for the Ste. Chapelle winery, Weston founded Weston Winery in 1982. Weston's main vineyard is at an elevation of 2,750 feet, one of the highest vine-

yards in the Northwest. Weston Winery, not far from the much larger Ste. Chapelle winery, is situated in the Sunnyslope area of the Snake River Valley, in the southwest corner of the state, the heart of Idaho's wine country.

The Chardonnays are fermented and aged in French Allier and Nevers oak barrels. Weston prefers the barrel fermentation over stainless steel fermentation for the vanilla and buttery qualities it imparts to the wine. Riesling, comprising 60 percent of the winery's production, is made in a variety of styles ranging from off-dry to intensely sweet.

Weston Winery

16316 Orchard Avenue
Caldwell, Idaho 83605
(208) 459-2631

Owner
Cheyne Weston

Winemaker
Cheyne Weston

Wine Production
6,000 gallons

Vineyard Acreage
14 acres

Year First Planted
1982

First Vintage
1982

Wines Produced
Chardonnay, Cabernet Sauvignon, Riesling, Late Harvest Riesling, Pinot Noir, Sauvignon Blanc

Most of Weston's wines are made from Idaho grapes, but some wines are made from Washington grapes. The wines Weston considers his best Idaho grape wines are released with label designs painted by his brother, Jeff, an Idaho artist. The ongoing label series depicts the lifestyle typifying Idaho high-country living.

About the Author

Ted Jordan Meredith has been writing about the wines of America's Northwest in books and in articles for national and regional publications since 1974. Other books by Meredith include *Northwest Wine Companion*, three previous editions of this book, and co-authorship of *A Dictionary of American Wines*, published by William Morrow, New York.

Born in Montana, now a resident of Washington, Meredith holds a bachelor's degree in Sociology and a master's degree in Philosophy. Recognizing his contributions to wine literature, Meredith was invited to join the prestigious International Authors and Writers Who's Who in Cambridge, England. Meredith's works are widely regarded as the authoritative references on the wines of America's Northwest.